THE HAMLYN
PICTORIAL ATLAS
OF THE WORLD

THE HAMLYN
PICTORIAL ATLAS
OF THE WORLD

A Philip/Salamander Book

Published by

HAMLYN

London · New York · Sydney · Toronto

A Philip/Salamander Book

This edition published 1976 by
The Hamlyn Publishing Group Limited
London · New York · Sydney · Toronto
Astronaut House, Feltham,
Middlesex, England

Fourth impression 1978

ISBN 0 600 39363 1

© Salamander Books Ltd.
Salamander House
27 Old Gloucester Street
London WC1N 3AF
United Kingdom

Maps © 1976 George Philip & Son Ltd

Credits

Filmset by
SX Composing, Leigh-on-Sea,
Essex, England

Colour reproduction by
Metric Reproductions Ltd,
Chelmsford, Essex, England

Printed by Henri Proost,
Turnhout, Belgium

All correspondence concerning the
content of this volume should be
addressed to Salamander Books
Limited.

Editorial consultant: Jack Tresidder
Geographical consultant: Dr John Salt
Project manager: Vivien Bowler
Design director: Chris Steer
Cartographic editor: Harold Fullard

The Geographical Consultant

Dr John Salt has been a lecturer in geography at University College London for ten years. A graduate of the University of Liverpool in 1963, he gained a PhD four years later. He teaches Human Geography, with particular reference to population studies. His research interests are in problems of employment and migration, and he has a number of publications in this field.

The Authors

Jack Tresidder, who was the editorial consultant on the atlas and wrote the sections on Asia, Australia, Oceania and the polar regions, was born in Whangarei, New Zealand, in 1931. He is married with four children and is a graduate of Otago University. He was formerly a newspaper foreign correspondent and leader writer and has travelled widely on reporting tours of South-East Asia. Now living in London, he is an author and editor with an international publishing firm.

Norman Barrett, who has an honours degree in Physics from Oxford University, is an experienced editor and writer on diverse subjects. He has worked on several international encyclopedias and particularly on publications connected with the sporting world.

Arthur Butterfield, who has lived and worked extensively in South America, has been a freelance journalist and author for many years. He has contributed a large number of articles on varied subjects to countless different publications and was a senior editor on *World Book Encyclopedia* in Britain and in the United States. His special subjects are Latin America, geography, natural history and sport.

Keith Lye has an honours degree in geography and is a Fellow of the Royal Geographical Society. Having lived and worked in Africa for several years, he then returned to London to become a writer, editor, lecturer and broadcaster on African affairs. He has also worked as an editor on *World Book Encyclopedia* both in Britain and in the United States and later as Publishing Manager in the Encyclopedic division of a major London company. He now concentrates on freelance writing and editing.

Right: Parpan, a village in the Swiss Alps.

Contents

Right: The Parthenon, Athens, at dawn.

Right: Dense undergrowth in the New Zealand bush.

Foreword

The present map of the world is a patchwork of countries with varying shapes and sizes and has evolved over a long period of time. Some parts of the pattern are old, many nations having long and honourable histories. The last three decades, however, have witnessed major change, with the number of independent states more than doubling in the wake of the process of decolonization. Independence has not always severed old ties and many of the new nations still retain social, economic, political and cultural links with a former 'mother' country.

One of the salient features of the twentieth century has been the emergence of three blocs of countries, grouped according to the political and social ideas they espouse and to their different standards of living. The western bloc, which includes North America, Western Europe, Australasia and Japan, is usually regarded as the First of these three 'worlds'. The eastern bloc, the 'Second World', comprises the USSR and Eastern Europe. The 'Third World' includes a wide range of countries, especially in tropical areas, which often have diverse characteristics but whose peoples generally have lower incomes than those of the other two worlds.

The emergence of so many newly independent countries marks a new phase in man's colonization of the world, the principal underlying feature of which is the uneven distribution of population over the earth's surface. For many millennia man has known of and lived in virtually all parts of the land area of the globe. Certain areas with favourable living conditions, such as the fertile, irrigated soils of the Nile valley and the deltas of southeast Asia, have long been foci of settlement. In contrast, three-fifths of the earth's surface has proved too rugged, too high, too cold or too dry to provide the means of livelihood. For over two million years man's numbers increased only slowly. Average length of life in Cromwell's England, 35–40 years, was little better than that of Neanderthal Man. But in the last two centuries, and especially in the last twenty years, man's numbers have shot up dramatically to the present 4000 million. What has happened is that the combined advances of hygiene and medicine have precipitated the retreat of death, while in much of the world a fall in birth rates has lagged behind. There are now no empty lands of opportunity to which people can migrate and the burden of massive population increment is becoming intolerable in many countries, particularly the poorer ones where the biggest increases are concentrated. At present rates, for example, Bangladesh's population will double to 150 million by the end of the twentieth century. At the same time, a massive redistribution of the world's people is in train. Man is becoming an urban rather than a rural animal and nowhere is this process currently more in evidence than in the Third World where towns and cities are becoming teeming ant-hills. In most of the more developed countries the bulk of population has for decades been town-based and here the principal tendency is for large city populations to fall as people prefer to live in surrounding villages.

Man's occupation of the earth has been marked by exploitation of its resources. Some of these, such as air and water, continually renew themselves. Others, such as the minerals and fossil fuels geologically laid down through the ages are non-renewable; once used they are gone for ever. While man's numbers were small and his industries primitive the need for materials was simply met, but more people and more industries have imposed increasing pressure on natural resources.

The availability of food has increasingly given cause for concern. Estimates vary, but it is commonly thought that at least one-sixth of the world's people are undernourished. In fact the food problem is not so much one of production as one of distribution.

Mineral and energy sources have long been prized and today their discovery and exploitation are major tasks of international concern. Larger amounts of raw materials needed, and the demands of new technologies, have meant a continual widening of the scope and intensity of man's search for natural resources. Parallel with the hunger for raw materials has been a thirst for energy, particularly fossil fuels such as oil, and in recent years the strong bargaining position of countries possessing these resources has become apparent.

One of the side effects of growing population and industrialization has been disturbance of the ecological balance in many areas. The ever increasing amounts of waste generated by man's activities have created serious problems of pollution. Rivers and even the sea have in parts been deprived of life and made dangerous to human health. The air in some places has become unpleasant to breathe; it has killed vegetation and poisoned soils as a result of emissions from some industrial processes. A consequence of increasing pollution has been a growing awareness of the need to conserve the environment and to pass on to future generations a natural heritage that is not ruined.

This brief introduction to the world's population and resource base serves as a reminder that each of the countries depicted and described in this atlas exists within two separate but related realms. The first is essentially national in that each country has its own individual, often unique, problems which arise from the management of its national territory and resources. The second realm is an international one. In a shrinking world, dominated by a complexity of trade, cultural and other links, no country can act for long in isolation. In the management of the earth's resources for the wellbeing of all its people each country owes some responsibility to the larger community of nations.

Dr John Salt

Right: Camels in Tunisia.

The World

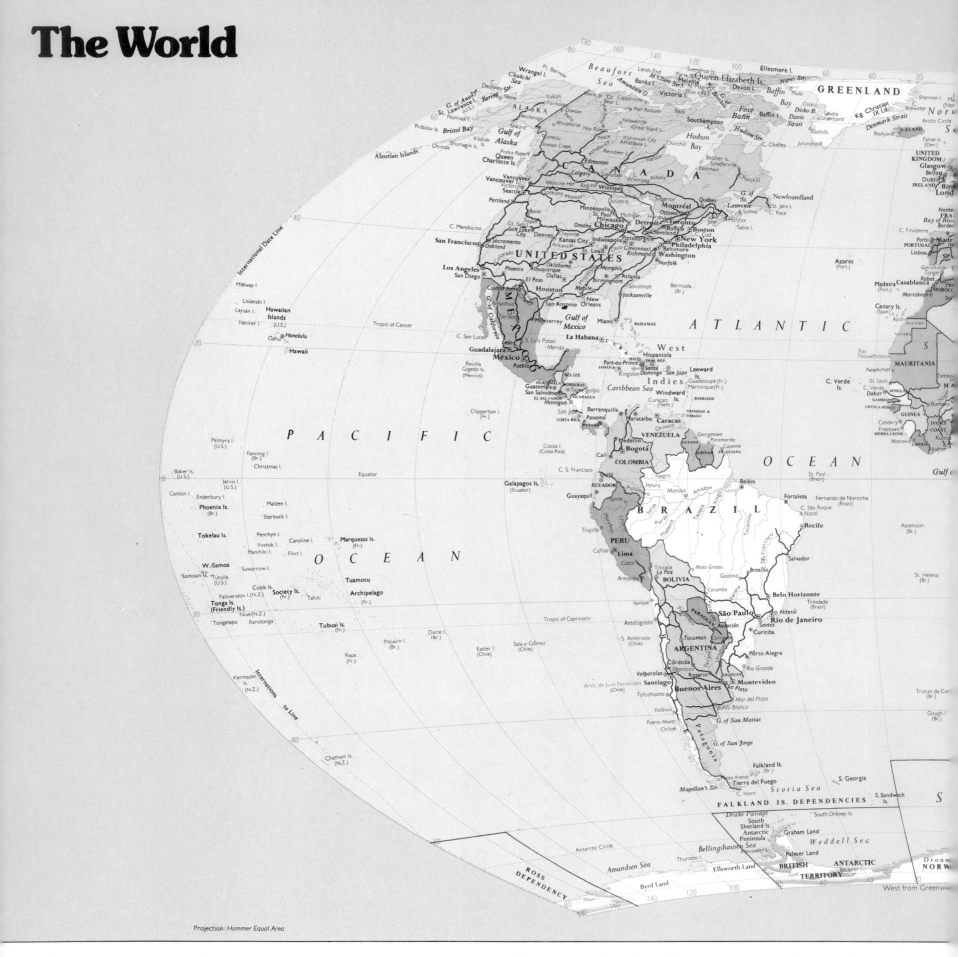

Projection: Hammer Equal Area

Introduction

A modern and comprehensive atlas has become indispensable both to students of geography and to general readers who want to understand the new economic and political shape of the world. This atlas is unique in that a concise, fascinating and authoritative text, illustrated with striking photographs, supports the fully detailed maps and graphs. The text and photographs relevant to each country fall as close as possible to the map of that country, and the Index to Principal Countries on page 144 gives the page number of both text and map. The text and maps are indexed separately, so the reader should consult the Index to the Text for information about a particular country or town and the Index to the Maps for its geographical location.

Spellings of place names are in the forms given in the latest official lists and generally agree with the rules of the Permanent Committee on Geographical Names and the United States Board on Geographic Names. The index contains over 18,000 entries.

The style of colouring chosen for the maps takes advantage of new developments in cartographic design and production. The inclusion of a hill-shading to complement the political colouring brings out clearly the character of the land and relief features without impairing the detail of names, settlement and communication. The opportunity of new reproduction was also taken to revise coastlines and rivers, boundaries and administrative divisions, railways, roads and airports from the results of the many recent surveys, and to express measures in metric form.

Attention is drawn to the policy adopted where there are rival claims to territory; international boundaries are drawn to show the de facto situation. This does not denote international recognition of these boundaries but shows the states which are administering the areas on either side of the line. The maps are not drawn to the same scale, but each one has its own scale clearly marked.

The majority of the maps are accompanied by a small selection of climate graphs. Where possible, towns have been chosen to reflect climatic differences within the area shown on the map, and principal towns are usually included. Complete temperature, pressure and rainfall statistics have been obtained for all except a few stations where pressure statistics were not available. Wherever possible the graphs show average observations based upon long period means, and in all other cases over as long a period as possible. The latest available statistics have been consulted throughout. The figure after the name of the station gives the height in metres of the station above sea-level, so that comparisons between stations can be made after allowing for elevation. For temperature, measurements are given in degrees centigrade; for pressure, millibars; and for precipitation (rainfall and snowfall), in millimetres.

The temperature graphs show the monthly means of daily maximum and minimum actual temperatures; from these the mean monthly actual temperatures can easily be determined by taking the mid point of the bar. The mean annual range of temperature is given above the temperature graphs. The pressure graphs show the mean monthly pressure at sea-level, except in cases of high-level stations, where the height to which the pressure has been reduced is noted. For both temperature and pressure graphs a uniform scale has been employed throughout.

The rainfall graphs show the average monthly rainfall, and above them is

COPYRIGHT. GEORGE PHILIP & SON, LTD.

given the average total annual rainfall. These graphs have been drawn to show the rainfall on the same scale for all stations to facilitate true comparisons between them. Where the rainfall graph extends over to the temperature graph it has been continued at the side of the graph.

GENERAL REFERENCE

Abbreviations of measures used — ft Feet; mm {Millimetres / Millimeters} cm {Centimetres / Centimeters} m {Metres / Meters} Km {Kilometres / Kilometers} mb Millibars

City and Town symbols in order of size

Sites of Archæological or Historical Importance

International Boundaries

International Boundaries (Undemarcated or Undefined)

Internal Boundaries

Principal Roads

Tracks, Seasonal and other Roads

Road Tunnels

Principal Railways

Other Railways

Railways under construction

Railway Tunnels

Principal Canals

Principal Oil Pipelines

3386 Principal Shipping Routes (Distances in Nautical Miles)

Principal Airports

Perennial Streams

Seasonal Streams

Seasonal Lakes, Salt Flats

Swamps, Marshes

Wells in Desert

Permanent Ice

Passes

▲ 8848 Height above sea-level } in metres
▼ 8050 Depth below sea-level }
1 34 Height of lake-level

CONVERSION SCALE
ft   m
30 000 ─ 9000
        ─ 8000
24 000 ─ 7000
        ─ 6000
18 000 ─ 5000
        ─ 4000
12 000 ─ 3000
9000   ─ 2000
6000   ─ 1000
3000   ─ 500
Sea Level 0 ─ Sea Level
        ─ 500
        ─ 1000
1000   ─ 2000
        ─ 3000
2000   ─ 4000
        ─ 5000
3000   ─ 6000
        ─ 7000
4000   ─ 8000
        ─ 9000
5000   ─ 10 000
        ─ 11 000
6000   ─ 12 000
7000
fathoms   m

The Arctic
Map 1

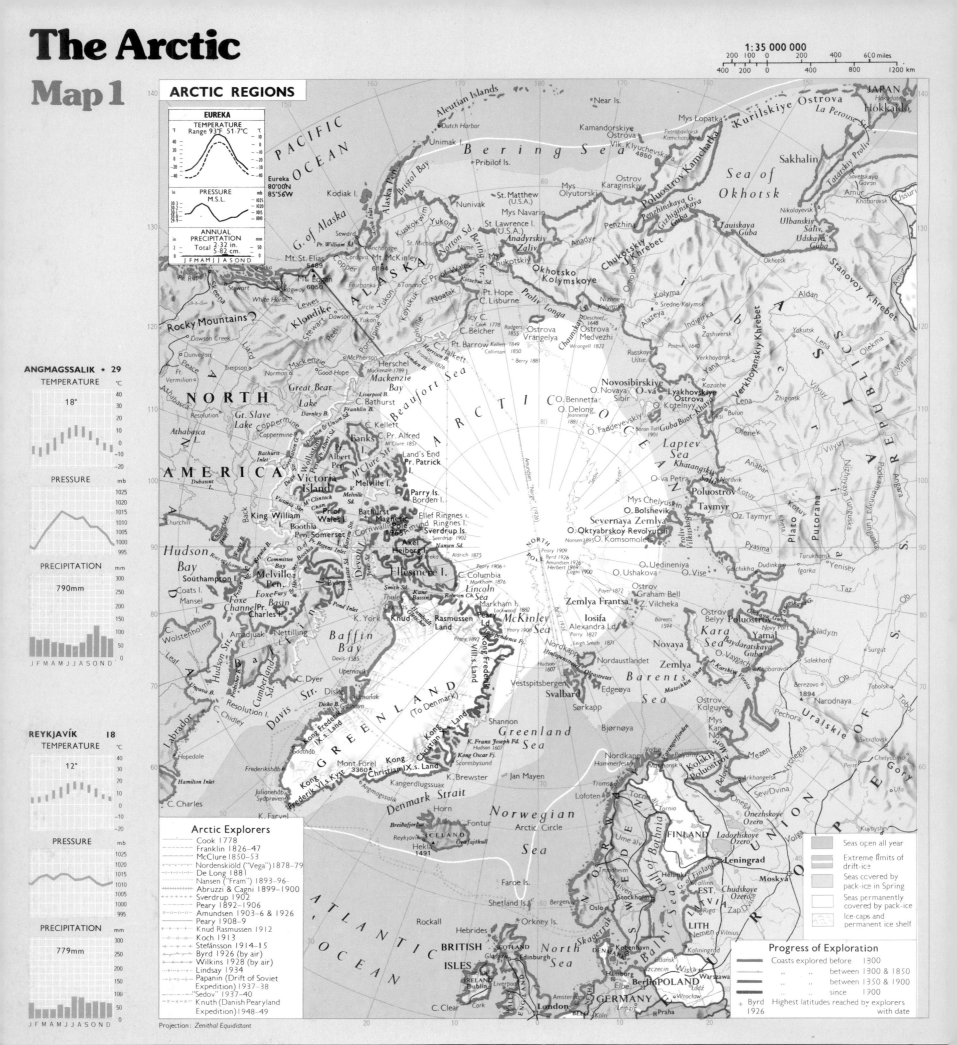

ARCTIC REGIONS

Arctic Explorers
- ———— Cook 1778
- ———— Franklin 1826–47
- ———— McClure 1850–53
- –·–·– Nordenskiöld ("Vega") 1878–79
- ········ De Long 1881
- ++++++ Nansen ("Fram") 1893–96
- +·+·+· Abruzzi & Càgni 1899–1900
- ———— Sverdrup 1902
- ———— Peary 1892–1906
- ———— Amundsen 1903–6 & 1926
- ———— Peary 1908–9
- ———— Knud Rasmussen 1912
- ———— Koch 1913
- +–+–+ Stefánsson 1914–15
- ———— Byrd 1926 (by air)
- ———— Wilkins 1928 (by air)
- ———— Lindsay 1934
- ········ Papanin (Drift of Soviet Expedition) 1937–38
- ———— "Sedov" 1937–40
- ———— Knuth (Danish Pearyland Expedition) 1948–49

Projection: Zenithal Equidistant

Seas open all year
Extreme limits of drift-ice
Seas covered by pack-ice in Spring
Seas permanently covered by pack-ice
Ice-caps and permanent ice shelf

Progress of Exploration
Coasts explored before 1300
" between 1300 & 1850
" between 1350 & 1900
" since 1900
+ Byrd 1926 Highest latitudes reached by explorers with date

ANGMAGSSALIK ★ 29
TEMPERATURE ℃
18°
PRESSURE mb
PRECIPITATION mm
790mm

REYKJAVÍK 18
TEMPERATURE ℃
12°
PRESSURE mb
PRECIPITATION mm
779mm

EUREKA
TEMPERATURE Range 93°F 51·7°C
PRESSURE M.S.L.
ANNUAL PRECIPITATION Total 2·32 in. 5·82 cm.
Eureka 80°00'N 85°56'W

The Arctic

The Arctic Ocean, with its vast area of pack ice, and the Arctic lands in northern America, Europe and Asia make up a total area of 14.2 million km² (5.5 million sq.m.). This bleak region of continuous cold today plays a vital role in meteorology and aviation and is increasingly being exploited for its minerals and fish.

Although the Arctic Circle itself lies along latitude 66°30'N, geographers usually define the Arctic limit as the northern tree line and this corresponds generally with a line where average midsummer (July) temperatures do not rise above 10°C (50°F). North of this line lie the island of Greenland, part of Iceland, belts of land in Alaska, Canada, Norway, Sweden, Finland and the USSR and many islands in the Arctic Ocean. Within this region, winter temperatures average –34°C (–30°F) and the sun rises only between March and September.

Rainfall is low, averaging 15-25cm (6-10in) but slow evaporation leaves the ground damp. Apart from Greenland, the land is generally free of ice but a thick layer of permafrost (mainly gravel) lies beneath the surface. Nevertheless, the topsoil thaws in summer and the plains (tundra) are covered with many species of plants, including moss, lichens, grasses, low shrubs and flowers. Apart from birds, wildlife includes polar bears, foxes, squirrels, hares, voles, lemmings and, during summer, large herds of reindeer and caribou. Some of the world's richest fishing grounds lie near Greenland and Iceland and the Arctic peoples also hunt whales and seals.

Mineral resources are widespread. Coal is found in Alaska, Canada, Greenland, Siberia and the Norwegian Svalbard Islands (Spitzbergen). There is iron, lead, nickel and petroleum in Canada and Russia, petroleum in Alaska, uranium and thorium in Canada, iron in the Scandinavian Arctic and some gold, copper and tin.

In the USSR, several cities lie within the Arctic, including the ice-free port of Murmansk and the mining centre of Norilsk. The largest group of Arctic peoples are the Yakuts of Siberia (300,000) and the Zyrians (300,000) who are a Finnish race, as are the Lapps (30,000). The Eskimos (100,000) are the most widespread group, living mainly in Greenland, Alaska and Canada. They have probably lived in the Arctic for at least 12,000 years. Although Nordic seamen established settlements from the 10th century, European exploration began in earnest only about 1500 and was directed mainly towards finding a short sea route to the Pacific. Robert E. Peary reached the North Pole in 1909. In 1958, the US submarine Nautilus travelled under the polar icecap, a distance of 2,945km (1,830 miles).

Today, world airline routes cross the Arctic as the shortest route from Europe to the Pacific. Strategic defence bases are maintained in the region by several nations, chiefly the US and USSR. Weather stations provide invaluable advance information on developments affecting America and Europe, especially the movement of low pressure areas lying between Siberia and Alaska (the Aleutian low) and Canada and northern Europe (the Icelandic low) which often send storms raging southward.

Right: Huge icebergs break off the glaciers of East Greenland, particularly between February and October. These awesome masses of floating ice reveal only one ninth of their total area and sometimes travel far down the coast of North America, presenting a menace to Atlantic shipping.

Greenland

Greenland, a province of Denmark with an area of 2,175,600km² (840,000sq.m.) is the world's largest island. It has a population of 58,000 and a capital at Godthaab (9,000). Most of the people are a mixture of Eskimo and Danish and the Greenlandic language is closely related to Eskimo. The island was settled by Eskimos from North America by the ninth century and was named Greenland by Norsemen who tried to attract settlers there after the tenth century. It became a Danish province in 1953 and elects two members to the Danish parliament.

Greenland has the world's only large deposit of cryolite (used for aluminium and ceramics). Its people live mainly by fishing, with some farming in the south-western coastal area. There is a US air base at Thule.

Geologically part of Canada, which is only 16km (10 miles) away at the nearest point, Greenland has mountains rising to 3,660m (12,000ft) in the north, west and east but is mainly a low plateau under a permanent icecap more than 1.6km (one mile) thick. It is deeply indented with fjords. Along the coasts, immense ice floes break off a series of glaciers, the widest of them the Humboldt Glacier, 97km (60 miles) across at the coast. Inland temperatures average −47°C (−53°F) in winter and −11°C (12°F) in summer, but coastal areas are warmer. ∎

Right: Beyond the steep approach to Narssarsuak, Greenland, high mountain ranges rise from the vast icecap.

Europe

[Map of Europe with scale 1:20 000 000, showing countries, cities, and physical features including ICELAND, UNITED KINGDOM, IRELAND, NORWAY, SWEDEN, FINLAND, DENMARK, GERMANY, POLAND, FRANCE, SPAIN, PORTUGAL, ITALY, YUGOSLAVIA, GREECE, TURKEY, UNION OF SOVIET SOCIALIST REPUBLIC, and others]

Projection: Bonne   West from Greenwich 0 East from Greenwich

COPYRIGHT: GEORGE PHILIP & SON

Europe

The continent of Europe has been a decisive influence on the economic, social and cultural history of much of the world for more than two thousand years. Since the peak of European power in the 19th century, two shattering wars, the dismantling of colonial empires and the rise of major world powers in America and the East have reduced the relative importance of Europe's political and technological leadership. But the continent includes many of the world's most prosperous economies, has an unmatched heritage of art, architecture, music, literature and science, and comprises a fascinating variety of peoples, languages and landscapes. It owes its position as the cradle of western civilization both to the energy and imagination of its people and to a fortunate combination of natural resources, both mineral and agricultural.

Europe is defined geographically as that part of the Eurasian land mass lying between the Atlantic Ocean in the west and the Ural mountains of Russia in the east and from the Mediterranean in the south to the Arctic Circle in the north. This huge peninsula has an area of 10,523,000km² (4,063,000sq.m.) and a population of about 680 million, grouped in 34 nations. Its highest peak is Mt Elbrus in the Caucasus, 5,633m (18,481ft), its longest river the Volga, 3,690km (2,293 miles) and its largest lake the Caspian Sea, 372,000km² (143,630 sq.m.). The climate of its milder

regions is governed by a warm air stream from the Atlantic moderating the severity of northern winters, although the continent grows colder towards the east. More than half the land is farmed and agriculture employs about a quarter of the workforce. The four main land forms are the ancient, eroded Northwest Mountains, the fertile rolling country of the Great European Plain, the Central Uplands stretching south of this through Central Europe to Portugal, and the Alpine Mountain System of Spain, Switzerland, Italy and the Balkans. Europe's leadership of the Industrial Revolution was based on vast deposits of coal and iron widely distributed through the continent (including Britain). The heavy industrial capacity of nations such as Russia, Poland, Czechoslovakia, Germany, Belgium, France and Britain is now supplemented by their highly developed lighter manufacturing industries.

Although the Cold War tensions that lined up western nations under Nato and eastern Europe under the Warsaw Pact have been reduced, the continent remains divided into two distinct political and economic blocs. Economically the socialist countries are grouped in the Council for Mutual Economic Aid (Comecon) while economic leadership of the west is taken by the European Economic Community (EEC). The EEC (France, West Germany, Italy, Britain, the Benelux countries, Denmark and Eire) is gradually moving towards greater economic, social and political integration.

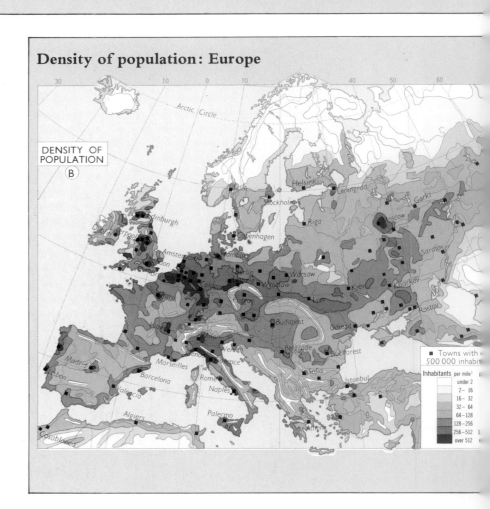

Density of population: Europe

DENSITY OF POPULATION

■ Towns with 500 000 inhabit.

Inhabitants per mile²
under 2
2 – 16
16 – 32
32 – 64
64 – 128
128 – 256
256 – 512
over 512

Above: Symbolizing postwar moves towards unity in Western Europe are the buildings of the European Economic Community in Brussels. 'Charlemagne' (left) is the seat of the Council, the EEC's decision-making body which comprises a delegate from each of the nine member states, Belgium, Britain, Denmark, France, Ireland, Italy, Luxembourg, the Netherlands and West Germany. 'Berlaymont' (right) houses the EEC Commission, the administrative branch which employs a staff of several thousand.

The British Isles

The British Isles consist of two main islands and a number of smaller islands off the northwest coast of Europe. They are separated from the continent by the English Channel which is 32km (20m.) across at its narrowest point. The larger of the two islands is made up of three countries—England, Scotland and Wales —known collectively as Great Britain. Together with Northern Ireland, which takes up the northeastern part of the second main island, these countries constitute the United Kingdom of Great Britain and Northern Ireland, and are united under one government. The United Kingdom is often referred to as Great Britain, or simply Britain.

The Republic of Ireland, formerly called Eire, is an independent nation occupying the whole of the smaller main island with the exception of the north-eastern portion. ∎

The United Kingdom

Area: *244,044km² (94,226sq.m.).*
Population: *56,427,000.* **Capital and largest city:** *London (7.5m.).*
Language: *English.* **Ethnic groups:** *British (descended from Celts, Romans, Angles, Saxons, Danes, Normans), and upwards of 1.5 million Commonwealth immigrants, mainly Asian and West Indian.* **Main exports:** *Engines, electrical machinery, ships, cars, aircraft, and other engineering products, textiles and clothing.* **Average temperatures:** *3°C (37°F) Jan, 18°C (64°F) July.* **Highest point:** *Ben Nevis 1,343m (4,406ft).*

Britain is a group of comparatively small islands and its peoples make up less than two percent of the world's population. But for nearly 500 years they have exercised a profound influence on world affairs. At the end of the 19th century the British ruled the seas and controlled the largest empire the world had ever seen. They started the Industrial Revolution; their legal system and democratic institutions became models for many other nations to copy; and their language and culture have spread to the remotest parts of the globe.

The English qualities of understatement and coolness in a crisis, combined with the fiery temperament of the Scots, and the poetic eloquence of the Welsh, have made up a blend of individualism and adventurousness that has produced some of the world's greatest explorers,

soldiers, scientists, statesmen, and writers.

The original ancestors of the British were the Iberians, people about whom little is known. They settled in the British Isles many thousands of years ago. Later came successive invasions of Celts, Romans, Angles, Saxons, Jutes, Norsemen, Danes, and Normans, each of whom left their mark. From the 1950s onwards, there was a substantial influx of Commonwealth immigrants, particularly from parts of black Africa, the West Indies, and India and Pakistan. Almost all of them settled in the poorer quarters of industrial centres in England and Wales and this resulted in problems of housing, education, employment, and racial discrimination, during the process of adjustment.

Britain is a densely populated country with nearly 230 people to the square kilometer. More than four-fifths of the people live in England, nearly four-fifths of them live in or near towns, and about a quarter of them are found within 80km (50m) of London.

Although English is the nation's official language, about a quarter of the people in Wales can speak some Welsh, and a few in Scotland and Northern Ireland speak Gaelic. Education is free, and is compulsory to the age of 16.

Britain's social welfare system is designed to look after its citizens 'from the cradle to the grave'. It includes free medical treatment (with certain exceptions), a nominal charge for prescribed drugs, sickness and unemployment benefits, and retirement pensions.

There are two established (official) churches—the Church of England (episcopal) in England and the Presbyterian

Church of Scotland in Scotland.

Most Britons are keen on sport but much of it is spectator-sport rather than active participation. Football (soccer) is the national winter game, and cricket takes over in summer. Rugby, tennis, golf, bowls, and boating also have large followings.

History and constitution

The Norman Conquest in 1066 marks the last time that the British Isles were successfully invaded. At that time the Channel Islands, which were part of Normandy, came under the English monarch and are today self-governing dependencies of the British Crown. This is also the present status of the Isle of Man, which was taken from Norway in 1266.

The Normans at first treated the conquered Anglo-Saxons as inferiors, but gradually the two peoples intermingled and became one in language and culture. In the century or so after the Norman Conquest a bitter conflict developed between the monarch and the barons, each jealously guarding their own rights. In 1215 the barons forced King John to accept the Magna Carta, a document that guaranteed many of the barons' rights.

In 1266 Norway gave up the Hebrides to Scotland, and in 1468 likewise surrendered the Shetland Islands and Orkney. In 1603 King James VI of Scotland succeeded England's Queen Elizabeth I as James I of England. Thus the two countries were finally united under one monarch. But political union had to await the Act of Union of 1707, which provided them with a common parliament as well as a single ruler. Together with Wales, the two countries from that

Above: The two houses of the British Parliament share Westminster Palace on the Thames, London.

Left: The rugged beauty of the Yorkshire Dales on the slopes of the Pennines at Malham.

time became known jointly as Great Britain. In 1801 came a full union of Ireland with England, Wales and Scotland.

Abroad, by the 18th century, Britain had become an imperial power, gaining Canada and India but eventually losing its American colonies. At home, new machines were invented, steam was harnessed as a source of power, and coke was used in the manufacture of iron. Agricultural workers flocked to the towns to take up better paid jobs in factories. The Industrial Revolution was on its way, and Britain became the workshop of the world, attaining a peak of power and wealth in the second half of the 19th century.

From 1914 to 1918 Britain played a leading role in World War I against Germany and her allies but was left exhausted and impoverished after victory. After the war, southern Ireland became a self-governing dominion, and in 1937 broke away completely as an independent republic.

From 1939 to 1945 Britain was once again on the winning side in World War II, against Hitler's Nazi Germany and Japan. After this even more debilitating conflict Britain tried slowly to adapt to a declining role as a world power and to modernize its industrial plant and outdated labour relations. Many of the old class distinctions began to disappear and a wide programme of socialization was initiated. The once-great empire quickly dissolved as one colony after another claimed and was granted its independence, with India leading the way. Most of them softened the blow by joining the British Commonwealth of Nations (later to be known simply as the Commonwealth), which is a free association of equal and independent states, together with a number of dependent territories, whose head is the British sovereign.

From 1969 onwards, violence in Northern Ireland, which had been simmering for many years, erupted in a series of shootings and bombings. A demand by the Roman Catholic minority there for power-sharing with the Protestant majority in this partly self-governing territory was backed by a terrorist campaign run by the illegal Irish Republican Army (IRA) which sought unification with the largely Roman Catholic republic across the loosely patrolled border. The Protestants, who strongly support the union with Britain, retaliated with bullets and bombs of their own. Britain established direct rule over Northern Ireland and sent large numbers of troops to the strife-torn area, but by the mid-1970s a solution seemed as remote as ever.

In 1973 Britain was formally admitted to the European Common Market after previous unsuccessful attempts to join. Facing severe inflation and a slice in the value of its currency, the country pinned much of its hopes for economic recovery on the prospects of North Sea oil flowing freely in the early 1980s.

Britain is a constitutional monarchy, with a largely unwritten parliamentary constitution based on well-tried ideas and practices. The House of Commons, with 635 elected members is the governing body. The House of Lords, which may delay but not defeat bills, has about 1,000 members, most of whom are hereditary

1:2 400 000

10   0   10   20   30   40   50 miles
10   0   10   20   30   40   50   60   70   80 km

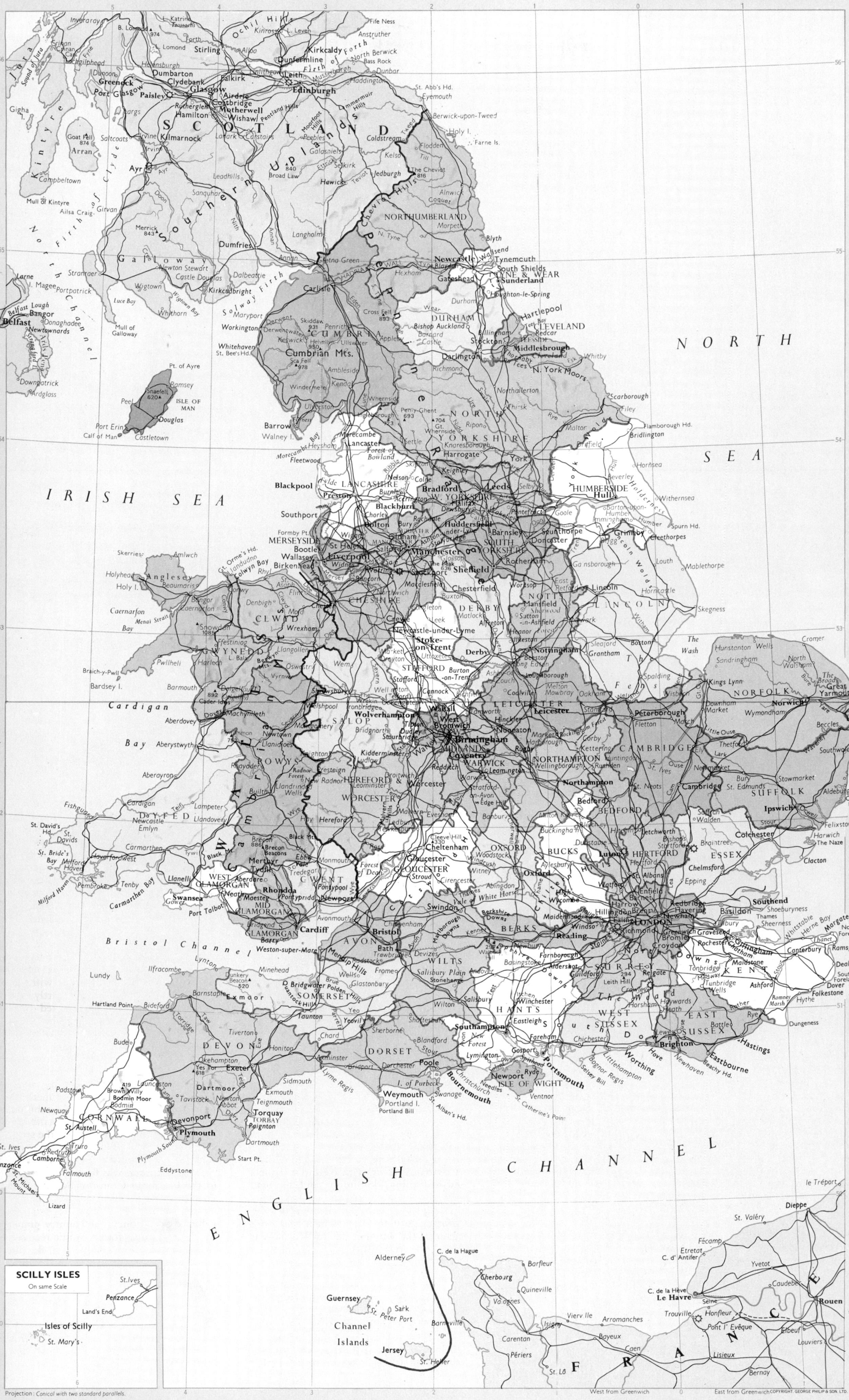

KEW   5
TEMPERATURE   °C
13°
                           40
                           30
                           20
                           10
                           0
                          −10
                          −20

PRESSURE   mb
                           1025
                           1020
                           1015
                           1010
                           1005
                           1000
                           995

PRECIPITATION   mm
593 mm
                           300
                           250
                           200
                           150
                           100
                           50
                           0
J F M A M J J A S O N D

ABERPORTH   133
TEMPERATURE   °C
11°
                           40
                           30
                           20
                           10
                           0
                          −10
                          −20

PRESSURE   mb
                           1025
                           1020
                           1015
                           1010
                           1005
                           1000
                           995

PRECIPITATION   mm
990 mm
                           300
                           250
                           200
                           150
                           100
                           50
                           0
J F M A M J J A S O N D

SCILLY ISLES
On same Scale
St. Ives
Penzance
Land's End
Isles of Scilly
St. Mary's

IRISH SEA

NORTH SEA

ENGLISH CHANNEL

Bristol Channel

Cardigan Bay

SCOTLAND

WALES

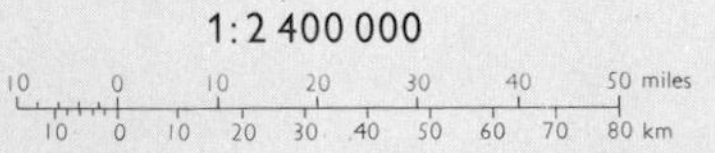

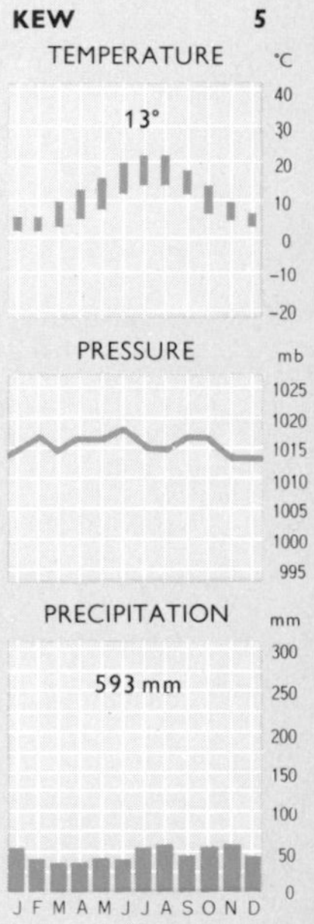

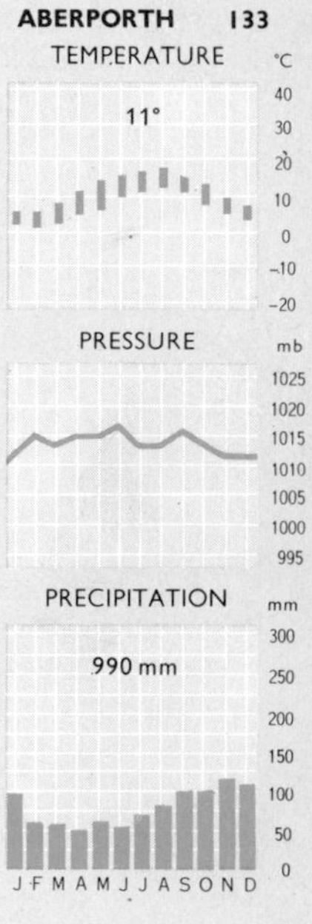

Projection: Conical with two standard parallels.

West from Greenwich   East from Greenwich COPYRIGHT GEORGE PHILIP & SON LTD.

19

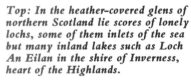

Top: In the heather-covered glens of northern Scotland lie scores of lonely lochs, some of them inlets of the sea but many inland lakes such as Loch An Eilan in the shire of Inverness, heart of the Highlands.

Above, left: Dolwyddelan Castle in Caernarvonshire is one of the most romantic and often-painted castles in Wales. Its keep, restored during the 19th century, may date back to the 12th century.

Above, right: The rivers of Scotland are renowned for their salmon fishing. Here an angler takes a fish from rapids near Gatehouse-of-Fleet, Kircudbrightshire, on Solway Firth.

peers and peeresses. The monarch is Head of State but the nation is governed by a Cabinet picked by the Prime Minister, usually the leader of the majority party in the Commons.

London is the capital of England, as well as the United Kingdom. The capitals of Wales, Scotland, and Northern Ireland are Cardiff, Edinburgh, and Belfast, respectively. There is increasing pressure for devolution of powers in Scotland and Wales.

Land and climate

Great Britain is a little under 960km (600 miles) long from north to south, and a little more than 480km (300 miles) wide at its widest point. The scenery is extremely varied for such a comparatively compact area. The Highlands rise in the north of Scotland. The Grampian Mountains form the chief range and include Ben Nevis, Britain's highest point. The land is craggy, desolate, and wind-swept, with deep fiords (sea lochs) cutting far inland from both the Atlantic

and the North Sea.

The Central Lowlands lie to the south of the Highlands, and are made up of the valleys of the rivers Tay, Clyde, and Forth. Rich coalfields and fertile farmland make this region a centre of population and industry. Farther south, the Southern Uplands rise in gently rounded hills. This is sheep-grazing country, and the valley of the Tweed is famous for its woollen mills. The Cheviot Hills, which mark the border between Scotland and England, rise at the southern limit of this region.

England's Pennine mountain chain runs southwards from the Scottish border to Derbyshire. It is often called 'the backbone of England' and its flanks are rich in coal. To the west of the Pennines, England's largest and most beautiful lakes are grouped together in the Lake District, a celebrated tourist attraction.

To the southwest of the Pennines a narrow lowland strip separates them from the magnificent Cambrian Mountains of

North Wales. South Wales has extensive coalfields, and much of Welsh industry is centred there.

To the south of Wales, across the Bristol Channel, lies the southwest peninsula. This is made up of Somerset, Devon and Cornwall and is noted for its mild climate and holiday resorts. The region is a huge granite plateau that in many places breaks off in spectacular cliffs where it meets the sea.

The remainder of England is known as the English Lowlands. They include the mainly treeless rolling downs of parts of the south and southeast; the low, flat landscape of East Anglia; and the mineral-rich Midlands plain, which makes up Britain's industrial heart. A third of the people live and work in the southeast and there, too, London is located.

Northern Ireland is a land of low hills and fertile lowlands. It is shaped almost like a saucer, with the hills round the coastal rim.

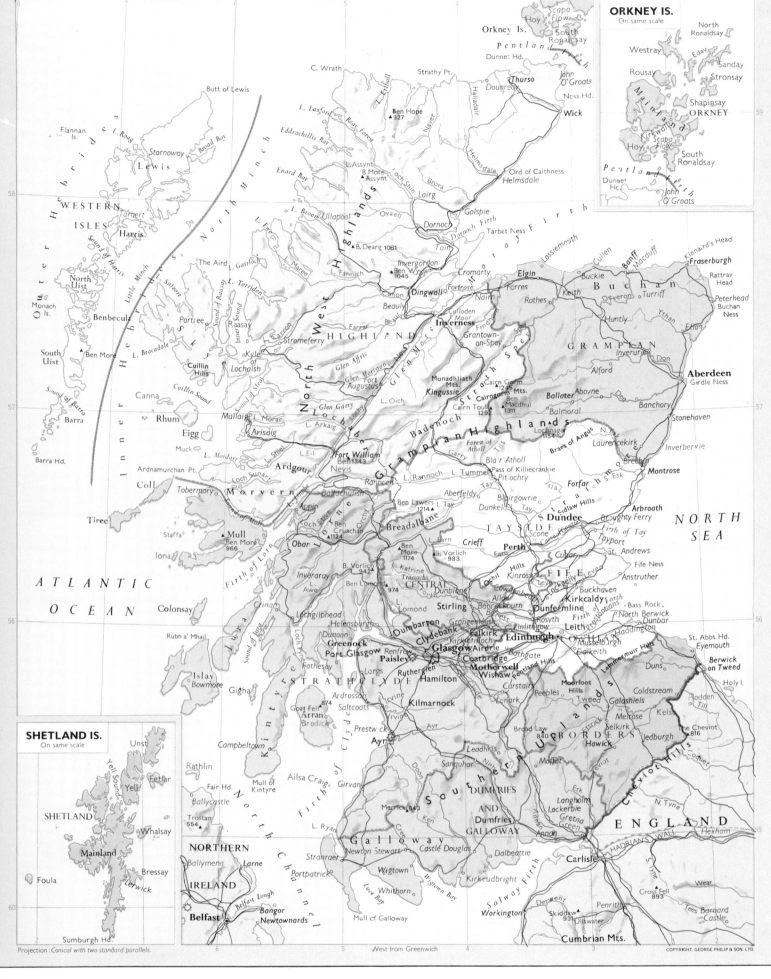

Britain's longest river is the Severn, which rises in Central Wales and flows about 354km (220 miles) into the Bristol Channel. The Thames drains southeastern England, and with London astride it, is the most important of Britain's rivers. The Clyde, Mersey, and Humber also have important estuaries with the ports of Glasgow, Liverpool, and Hull, respectively, located on their banks. The largest lake in the British Isles is Lough Neagh in Northern Ireland, with an area of 398sq.km (153sq.m.).

In spite of its northerly latitude, which is the same as that of icy Labrador, Britain has a temperate climate. In winter the temperature rarely drops as low as −12°C (10°F) or reaches as high as 32°C (90°F) in summer. Its mildness is due to the North Atlantic Drift, which warms the prevailing westerly winds. Rain falls during every month of the year, most of it in the northwest of the country. February and August are the wettest months.

Natural resources

Coal has been Britain's most important natural resource since the early 1600s and reserves are expected to last for at least another 200 years. But the best and easiest seams have already been worked out and new and deeper seams are constantly being explored while older pits are closed. Although annual coal production has been declining it is still the basis of most electrical power. The main coalfields are located in South Wales, in the Central Lowlands of Scotland, along the edges of the Pennines in the north of England and in the East Midlands.

Britain's iron ore is abundant but of poor quality. As a result, higher grades are imported in large quantities. Fine china clay for making pottery is found in the southwest of England, and chalk and limestone, for making cement, are plentiful in the southeast.

There are large natural gas fields in the North Sea. Supplies were already widely in use by the early 1970s. Huge oil deposits were discovered in the bed of the North Sea in the late 1960s, and by the early 1980s Britain is expected to meet all its own needs for oil and have a surplus left for export. Its present import bill for oil and gas imposes a heavy economic burden.

Farming, fishing and forestry

British farmers are unable wholly to feed the country because there is not enough fertile land available. In spite of efficient farming methods and much recent modernization, nearly half Britain's food is imported. The main arable area is in the eastern part of the country, while in general the west is given over to livestock rearing. The principal agricultural products are barley, wheat, oats, potatoes, and sugar beet. Britain's beef, especially Scottish beef, is world famous. Sheep are reared more for their meat than for their wool. British breeding cattle and sheep are in demand all over the world and are often used to improve stock.

The more sheltered parts of the south favour fruit, flower, and vegetable growing, much of it for the London market. Kent, in the southeast corner of England, has been called 'the garden of England'.

Northern Ireland's specialized and highly mechanized farms produce milk, butter, cheese, beef, bacon, eggs, and poultry.

Fishing has been a traditional industry for centuries. British fishing fleets regularly sail from ports such as Fleetwood, Hull, Grimsby, and Aberdeen to grounds in the North Sea and as far away as the Grand Banks off Newfoundland. Catches include cod, plaice, sole, haddock, hake, herring, and skate. But in the mid-1970s Iceland unilaterally widened the boundaries of her territorial waters to a radius of 320km (200 miles). Foreign fishing was strictly limited within this area. Britain refused to accept this decision and this led to a non-shooting 'cod war' between the two nations. As a result, Iceland severed diplomatic relations with Britain early in 1976.

About 7 percent of Britain is forested, but much of this is privately owned. The country imports most of its timber.

Manufacturing industries

Manufacturing accounts for about 35 percent of Britain's gross national product, and in spite of the loss of captive markets and valuable sources of raw materials with the dissolution of the empire, the country is still one of the leading exporters of engineering products and other manufactured goods. Britain is fifth in the world in steel production and has large new development projects in hand.

In addition to being the centre of politics, administration, law, insurance, banking, the arts, and fashion, London is also at the heart of the nation's network of transport and communications. Among its major industries are chemicals, clothing, printing, food processing, paper, furniture, plastics, and electrical and mechanical engineering.

The Midlands, stretching outwards from the sprawling conurbations of Birmingham (2,275,000) [Britain's second city], Wolverhampton (269,000), and Coventry (336,000), is traditionally the heartland of British industry. The major industries are motor vehicle manufacture, metal products, tractors, and bicycles, and a wide range of other engineering products, as well as pottery. Lancashire has a flourishing textile industry (formerly cotton but now mainly man-made fibres), and oil refining, shipbuilding, food processing, chemicals, glass-making, paper, and printing are also important. The largest cities in that region are Greater Manchester (2.4m) and Greater Liverpool (1.2m).

The Yorkshire textile industry is better known for its woollen goods and carpets. Sheffield (513,000) is celebrated for its steel and cutlery. Coal, iron and steel, chemicals, and shipbuilding are the major industries of northeastern England. The Central Lowlands of Scotland, with the centre of Glasgow (1.7m) at its hub, produces ships, iron and steel, and woollen goods. Northern Ireland has the largest shipbuilding yards in Britain at its capital, Belfast (360,000). High-quality Irish linen manufacture and tobacco processing are other important industries of the Province.

Many British industries are nationalized (government-owned); they include transport, coal, electricity and gas, and the steel industry. They also include the advanced nuclear energy stations that lead the world in production of electricity from nuclear power.

Trade and external affairs

Britain is one of the world's leading trading nations. Its chief partners are the United States, West Germany, Belgium, Denmark, France, Canada, Australia and New Zealand. Although it imports more than it exports, it is a key financial centre, providing banking, shipping, insurance and other commercial services whose 'invisible' earnings make a significant contribution to its balance of payments. Tourism is another important foreign exchange earning industry.

Although Britain has lost much of its former power and prestige, its experience in statesmanship and its diplomatic finesse is valued abroad in delicate international situations and it has often been called on in the role of 'honest broker'. In addition to the influence it exercises through its world-wide Commonwealth, it retains numerous protectorates, colonies or associated territories. Gibraltar, Hong Kong and most of its holdings in Oceania and the West Indies are discussed in other articles. Some of its territories, such as the Seychelles in the Indian Ocean are moving towards independence; a few are in dispute with other nations, such as Gibraltar (with Spain), Belize (with Guatemala) and the Falkland Islands (with Argentina). A serious diplomatic problem has been Rhodesia whose unilateral declaration of independence in 1965 was not recognized by Britain and whose security is increasingly under threat from guerilla movements sympathetic to its disadvantaged African majority. ■

Above: Dublin, capital of Ireland is attractively laid out around the River Liffey with its quays and bridges.
Below: Ancient stone turrets form a farm gateway in Londonderry, one of the six counties of Northern Ireland.

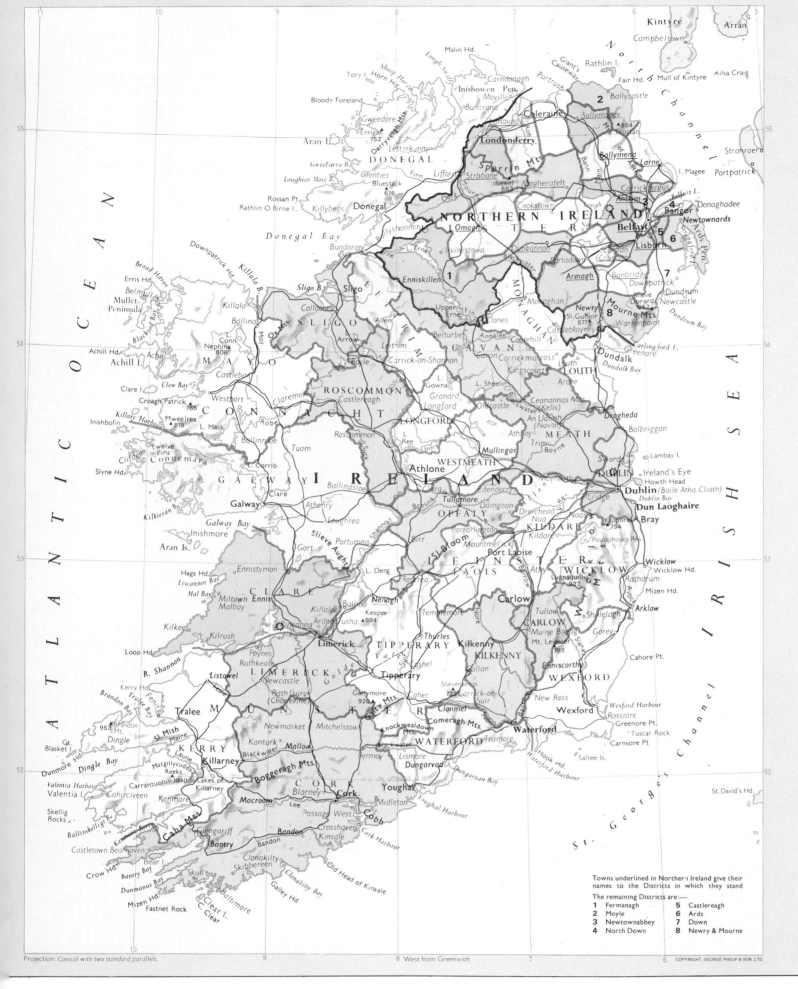

The Republic of Ireland (Eire)

Area: *70,282km² (27,136sq.m.).*
Population: *3 million.* **Capital and largest city:** *Dublin (556,000).*
Languages: *Irish (Gaelic) and English.* **Ethnic groups:** *Irish, with Anglo-Irish minority.* **Main exports:** *meat, livestock, textiles, machinery, transport equipment, dairy products.*
Average temperatures: *5.6°C (42°F) Jan, 13.9°C (57°F) July.*
Highest point: *Carrantual, 1,014m (3,414ft).*

The Irish people are descended from a branch of an ancient Celtic tribe called the Gaels. They are a deeply patriotic and religious people, loquacious, artistic and musical. More than 90 percent of the people are Roman Catholics and large families are generally the rule. The name of the country in Gaelic is *Eire.* Although small in size, Ireland's influence on the outside world has been remarkable, especially through the work of writers such as Joyce, Yeats, Wilde, Shaw and O'Casey.

Most of Ireland's history is taken up with the people's bitter struggle against British rule. From 1845 to 1849 a disease wiped out the Irish potato crop, and as a result more than a million people died of disease and starvation. Many of the survivors emigrated to the United States and other countries.

Rebellion against the British erupted sporadically from 1916 to 1921, after which Britain granted the country the status of a dominion. Civil war raged during the following two years. In 1949 Ireland severed its last ties with the British Commonwealth and declared itself an independent republic.

Since that time the Irish Republican Army (IRA), an illegal organization opposed to the partition of Ireland, has been a thorn in the side of the Irish government, particularly with its stepped-up campaign of violence in Northern Ireland in the 1970s.

Land, climate and economy

Ireland's plentiful rainfall has made the land so green that it is often called the *Emerald Isle.* The North Atlantic Drift comes close to the west coast and keeps the climate mild. Physically, Ireland consists of a large central lowland surrounded by a rim of plateaus and hills. Most of the low lying land is used for agriculture cultivation or pasture, although some of it is peat bog.

The Shannon, which flows for 386km (240 miles), is the longest river in the British Isles. Among the country's many lakes, pride of place goes to Killarney, famous in literature and song, and a great tourist attraction.

Politically, the island consists of four provinces—Connaught, with 5 counties; Leinster, 12 counties; Munster, 6 counties; and Ulster, 9 counties. Twenty-six of these 32 counties are in the Irish Republic and 6 form the Six Counties of Northern Ireland.

Ireland's greatest resource is its fertile soil. The most important crops are oats, potatoes, barley, wheat, turnips, and beet. Cattle, sheep, pigs, and horses are reared. In the 1960s and 1970s there was considerably increased investment of foreign capital in a number of industrial undertakings such as oil-refining, shipbuilding, fertilizer manufacture, and electronics. Among traditional industries, glass-making at Waterford, and weaving and hand-knitting are well known. Tourism and travel are also major sources of income.

Ireland's major trading partners are the United Kingdom, the United States, West Germany and the Netherlands. Ireland joined the European Common Market in 1973. ■

23

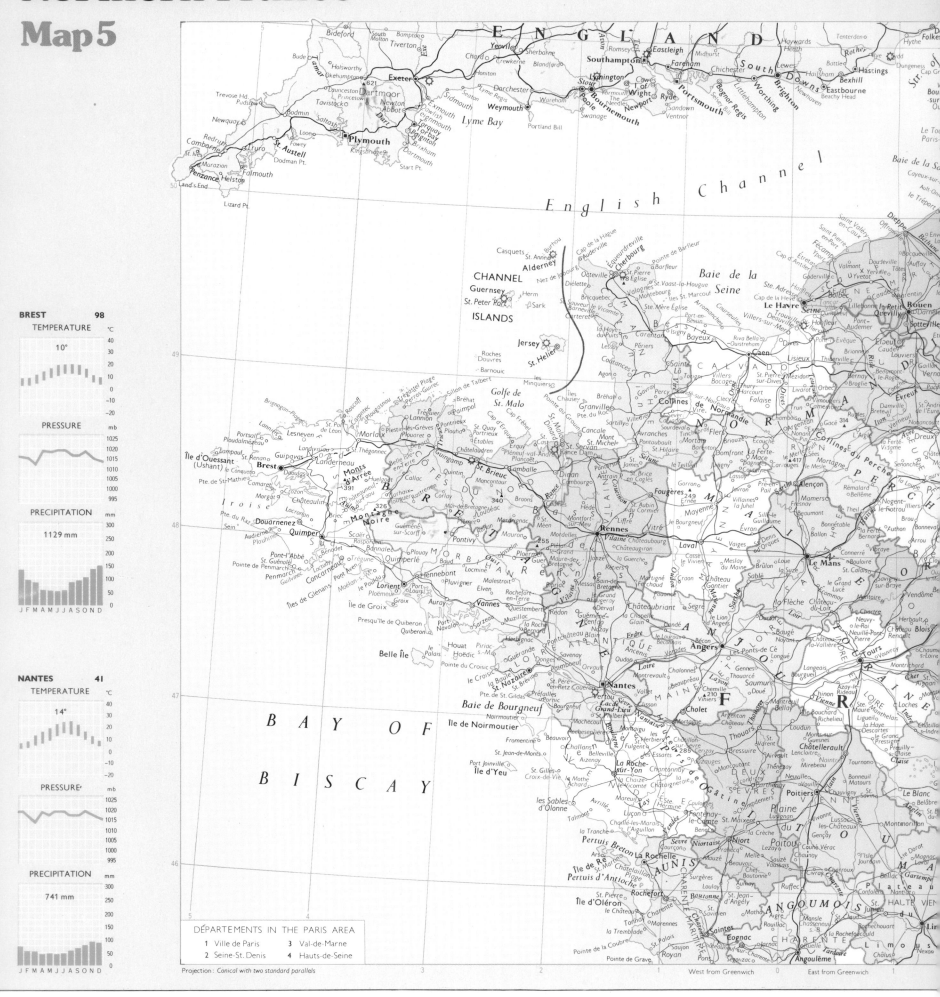

BREST 98
TEMPERATURE °C
10°
PRESSURE mb
PRECIPITATION mm
1129 mm
J F M A M J J A S O N D

NANTES 41
TEMPERATURE °C
14°
PRESSURE mb
PRECIPITATION mm
741 mm
J F M A M J J A S O N D

DÉPARTEMENTS IN THE PARIS AREA
1 Ville de Paris 3 Val-de-Marne
2 Seine-St. Denis 4 Hauts-de-Seine

Projection: Conical with two standard parallels

France

Area: 547,026km² (211,207sq.m.).
Population: 53,074,000. Capital:
Paris (city, 2.59m., metropolitan area,
8.2m.). Languages: French, Basque,
Breton, Catalan, German, Provençal.
Ethnic groups: French, Basques,
Bretons, Catalans, Flemings. Main
exports: chemicals, iron and steel
goods, machinery including cars, textiles,
wines and spirits, luxury goods, beef.
Average temperatures: Paris, 2°C
(36°F) Jan. 18°C (65°F) July;
Marseille, 6°C (43°F) Jan. 22°C
(72°F) July. Highest point: Mont
Blanc, 4,810m (15,781ft).

France is one of the most beautiful and
varied of western European nations. It
contains temperate fertile plains and

*Left: The Place des Vosges, Paris, is
the oldest formal square in Europe.*

rugged, scenic coastlines in the north,
plateaus and high mountain scenery, and
sunny Mediterranean beaches.

Each region has its own special character, culture and cuisine. France's elegant,
cosmopolitan capital, Paris, is one of the
world's leading cultural centres and the
country has pioneered many artistic developments in architecture, literature,
music and painting. French cuisine,
cheeses, fashions, perfumes and wines are
world-renowned.

After France was liberated from
German occupation in 1944, it suffered
crippling colonial wars and, as a consequence, political instability. But it has
recovered quickly and it has made a major
contribution to the development of the
European Economic Community, of
which it was a founder member.

People
The French people are a mixture of
various groups, including the original
Celts. Throughout history, France has
been subjected to Roman and, later,

Map 6

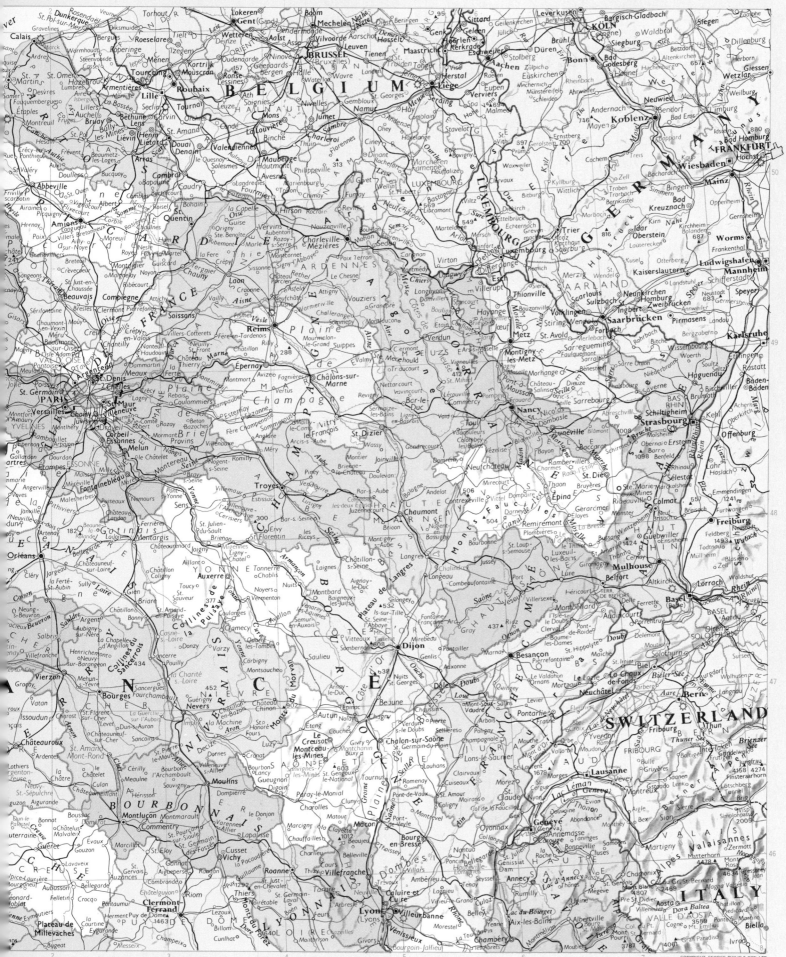

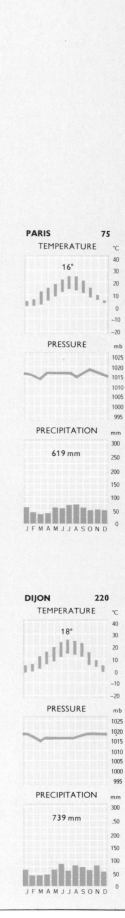

Moorish and Italian influences from the south. From the north came Norse, Germanic and other influences.

French is a Romance language. A Celtic language, Breton, survives in Brittany and forms the basis of separatist aspirations. Breton nationalism, however, probably owes more to geographical remoteness and the relative poverty of its farming and fishing people.

In the southwest, the Basques form a distinctive group, quite different from Frenchmen or Spaniards. The Basque language is of very ancient origin. At the western end of France's border with Spain live the Catalans, whose Romance language resembles that of Provençal. German is spoken in Alsace, which was returned to France from Germany after World War I, and some French-speaking Flemings live in the region bordering Belgium.

In about 1800, France had a population of 27 million—the largest in Europe except for Russia. By 1900 it had in-

creased to 39 million but, in the early 1900s, the birth rate fell. The two World Wars caused the deaths of many of France's active, working male population and this created a serious shortage of workers.

Partly in consequence, after 1945, proportions of children and elderly people had increased relative to those of working age. By 1960, only 56 percent of the people were between 20 and 64 years of age, compared with about 60 percent in that age range from 1920 to 1940. Immigrant workers filled the gap in the labour force and, in the late 1960s, there were more than 2½ million foreign workers in France—especially Algerians, Spaniards, Portuguese and Italians. Today the annual rate of population increase is about average for western Europe— about 0.9 percent, or an increase of about 48,000 people per year.

In recent times, France's urban population has increased rapidly. The nation has five conurbations with more than

500,000 people: Paris, Lyon (1.07m.), Marseille (0.96m.), Lille (0.88m.) and Bordeaux (0.56m.). However, France remains a major farming country. Although the proportion of people engaged in farming has been steadily decreasing, about 13 percent of the labour force still work in farming, forestry and fishing, as opposed to 7 percent in West Germany.

There is no state religion in France, but most people are Roman Catholics. About 750,000 people are Protestants.

History and constitution

Between 58 and 51 BC, Julius Caesar conquered the region that is now France, which the Romans called Gaul. The Celtic population were Romanized and Gaul became a prosperous province. The decline of Roman rule was heralded by border fighting with Germanic tribes.

Finally, a Frankish king, Clovis, overthrew the Roman governor and became the Christian king of the so-called Frankish realm in AD 486. (The name

France is derived from the term Frankish.) This realm at first included Aquitaine, northern Gaul and some areas east of the Rhine. Later, the Merovingian dynasty, established by Clovis, added Bavaria, Burgundy, Provence and Thuringia.

The Merovingian dynasty gradually declined in the 600s and, in 751, it was replaced by the Frankish Carolingian dynasty. The second Carolingian ruler, Charlemagne, became extremely powerful and was made emperor of the Romans by the pope. Charlemagne died in 814 and, in 843, his empire was divided into three kingdoms. The area containing much of modern France came under Charles the Bald, one of Charlemagne's grandsons.

In 987, the Capetian dynasty replaced the Carolingian. The Capetians controlled the centre of France around Paris and Orléans. But Normandy was a separate feudal state. Under Duke William of Normandy the Normans began their conquest of Britain in 1066.

Above: A ruined castle in Normandy recalls a formidable military strength.

The Capetian dynasty ruled France until 1328. It had a strong, centralized monarchy and extended French territory. But Philip VI's accession in 1328 was challenged by Edward III of England. Fighting broke out between France and England in 1337 and continued, off and on, until the French, under Joan of Arc, defeated the English at Orléans in 1429, weakening their rule in France which ended at last in 1453.

A powerful monarchy gradually emerged and new territories were occupied. However, French conquests in Italy were ended when the French were defeated in the 1500s. Religious conflict between Roman Catholics and Protestant Huguenots occurred in France in the 1500s, but religious freedom for Protestants was granted by the first Bourbon monarch, Henry IV, in 1598.

The Bourbon monarchy became extremely powerful but it was overthrown by the French Revolution in 1789. In 1792 the First Republic was established, but seven years later Napoleon Bonaparte seized power. After brilliant military successes, Napoleon was finally defeated in 1815. The Bourbon monarchy was re-established. But in 1848, Louis Philippe was exiled and the Second Republic was proclaimed.

This republic was short-lived. In 1851 Louis Napoleon, nephew of Napoleon Bonaparte, took power and became emperor in 1852. In 1870-1871, France lost the Franco-Prussian War and surrendered Alsace and part of Lorraine to Germany.

A provisional republican government was set up in 1871 and the Third Republic began in 1875. France's territorial losses aroused Franco-German hostility and, in 1904, France established close relations with Britain through the Entente Cordiale. In 1907 France, with Britain and Russia, formed the Triple Entente which lined up against Germany

and Austria-Hungary in 1914. France suffered greatly during World Wars I and II.

In 1946 the Fourth Republic came into being. But post-war recovery was hindered by expensive colonial wars, especially in Indo-China and later in Algeria. Successive governments failed to solve the nation's problems.

Finally, the war-time leader Charles de Gaulle was elected president in 1958 under a new constitution establishing the Fifth Republic. The chief feature of the constitution was that it greatly extended the president's powers.

The president is directly elected by universal suffrage for seven-year terms. He nominates and dismisses the prime minister and other ministers. There are two houses of parliament: the National Assembly and the Senate. The National Assembly is directly elected. It can be dissolved by the president after consultation with the prime minister. The Senate is comprised of delegates from the National Assembly, the communes (units of local government) and other groups.

The presidential elections are supervised by a nine-member constitutional council, which acts as a guardian of the constitution. Three members are nominated by the president, three by the president of the National Assembly and three by the president of the Senate.

The new constitution brought stability to France. Under President de Gaulle, the nation rapidly disengaged from colonialism and pursued an independent attitude in foreign affairs. Through the European Economic Community, France became increasingly prosperous.

Physical features and climate
The landscapes of France are very varied, and mainland France can be divided into eight main regions.

The northwest peninsula contains Brittany, which is a hilly scenic region of ancient rocks. Brittany's coast is deeply indented by drowned river valleys. In the north, the region extends into western

Normandy and in the south into Anjou and La Vendée. The climate is mild and the rainfall, which occurs all the year round, supports lush grasslands which are used especially for dairy farming. Many coastal peoples are engaged in fishing or in the flourishing tourist trade. Industry is increasingly important.

The Paris basin includes the basins of the Seine, Somme and middle Loire rivers. The region is a synclinal depression consisting of circular belts of limestone, chalk and sandstone hills, separated by clay vales. The hills are mostly bordered by steep, outward-facing scarps, but they dip gently towards the centre of the basin, where Paris, a great route centre, straddles the Seine. The original site of Paris was an island in the Seine called the Ile de la Cité.

Within the Paris basin, there are several distinctive sub-regions. Southwest of Paris is the loam-covered, dry limestone Beauce region which is im-

Above: The monastery at Gorges de Galamus, Aude, is built into a cliff.

portant for wheat and sheep-grazing. To the southeast, the limestone Brie plateau is mostly covered by clayey soils. Brie is known for its dairy produce and sugar-beet farming. To the east, vine-growing regions include the chalk Champagne district. North of Paris is a region of chalk hills where fruits and dairy products are important. In the far south, the middle Loire valley contains industrial centres that were once picturesque market towns, such as Orléans and Tours. In the north, near the Belgian frontier, there is a major industrial region, based on an extension of the Belgian coalfield into France. The largest industrial city here is Lille.

The eastern borderlands are a low, broken plateau region between the Meuse and Rhine rivers. The Vosges mountains are in the southeast. The im-

portance of the eastern borderlands lies in the vast iron ore deposits which stretch from Nancy to the Belgium-Luxembourg frontier. This region is a great industrial area. The Ruhr supplies coking coal for iron and steel production.

The central plateau occupies the heart of France. It covers about one-sixth of the country. The central plateau averages 914m (3,000ft) above sea level and winters are severe. The plateau is partly volcanic in origin and there are remains of volcanic cones, called *puys*, in the northwest. These volcanic remnants reach heights of more than 1,830m (6,000ft) above sea level. In the west and south, limestone massifs have typical karst scenery, with little surface drainage, potholes, disappearing streams, gorges and large cave networks. The thinly-populated central plateau contains the headwaters of the Dordogne, Garonne, Loire and Seine rivers.

The Rhône-Saône basin is flanked by the central plateau in the west, the Jura mountains in the northeast, and the foothills of the French Alps in the southeast. Lyon stands on the junction of the Rhône and Saône. North of Lyon, there is a rich farming region which includes the famous vineyard country of Burgundy. Summer temperatures are fairly hot but there is some summer rain. To the south of Lyon, the Rhône valley becomes increasingly dry and Mediterranean in character.

In southwestern France, the Aquitaine basin is a low-lying area that broadens to the south. It rises eastwards to the central plateau and southwards to the lofty Pyrenees. Sand dunes and a belt of sandy soils border the coast of Aquitaine (the Landes), but farther inland the plains and river valleys are fertile.

Mediterranean France is growing in industrial importance. Much of the coastlands west of Marseille are marshy, but rice, cattle and wine production are important activities. Oil refining and petrochemicals are among industrial activities

Above: A vineyard stretches out in front of early fortifications at Carcassone.

and there is a large complex around the steel plant at Fos-sur-Mer. East of Marseille is a rich coast belt, including the tourist Riviera region. Also on the Riviera is the small independent principality of Monaco.

Monaco covers an area of only 189 hectares (467 acres) and has a population of 26,000. Apart from its famous princess, the former film actress Grace Kelly, Monaco is known for its casino at Monte Carlo.

The French Alps rise behind the southeastern coastlands. The highest point is Mont Blanc on the Franco-Italian border. The swift-flowing streams of the French Alps are utilized for hydro-electric power.

Corsica (Corse in French) is a wild mountainous island in the Mediterranean Sea, some 14½km (9 miles) north of the Italian island of Sardinia. Corsica covers 8,723km² (3,368sq.m.) and has a population of 219,000.

The climate of maritime northwestern France is mild and moist all the year round, although most of the rain falls in winter. To the east, the climate becomes more continental in character and annual temperature ranges steadily increase. To the south, the average temperatures gradually rise. The Mediterranean coastlands have hot, dry summers and mild, moist winters. The mountain and plateau regions have more severe climates than surrounding lowland areas.

Minerals

France's most important mineral resource is iron ore. The chief mining area is in Lorraine, where Europe's largest deposits occur. Although the Lorraine ore is low grade, it is easily mined. Some is exported to West Germany. The second

Right: The beautiful carved and decorated façade of this house in Joigny, Yonne, sums up the historic charm of French domestic architecture.

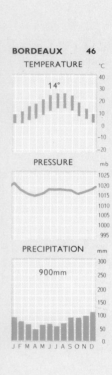

BORDEAUX   46
TEMPERATURE
14°
PRESSURE
PRECIPITATION
900mm

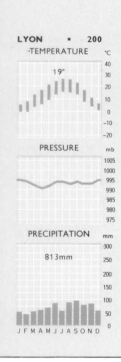

LYON ★ 200
TEMPERATURE
19°
PRESSURE
PRECIPITATION
813mm

iron ore area is around Caen in Normandy.

Coal is mined in the northeast, in Lorraine and in some areas around the central plateau. The coalfield in the northeast, an extension of the Belgian coalfield, produces mainly steam coal, which is unsuitable for metallurgical industries. The Lorraine coal, although abundant, is not of coking quality and the deposits around the central plateau are mainly of local importance. As a result, France has to import coal.

France produces some petroleum, mainly from the Landes in the southeast and some natural gas is obtained from the Lacq region in the foothills of the Pyrenees. Some bauxite and other metal ores, potash, salt and sulphur are also mined.

Industry and communications
France has always been known for its wines and quality goods, such as silks, particularly from Lyon, lace and fine porcelain (Limoges and Sèvres). Luxury

goods, such as perfumes, were famous products of Paris. Today France still produces all these items and is the world's leading wine producer in some years.

Since 1945, the growth of France's heavy industry capacity has been rapid and about 27 out of every 100 working people are employed in manufacturing— twice as many as in farming, fishing and forestry. In the late 1960s and early 1970s, progress was spectacular and industrial production was increasing by between 7 and 8 percent per year.

Today France's leading industrial goods are cars, chemicals, mechanical engineering products and textiles. The chief industrial areas are situated in Paris, where traditional luxury industries thrive alongside heavy industries, on and around the mining areas, and in the major ports where imported raw materials are used. Although oil has been the major stimulus to industrial expansion, the development of hydro-electric power in the Alps, Pyrenees, Vosges and the central plateau

has helped new industrial centres to arise in these and adjacent areas.

France has one of the best developed transport systems in Europe, with more than 70,000km (491,000 miles) of roads and 35,600km (22,100 miles) of railways. Canals are important in the northeast and some rivers, such as the Seine below Paris, are used to transport heavy goods and materials. Navigable waterways total 7,600km (4,720 miles). The chief ports are Marseille, Le Havre and Rouen, which together handle more than half of France's seaborne trade. Dunkirk, Bordeaux, Nantes, Saint-Nazaire and Caen are also important ocean ports and Strasbourg is an important inland port.

Agriculture, forestry and fishing
Because of France's differing climates, its agriculture is also varied. Only about 14 percent of the country is unproductive, and France's chief natural resource is its fertile soil.

Cultivated fields cover 31 percent of the country, pasture 26 percent, and

vineyards about 2½ percent. Forests cover 26 percent, especially in highland areas, and timber is used to manufacture a wide range of wood products.

The chief crops, by area, are wheat, barley, maize, rice, sugar-beet, tobacco and potatoes. Many fruits, including apples, pears, plums, peaches and apricots are grown. Livestock raising is extremely important and there are 22.5 million cattle, 11.4m pigs and 10.2m sheep. The chief dairy farming regions are in the northwest.

The chief wheatlands are in the Paris and Aquitaine basins. The leading wine-producing areas are the lower Loire valley, the lowlands of the Charente and Garonne rivers in Aquitaine, the Champagne district, the Burgundy region and the Mediterranean-facing southern slopes of the central plateau and the Languedoc plains. Brandies from Armagnac and Cognac are well-known and France produces a variety of liqueurs. Normandy is known for its cider and Alsace

Map 8

1:2 500 000

MARSEILLE 4
TEMPERATURE
17°

PRESSURE

PRECIPITATION
546mm

PERPIGNAN 43
TEMPERATURE
16°

PRESSURE

PRECIPITATION
639 mm

COPYRIGHT, GEORGE PHILIP & SON. LTD.

produces beer.

French agriculture was traditionally a peasant industry and it was relatively under-developed. Many changes have occurred in the last 25 years. Many small farms have been consolidated, fertilizers are more widely used and many farms have been mechanized. As a result, France often has agricultural surpluses. France has tried to dispose of the surpluses through the European Economic Community. However, problems have arisen because West Germany, a food importer, has wanted to protect its farmers from French competition.

Fishing is important, especially around the northwestern peninsula, where sardine canning is a thriving industry in the

coastal towns, and in the Mediterranean. France has more than 34,000 fishermen and about 14,000 fishing vessels.

Trade and foreign relations

France's chief trading partners are West Germany, Belgium-Luxembourg and Italy. Trade with the French Community (former French overseas territories), the US, the Netherlands, the UK and Switzerland is also important.

Despite the loss of most of its overseas empire, France has sought to re-establish its world status by seeking, through the EEC, to make Europe a united world power, independent of the super-powers, the US and the USSR. France has pursued an independent policy in foreign affairs and has tended to challenge the leadership of the US. It has attempted to establish good relations with communist countries, including China. In addition to its overseas territories there are four overseas departments in non-metropolitan France — Martinique, Guadeloupe, Réunion and Guiana. ∎

Left: The picturesque boat harbour at Calvi, Corsica, was once heavily fortified. An important sea port in the north-west of the island, the town was founded in 1268 and in the 16th century fiercely repulsed a French invasion.

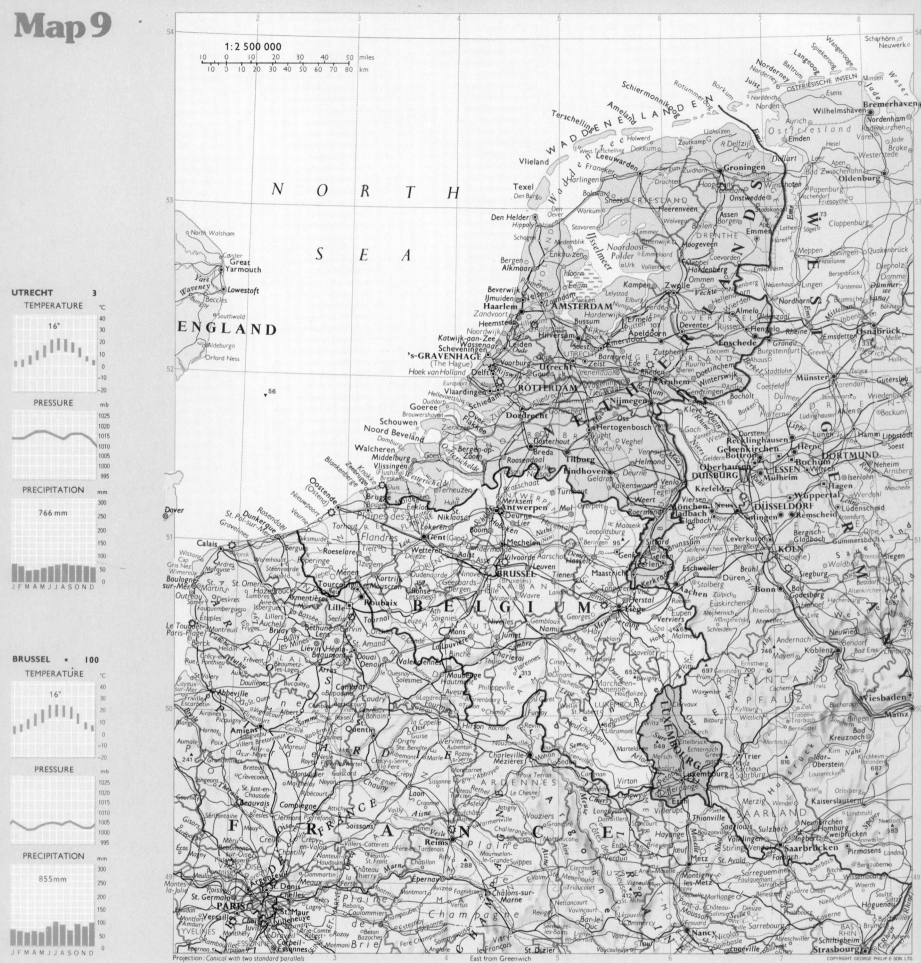

1:2 500 000

UTRECHT 3
TEMPERATURE °C
16°
PRESSURE mb
PRECIPITATION mm
766 mm

BRUSSEL ★ 100
TEMPERATURE °C
16°
PRESSURE mb
PRECIPITATION mm
855mm

Projection: Conical with two standard parallels   East from Greenwich   COPYRIGHT. GEORGE PHILIP & SON LTD.

The two monarchies of Belgium and the Netherlands, with the Grand Duchy of Luxembourg, are commonly called the Low Countries, although southeastern Belgium and much of Luxembourg contain uplands. These countries are also described as the Benelux countries after the Benelux Customs Union, established in 1947, which led to the creation of the Benelux Economic Union by the three countries in 1960. Their economies have also become increasingly integrated through the EEC.

The three small territories possess thriving industries and fertile farmlands and they are centres of trade. ■

Left: Chassepierre is typical of many villages and towns in the river valleys of the Ardennes region of Belgium. The Semois River, shown here, runs close to the French border and French is the language of the Walloon people of this region. The Ardennes is an area of small farms, although dense forests still cover much of the land.

The Netherlands

Area: *40,844km² (15,770sq.m.).*
Population: *13,708,000.* **Capital:** *Amsterdam (1m.).* **Largest city:** *Rotterdam (1.04m.).* **Language:** *Dutch.* **Ethnic group:** *Dutch.* **Main exports:** *chemicals, electrical equipment, flower bulbs, machinery, meat, petroleum products.* **Average temperatures:** *4°C (39°F) Jan. 17°C (63°F) July.* **Highest point:** *on the German border near Aachen, 322m (1,057ft).*

The Netherlands is a delta formed from sediments deposited by rivers, including the Maas, Rhine and Scheldt. Water covers about 17 percent of the country and about two-fifths of the land is below sea level. Large, low-lying areas called *polders* have been enclosed by dykes (sea walls), drained and reclaimed from the sea. Despite more than 140 floods in the

last 700 years, the Dutch people have never ceased in their struggle to enlarge their country by reclamation.

On the reclaimed land, they have practised highly efficient agriculture and, in recent years, manufacturing has developed quickly. Despite the post-war loss of its overseas empire, the Netherlands is now a prosperous, densely-populated country.

People, history and constitution
The Dutch language belongs to the Germanic group and most of the people are of Germanic origin. The country has come under Roman, Frankish (Germanic), French and Spanish influence. Largely independent from 1581, it rose to world prominence in the 17th century as a commercial and colonial power and as an artistic centre. A constitutional monarchy was established in 1815, but, in 1830, the southern part broke away to become the independent kingdom of Belgium.

The Netherlands, neutral in World War I, was occupied by Germany in World War II. Tremendous damage was done when the Germans were driven out, but post-war recovery was rapid. The Netherlands has an hereditary monarchy. Its parliament consists of two chambers. The Upper or First Chamber has 75 members, elected indirectly by the provincial states. The Second Chamber has 150 directly-elected members. The seat of government is at The Hague.

Physical features and climate
The polder region, which covers 40 percent of the Netherlands, lies behind a narrow, sandy coastal strip. Although flat, this region is an attractive patchwork of fields, criss-crossed by canals. The towns, mostly old, are picturesque. Glacial deposits cover much of the east, with peat bogs in places. But much of this mostly infertile land has been reclaimed. The Netherlands has cool summers and mild, moist winters.

Mining, industry and communications
The Netherlands has a little coal but some petroleum and a valuable field of natural gas. Its chief industrial resource is a highly-skilled workforce with a long tradition of craftsmanship. Many of the materials needed for heavy industry are imported. Amsterdam and Rotterdam are the main industrial centres. Some industries process farm products and others use imported materials, such as cocoa for chocolate.

The country has an excellent network of roads, railways and canals. Rotterdam and its outport, Europoort, handle much West German traffic.

Agriculture and fishing
Farmland covers 62 percent of the land and two-thirds of it is pasture. Cattle-raising for butter, cheese and meat is important and the dairy industry is highly efficient. The nation has 4.6 million cattle and, with Belgium, has more cattle per square kilometre than any other country. There are also 0.7m sheep, 6.4m pigs and 60m poultry. The chief crops are cereals, sugar-beet, potatoes and flower bulbs. Sea and inshore fishing are important industries.

Trade and foreign relations
The country's chief trading partners are EEC nations and the US. The Netherlands, like Belgium, is a member of West European institutions, such as the EEC and NATO. ■

Luxembourg

Area: *2,586km² (998sq.m.).*
Population: *358,000.* **Capital:** *Luxembourg (78,000).* **Languages:** *French, German, Luxembourgeois.* **Ethnic groups:** *mixed French, Belgian, Dutch and German.* **Main exports:** *iron and steel, farm products.* **Average temperatures:** *3°C (37°F) Jan. 23°C (73°F) July.* **Highest point:** *565m (1,854ft).*

Luxembourg is a small Grand Duchy, with a Grand Duke or Duchess as head of state. It was occupied by Germany between 1940 and 1944. Luxembourg has

Above: Luxembourg is famous for the fortified towns along its steep valleys.

major iron ore deposits and steel manufacturing is very important, although farming still provides a useful source of income. The Grand Duchy also earns 'invisibles' from foreign companies registered in the country, tourism and its commercial radio. ■

Belgium

Area:: *30,513km² (11,781sq.m.).*
Population: *9,835,000.* **Capital:** *Brussels (1.06m).* **Languages:** *Dutch, French, German.* **Ethnic groups:** *Flemish, Walloons, with some German-speaking people in the southeast.* **Main exports:** *manufactured goods including chemicals, machinery, foodstuffs, textiles.* **Average temperatures:** *Brussels, 4°C (39°F) Jan. 23°C (73°F) July.* **Highest point:** *Botrange Mt., 693m (2,274ft).*

Belgium is one of western Europe's most densely-populated and leading industrial nations. It is a prominent member of West European institutions, including the Benelux Economic Union, the EEC, NATO, the Council of Europe and the West European Union. Brussels is the headquarters of the EEC and NATO.

People and language
Belgium's official languages are Dutch, French and German. The two major language groups are the Flemings in the north, who speak a Dutch dialect and the French-speaking Walloons in the south. Brussels is bilingual, but language divisions have created communal conflict. To reduce conflict, the government has granted the language groups more autonomy. Most people are Roman Catholics.

History and constitution
Belgium declared its independence from the Netherlands in 1830. It was occupied by Germany in World Wars I and II. Since then, it has recovered quickly, despite the loss of its colonial territories, especially Zaïre. Belgium is a constitutional monarchy. The Senate is partly elected directly by the people and partly by provincial councils, for four-year terms. The directly-elected Chamber of Representatives also sits for four years.

Physical features and climate
Sand dunes fringe Belgium's short coastline. Behind the coastal strip is a rich, flat area which is largely reclaimed marshland. The central plains form the largest region. They include the basin of the River Scheldt and its tributaries. The Campine region near the Dutch frontier is Belgium's chief coal-mining area. The south Belgian coalfield, which has declined in recent times, extends from Mons, along the Sambre-Meuse valley, to

the industrial city of Liège. South of this coalfield are the southern highlands which rise to the Ardennes plateau. Belgium has a mild, moist climate.

Minerals, industry and communications
Belgium's large coal and iron deposits form the basis of prosperous engineering and metal-working industries. Some industries process farm products and the woollen and linen textile industries of Flanders have been important for centuries. Brussels, like Paris, is known for its luxury goods. New industries have recently been established in the port of Antwerp and other northern centres as a result of imported petroleum and the development of coal mining in the Campine. This has led to a relative decline of the southern industrial area in the Sambre-Meuse valley. Belgium has the world's

Above: Six windmills at Kinderdijk recall the 19th century when the Netherlands had more than 1000 big corn mills. Experiments are now being carried out to develop an economic means of harnessing their surplus energy to generate electricity.

greatest density of railways and a good road system.

Agriculture, forestry, fishing, trade
Only 4 percent of the active population work in farming, forestry and fishing. The chief crops are cereals, especially wheat and barley, sugar-beet and potatoes. Livestock are also important, but Belgium imports food. Forests cover nearly one-fifth of the land and forestry and fishing are both important. Belgium's chief trading partners are its EEC partners and the United States. ■

BERLIN ★ 55

TEMPERATURE

PRESSURE

PRECIPITATION

603mm

JFMAMJJASOND

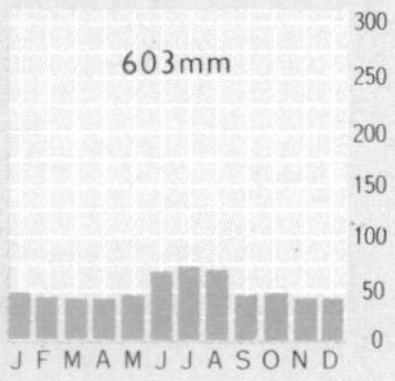

MÜNCHEN ★ 524

TEMPERATURE

PRESSURE

PRECIPITATION

957mm

JFMAMJJASOND

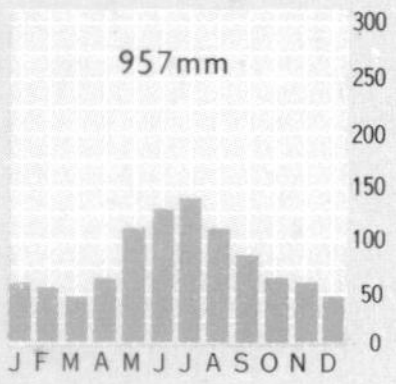

GENÈVE ★ 405

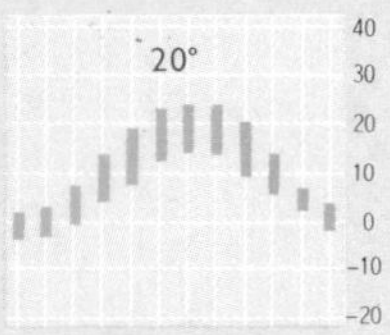

TEMPERATURE

PRESSURE

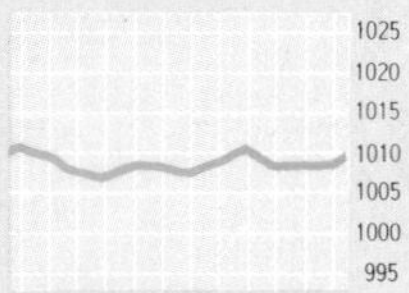

PRECIPITATION

853mm

JFMAMJJASOND

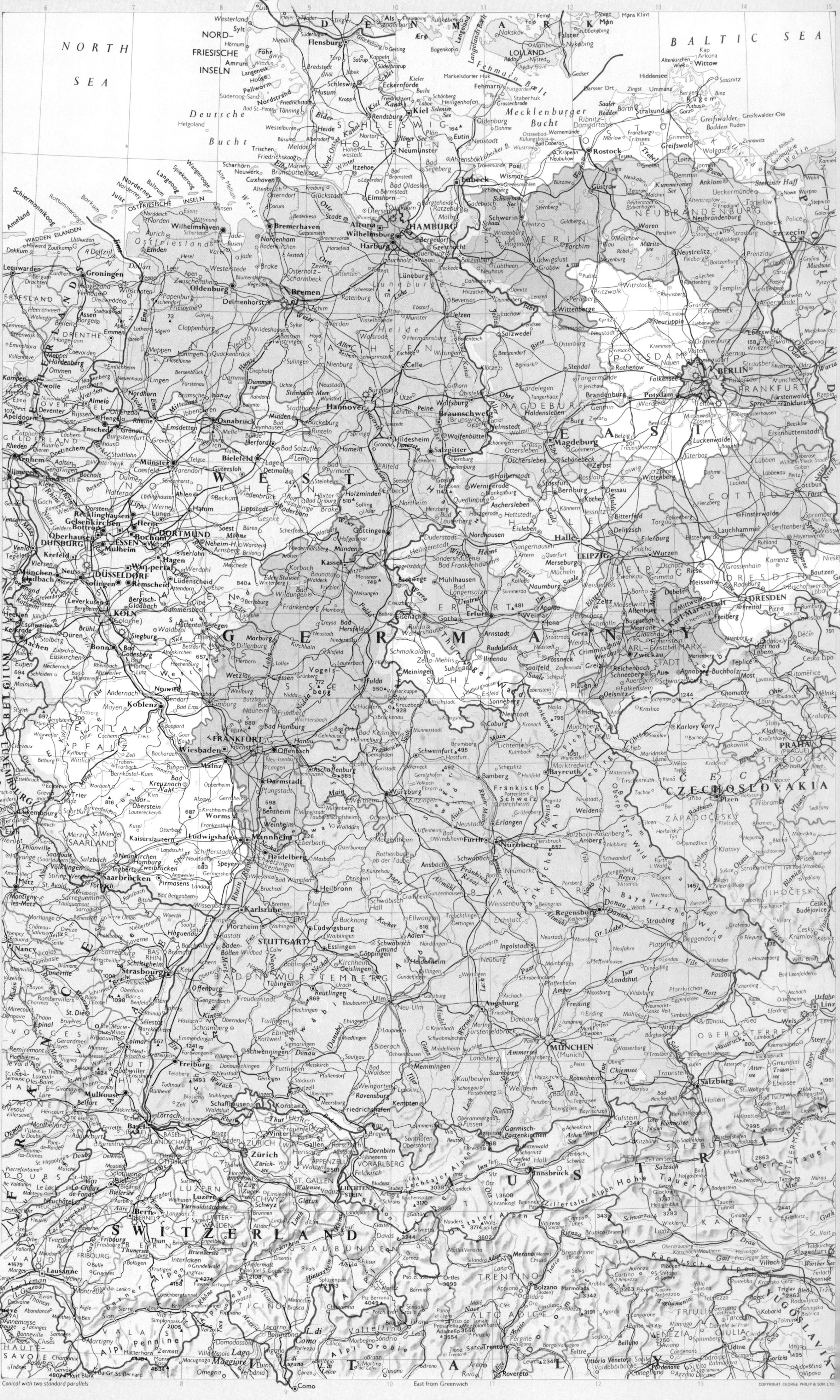

NORTH SEA

BALTIC SEA

DENMARK

HAMBURG

BERLIN

GERMANY

SWITZERLAND

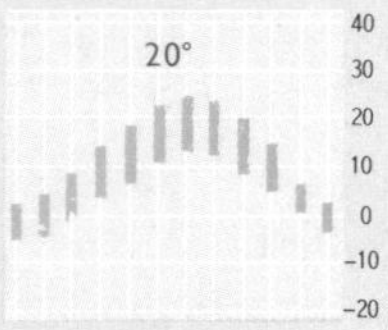

CZECHOSLOVAKIA

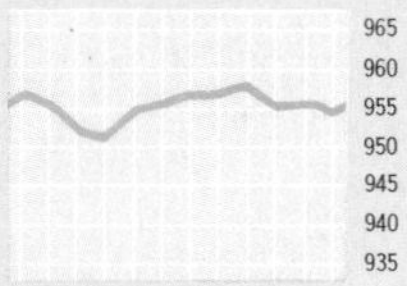

AUSTRIA

ITALY

FRANCE

MÜNCHEN (Munich)

STUTTGART

FRANKFURT

KÖLN (Cologne)

DÜSSELDORF

DORTMUND

BREMEN

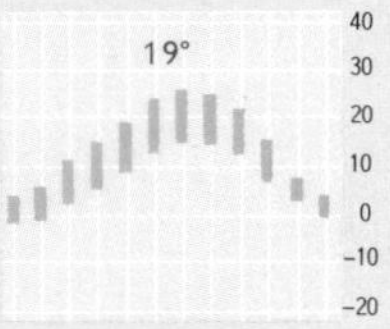

HANNOVER

MAGDEBURG

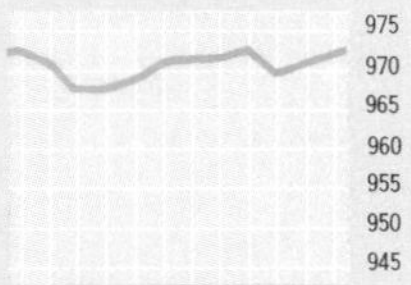

LEIPZIG

DRESDEN

NÜRNBERG

ZÜRICH

BERN

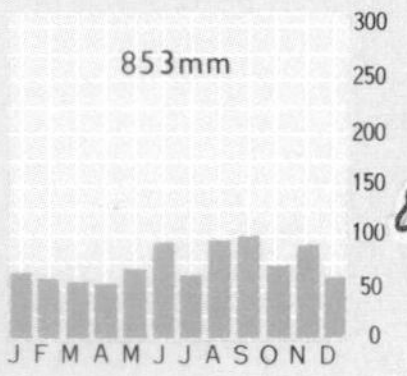

Germany

Before 1800 the German people were divided into more than 300 states. But, after the defeat of Napoleon, the number of states was reduced to 39, including Prussia. Between 1814 and 1871, these states were loosely confederated. Following the success of Germany in the Franco-Prussian War (1870–1871), a federated German empire, or *Reich*, was established with the King of Prussia as its *Kaiser* (emperor). The united Germany rapidly expanded its industries and military power, and colonized overseas territories.

In World War I, Germany, Austria-Hungary, Bulgaria and Turkey formed a powerful central European alliance. But, after their defeat in 1918, Germany lost its overseas empire, and, in Europe, it lost territory to Belgium, Czechoslovakia, Denmark, France, Lithuania and Poland. East Prussia was separated from Germany by the Polish Corridor.

In the 1920s, Germany suffered appalling inflation and unemployment and, finally, Adolf Hitler and the National Socialist party established an absolute dictatorship in 1933. Germany began to recover lost territory. It occupied the Rhineland in 1936. In 1938 German troops took Austria and, later, seized the German-speaking parts of Czechoslova-

kia. In 1939, Germany took the rest of Czechoslovakia and Memel from Lithuania. Finally, the German invasion of Poland on September 1, 1939, precipitated World War II

After Germany collapsed in 1945, it lost the territories it had seized and a large area of eastern Germany was taken by Poland. The eastern border of Germany was fixed along the Oder-Neisse rivers. Some 10 million Germans were expelled from East Prussia, Poland, Czechoslovakia and other counties and these refugees went mainly to western Germany.

Germany was partitioned into American, British, French and Russian zones. Berlin, the capital, lay within the Russian zone, but it, too, was partitioned into four occupation areas. At that time, the occupation was considered to be temporary. German reunification was expected before long. By 1948 the American, British and French zones had become one unit, West Germany. But the Russians kept control of their zone.

In 1949 West Germany became a federal republic, but a communist regime was established in East Germany. Since 1949 West and East Germany have developed as separate countries. Berlin remains divided. West Berlin, comprising the former American, British and French zones, has its own government, but it is effectively part of West Germany. East

Berlin is the capital of East Germany.

Both West and East Germany have made remarkable recoveries since 1945. But the methods adopted have differed greatly. ∎

West Germany

> **Area:** *248, 577km² (95,976sq.m.).*
> **Population:** *62,838,000.* **Capital:** *Bonn (283,000).* **Largest city:** *West Berlin (2m.).* **Language:** *German.*
> **Ethnic group:** *Germans.* **Main exports:** *automobiles, machinery, iron and steel products, chemicals, electrical equipment, textiles, processed food.*
> **Average temperatures:** *4°C (40°F) Jan. 21°C (70°F) July.*
> **Highest point:** *Zugspitze, 2,968m (9,738ft).*

The German language belongs to the same family as Danish, Dutch, English, Norwegian and Swedish. Ethnically, the Germans are a mixed people, although two main types may be distinguished: the long-skulled, fair, tall, blue-eyed Nordic people; and the broader-skulled, short, sturdy, dark-haired and dark-eyed Alpine people.

The population of West Germany increased rapidly after 1945. First came

Above: Medieval castles such as this once enforced tolls on the Rhine.

about 8.5 million German refugees, most from the lost territories in the east. Later, many more East Germans entered West Germany. East German refugees totalled about two million between 1955 and 1961. Despite East German efforts to prevent emigration, an average of 21,000 people left East for West Germany each year between 1965 and 1973. Most refugees were absorbed into industrial employment. West Germany's largest cities are West Berlin (2m.), Hamburg (1.75m.) and München or Munich (1.34m.).

Protestants form 49 percent of the population and Roman Catholics 44.6 percent. At the end of 1975, there were about 2.2m. foreign workers employed in West Germany. These *Gastarbeiter* (guest-workers) came from Turkey, Yugoslavia, Italy, Greece, Spain and other countries.

History and constitution

The Bundesrepublik Deutschland, or the Federal Republic of Germany, came into existence in 1949. When Britain, France and the US revoked the Occupation Statute in 1955, West Germany became an independent democratic country.

The Federal Republic is divided into Länder (states), each of which has its own Government. The federal govern-

ment controls such matters as citizenship rights, currency, federal communications and foreign affairs.

The federal parliament consists of two houses. The members of the lower house, the Bundestag (Federal Diet), are elected for four-year terms. Berlin sends representatives but they have no vote. The upper house is the Bundesrat (Federal Council). It consists of representatives of the governments of the Länder. The federal president is elected by the Federal Assembly for five-year terms. This assembly consists of all the members of the Bundestag with an equal number of representatives from the Länder. The president may only serve two terms.

The government is led by the federal chancellor, who is proposed by the president and elected by the Bundestag. The chancellor selects federal ministers who are appointed by the president. The chief political parties are the Social Democrats, the Christian Democrats and the Free Democrats.

Physical features and climate

West Germany has four main physical regions: the north German plain; the central uplands, south-west Germany; and the southern uplands.

The North German plain is largely covered by glacial deposits and much of it is poorly drained. In some parts the soils are infertile, especially the sandy heathlands, such as Lüneburger Heide (Lüneberg Heath). The northwest coast is deeply indented by drowned river valleys, such as those of the Elbe and the Weser.

Central Germany is a region of plateaus, low hills and block mountains. It includes the Ruhr coalfield, West Germany's chief industrial region.

Southwest Germany contains the Rhein, or Rhine, highlands which are divided by the Rhine and its tributaries. To the south, the Rhine occupies a deep trough flanked in the west by the Odenwald and Schwarzwald (Black Forest) uplands.

Southeastern Germany is an area of varied relief. It contains the limestone plateaus of the Swabian and Franconian Jura and in the south it rises to the Alps which border Austria.

The high parts of the southern uplands have a severe climate, but most of West Germany enjoys a mild climate, because of its relative proximity to the sea.

Minerals and industry

West Germany is a major producer of coal. The chief coalfields are in the Ruhr, Saar and Aachen areas. The country produces some iron ore, potash, salt and various metals. Petroleum is also extracted, but much is imported, particularly by pipeline from the south. West Germany is a major industrial nation. Manufacturing first grew up around the coalfields and ports, but its spread to other areas has accelerated since 1958 because of the increasing use of petroleum and availability of electricity generated by coal and distributed by a grid system. Munich and Nürnberg, or Nuremburg are notable examples of major industrial areas without nearby coalfields. Machinery, electrical engineering, chemicals and textiles are all important industries in West Germany. The establishment of new industrial plant has been rapid since 1945, especially in some areas that formerly had only limited industrial capacity, such as Bavaria and

Above: 'Checkpoint Charlie' is the main road crossing point between West and East Berlin, regulated since 1961.

Right: A view over the rooftops of Lübeck to the Holstentor, a monumental gate built between 1467 and 1478.

Baden-Würtemberg.

West Germany's industrial revival after 1945 was based on such factors as the availability of refugee labour, a world shortage of coal and steel, and the necessity of replacing destroyed plant with new machinery. Although the country benefited from US aid, the Germans worked hard to rebuild their wealth.

West Germany is well provided with roads, railways and waterways.

Agriculture, forestry and fishing

The proportion of people engaged in farming dropped from 20 percent of the labour force in 1939 to 7 percent in 1973. More than half of the land is used for farming. The chief cereals are barley, wheat, oats and rye. Potatoes, sugar beet, wine, dairy products and meat are all important. The richest farming region is the rift valley of the middle Rhine.

Forests cover nearly 30 percent of the land and forestry, based on scientific methods, is a major industry, especially for timber used in construction. The northern ports of West Germany have sizeable fishing fleets.

Trade and foreign relations

West Germany's leading trading partners are France, the Netherlands, Belgium-Luxembourg, the US, Italy, Switzerland and the UK. West Germany was a founder member of the European Economic Community.

Because of its position between East and West, West Germany occupies a key role in western defence strategy and it is a member of NATO. In 1970 it recognized the Oder-Neisse line as Poland's permanent frontier with East Germany and it later sought to relieve tensions with its communist neighbour through agreements on Berlin. A treaty, signed in 1972, established the basis for relations between West and East Germany. ∎

East Germany

Area: *108,178km² (41,768sq.m.).*
Population: *16,902,000.* **Capital:** *East Berlin (1.09m.).* **Language:** *German.* **Ethnic group:** *Germans.* **Main exports:** *manufactured products, chemical products, coal (lignite).* **Average temperatures:** *0°C (32°F) Jan. 18°C (65°F) July.* **Highest point:** *Brocken, 1,142m. (3,747ft).*

The people of East Germany differ from West Germans only in their political institutions. Religion is officially discouraged. But, in the 1964 census, nearly 60 percent of East Germans were reported to be Protestants and about 8 percent Roman Catholics.

History and constitution

Following the establishment of the Federal Republic of Germany, the communist German Democratic Republic (GDR) was set up in 1949.

Today the GDR has a People's Chamber consisting of 500 deputies. The People's Chamber elects the Council of

State which was set up after the office of president was abolished in 1960. The Council of State consists of a chairman, who represents the country in international law, six deputy chairmen, 18 members and a secretary. The People's Chamber also elects the Council of Ministers, the National Defence Council and Supreme Court judges. For local government, the country is divided into 14 districts, which have replaced the original six Länder.

Physical features and climate
The northern part of the GDR is a section of the North European plain. The Baltic coastline is sandy and fringed by sand bars which enclose lagoons. To the south, moraine hills alternate with lakes and marshes. Soils are low in fertility. South of the moraine belt is a flat, poorly-drained depression. The rivers occupy southeast-northwest valleys which were formed by melt water when the glaciers receded at the end of the Ice Age. Berlin is situated in one of these glacial valleys.

The southern part of East Germany is a hilly region enclosed by ancient upland areas. It is by far the most populous and wealthy part of the country, both agriculturally and industrially. The uplands include the Harz mountains in the east, the Thüringer Wald uplands in the southwest and the Erzgebirge in the southeast along the border with Czechoslovakia. East Germany's climate is more continental than that of West Germany and winters are distinctly colder.

Minerals and industry
East Germany is the world's most important lignite producer. It also has massive reserves of potash, which is used in chemical industries, and some rare metals, including antimony, arsenic and uranium. However, East Germany lacks iron ore, non-ferrous metals and petroleum. All these items are imported.

Before World War II, the economy of what is now the GDR was essentially agricultural. But today manufacturing contributes two-thirds of the country's national income. All manufacturing industries are nationalized. They produce fertilizers, chemicals, synthetic rubber, cement, textiles, shoes and iron and steel. Apart from Berlin, the chief industrial areas are in the southeast, including Karl-Marx-Stadt and Zwickau. Other industrial centres include Halle, Leipzig, Magdeburg, Stassfurt and the northern port of Rostock. Communications in East Germany are generally less well developed than those in West Germany.

Agriculture, forestry and fishing
Agriculture has been largely collectivized and has made less progress in manufacturing since 1945. Arable farming for wheat, rye, barley, oats, potatoes and sugar-beet is relatively more important than in West Germany. Livestock include 5.5m. cattle and 10.8m. pigs.

Forests cover about 27 percent of the land. Sea fishing and inland fishing, especially for carp, are important.

Trade and foreign relations
More than 68 percent of the GDR's trade is with communist countries and only 7 percent with West Germany. The GDR is a member of the communist military Warsaw pact alliance and also of COMECON. ∎

Switzerland

> **Area:** 41,288km² (15,941sq.m.).
> **Population:** 6,603,000. **Capital:** Bern or Berne (282,000). **Languages:** German, French, Italian, Romansh. **Ethnic groups:** Swiss nationals include German-speakers (74.5 percent), French-speakers (20.1 percent), Italian-speakers (4 percent), Romansh-speakers (1 percent), others (0.4 percent). More than 1m. foreigners also live in Switzerland. **Main exports:** machinery, chemicals, clocks and watches, textiles, scientific instruments, dairy produce. **Average temperatures:** 0°C (32°F) Jan. 20°C (68°F) July. **Highest point:** Monte Rosa, 4,634m. (15,203ft).

The Swiss are mostly people of Germanic or Latin origin. The largest group speak Schwyzerdutsch. French is spoken in the west and Italian in south-central areas. German, French and Italian are the official languages. Romansh, a Rhaeto-Romantic language related to Latin, is spoken in the southeast.

The people are divided into Roman Catholics (49.4 percent), Protestants (47.7 percent) and others (2.9 percent). The foreign residents are mostly immigrant workers, but some work for international organizations, such as agencies of the UN.

History and constitution
In 1291 the people of two forest areas, Schwyz and Uri, united with neighbouring Unterwalden and declared their independence from the Austrian rulers of the House of Hapsburg. From this beginning, a league of loosely-allied independent cantons (states) grew up and the league's independence was finally recognized in 1648.

France conquered the area in 1798 and established the Helvetic League, a federal republic of 19 cantons. But, after Napoleon lost power, the Swiss reverted to their previous loose alliance. In 1805 Swiss neutrality was guaranteed by the Congress of Vienna.

The country's present constitution dates from 1874. Switzerland is now a federal republic, containing 22 cantons each of which has its own government for local matters. The federal government controls such things as defence, the coining of money, the railways and the planning of national public works.

The federal parliament consists of two houses. The Nationalrat (National Council) contains 200 national councillors, directly elected in proportion to the population of the cantons. The Ständerat (Council of State) has 44 members—two being chosen by each canton. Executive authority is vested in the Bundesrat (Federal Council), which is chosen by a joint session of the federal parliament. There is no head of state. The president of the Bundesrat may not serve terms of two consecutive years.

Physical features and climate
Switzerland has three distinctive regions. The Jura mountains run northeast to southwest in western Switzerland. They reach heights of about 1,520m. (5,000ft) above sea level. The central plateau lies between 460 and 910m. (1,500–3,000ft). Although it covers only one-quarter of the country, it contains nearly three-quarters of the population. The lofty, snow-capped Alps cover more than half of Switzerland. They contain magnificent glaciated scenery which attracts many tourists to mountain resorts. Switzerland's climate varies greatly according to the altitude. The central plateau has warm summers and cool winters, but the mountains are much colder and wetter.

Industry and agriculture
Switzerland is a highly industrialized nation. Because it lacks minerals (apart from salt deposits), it has concentrated on processing industries and metal industries, such as clock-making and precision instrument manufacture, that require few raw materials but highly-skilled labour. Yet machinery products and chemicals have become increasingly important. Processing industries produce butter, cheese, meat, sugar, textiles and tobacco. Although use of oil is increasing most of the country's power comes from hydro-electric stations.

Because of its position in central Europe, the most important routes are north–south roads and railways which use passes such as the St Bernard or tunnels such as the St Gothard. About 6 percent of the land is arable, meadows and pastures are 46 percent, forests 24 percent and unproductive land 24 percent. Livestock farming, especially for dairy products, is extremely important with upland pastures used in summer. Wheat and other cereals, potatoes, sugar beet and vegetables all grow in the central plateau.

Trade and foreign relations
Switzerland's main trading partners are West Germany, France, Italy, the US, the UK and Austria. Switzerland's neutrality, stability and good government have given it a special reputation in the world. Its currency is highly respected and it is a major centre of international commerce, banking and insurance. ∎

Left: Switzerland, with its soaring peaks, matchless snowfields and sparkling mountain air is almost synonymous with winter sports. Parpan, Graubunden, is only one of hundreds of resort villages snugly enclosed in the deep valleys of the Swiss Alps. From being the prerogative of the rich, skiing has become a universal sport and Switzerland's efficient tourist industry has exploited its earning potential by attracting millions of visitors.

Austria, Czechoslovakia and Hungary
Map 11

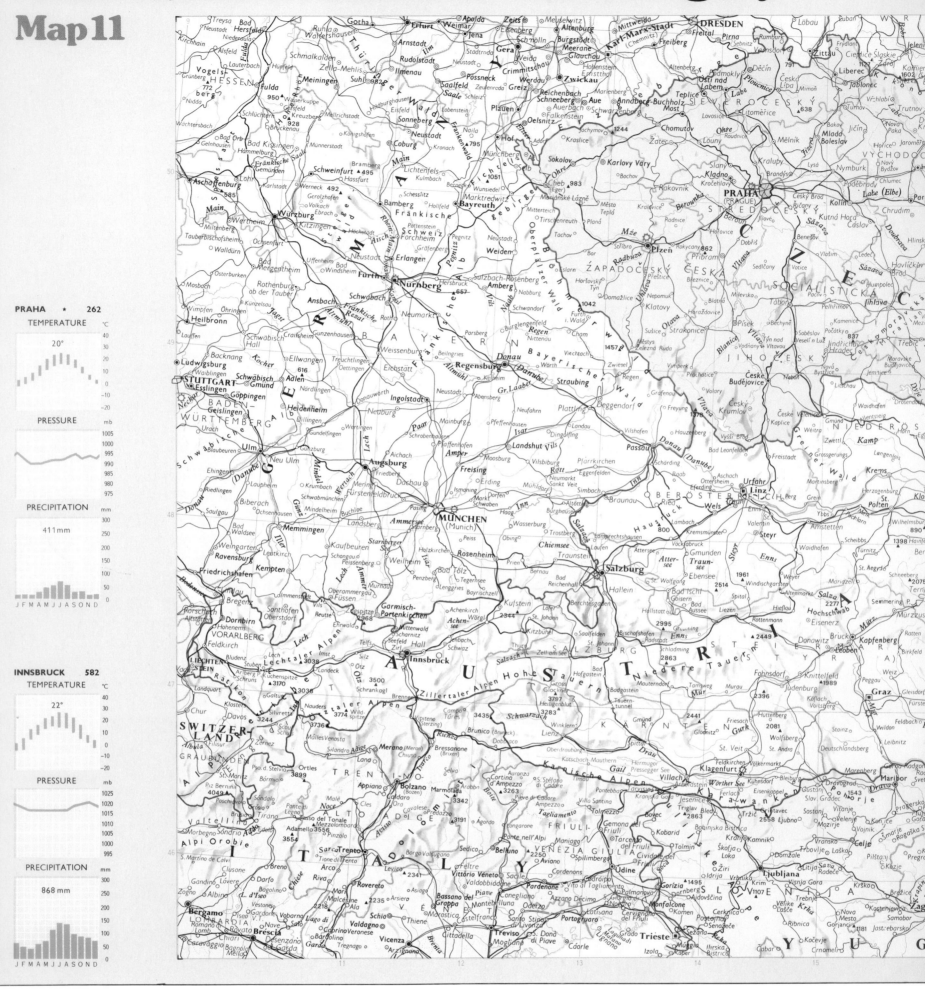

PRAHA ★ 262
TEMPERATURE
20°

PRESSURE

PRECIPITATION
411mm

J F M A M J J A S O N D

INNSBRUCK 582
TEMPERATURE
22°

PRESSURE

PRECIPITATION
868 mm

J F M A M J J A S O N D

Austria

Area: *83,849km² (32,374sq.m.).*
Population: *7,611,000.* **Capital:**
Wien (Vienna) (1.6m.). **Language:**
German. **Ethnic groups:** *German-speaking Austrians. There is a small Slovene minority.* **Main exports:** *iron and steel goods, machinery, timber, wood pulp, paper, chemicals.* **Average temperatures:** *−2°C (29°F) Jan. 19°C (67°F) at Wien.* **Highest point:** *Gross Glockner, 3,797m. (12,457ft).*

Austria was once the centre of the great Hapsburg empire. Croats, Czechs, Hungarians, Italians, Poles, Rumanians, Ruthenians, Serbs, Slovenes and Slovaks settled there and today the population is a mixture of these ethnic groups. The official language is German and about 88 percent of the people are Roman Catholics.

From 962, Austria was part of the Holy Roman Empire. In the 1200s, Austria became a possession of the Hapsburg family and, after 1438, successive Hapsburgs served as Holy Roman emperors. Vienna became one of the most glittering cultural centres in Europe. In 1806 the Holy Roman Empire came to an end and the ruler becoming the emperor of Austria and (from 1867) the dual monarchy of Austria and Hungary.

The country's power gradually declined during the 1800s. In 1919, the Austro-Hungarian empire was broken up and Czechoslovakia and Yugoslavia became separate countries. In its truncated form, Austria faced many problems and offered no resistance when Germany took it over in March 1938.

After World War II, Austria, like Germany, was divided into American, British, French and Russian zones. Austria became independent in 1955 as a neutral federal republic. There are nine federal states, each of which has an elected provincial assembly. The *Nationalrat* (national council) and the *Bundesrat* (federal council) together form the National Assembly.

Physical features and climate
Most of Austria is mountainous. The east-west Alpine ranges cover 70 percent of the country. The Alps are loftiest in the west, where winter sports attract many tourists who provide an important source of revenue. In the east, the Alps are more open and support rather more people than the west. In the north, the Alps descend to a low plateau, which is crossed by the Danube. The Wien basin in the northeast forms a small but thickly-populated lowland.

The country has a climate similar to that of Switzerland, with severe winters, especially in the mountains, and warm summers in low-lying areas.

Minerals, industry and communications
Austria produces large quantities of iron ore and lignite and some magnesite, lead, zinc and petroleum. It is also a major producer of high-grade graphite.

Manufacturing is becoming increasingly important in Austria and Wien is the chief centre. Hydro-electricity is widely used because of the shortage of coal. The chief manufacturing and power companies have been nationalized. Manufactured products include steel, iron and steel products, electrical machinery and textiles.

Communications are hampered by the Alps. East-west communications run along the Danube, an important waterway in the north, and along east-west valleys in the south. North-south routes are through mountain passes, such as the rail crossing at the Brenner Pass, linking Innsbruck with Italy.

Agriculture and forestry
Some farming is practised in the eastern Alps and the Alpine forelands, but the chief farming area is the Wien basin. Only about 17 percent of Austria is cultivated and the chief crops are barley,

Map 12

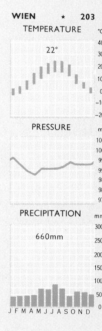

WIEN ★ 203
TEMPERATURE °C
22°

PRESSURE mb

PRECIPITATION mm
660mm

J F M A M J J A S O N D

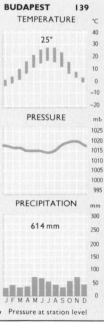

BUDAPEST 139
TEMPERATURE °C
25°

PRESSURE mb

PRECIPITATION mm
614 mm

J F M A M J J A S O N D

★ Pressure at station level

oats, potatoes, rye and wheat. Cattle, pigs and sheep are kept in large numbers. However, Austria has to import much of its food.

Forests cover nearly 40 percent of Austria and timber-using industries produce furniture, wood pulp and paper.

Trade and foreign relations

West Germany, Italy and Switzerland are major trading partners of Austria, which is a member of the European Free Trade Association.

Austria is culturally German, but it had strong historic links with eastern Europe. These links have been weakened since World War II. Neutral Austria has received much US aid and has become increasingly oriented towards the west. ∎

Left: Winter sports provide important foreign earnings for Austria. Heiligenblut in the Hohe Tauern region of the Austrian Alps is a characteristically picturesque village offering simple hospitality.

Liechtenstein

Area: *157km² (61sq.m.).*
Population: 23,000. Capital: *Vaduz (4,300).* **Language:** *German.* **Ethnic group:** *Alemannic.*
Main exports: *manufactured products.*
Average temperatures: *0°C (32°F) Jan. 20°C (68°F) July.* **Highest point:** *Naarkopf, 2,570m. (8,432ft).*

Liechtenstein is a small, neutral principality which originated in 1342, although its present frontiers were not fixed until 1434. Swiss currency is used and Liechtenstein has been part of a customs union with Switzerland since 1923. Formerly an agricultural country, Liechtenstein has become highly industrialized in the last 30 years. Light industries predominate. They manufacture an enormous variety of products. ∎

Czechoslovakia

Area: *127,869km² (49,370sq.m.).*
Population: 14,753,000. Capital: *Praha or Prague (1.09m.).*
Languages: *Czech, Slovak.* **Ethnic groups:** *Czechs, including Moravians, Slovaks. Minorities include German-speaking peoples mainly in Bohemia, and Magyars in Slovakia.* **Main exports:** *machinery, industrial consumer goods, raw materials and fuels.*
Average temperatures: *−7°C (20°F) Jan. 20°C (70°F) July.*
Highest point: *Gerlachovka, 2,655m. (8,711ft).*

Formerly part of the Austro-Hungarian empire, Czechoslovakia became a separate state in 1918, uniting the Czechs and Slovaks in a new republic. The boundaries were fixed by treaty in 1919.

In 1938, Hitler demanded that Sudeten-

Right: Prague, capital of Czechoslovakia and centre of the beautiful Bohemian region, was founded in the 9th century. Hradcany Castle, whose massive walls rise on the left bank of the Vltava River, is equally ancient. Charles Bridge, the most remarkable of many bridges in the city, was built in 1357 and reconstructed in 1970. Prague is one of Europe's most enchanting cities.

land, the German-speaking area, should be handed over to Germany. Britain, France, and Italy agreed to satisfy Hitler's demands in September 1938. At the same time, Poland took Teschen and Hungary took southern Slovakia. The dismemberment of the country was completed in March 1939, when Germany took what remained of the country. Bohemia and Moravia became part of Germany, Slovakia became a German puppet state and Ruthenia went to Hungary. Czechoslovakia was liberated by Russian troops in 1945. The original frontiers were restored except for Ruthenia which went to the USSR. More than three million German-speaking people were expelled.

Elections in 1946 resulted in the communist party emerging as the largest single party. In 1948 the communists seized power. In 1968 pressure for liberalization culminated in Bulgarian, Hungarian, Polish and Soviet forces occupying Czechoslovakia. But in 1970, a 20-year Czechoslovak-Soviet friendship, co-operation and mutual assistance treaty was signed.

Today Czechoslovakia is a federal socialist republic, containing the Czech Socialist Republic and the Slovak Socialist Republic, each having equal authority. But power basically rests in the communist party.

In 1973 the Czechs, who live mainly in Bohemia and Moravia in western Czechoslovakia, accounted for 64 percent of the population. The Slovaks, who live in the east, made up another 30 percent. The remainder included Hungarians, German-speaking people, Poles, Russians and gypsies. Nearly three-quarters of the population are Roman Catholics.

Physical features and climate
In Bohemia, the rich farming basin of the River Elbe is almost enclosed by mountains. Praha stands on the Vltava, a tributary of the Elbe. To the east are the plains of Moravia. Slovakia is a forested mountainous region, except for the Danube lowlands around the river port of Bratislava. Czechoslovakia has cold winters, warm summers and moderate rainfall.

Minerals and industry
Czechoslovakia has large deposits of hard and soft coal. Some iron ore and other metals are extracted but many raw materials are imported.

The country's manufacturing industries recovered and expanded rapidly after 1945. Today about 39 percent of employed people work in manufacturing, as opposed to 15 percent in agriculture and forestry. All industries are nationalized. Products include iron and steel, chemicals, cars, sugar, beer, textiles and shoes. The country's terrain has made communications difficult, but efforts have been made to open up less accessible highland areas.

Agriculture and forestry
About 55 percent of the land is used for farming. The chief crops are sugar beet, potatoes, wheat, maize, oats and rye. Czechoslovakia has about 4½ million cattle and more than 6 million pigs. Most farms are collectives or state farms, but private plots still exist on the collectives.

Forests of spruce, beech, pine and oak cover about 35 percent of the land. Paper making is a major industry.

Trade and foreign relations
Some 69 percent of Czechoslovakia's trade is with communist countries. The largest non-communist trading partners are West Germany, Austria and the UK. In 1973 Czechoslovakia signed a treaty with West Germany, anulling the 1938 Munich agreement and normalizing relations. ■

Hungary

Area: 93,030km² (35,919sq.m.). **Population:** 10,453,000. **Capital:** Budapest (2.04m.). **Language:** Magyar (Hungarian). **Ethnic groups:** Magyars; minorities include Germans, Slovaks, Rumanians, Croats, Serbs, gypsies. **Main exports:** machinery, industrial consumer goods, raw materials, food. **Average temperatures:** −1°C (30°F) Jan. 21°C (70°F) July. **Highest point:** Mt Kékes, 1,015m. (3,330ft).

The Magyars (Hungarians) are people of Finnish-Ugric and Turkish descent, although they have mixed with local people. Some 48 percent of the people live in urban areas, the largest city by far being Budapest. Nearly 60 percent of the people are Roman Catholics.

Hungary and Austria jointly controlled the Austro-Hungarian empire from 1867 until it was dismembered after World War I. In 1918 Hungary was proclaimed a republic and, in 1919, there was a brief spell of communist rule. However, Admiral Horthy re-established Hungary as a monarchy, although there was no monarch. Horthy proclaimed himself regent.

In the 1930s, Hitler supported some of Hungary's claims for the recovery of its lost territories. In 1939 and 1940, Hungary was granted areas seized by Germany, including southern Slovakia, Ruthenia and part of Transylvania. Hungary supported Germany but later tried to negotiate a separate armistice with the Allies. Germany invaded Hungary but Russian troops drove the Germans out by 1945.

Hungary's area was reduced to its pre-1938 size. In 1948 the communists, aided by the Russians, took power. In 1956 an anti-Stalinist revolution was suppressed by Russian troops. Today

Above: Budapest, on the Danube, is the chief city of Central Europe.

Hungary is a communist people's republic. Power is vested in the 352-member parliament, which elects the presidential council, whose chairman is the head of state.

Physical features and climate
The limestone Bakony Forest ridge separates the hilly Little Alföld in the northwest from Transdanubia in the southwest and the flat Great Alföld, or the Hungarian plain, in the east. Mountains occur only in the far north. Hot dry summers and cold winters are the chief features of the climate. Most rain falls in autumn and winter.

Minerals and industry
Hungary lacks large mineral reserves and imports much of what it needs for manufacturing. It produces some coal, lignite,

1:2 500 000

BUCUREŞTI ★ 92

TEMPERATURE ℃

26°

PRESSURE mb

PRECIPITATION mm

592mm

JFMAMJJASOND

Projection: Conical with two standard parallels

East from Greenwich

COPYRIGHT. GEORGE PHILIP & SON. LTD.

bauxite and iron ore, and petroleum and natural gas deposits have been discovered.

Manufacturing has been the fastest developing sector of the economy since 1945. Food processing is important but metal, chemical and textile industries have been expanding quickly. About 36 percent of employed people now work in manufacturing, and Hungarians have been an important source of skilled man-power for Soviet industry. Hungary is well provided with roads, railways and waterways.

Agriculture, forestry and fishing

About 25 percent of the labour force work in agriculture. A high proportion of Hungary is farmed. Most land is collectivized or run by state farms. Hungary has nearly 2 million cattle, more than 2 million sheep and nearly 7 million pigs. Vineyards on the northern mountain slopes produce *tokay* wines.

Forests cover 16 percent of the land. Fishing takes place on the Duna (Danube) and Tisza rivers and also in Lake Balaton.

Trade and foreign relations

Some 62 percent of Hungary's trade is with COMECON countries, especially the USSR. After the uprising in 1956, Hungary restored its close relations with Russia and Hungarian troops were used in the 1968 invasion of Czechoslovakia.

Rumania

Area: 237,500km² (91,699sq.m.).
Population: 21,205,000. **Capital:** *Bucureşti or Bucharest (1.6m.).*
Language: *Rumanian.* **Ethnic groups:** *Rumanians; minorities include Hungarians, Germans, Russians, Bulgarians, Turks.* **Main exports:** *cement; cereals; equipment for oilfields; engineering and construction products; fuel oil; ships; tractors.* **Average temperatures:** −4°C (25°F) Jan. 24°C (75°F) July in Bucureşti.
Highest point: *Moldoveanu, 2,543m. (8,343ft).*

Rumanians are descended from a mixture of peoples, including early Dacian tribesmen, Romans and some Turkish and Slavic peoples. The language is based on Latin. About 42 percent of the people live in urban areas and the largest church is the Rumanian Orthodox.

After being a Roman province, the area was conquered by Asian tribes.

Right: Sucevita Monastery, Rumania, was founded in 1585. Of 15 churches, the Orthodox Church is the largest.

Rumania came into being as a monarchy following a union of Moldavia and Walachia in 1861. In World War I, Rumania supported the Allies and, after the war, its territory was extended following the break-up of the Austro-Hungarian empire. In 1940 Rumania lost much territory to Bulgaria, Hungary and the USSR. It finally joined the Allies in 1944.

The communists took power after World War II and King Michael was forced to abdicate in 1947. Today

Rumania is a socialist republic, controlled by the communist party.

Physical features

Transylvania forms the heart of Rumania. It consists of a central plateau ringed by the Carpathian mountains in the east, the Transylvanian Alps in the south, and the Bihor massif in the west. Transylvania is flanked by fertile plains in the west. The Walachian plains and Moldavia are in the south and east. The climate is continental with hot summers and cold winters. The rainfall averages 625 milli-

Above: The imposing Printing Works Palace at Bucharest, Rumania, is seen here from Herastrau Lake.

metres (25 inches) and much of it falls in summer.

Minerals and industry

Rumania produces oil and natural gas, salt, lignite and various metals, but it imports large quantities of coke, iron ore and other metals.

Manufacturing has increased greatly since 1945 especially with the develop-

Above: Main Square, Krakow, centre of Poland's third most important city, was constructed in the 13th century.

ment of the Ploesti oilfield and manufactures are now the most valuable exports. They include steel and steel products, chemicals, textiles and processed farm products. Consumer goods are increasing in importance. Rumania's internal communications are poor. Its main Black Sea port is the artificially constructed harbour at Constanţa.

Agriculture and forestry

Agriculture still employs about 42 percent of the labour force. The chief crops of this fertile country are maize, potatoes, sugar beet and wheat. Rumania has about six million cattle, nine million pigs and 14 million sheep. Most land is collectivized or run by state farms.

Forests cover 27 percent of the land. The pine and oak forests of Transylvania support a flourishing timber industry.

Trade and foreign relations

About 60 percent of Rumania's trade is with COMECON countries. But recently Rumania has been looking beyond the Soviet bloc. In the 1970s it signed trading agreements with the UK, China and the US.■

Poland

Area: 312,677km² (120,725sq.m.).
Population: 33,964,000. **Capital:** *Warszawa* or Warsaw (1.39m.).
Language: *Polish.* **Ethnic groups:** *Poles; minorities include Russians, Jews, Slovaks and Lithuanians.* **Main exports:** *Coal, lignite, coke, fertilizers, ships.* **Average temperatures:** −1°C (30°F) Jan. 21°C (70°F) July. **Highest point:** *Rysy Peak, 2,503m. (8,212ft).*

Most Poles belong to the Western Slavic group. Although a communist country, Poland has strong religious traditions

1 : 2 500 000

WARSZAWA ★ 110
TEMPERATURE
PRESSURE
PRECIPITATION
555mm

and it is estimated that 80 percent of the people are active Roman Catholics. The rest are Orthodox or Protestant. There are only a few Jews, because three million perished during Word War II.

Poland became an independent kingdom in 1025, but since then it has suffered many partitions and boundary changes. Twice, in 1795 and 1939, it disappeared from the map.

In World War I, the Poles were forced to fight for opposing Russian and German and Austrian armies. But in 1918, Poland became an independent republic. It contained large German, Russian, Lithuanian and Jewish communities. Following Germany's invasion of Czechoslovakia in March 1939, Hitler demanded special privileges for the Germans in Poland and transport rights through the Polish corridor—the area between East Prussia and the rest of Germany which gave Poland access to the Baltic Sea. The Germans attacked Poland in September 1939 and, despite brave resistance, the country fell. It was partitioned between Germany and the USSR.

After liberation in 1945, Poland lost territory in the east to the USSR, but

gained territory from Germany. About 2½ million Germans were expelled from Poland and another 2 million from East Prussia. Most of them went to West Germany. Poland's eastern border, the Oder-Neisse line, was not recognized by West Germany until 1970. The post-war communist government launched a rapid programme of industrialization, nationalization and collectivization. However, the communists were unable to break the power of the churches and collectivization was eventually abandoned. Today more than 80 percent of the farmland is privately owned. Anti-Russian riots in 1956 led to anti-Stalinists taking control of the communist party. Further rioting and strikes occurred in 1970, in opposition to rises in food prices. These, too, led to changes in the communist party leadership.

Today Poland is a communist people's republic, with power effectively in the hands of the communist party. The country has a 460-member Sejm (parliament) and a 15-member Council of State.

Physical features and climate
Northern Poland is largely covered by glacial deposits and the soils are poor.

Although poorly drained, the central lowlands are more fertile. The southern plateau, which rises above 183m. (600ft), contains Poland's best farmland and most important mineral deposits, especially the Upper Silesian coalfield. In the southeast, the plateau rises up to the Carpathian mountains which border Czechoslovakia. Poland has cold winters and mild summers, although conditions become more extreme from west to east and from north to south. The average annual rainfall varies between 508 and 1,016 millimetres (20–40 inches).

Minerals and industry
Poland is Europe's leading coal exporter and a major copper producer. Poland also extracts iron ore, lead, salt and zinc.

Since 1945 Poland has become a major industrial nation. Large manufacturing centres, such as Gliwice and Katowice, stand on the Upper Silesian coalfield. Away from the coalfields, major industrial centres include Krakow, Lódź, Warszawa and Wrocław. Steel and steel products, fertilizers, locomotives, metals, ships and textiles are among the varied manufactures produced in Poland.

In addition to a good road and rail network, waterways, including the rivers Odra and Vistula, are important lines of communication. The chief seaports, Gdánsk (Danzig), Gdynia and Szczecin (Stettin), are also centres of ship-building and other industries.

Agriculture, forestry and fishing
Before 1939 Poland depended mainly on farming, but agriculture now employs only 29 percent of the labour force. The chief crops are rye, potatoes, wheat, oats, barley and sugar beet. Poland has 12 million cattle, 20 million pigs and 3 million sheep.

Forests, mostly coniferous, cover more than 25 percent of the land. Timber forms the basis of a major paper industry. In 1973 Poland had a deep-sea fishing fleet consisting of 131 vessels.

Trade and foreign relations
About 62 percent of Poland's trade is with COMECON countries, and West Germany and the UK are also important trade partners. Western companies are encouraged to set up operations in Poland, taking up to 49 percent of the shares. In the 1970s, Poland signed trade agreements with the US and the USSR. ■

1:3 000 000

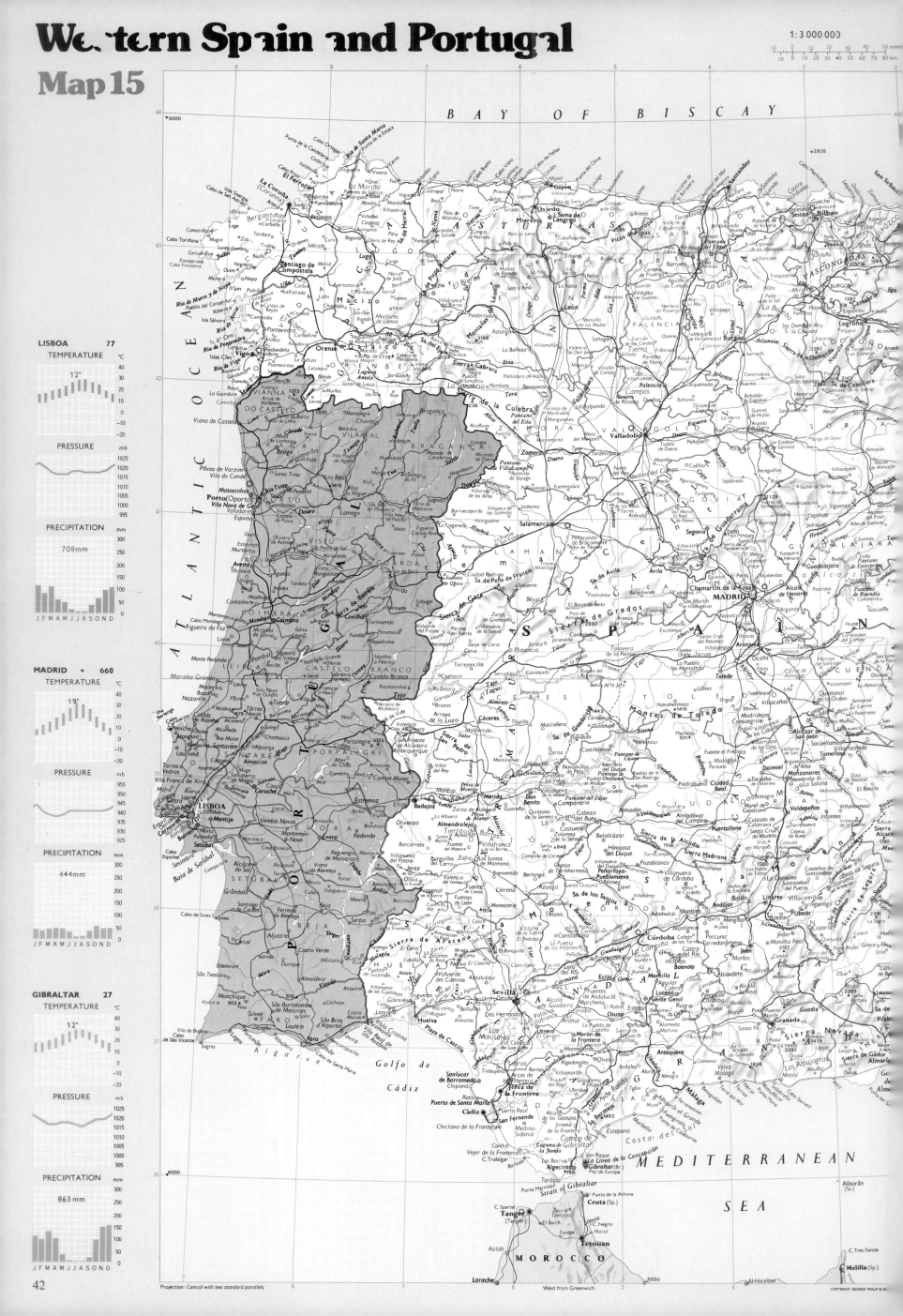

LISBOA   77
TEMPERATURE   °C
12°
PRESSURE   mb
PRECIPITATION   mm
708mm
J F M A M J J A S O N D

MADRID ★ 660
TEMPERATURE   °C
19°
PRESSURE   mb
PRECIPITATION   mm
444mm
J F M A M J J A S O N D

GIBRALTAR   27
TEMPERATURE   °C
12°
PRESSURE   mb
PRECIPITATION   mm
863 mm
J F M A M J J A S O N D

BAY OF BISCAY

ATLANTIC OCEAN

MEDITERRANEAN SEA

MOROCCO

Projection: Conical with two standard parallels   West from Greenwich   COPYRIGHT GEORGE PHILIP & SON

Portugal

Area: *92,082km² (35,553sq.m.).*
Population: *8,496,000.* **Capital:**
Lisboa or Lisbon (1.03m.). **Language:**
Portuguese. **Ethnic group:**
Portuguese. **Main exports:** *wine, cork,
textiles, wood pulp, resin, sardines.*
Average temperatures: *10°C
(50°F) Jan. 21°C (70°F) July.*
Highest point: *Malhao, 1,991m.
(6,532ft).*

The Portuguese are a mixture of the original Iberians and later invaders, including Carthaginians, Celts, Germanic tribes, Greeks, Moors and Romans. The Portuguese language developed from Galician and is similar to Spanish.

The people are mostly Roman Catholics. Their economy depends mainly on agriculture, forestry and fishing and many people are poor and illiterate. The distribution of population is unbalanced with many more people living in the north than in the south. Emigration, especially to Brazil, has long been an important demographic safety valve and more recently many Portuguese workers have migrated to France.

History and constitution
The early history of Portugal is similar to that of Spain. But Spain recognized Portugal as an independent kingdom in 1385. In the 15th century, mainly through the activities of Prince Henry the Navigator, the Portuguese led the way to the exploration of the African coastline and the search for a sea route to India. Vasco da Gama finally reached India in 1498. Portugal's overseas empire grew quickly, including the colonization of Brazil. However, conflict with Spain and rivalry with other European powers gradually weakened Portugal and Brazil was lost in 1822.

Portugal became a republic in 1910, but this impoverished country suffered from political unrest. In 1928 Antonio de Oliveira Salazar became finance minister and, in 1932, prime minister. Effectively a dictator, Salazar remained in power until he died in 1970, when Dr Caetano succeeded him.

Wars in the overseas possessions of Portugal—Angola, Guinea-Bissau and Mozambique—were a great strain on the country's resources. Finally, in 1974, Caetano was overthrown by army officers led by General Antonio de Spinola. Political conflict between army leaders and the revived political parties caused the moderate Spinola to resign as president and he went into exile in 1975.

Portugal is governed by a Supreme Revolutionary Council and a Constituent Assembly. In April 1975, the Socialists emerged as the largest single party in elections to the Assembly. However, by early 1976 Portugal faced many problems, some concerned with soaring inflation, others with disagreements between the military leaders and the party politicians.

Physical features and climate
Northern Portugal is a westward extension of the Spanish meseta. It is fringed by a narrow coastal lowland. The lowlands broaden to the southwest, where the capital and chief port Lisbon stands on the estuary of the River Tagus.

Minerals and industry
Portugal has various mineral resources which are generally under-exploited. The country produces some coal, copper, wolframite and other metals.

Efforts have been made to increase the importance of manufacturing. The chief industries are wine-making, sardine-canning and textile manufacturing, but Portugal has begun to develop a steel industry. Lisbon is the chief manufacturing centre. Portugal has more than 30,000km (18,640m.) of roads and 3,500km (2,170m.) of railways. Tourism has been growing in importance but it suffered a setback in the mid-1970s because of political unrest.

Agriculture, forestry and fishing
Agriculture remains the basis of Portugal's economy. Wheat, maize and vines are important and Portugal has about

Above: River water and sunlight achieve a whiter wash in the Algarve, Portugal.

Right: A placid convent garden in Lisbon.

2 million pigs and 1.1 million cattle.

Forests of pine, cork oak and other oaks, eucalyptus, chestnuts and other trees cover about one-third of the land. Portugal is the world's chief supplier of cork. Sardine fishing is of great importance and canned sardines are a leading export.

Trade and foreign relations
Portugal's chief trading partners are the UK, West Germany, the US and France. After the coup of 1974, Portugal recognized the USSR and COMECON countries for the first time, but trade with communist countries is small. Most of the aid that Portugal has recently received has come from EEC countries and the US.∎

The Azores Islands
The Cape Verde Islands
The Madeira Islands

These three island groups in the Atlantic Ocean were governed by Portugal until 1975, when the Cape Verde Islands became an independent republic. Nationalist demands for independence have also been made in the Azores and Madeira islands.

The northernmost group, the Azores, are about 2,070km (800m.) from Portugal. Administratively, they form three Portuguese districts. The Madeira Islands lie west of Morocco. The largest island, Madeira, is fertile and renowned for its wine. The Cape Verde Islands lie west of Senegal.

The **Azores Islands** consist of nine islands with an area of 2,313km² (893sq.m.) and 330,000 people, and are of great strategic value.

The **Cape Verde Islands** consist of 10 islands and five islets. They have an area of 4,033km² and 272,000 people. The capital is Praia.

The **Madeira Islands** cover 798km² (308sq.m.) and have 270,000 people. There are two main islands, Madeira and Porto Santo, and two uninhabited island groups, the Desertas and Selvagens.

Spain

Area: *504,782km² (194,896sq.m.), including the Balearic and Canary islands.* **Population:** *35,628,000.* **Capital:** *Madrid (3.15m.).* **Languages:** *Spanish (Castilian), Basque, Catalan, Galician.* **Ethnic groups:** *Spaniards, Basques, Catalans, Galicians.* **Main exports:** *manufactured goods; food, drink and tobacco.* **Average temperatures:** *5°C (41°F) Jan. 26°C (78°F) July on central plateau, but cooler in the north and warmer on southern and eastern coasts.* **Highest point:** *Mulhacén, 3,478m. (11,411ft).*

The early people of Spain, the Iberians, mixed with later invaders who included Carthaginians, Celts, Germanic tribes, Moors and Romans.

The Spanish language is Castilian. There are three other languages. Basque is spoken in the Spanish provinces bordering the Bay of Biscay and the French frontier. Some Basques live in France. Basque is an ancient tongue, quite unlike French or Spanish. The Basque people are also ethnically different from Frenchmen and Spaniards. They are of medium height with narrow faces.

Two other languages, Catalan and Galician, developed from Romance languages, as did Castilian. Catalan is spoken in the northeast. It resembles the Provençal language of southern France. Galician is spoken in the northwest. It is the language from which Portuguese developed. Many Basque and Catalan-speaking people, although bilingual, have their own culture and have supported separatist policies. The state religion in Spain is Roman Catholicism.

History and constitution
From about 480 BC, Spain was held successively by the Carthaginians, the Romans and Germanic tribes. The Moors invaded Spain in AD 711 and much of the peninsula fell under Moslem influence, apart from Christian outposts in the north. The Moors left their mark on Spain and some of their superb palaces and fortresses, still survive, such as at Cordoba and Granada. A Christian revival began in the 1100s and by 1276 the Moors held only Granada.

Castile emerged as the leading kingdom in the late 1300s and in 1469 Castile was united with Aragon through the marriage of Ferdinand of Aragon and Isabella of Castile. From this union, the other independent kingdoms of Spain were gradually welded into one nation.

Columbus's voyage in 1492 began the rapid emergence of Spain as a great world power. Even today, the Spanish language is spoken throughout most of central and South America, except for Brazil. However, from the late 1500s, Spanish power gradually began to decline and Spanish sea power was finally destroyed at the Battle of Trafalgar in 1805.

By the 1900s, Spain was a poor farming country beset with many problems. In 1923 Spain became a dictatorship under Primo de Rivera, with the king's approval. In 1930 the king and the army brought the dictatorship to an end, but in 1931 Spain became a republic. The royal family left Spain and the nation became increasingly divided politically. Finally, the bitterly-fought Civil War (1936–1939) brought General Francisco Franco to power. Franco ruled as a dictator. He restored the institution of the monarchy but there was no monarch.

However, when Franco died in 1975, his designated successor, Prince Don Juan Carlos de Borbon, became king and head of state. In January 1976, the government announced that it planned to introduce reforms and that there would be elections to a new two-chamber parliament in 1976.

Physical features and climate
Five-sixths of Spain is a plateau, called the *meseta*. It is bordered by mountains and generally narrow coastal plains.

Northern Spain is mountainous. Galicia in the northwest is a rugged area, resembling Brittany. The Cantabrian

Above: Olive trees flourish in the dry climate of southern Spain. The country leads the world in production of olive oil.

mountains, extending eastwards from Galicia to the French border, reach 1,800m. (6,000ft) above sea level. The Pyrenees in the northeast contain peaks of more than 3,350m (11,000ft).

The Spanish meseta is mostly between 600 and 900m (2,000–3,000ft) above sea level. It is broken by high ridges called *sierras*. To the southeast is another mountain range which contains Spain's highest peak, Mulhacén.

The largest plains are in Andalusia and Aragon. The Andalusian plain in the southwest is rich and well-watered, whereas much of the Aragon plain in the northeast is arid. The south and east are fringed by a series of coastal plains. Several, including those around Alicante and Valencia, are fertile after irrigation. The northeast coast is rugged in places.

The entire Mediterranean coast has become a great centre for about 35 million tourists per year. Coastal regions have hot, dry summers and mild winters. The northern mountains have cool summers and mild winters with rain falling throughout the year. The interior meseta has a severe, almost continental climate, with a large annual temperature range.

Minerals and industry
Spain has important mineral resources, but many are only partially developed. However, Spain produces coal, iron ore, lead and zinc. It also leads the world in mercury production.

Manufacturing has been steadily increasing in importance. Today about 27 percent of the workforce are in manufacturing as opposed to 30 percent in agriculture and fishing. The chief industries include textiles, especially cotton and woollen goods, iron and steel, shipbuilding, paper-milling, cork and cement. Engineering industries in general are increasing. Wine-making is a major industry especially sherry from the Jerez region in the south. The chief industrial

regions are in the northwest around Bilbao and in Cataluña, especially around Spain's second city and largest port, Barcelona (1.75m.).

In some areas, communications are poorly developed and travel is difficult.

Agriculture, forestry and fishing
Agriculture is still Spain's chief activity. Cereals, especially wheat and barley, vines, maize, potatoes and vegetables are important. Typical Mediterranean crops, such as oranges and olives, flourish in such areas as the plains of Andalusia and other coastal areas. Livestock farming is a major industry. Spain has more than 16 million sheep, 9 million pigs and 4.8 million cattle. Sheep-raising is the chief activity on the meseta.

Forestry contributes about 7 percent of the value of agricultural production. Fishing, especially for sardines, tunny fish and cod, contributed about twice the value of forest products in 1972.

Trade and foreign relations
France, the US, West Germany, the UK and Italy are Spain's chief trading partners. Because of its conservatism and undemocratic form of government, Spain has tended to be isolated from the mainstream of European development. However, Spain has been a major source of migrant workers to France and West Germany. Its ambitions to join the EEC could be achieved if political liberalization occurs in the second half of the 1970s. ∎

The Balearic Islands
The Canary Islands

These Spanish island groups contain popular holiday resorts. The 15 Balearic islands in the Mediterranean form a province of Spain. They include Mallorca (Majorca), the largest, Menorca (Minorca) and Ibiza. The chief tourist centres in the Canary Islands, which number 13,

are Palma and Tenerife. Six of the Canary Islands are barren and uninhabited. The Canary Islands form two provinces of Spain: Santa Cruz de Tenerife (capital, Tenerife); and Las Palmas de Gran Canaria (capital, Palma).

The **Balearic Islands** have an area of 5,014km² (1,936sq.m.) and 558,000 people. The provincial capital is Palma de Mallorca (234,000).

The **Canary Islands** have an area of 7,273km² (2,808sq.m.) and 1,139,000 people. ∎

Andorra, Gibraltar

These two small territories are both in the Iberian peninsula. They rely very much on tourism as a source of revenue.

Andorra covers an area of 453km² (175sq.m.) and has a population of 24,000. Its capital is Andorra la Vella. This mountainous, landlocked country nestles in the Pyrenees. France is to the north and Spain to the south. Andorrans speak Catalan, French and Spanish. Andorra is a co-principality, technically ruled by the Spanish Bishop of Urgel and the French president. In fact, French and Spanish delegations are appointed and the legislature is the General Council of the Valleys. There is some farming but tourism is the main activity.

Gibraltar has an area of 6km² (2.3sq.m.) and a population of 27,000, occupying a rocky peninsula. It has been a British fortress since 1704. Spain has demanded its return but, in 1967, 99.6 percent of the people voted to remain British. The governor rules with the Gibraltar Council and an elected House of Assembly. Gibraltar has a ship repair yard and an airfield, and an important strategic position. ∎

1:3 000 000

BAY OF BISCAY
Golfe de Gascogne

FRANCE

SPAIN

ANDORRA

PYRENEES
ROUSSILLON

MADRID

Zaragoza (Saragossa)

BARCELONA
Hospitalet de Llobregat
Badalona
Sabadell
Tarrasa

VALENCIA
Valencia

Castellón de la Plana

Alicante
Elche
Orihuela
Murcia
Cartagena
Lorca
Almería

Albacete

Cuenca
Teruel

Huesca
Lérida

Pamplona
Logroño
Burgos
Vitoria
Bilbao
San Sebastián
Santander

Perpignan
Toulouse
Narbonne
Béziers
Carcassonne

ISLAS BALEARES ISLANDS

Mallorca (Majorca)
Palma
Menorca (Minorca)
Ciudadela
Mahón
Ibiza (Iviza)
Formentera

Golfo de Valencia

MEDITERRANEAN SEA

Costa Brava
Costa Dorada
Costa Blanca

Mar Menor

ALGERIA
Orán
Mostaganem
ALGER (Algiers)
Blida

MOROCCO
Melilla (Sp.)
Nador

Sierra Nevada
Mulhacén 3478

ALICANTE ★ 81
TEMPERATURE °C
15°
PRESSURE mb
PRECIPITATION mm
328mm
J F M A M J J A S O N D
★ Pressure at station level

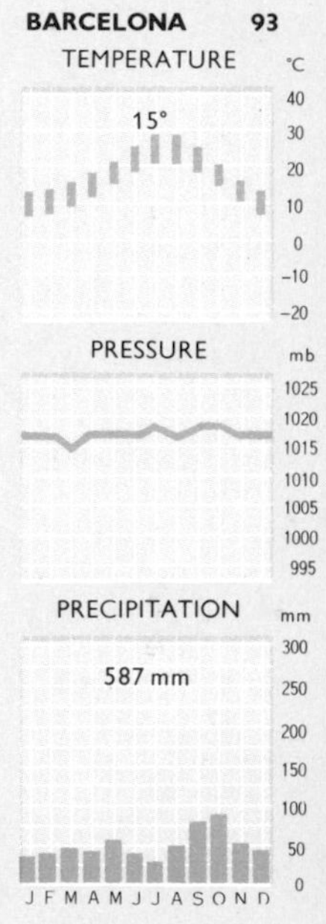

BARCELONA 93
TEMPERATURE °C
15°
PRESSURE mb
PRECIPITATION mm
587 mm
J F M A M J J A S O N D

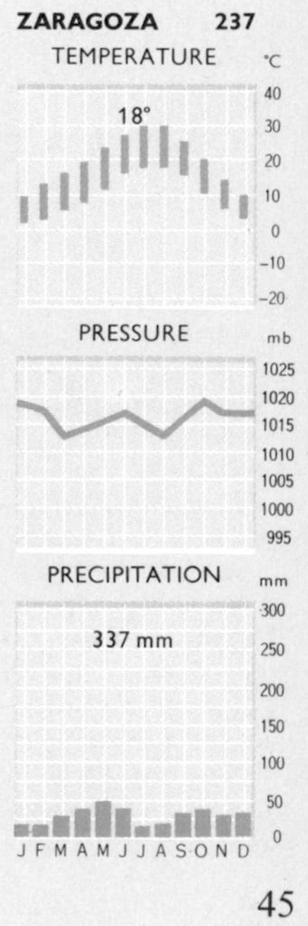

ZARAGOZA 237
TEMPERATURE °C
18°
PRESSURE mb
PRECIPITATION mm
337 mm
J F M A M J J A S O N D

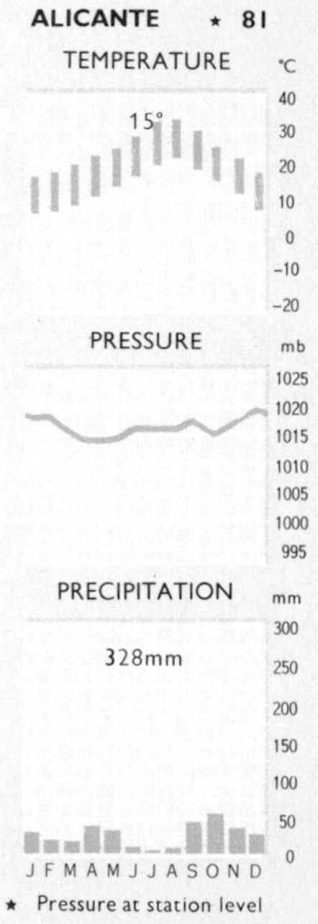

Projection: Conical with two standard parallels

West from Greenwich   East from Greenwich

COPYRIGHT: GEORGE PHILIP & SON LTD.

45

MILANO 121
TEMPERATURE °C
22°
PRESSURE mb
1025
1020
1015
1010
1005
1000
995
PRECIPITATION mm
1017mm.
JFMAMJJASOND

AJACCIO 4
TEMPERATURE °C
14°
PRESSURE mb
1025
1020
1015
1010
1005
1000
PRECIPITATION mm
672 mm
JFMAMJJASOND

Projection: Conical with two standard parallels

East from Greenwich

Italy

Area: *301,262km² (116,318sq.m.)*
Population: *56,240,000.* **Capital:**
Rome (2,833,103). **Language:**
Italian. **Ethnic groups:** *Italian (99
percent), German, Albanian.* **Main
exports:** *motor vehicles, transport
equipment, engineering products,
refrigerators, washing machines,
chemicals, clothing, textiles, foodstuffs,
wine, fruit and vegetables.* **Average
temperatures:** *24°C (75°F) in July,
9°C (48.2°F) in January in Rome.*
Highest point: *Grenzgipfel Peak on
Mt. Rosa 5,539m (15,194ft).*

Italy is regarded as one of the most
beautiful countries in the world, both
for its natural surroundings and for its
cultural heritage. Within its graceful
peninsula shaped like a slender boot are
snowcapped mountains, plains and valleys and a 4,313km (2,681m.) coastline
ranging from golden beaches to steep
cliffs.

The cities match the splendour of their
natural setting. Venice with its maze of
canals, is unique. Florence, where
Renaissance art reached its greatest peak,
is one of the world's best loved and most
visited places. Rome combines cosmopolitan flair with echoes of past imperial
grandeur.

No country has contributed more to
the arts and sciences. Names such as
Dante, Leonardo, Michelangelo, Machi-
avelli, Galileo, Columbus and Verdi all
testify to Italy's signal achievements in
literature, painting, sculpture, music and
learning.

The land
The Italian peninsula extends south for
1,223km (760m.). Its average width from
the Mediterranean in the west to the
Adriatic in the east is about 241km
(150m.).

The Alps in the north separate Italy
from France, Switzerland, Austria and
Yugoslavia.

South of the Alps lies the broad Plain
of Lombardy, Italy's most densely populated region. The plain is fertile and it
also contains the major industrial centres.

The Apennines begin south of the
Plain. They rise more than 2,438m
(8,000ft) in places and form a backbone
that runs the entire length of the peninsula, continuing into Sicily. In the northwest, the Apennines include the white
marble quarries of Carrara which have
been worked for their beautiful stone for
more than 2,000 years.

Sicily, a triangular island and the largest in the Mediterranean, lies close to the
toe of the peninsula. It consists mainly of
a rugged plateau surrounded by a coastal
plain dotted with cities such as Palermo,
Messina and Catania. Sardinia, Italy's
other main island lying 241km (150m.)
to the west, is also mountainous.

The Po flows westward across the
Lombardy Plain into the Adriatic. Its
delta is subject to flooding and major
drainage schemes have been undertaken
during this century. The Arno rises in
the Apennines and flows westward
through Florence and Pisa into the
Mediterranean. The Tiber, the river of
Rome, also flows into the Mediterranean.

Glaciers advancing south from the
Alps during the last ice age scooped out
huge hollows which now form the
beautiful lakes of Como, Maggiore and
Garda at the foot of the mountains. In
central Italy, the lakes of Trasimeno,
Bracciano and Bolsena fill the circular
craters of dead volcanoes.

Italy still has three active volcanoes.
Vesuvius 1,277m (4,190ft) is near Naples.
Stromboli, 926m (3,038ft) stands on the
island of the same name between the
Italian mainland and Sicily. Etna, 3,390m
(11,122ft) is situated on the north-east
corner of Sicily. Cataclysms and volcanic
eruptions have engulfed ancient cities
like Pompeii and Herculaneum in past
holocausts.

Map 18

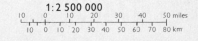

1:2 500 000

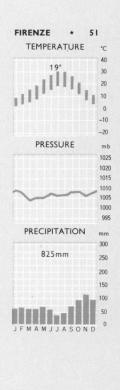

FIRENZE ★ 51

TEMPERATURE °C
19°

PRESSURE mb

PRECIPITATION mm
825mm

J F M A M J J A S O N D

TRIESTE II

TEMPERATURE °C
20°

PRESSURE mb

PRECIPITATION mm
1023 mm

J F M A M J J A S O N D

COPYRIGHT. GEORGE PHILIP & SON. LTD.

Italy, with its long, hot summers, is generally thought of as a sunny land. However, fierce squalls called *temporali* often cause severe damage in summer. Winters, although warmer in the south, bring deep snow to high regions and temperatures drop to below freezing. The Milan region is one of the foggiest in Europe, a combination of the physical nature of its site and its industrialization.

Italy is poor in minerals, although it is a leading producer of mercury and has useful deposits of natural gas in Lombardy. Other minerals include coal, lignite, sulphur and petroleum but these are produced in modest quantities. Some hydro-electricity is produced in the Alps. But oil and coal imports are a heavy economic burden.

The people

The ancestors of the Italians include the

Left: The ruins of several Roman temples are preserved in the Forum, a large area in the heart of Rome.

barbarians who swept into the land in the 5th century with the decline of Rome. Teutonic and Slavonic people also settled in Italy. Carthaginians, Greeks, Arabs and Normans were among the earliest inhabitants of Sicily.

A small German-speaking minority lives in the Alto Adige region near the Austrian border. In the south-east there is a tiny community of Albanian-speaking people.

Milan (1,743,427) is the commercial and financial centre. Every Italian city has its own highly individual history and character. Among the best known in addition to Rome, Florence and Turin are Naples (1,221,859), Genoa (813,256), and Bologna (493,933).

The cities, where the people are mainly apartment dwellers, are full of noise and movement. Rural life is enlivened by feast days celebrating some local saint or religious occasion with processions, ceremonies, fairs and carnivals. Dramatic and energetic sports, such as football and

motor racing, are popular. More than 90 percent of the people are Roman Catholic.

Italian food is appreciated throughout the world, particularly the many kinds of *pasta* and the sauces that adorn them and the universally popular *pizza*.

Agriculture and industry

A major economic problem for Italy is the disparity of wealth between the people of the industrialized north and the poor small-farmers of the rural south. About two-thirds of the land is under cultivation but only one Italian in five now works in farming. Much of the terrain makes agriculture difficult and Italy is not self-sufficient in food. Although about a fifth of the land is forested, Italy also has to import timber.

Wheat grows throughout most of the country. Other important crops include maize, rye, barley, oats and olives. Italy is a major producer of olive oil. Vineyards occur widely. With France, Italy is one of the two leading producers of wine in the world. Fruits and vegetables are also major crops but the meat and dairying industries are small. From mostly indifferent pastures, Italian cattle produce the milk that makes two famous cheeses: Parmesan and Gorgonzola.

Italy's chief industrial region is in the triangle formed by Turin, Milan and Genoa. Turin and Milan are centres of the motor industry. Fiat (Europe's second biggest producer of vehicles), Alfa Romeo, Ferrari, Maserati and Lamborghini are names known worldwide.

Italy's big oil-refining plants have encouraged the growth of petro-chemical manufactures. Other industrial products include textiles, typewriters, synthetic fibres, domestic electrical appliances and ships. Major efforts are being made to develop industry in the south, particularly petro-chemicals and steel production.

Above: The hill towns of Tuscany are among the most attractive in Italy. The region is famous for Chianti wine.

Right: Michaelangelo's Dawn graces a tomb in the Medici Chapel, Florence.

Italy is famous for its craft industries. These include the gloves and shoes of Florence's leather trade, ornate glass and delicate lace from Venice, silks from Milan and finely carved cameos from Naples.

Tourism is a major source of foreign earnings with more than 30 million visitors each year.

There are some excellent roadway systems. The Autostrada del Sol runs the length of the peninsula. Motorways connect Milan with Turin, Genoa and Venice. The major ports are Genoa, Venice, Naples, La Spezia and Cagliari in Sardinia.

Government

Italy is a republic with a president who serves for seven years. Elections are scheduled every five years for the two-chamber parliament consisting of the senate and the chamber of deputies.

Two small independent states lie within Italian territory. The Vatican, the smallest independent state in the world, has a population of about 1,000, most of them ecclesiastical officials. Its head of state is the pope who is also head of the Roman Catholic Church. St Peter's, the largest church in Christendom, is situated in the Vatican which is on the right bank of the Tiber in Rome.

San Marino, which claims to be the oldest republic in the world, is situated south-west of Rimini near the Adriatic. Traditionally dating from the 5th century, its independence was recognized by Pope Urban VIII in 1631. Tourism and the sale of postage stamps are important sources of revenue, although there is

some farming and manufacture.

The arts

Italy has a unique place in the history of the arts as the birthplace of Renaissance humanism which began to develop during the 14th century with the support of prosperous merchant and banking families such as the De Medici in Florence. The pioneers were Giotto (1266–1337) in painting, Petrarch (1304–1374) in poetry and Giovanni Boccaccio (1313?–1375) in prose.

Giotto broke away from the stiff conventions of medieval religious painting. Petrarch revived the ideals of ancient Greek and Roman literature and made the Italian language into a literary vehicle. Boccaccio, with his lively tales of the *Decameron*, was the father of modern prose literature.

These three were followed by geniuses such as Leonardo da Vinci (1452–1519), painter, architect, inventor and scientist; Michelangelo (1465–1564) sculptor, painter, architect and poet; and many others who brought the High Renaissance to a peak of unsurpassed glory. Since then, Italy has made outstanding contributions in the field of music and, more recently, the cinema.

History

Italy has one of the oldest civilizations in Europe but is one of that continent's youngest nations.

About 500 BC, the Romans began building their empire which lasted until the 5th century. After the barbarian invasions from the north, Italy disintegrated into a collection of rival states which included duchies, principalities, city-states and the Papal lands occupying a third of the peninsula.

This situation, in which much of Italy was dominated by foreign powers such as Austria, France and Spain, continued until the mid 1800s. The Risorgimento or resurgence of the desire for unifica-

Above: Gran Sassa, in the Italian Alps.

Right: Raphael designed the Old Testament scenes in the Logge, Vatican.

tion, began in 1860. The philosopher was Giuseppe Mazzini. The political architect was Count Camillo Cavour. The liberator-hero and brilliant general was Giuseppe Garibaldi.

Through the efforts of this triumvirate, Italy was declared an independent kingdom in 1861. Total unification took another decade when the Papal lands were seized and the pope withdrew to the Vatican.

Italy entered World War I on the side of the Allies against Austria and Germany. It suffered severe losses. In the discontent that followed, the Fascists, led by Benito Mussolini, came to power in 1922 and ruled the country until 1943.

The Fascist regime embarked on an empire-building campaign in North Africa and Abyssinia (now Ethiopia) and Italy entered World War II on the side of Germany against Britain and France.

Serious defeats in Greece and north Africa helped to topple Mussolini and the dictator was captured and executed by partisans in 1945.

In 1946 the Italian people decided in a referendum to abolish the monarchy.

Italy became a member of the United Nations in 1955, a founder member of the North Atlantic Treaty Organization in 1949 and a founder member of the European Economic Community in 1958.

From the 1950s onward, the Italian economy developed rapidly. The country which had once been preponderantly agricultural, became one of Europe's important industrial nations. Emigration, which was very heavy to the US in the late-19th and early-20th centuries continues to be a demographic safety valve

ROMA 17

TEMPERATURE °C

17°

PRESSURE mb

PRECIPITATION mm

744 mm

J F M A M J J A S O N D

PALERMO 31

TEMPERATURE °C

14°

PRESSURE mb

PRECIPITATION mm

512 mm

J F M A M J J A S O N D

Projection: Conical with two standard parallels

East from Greenwich

Left: The amphitheatre at Cagliari, capital of the island of Sardinia.

and since 1945 many Italians have gone to Australia or France, West Germany and Switzerland. Extensive regional development schemes are being undertaken to increase labour opportunities in the south through industrialization. ■

Malta

Area: *316km² (122sq.m.).*
Population: *298,252.* **Capital**: *Valletta (14,152).* **Languages**: *Maltese, English, Italian.* **Ethnic groups**: *Maltese 95 percent, English, Italian.* **Main exports**: *Textiles, wine, flower seeds, potatoes, scrap metal.* **Average temperatures**: *12°C (53°F) Jan., 25°C (77°F) July.* **Highest point**: *Tas-Salib, 244m. (800ft).*

Malta is an independent state in the Mediterranean. It consists of five islands: Malta which is the largest, Gozo Comino and the uninhabited Comminotto and Filfla. The islands are about 92km (58m.) south of Sicily.

The landscape is hilly with cultivated terraces. The climate is Mediterranean with mild winters and warm summers although strong westerly winds blow in autumn.

Malta's only mineral resource is limestone, used for cement manufacture. Lack of space and poor soil hamper agriculture and much of the food has to be imported. The country's chief assets are its fine harbour at Valletta and its strategic location as a military base and a fuelling point for shipping. The tourist trade is also an important source of foreign earnings.

The people are descended from many previous settlers: Phoenicians, Greeks, Normans, Spaniards, Arabs and Italians. Maltese is a west Arabic dialect with

Map 20

1 : 2 500 000

NAPOLI 110
TEMPERATURE °C
16°
PRESSURE mb
915 mm
PRECIPITATION mm

MESSINA 54
TEMPERATURE °C
15°
PRESSURE mb
PRECIPITATION mm
902 mm

Italian admixtures mainly from the Sicilian dialect. Roman Catholicism is the state religion.

Emigration has led to a downward trend in the population. Some industries such as brewing, textiles and the manufacture of certain consumer goods were developed from the late 1960s and may halt population loss.

Remains of the stone and bronze ages and various ancient buildings testify to the antiquity of human settlement on Malta. After being ruled by Normans, the Holy Roman Empire, Spain, and France, Malta became a British colony in 1814. During World War II it was a much-bombed and beleaguered fortress for which it was awarded the George Cross, Britain's highest decoration for civilian valour. Malta became independent in 1964. ∎

Right: Valetta, capital of Malta, has resisted many invasions. This view looks towards the harbour entrance.

BEOGRAD ★ 132

TEMPERATURE ℃

23°

PRESSURE mb

PRECIPITATION mm

700mm

J F M A M J J A S O N D

ŠIBÉNIK 77

TEMPERATURE ℃

18°

PRESSURE mb

PRECIPITATION mm

877mm

J F M A M J J A S O N D

Projection: Conical with two standard parallels

East from Greenwich

Yugoslavia

Area: 255,804km² (98,766sq.m.).
Population: 21,377,000. **Capital:**
*Beograd or Belgrade (770,000, met.
area 1.2m.).* **Languages:** *Serbo-
Croat, Slovene, Macedonian,
Albanian.* **Ethnic groups:** *Serbs,
Croats, Slovenes, Macedonians.
Minorities include Albanians,
Hungarians, Rumanians and Turks.*
Main exports: *machinery and metal
products, non-ferrous metals, textiles,
chemicals, ships, timber.* **Average
temperatures:** *8°C (46°F) Jan.
25°C (77°F) July on coast, but cooler
in inland mountain valleys.* **Highest
point:** *Triglav, 2,863m. (9,393ft).*

Most people in Yugoslavia are South
Slavs, but there are non-Slav minorities.
The Serbs and the Croats are the largest
groups. Politically divided centuries ago,

they came under different influences,
principally religious, but their language,
Serbo-Croat, is the same. The Slovenes
live in the north and speak another Slav
language, while the Macedonians in the
south speak a language which is close to
Bulgarian.

The non-Slavs live mainly in the south
and east. The largest groups are the
Albanians in the south, and the Hungarians and Rumanians in the east. Small
Turkish areas are in the central and
southern regions and there are pockets of
Vlachs (related to Rumanians) scattered
over the country. In northeast Serbia,
there are small groups of Slovaks and
Ruthenes, who belong to the Western
Slav group. The German minority was
expelled after World War II.

The Croats and Slovenes are Roman
Catholics and use the Latin alphabet. The
Serbs and Macedonians are Orthodox
and use the Cyrillic alphabet. The
Albanians are mostly Muslims and some
Muslim Serbs live in Bosnia. The other

minorities are divided between
Roman Catholic and Orthodox.

History and constitution
Yugoslavia was founded in 1918 as a
union of the South Slavs. Before that
time, the Croats and Slovenes were part
of the Austro-Hungarian empire, while
the Serbs and Macedonians had been
Turkish subjects. In Crna Gora (Montenegro), some Serbs had remained independent. Serbia regained its freedom in
the 1800s and gradually expanded its
territory.

After World War I, the Serbs of Montenegro united with the Kingdom of
Serbia, and the Croats, Slovenes and
Macedonians joined the new nation. For
two decades, there were many problems,
particularly the wish of the Roman
Catholic Croats for more autonomy
from the Orthodox Serbs.

In 1941 Germany and its allies, Bulgaria, Hungary and Italy, attacked Yugoslavia. The country was divided between

the victors, although a semi-independent
state of Croatia was established. Partisan
groups fought the Germans and the communist leader, Josip Broz (Tito) soon
took over the leadership of the resistance.

After the war, the monarchy was
abolished and Yugoslavia became a
socialist federal republic, notable in East
Europe for its independent stance
towards Russia. It contains six republics,
Serbia, Croatia, Slovenia, Montenegro,
Bosnia-Herzegovina and Macedonia. The
Serbian republic has two autonomous
provinces, Kosovo and Vojvodina. The
first is the home of the Albanian minority.
The other includes most of the other
minorities.

Physical features and climate
The Dalmatian coast of Yugoslavia
borders the Adriatic Sea. The coastline
has sunk and former mountain ranges
which parallel the coast now form long,
narrow islands. Former valleys are now
large harbours. The coast has a Mediterranean climate and it attracts more than

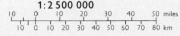

1 : 2 500 000

VARNA ★ 35
TEMPERATURE °C
22°
PRESSURE mb
PRECIPITATION mm
476 mm
J F M A M J J A S O N D

SOFIYA ★ 550
TEMPERATURE °C
22°
PRESSURE mb
PRECIPITATION mm
661 mm
J F M A M J J A S O N D

COPYRIGHT GEORGE PHILIP & SON LTD.

---

five million tourists a year.

Inland, the Dinaric Alps run the whole length of the country. Bare limestone outcrops give rise to the characteristic *karst* landscape, which includes swallow holes, gorges and underground cave networks. Beyond the mountains, the land descends through a forested hilly zone to the interior plains. The plains have a continental climate. The capital, Belgrade and the second city Zagreb (602,000) are both situated on the interior plains.

Minerals and industry

Yugoslavia has considerable mineral resources and it produces coal, iron ore, gold, copper, lead, chrome, manganese and other minerals. Crude petroleum production is increasing.

Most industry is in the northwest. The country produces cement, chemicals,

Left: Towns such as Budva make the Adriatic shores of Yugoslavia one of Europe's most enchanting coasts.

fertilizers, pig-iron, steel and textiles. Yugoslavia has extended its road system and railways since 1945. Communication with the interior is obstructed by the mountain ranges which parallel the coast.

Agriculture, forestry and fishing

Agriculture is still the chief occupation of most Yugoslavs. The land produces barley, fruit, maize, rye, tobacco and wheat. Livestock farming, especially sheep and pig-raising, is important.

Timber is an important export. The country's forests are mainly beech, fir and oak. Fishing, both coastal and inland, employs a large number of people.

Trade and foreign relations

Yugoslavia's main trading partners are the USSR, West Germany and Italy. Since 1948, Yugoslavia has remained outside the two power blocs and has identified itself with the non-aligned nations. A long-standing dispute with Bulgaria over Macedonia is dormant, but Bulgaria still claims the area. Yugoslavia has a history of emigration. Since the early 1960s an estimated 1.5 million Yugoslavs have left the country mainly to work in northern Europe, especially West Germany. ■

Bulgaria

Area: *110,912km² (42,823sq.m.).*
Population: *8,705,000.* **Capital:** *Sofiya or Sofia (946,000).*
Languages: *Bulgarian, Turkish.*
Ethnic groups: *Bulgarians, Turks, Greeks, Macedonians, Armenians, Gypsies.* **Main exports:** *food products, tobacco, iron, leather, textiles, machinery.* **Average temperatures:** *4°C (40°F) Jan. 21°C (70°F) July.* **Highest point:** *Musala, 2,925m. (9,592ft).*

The original Bulgars were an Asian tribe who conquered, and were absorbed by, the Slavs living south of the Danube. The Bulgarian language is Slav. The so-called Pomaks are Bulgarians who became Muslims when Turkey ruled the country.

A Bulgarian empire existed in the 10th century, but the country was then ruled by the Greeks and, later, by the Turks. After pressure from European powers, an autonomous principality was set up in the 1870s and Bulgaria became an independent kingdom in 1908. In World War I, Bulgaria fought with Germany and lost territory in 1919. It again joined Germany in 1941 and attacked Yugoslavia and Greece. The USSR occupied Bulgaria in 1944 and a communist people's republic was set up in 1946.

Physical features and climate
The Balkan mountains cover much of northern Bulgaria. In the far north, the land descends to the Danube lowlands. Between the Balkan mountains and the undeveloped Rhodope mountains in the southwest is the central lowland—Bulgaria's most productive area. Bulgaria's climate is transitional between Mediterranean in the south and continental in the north.

Minerals and industry
Bulgaria has deposits of copper, iron ore, lead, manganese and zinc. Coal is also mined. Petroleum is extracted in the northeast and there is offshore drilling in the Black Sea.

About a third of the people work in manufacturing industries. All industry is nationalized and manufactured products include coke, fertilizers, steel and textiles. Hydro-electric stations provide power and the USSR is helping to build an atomic power station on the Danube. Bulgaria has two large Black Sea ports, Varna and Burgas. It has a large merchant fleet and an extensive road and rail network.

Agriculture and forestry
By 1958 all farmland was collectivized. But the government plans to merge state and co-operative farms into new industrial-agricultural complexes (agro-towns). The main farm products are wheat and other cereals, sunflower seeds, cotton, tobacco, fruit and vegetables. Bulgaria is the world's leading supplier of attar of roses. Cattle, sheep, pigs and poultry are raised, together with large numbers of horses and asses.

Almost two thirds of Bulgaria's forests are of hardwoods and timber production is increasing. Fishing is important for local consumption.

Trade and foreign relations
Four-fifths of Bulgaria's trade is with other COMECON countries, mostly with the USSR. Italy is the biggest non-communist trading partner. Recent agreements allow for Soviet oil and natural gas to be piped to Bulgaria in exchange for food, clothing and electronic components. Bulgaria and the UK recently signed a long-term economic, scientific and technological agreement. Since 1946 Bulgaria has been the closest of the USSR's allies. Bulgaria's long-standing dispute with Yugoslavia over Macedonia, which is mostly in Yugoslavia, arises because of the close similarities between Macedonians and Bulgarians. ■

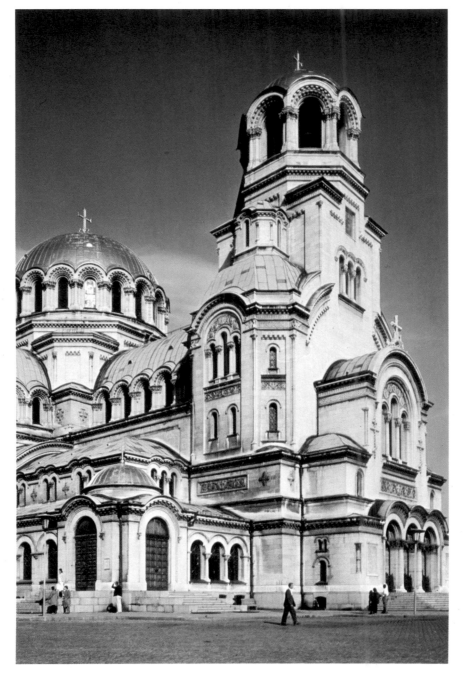

Above: Jajce, with its pretty waterfall on the Vrbas River, lies in a valley of Bosnia, Yugoslavia.

Left: Alexander Nevsky church in the Bulgarian capital, Sofia, commemorates historic links with the Russian Slavs.

Greece

Area: *131,944km² (50,944sq.m.).*
Population: *8,793,000.* **Capital:** *Athinai or Athens (2.5m.).* **Language:** *Greek.* **Ethnic groups:** *Greeks with Turkish and Slav minorities.* **Main exports:** *manufactured goods, chemicals, foodstuffs, especially fruit, tobacco, cotton, wine.* **Average temperatures:** *9°C (48°F) Jan. 28°C (80°F) July in Athinai.* **Highest point:** *Oros Olimbos or Mt Olympus 2,917m (9,570ft).*

Greece has a unique heritage as the cradle of the most brilliant culture of the ancient world. Classical Greek philosophy, art, literature and scientific method permeates Western civilization and Athenian democracy has been a model for many nations. Although today one of Europe's less prosperous countries with a high level of emigration, Greece continues to exercise a powerful attraction through the beauty of the warm Aegean islands and the vitality and exuberance of its people.

History and people
The history of ancient Greece began about 3000 BC with the rise of the Aegean (Cycladic) civilization. This reached a peak in the Minoan culture of Crete, which gave way to the warrior state of Mycenae and ended about 1100 BC with successive waves of invaders. Emigrants from mainland Greece established many settlements throughout southern Europe on sites that were later to develop into great cities, such as Constantinople and Odessa. Trade with these colonies greatly increased the wealth and power of the mainland.

Athens emerged as the foremost Greek power with the repulse of Persian invaders. The 5th century BC saw a remark-

able flowering of the arts, science and philosophy which continued even after power passed to the Spartans and Thebans. In the 4th century the rise of Macedonia culminated in Alexander the Great's conquest of the Persian empire. Roman rule was established by 146 BC and in AD 395, Greece became part of the East Roman or Byzantine empire. This fell in 1453 when the Turks took Constantinople (Istanbul).

But the spirit of Greek nationalism was never extinguished. The Greek Orthodox Church (to which 97 percent of the population belong) and the Greek language were both preserved. The spoken Greek language, *demotike,* is pronounced quite differently from ancient Greek. But today's official documents and newspapers are written in *katharevousa,* a revival of classical Greek. In 1821 the Greeks rebelled against Turkish rule and proclaimed their independence. Following a long struggle, Greek independence was ratified by treaty in 1830 and the country became a monarchy. Throughout the 1800s, Greek territory was gradually extended. Wars against Turkey in 1912 and 1913 resulted in Greece taking much of Macedonia, Crete and several Aegean islands.

Greece fought on the side of the Allies in World War I. After the war, Greece lost Smyrna to Turkey and, in 1923, there was a large transfer of population between the two countries. In 1924 Greece became a republic, but the monarchy was restored in 1935. In World War II, Greece forced back Italian invaders, but fell to the Germans in 1941. After the Germans were defeated in 1944, a civil war broke out which continued until 1949.

A revolution in 1967 led to the departure of the king and the establishment of a military dictatorship. A referendum in 1973 resulted in a majority in favour of a republic. The military regime was overthrown in 1974 but, in another referendum, the Greeks voted against the restoration of the monarchy, and the country is now a constitutional republic.

Physical features and climate

Makedonia or Macedonia and Thraki or Thrace occupy northern and northeastern Greece. Behind flat coastal plains, hills rise gradually towards the mountains along the Bulgarian and Yugoslav borders. Northern Greece has a mild climate but winters are colder than in southern Greece and frosts often occur.

Most of Greece is a peninsula, which is almost divided into two by deep gulfs. In fact, the gulfs are connected by the artificial Corinth Canal which is about 6½km (4m.) long. The northern part of the peninsula contains the rugged central Pindus mountain range, where the rainfall is heavy. West of this range lies a lower region with a Mediterranean climate. To the east lies the large alluvial plain of Thessalia, to the north of which is Greece's highest mountain, Oros Olimbos. To the south of Thessalia is eastern Greece, the most famous historical region which contains Athinai. This region has broken relief and a Mediterranean climate.

The southern extension of the peninsula, Peloponnisos, is mainly mountainous with a number of fertile coastal plains and valleys. Peloponnisos contains the sites of many classical cities, including Sparta. It has hot summers and mild, moist winters. Many of the original forests have been cleared and soil erosion has damaged many areas.

The largest Greek island is Crete. It covers 8,331km² (3,217sq.m.) and has a population of 457,000. Although mainly mountainous, Crete has some narrow coastal plains in the north. There are six other main groups of Greek islands. In the west, the seven *Ionian islands* are rugged, although Kerkira or Corfu is a popular tourist centre. In the northeastern Aegean Sea, the *Thracian islands,* including Thasos and Samothraki are mountainous, but Limnos is mostly flat. Off the eastern coast of Greece, the *Sporadhes* are a group of small rocky islands. The *Kikladhes,* or Cyclades, contain more than 20 islands, the largest of which is Naxos. In the south, Thira or Santorin contains Minoan sites which were buried during a tremendous volcanic eruption. The *eastern Aegean islands* include Lesvos or Lesbos, Khios or Chios, and Samos. The Dodecanese group was acquired from Italy in 1945.

These hilly islands, lying close to the Turkish mainland, include Rodhos or Rhodes.

Minerals and industry

Mining is of relatively little importance in Greece. The country has little coal, but some petroleum, iron ore and various other minerals are produced. Manufacturing has increased rapidly in recent years. For example, manufactured products accounted for only 17 percent of Greece's exports in 1960, but they had risen to 45 percent in 1970. Many industries are concerned with processing farm products. For example, wine and olive oil are important exports. But Greece now has many varied industries, including chemical and metal industries. About 19 out of every 100 employed people work in manufacturing. Athinai, including the port of Piraievs (Piraeus) and Thessaloniki, or Salonica, are the chief manufacturing centres. Inland communications are hampered by the rugged relief, but no part of the country is more than 130km (80m.) from the sea. Sea transport has always been important and today Greece has one of the world's largest merchant navies. Many Greek

Above: The harbour at Áyios Nikolaos, Crete, is the attractive centre of a rapidly expanding tourist industry.

Top: The Parthenon, Athens, seen at dawn, was built under Pericles in the 5th century BC when the city rose to lead Greece into its great classical period.

ships also fly under foreign flags and shipping is an important source of revenue. Another indirect source of income comes from the expanding tourist industry. More than three million tourists visited Greece in 1973, some attracted by the mainland and island beaches, and others by the superb historical sites.

Agriculture, forestry and fishing

Nearly half of all employed people work in agriculture. However, only about one-third of the country can be cultivated, the rest being too rugged. Maize, wheat and other cereals are grown for home consumption. Cotton, tobacco and typical Mediterranean crops, such as apricots, citrus fruits, grapes, melons and olives, are exported. Greece has more than seven million sheep, four million goats and nearly one million cattle.

Much of Greece's original forest has been destroyed and this has resulted in severe soil erosion in many areas. Forests now cover only about 19 percent of the country. Fishing is a more important industry than forestry and sponges are an important product.

Trade and foreign relations
Greece's leading trading partners are West Germany, Japan, Italy, France and the US. Because of its increasing trade with the European Economic Community, Greece has applied for membership.

In foreign affairs, Greek-Turkish hostility continues. For example, an attempted Greek coup in Cyprus in 1974 led to a Turkish invasion of that island. Another vexed problem is the allocation of petroleum prospecting rights in the Aegean. ∎

Albania

Area: *28,748km² (11,100sq.m.).*
Population: *2,250,000.* **Capital:** *Tirana (175,000).* **Language:** *Albanian.* **Ethnic groups:** *Albanians, Greeks, Vlachs.* **Main exports:** *chrome ore, copper wire, crude oil, fruit, tobacco, vegetables.* **Average temperatures:** *4°C (40°F) Jan. 27°C (81°F) July.* **Highest point:** *Mt Korab, 2,746m. (9,068ft).*

The Albanians are descendants of Illyrian tribes who lived in the Balkans before the Slavs. They are divided into two groups—the Ghegs and the Tosks. The Ghegs live north of the Shkumbini river and the Tosks to the south. There are some differences between their dialects and the official language is based on Tosk pronunciation. Albanians also live in adjacent areas in Yugoslavia and Greece. Albania has a small Greek minority in the south and groups of Vlachs are scattered in central and southern Albania. Vlachs speak a Latin language related to Rumanian.

History and constitution
When the Romans conquered the Balkans, they used Illyrians in their armies. Some Illyrians even became Roman emperors.

The Slavs later pushed the Illyrians back into what is now Albania and, later, the Turks conquered them. Most Albanians became Muslims, but there were Roman Catholic and Greek Orthodox minorities. Albanians held important positions in the Turkish empire, but their homeland was backward.

In 1913 they declared their independence, but there was no strong central ruler until a kingdom was established under King Zog I in 1925. Italian influence was very strong and Italy invaded Albania in 1939. Albania remained a monarchy under the Italian king. Partisan groups fought the Italians and communists soon dominated the resistance movement. After liberation, a communist republic was set up. By 1961 Albania had quarrelled with the USSR and China became its closest ally. In 1967 the government closed all mosques and churches and declared Albania the world's first atheist state.

Physical features and economy
Albania is largely mountainous, but there are fertile regions in the centre. The climate is temperate. The coast is dry, but mountain areas are well-watered.

Albania has considerable mineral wealth but it has only recently begun to develop it. Coal, chromium ore and copper are worked and ferro-nickel ore output is increasing. Salt and bitumen are also produced. The oil industry is becoming important. An oil pipeline connects the central Albanian oilfields to the port of Vlora.

Left: Pelekas in western Corfu, is a typical village on this comparatively closely settled island, Corfu (Kérkira in Greek) is one of the most northerly of the Ionian islands and tourism is a major source of income.

Above: The temple of Áthene at Delphi, Greece, was dedicated to the goddess of both life and death. Apart from Apollo, who presided over the oracle, she was the only divinity so honoured at Delphi, the most sacred site of ancient Greece. The sanctuary and oracle, on the lower slopes of Mount Parnassus, drew worshippers from throughout the ancient world. With its broken columns set among bare, eroded hills, Delphi retains a brooding sense of mystery.

All industry in Albania is nationalized, even the smallest workshop. The chief industries are food processing, textiles, petroleum products and cement. The government is developing chemical and engineering industries and an iron and steel works is being built at Elbasani in central Albania. The country's 151km (94m.) of railways have all been built since 1947. The 3,100km (1,926m.) of roads serve all except the mountain districts in the north where pack ponies and donkeys are still essential. Albania has a merchant navy.

Most Albanians work in agriculture but, because of its wild and rugged terrain, arable land is confined mainly to the coast and the Korca basin. All land is owned by the state and farming is largely collectivized. The main crops are cotton, fruit, grains, potatoes, sugar beet and tobacco. Livestock farming is mainly carried out on state farms.

Almost half of Albania is forested, mainly with chestnut, elm, oak, pine and walnut, and timber is a major resource. Fishing is not an important industry and catches are for local consumption.

Trade and foreign relations
About 70 percent of Albania's trade is with China and the rest with other communist countries (not the USSR) or Italy. Relations with the USSR were broken in 1961 and in 1968 Albania left the Warsaw Pact but, in early 1976, the USSR made friendly overtures. ∎

1:3 000 000

ATHÍNAI 107
TEMPERATURE °C
18°
PRESSURE mb
PRECIPITATION mm
402mm
JFMAMJJASOND

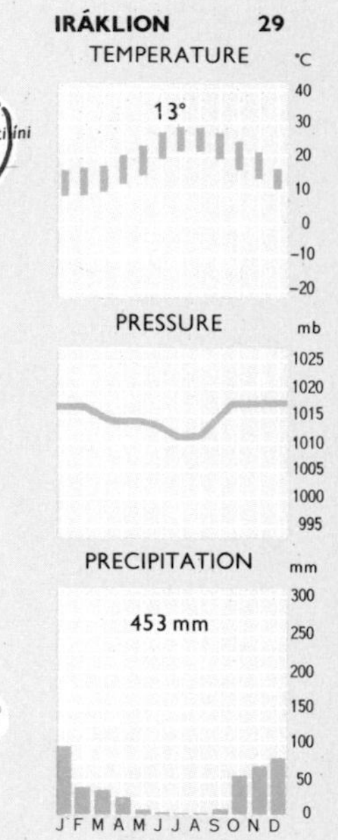

IRÁKLION 29
TEMPERATURE °C
13°
PRESSURE mb
PRECIPITATION mm
453 mm
JFMAMJJASOND

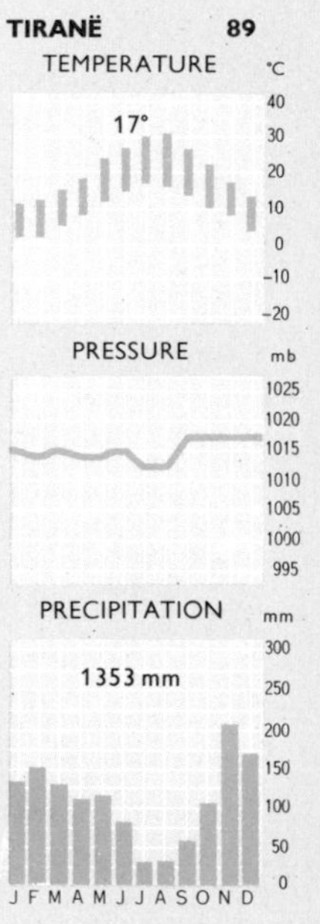

TIRANË 89
TEMPERATURE °C
17°
PRESSURE mb
PRECIPITATION mm
1353 mm
JFMAMJJASOND

Selected labels across the map:

YUGOSLAVIA — CRNA GORA (MONTENEGRO) — Titograd — Skopje (Skopji) — Priština — Kosovo — MAKEDONIJA

ALBANIA (ALBANIJA) — TIRANA-DURRESI — Tiranë — Durrës (Durazzo) — Vlora (Valona) — Shkodra (Scutari) — Korça — ELBASANI-BERATI — VLORA — Berat

BULGARIA — Sofia (Sofija) — Plovdiv — Stara Zagora — Rodopi — Perník

GREECE — THESSALONÍKI (Salonica) — MAKEDHONÍA — THRÁKI — Kaválla — Dráma — Sérrai — Xánthi — Komotiní — Samothráki — Thásos — Límnos — Lésvos (Lesbos) — Khíos (Chios) — Psará

Thrakikón Pélagos — Saros Körfezi

ÍPEIROS — Ioánnina — Kérkira (Corfu) — THESSALÍA — Lárisa — Vólos — Tríkkala — Kardhítsa — Olimbos (Olympus)

STEREÁ ELLÁS — AKARNANÍA — AITOLÍA — FOKÍS — Agrínion — Mesolóngion — Lamía — Pátrai — Korinthós (Corinth) — Corinth Canal — ATHÍNAI (ATHENS) — Piraiévs (Piraeus) — ATTIKÍ — Khalkís (Chalcis) — Évvoia (Euboea)

PELOPÓNNISOS — Trípolis — Kalamáta — Spárti (Sparta) — Pírgos — ARKADHÍA — MESSINÍA — LAKONÍA — ACHAÍA

Voríai Sporádhes (Northern Sporades) — Skíros — Skópelos — Skíathos — Skantzoúra

KIKLÁDHES (CYCLADES) — Ándros — Tínos — Síros — Náxos — Páros — Mílos — Íos — Thíra — Amorgós — Astipálaia — Sérifos — Sífnos — Kímolos

Zákinthos (Zante) — Kefallinía (Cephalonia) — Itháki (Ithaca) — Levkás (Santa Maura)

SEA OF CRETE (Sea of Candia) — KRÍTI (CRETE) — Khaniá (Canea) — Iráklion (Candia) — Réthimnon — Khersónisos Akrotíri — Kíthira (Cerigo)

DHODHEKÁNISOS (DODECANESE) — Ródhos (Rhodes) — Kos — Kárpathos — Astipálaia — Léros — Pátmos — Nísiros — Sími

Sámos — Ikaría — Sámsun Daği — MUĞLA — AYDIN — Marmaris — Bodrum (Halicarnassus) — Kerme Körfezi

Continuation Eastwards on same scale

Projection: Conical with two standard parallels
East from Greenwich
COPYRIGHT. GEORGE PHILIP & SON. LTD.

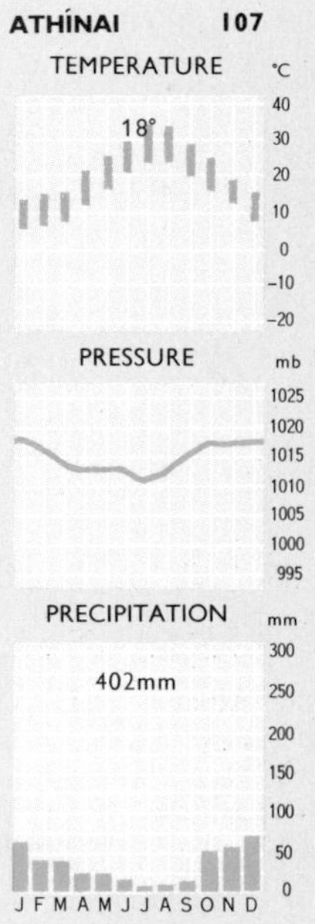

57

1:6 000 000

20 10 0   50   100 miles
40 20 0   40   80   120   160 km

Climate charts

TRONDHEIM   58
TEMPERATURE °C
19°
PRESSURE mb
PRECIPITATION mm
870mm
J F M A M J J A S O N D

HELSINKI   46
TEMPERATURE °C
24°
PRESSURE mb
PRECIPITATION mm
688mm
J F M A M J J A S O N D

BERGEN   43
TEMPERATURE °C
14°
PRESSURE mb
PRECIPITATION mm
1930mm
J F M A M J J A S O N D

ICELAND
on the same scale
as general map

NORWEGIAN SEA

Arctic Circle

NORWAY   SWEDEN   FINLAND   DENMARK   GERMANY   POLAND

NORRBOTTEN   VÄSTERBOTTEN   LAPPLAND

GULF OF BOTHNIA

BALTIC SEA

Skagerrak   Kattegat   The Sound

Oslo   Stockholm   Helsinki   Trondheim   Bergen   Göteborg   Köbenhavn   Hamburg

ESTONIAN S.S.R.   LATVIAN S.S.R.   LITHUANIAN S.S.R.   R.S.F.S.R.

Gulf of Riga

Projection: Conical with two standard parallels   East from Greenwich

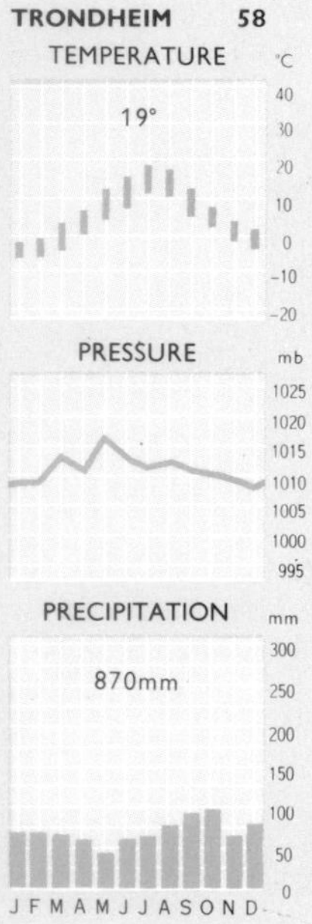

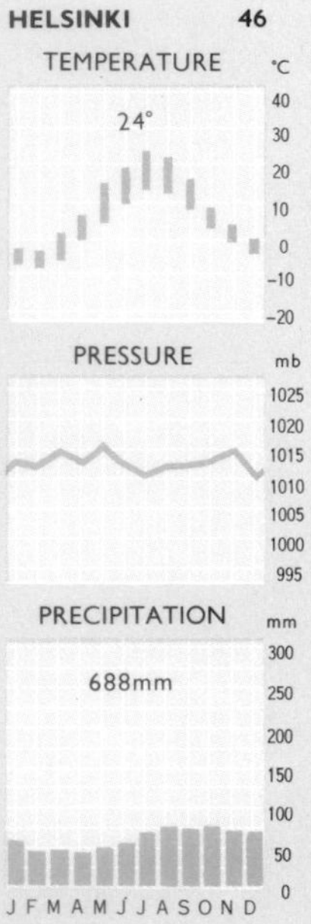

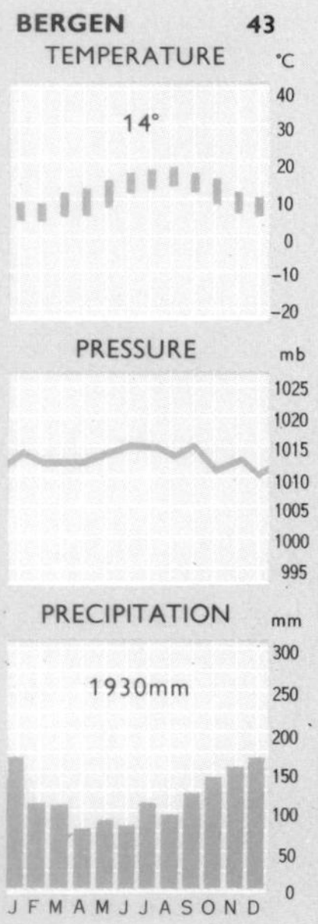

Iceland

Area: *103,000km² (39,770sq.m.).*
Population: *219,000.* **Capital:**
Reykjavik (90,000). **Language:**
Icelandic. **Ethnic groups:**
Norwegians, Lapps, Finns. **Main**
exports: *fish and fish products.*
Average temperatures: *−1°C*
(30°F) Jan. 11°C (52°F) July in
Reykjavik. **Highest point:**
Hvannadalshnukur 2,119m (6,952ft).

The republic of Iceland is a rugged island
lying 1,050km (650 miles) west of
Norway in the North Atlantic Ocean
just south of the Arctic Circle. Despite
its northerly latitude the warming influence of the North Atlantic Drift provides it with a comparatively temperate
climate and it has a growing population
that has achieved economic prosperity
based on a single major export, fish.

Iceland was settled from Norway
about AD 850. Its literary tradition extends back to the sagas and its parliamentary assembly, the Althing, has a
1,000-year history. Formerly ruled by
Denmark, the country was largely self-
governing from 1918 and an independent republic was established in 1944.

The island is of volcanic origin and is
subject to frequent earthquakes and volcanic eruptions, one of which destroyed
a large part of the fishing port of Vest-
manaeyjar on Heimaey Island in 1973.
Grassy coastal lowlands rise to a largely
barren inland plateau with volcanic
peaks, and several glaciers extend to
fiords. Precipitation averages 76cm (30in)
at Reykjavik. The lowlands carry sheep
and dairy and beef cattle. Industries include diatomite mining and aluminium
smelting but the main industry is fishing
and processing, which employs a sixth of
the workforce.

Icelandic waters where warm and cold
currents mingle are rich in cod, haddock,
herring and other fish. These valuable
fishing grounds have been the subject of
several recent disputes over territorial
rights. Iceland's progressive extension of
its fishing limits out to 320km (200 miles)
was contested by other nations who
traditionally fished there, notably Britain
whose disagreement with Iceland on
catch limitations led to so-called 'cod-
wars' with Icelandic gunboats cutting
British trawler wires. ■

Finland

Area: *337,000km² (130,000sq.m.).*
Population: *4,712,000.* **Capital:**
Helsinki (700,000). **Languages:**
Finnish, Swedish. **Ethnic groups:**
Finnish, Lappish (2,500). **Main**
exports: *Timber and timber products,*
metals and machinery, textiles.
Average temperatures: *18°C*
(64°F) July; −6°C (21°F) Feb. in
Helsinki. **Highest point:**
Haltiatunturi 1,328m (4,357ft).

Apart from Iceland, Finland is the most
northerly country in the world. A third
of its area lies within the Arctic Circle.
It has some 60,000 lakes, and 80,000
islands lie along its rocky, jagged coastline. The Finns are a proud and hardy
people. They have fought 42 wars against
the Russians—and lost them all. After
World War II, they had a reparations bill
of £180 million from Moscow. Yet they
have emerged with a vigorous economy
and a prosperous society.

Land and climate
Coniferous forests cover 71 percent of
Finland. The landscape is heavily glaciated, and lakes and waterways cover 10
percent of the total area. Inland, water
remains frozen from December to May.
Most of the country is a flat low-lying
plateau, dropping to a lower plain along
the south and west coasts. The thousands
of offshore islands make navigation
difficult. In the north, Finland extends
into Lapland, which rises in places to
over 1,000m (3,300ft).

Economy
The economy of Finland is based largely

on its forests, which contain valuable
reserves of pine, spruce, birch, and fir
trees—Finland's 'green gold'. The forest
industries include the manufacture of
cellulose, paper, board, woodpulp, plywood, and finished articles ranging from
spools to furniture and prefabricated
houses. A fifth of the working population is engaged in agriculture. The
average farm is small. Cattle are usually
raised, and the chief crops are oats,
barley, wheat, rye, and potatoes. Another
fifth of the work force is employed in
manufacturing industries, although few
plants have more than 500 workers.
Metal-processing has overtaken wood-
processing in the numbers employed. The
foodstuff and textile industries are also
important to the economy. Finland is
renowned for its design, including glass,
ceramics, tableware, and furniture.

A tall, fair people, the Finns place
much emphasis on improving mind and
body. They have produced many fine
writers and a foremost composer in
Sibelius, and are well known for their
sporting accomplishments, particularly
athletics. More than a million Finns
compete in cross-country skiing. Another

passion is the *sauna*, a steam bath that is
now becoming popular in many other
countries.

History and constitution
The Finns call their country *Suomi*.
Unlike the other Scandinavian nations,
Finland is not a monarchy. The head
of state is a president, and there is a one-
house parliament. Finland is neither part
of a western alliance, nor is it a Soviet
satellite.

Finland has been fully independent
only since 1917. The Finns had lived as
separate clans for a thousand years before
they became part of Sweden in the 12th
century. The Swedes and the Russians
fought many battles on Finnish land, and
the Russians seized control in 1809. But
Finland finally broke away after the
Russian Revolution in 1917. Civil war
followed but with the help of Germany
Finland was saved from becoming a
communist state. The Finns again found
themselves on the German side in World
War II, when Russia attacked them.
Remarkably, they survived both the war
and their enormous war debts, and
emerged as a proud and prosperous
nation. ■

Top: Repeated and widespread flows of
lava in Iceland have produced many
striking rock formations such as this
one at Lake Myvata.

Above: Vast forests of pine, birch and
spruce strewn with lakes cover much of
Finland, providing its industrial base. –

Norway

Area: *323,886km² (125,053sq.m.).*
Population: *4,045,000.* **Capital:**
Oslo (500,000). **Languages:** *Bokmål*
(or Riksmål), Nynorsk (or Landsmål).
Ethnic groups: *Norwegian, Lappish*
(20,000). **Main exports:** *machinery*
and transport equipment, metallurgical
products, pulp and paper, fish and fish
products, chemicals, oil. **Average**
temperatures: *17°C (63°F) July;*
−5°C (23°F) Jan. in Oslo. **Highest**
point: *Galdhøpiggen 2,469m*
(8,100ft).

A long, narrow country that occupies the
western part of the Scandinavian Penin-

Above: Sogne Fjord, Norway, reaches 175 km (110 miles) into the heart of Norway, and is the largest in the world.

sula, Norway is a seafaring nation. About 80 percent of all Norwegians live within 20 kilometres (12 miles) of the sea. A proud and nationalistic people, the Norwegians enjoy one of the highest standards of living in the world. And despite industrialization, they have managed to preserve the country's natural beauty—seen most strikingly in its mountains, valleys, and fiords.

Land and climate
More than a third of Norway lies within the Arctic Circle. Most of the country is a high, mountainous plateau covered by bare rock smoothed out by ancient glaciers. There are lowlands in the southeast and around Trondheim.

The most notable physical features of Norway are the fiords, the long, narrow sea inlets that indent the coast. Some 150,000 islands lie off the coast. The climate of Norway is mild for such a northerly country, especially along the west coast. There, the warm North Atlantic Drift keeps most of the seaports ice-free. Inland, it is colder, because the mountains block the warm west winds.

Economy
Only 5 percent of the land is used for agriculture or grazing. Nearly 75 percent consists of mountains and moorland. Most of the people live in the countryside, many in the small settlements scattered along the valley floors of the interior and in the small pockets of flat land to be found in the Atlantic fringe.

A land of few natural resources, Norway has built its economy on human resources. The people have harnessed the rushing streams to provide cheap and abundant hydroelectric power, they have built ships to import a wide variety of raw materials, and they have earned a reputation for the manufacture of quality goods that they can market throughout the world. The exploitation of North Sea oil in the 1970s promises further economic advances.

About half of Norway's factories are in the Oslo area. Products include chemicals, metals, processed foods, and paper and wood pulp. Fishing and forestry are also important. Much of the fish caught, chiefly cod and herring, is processed for export.

The Norwegians are an outdoor people. Skiing is the national sport, and the country boasts some 10,000 ski jumps. The leading exponents are national idols. The Norwegians have also excelled in the arts, producing such giants as the playwright Henrik Ibsen, composer Edvard Grieg, and expressionist painter Edvard Munch. But perhaps the most famous of all Norwegians are their explorers—Leif Eriksson, who probably discovered America some 500 years before Columbus, Fridtjof Nansen, who became a great diplomat and humanitarian, Roald Amundsen, the first man to reach the South Pole, and Thor Heyerdahl of *Kon Tiki* fame.

A constitutional monarchy, Norway has a prime minister and a one-house parliament called the *Storting*. The country was first united in about AD 872 by King Harold Fairhair. Previously,

Norwegian Vikings had colonized Iceland. Norway has been fully independent only since 1814, after 495 years as an overshadowed member of Nordic unions with Sweden and Denmark.

Norway suffered greatly in World War II. Invaded by Germany in 1940, its people resisted bravely. When finally overcome, they set up a government-in-exile in Britain, and the people continued to resist the Nazis in every conceivable way. American aid helped Norway recover after the war, and the fierce independence of the people restored the country's prosperity. Active regional development programmes are aimed at developing the economic and social potential of the whole country. ■

Sweden

Area: *449,790km² (173,665sq.m.).*
Population: *8,210,000.* **Capital:** *Stockholm (1.4m).* **Language:** *Swedish.* **Ethnic groups:** *Swedish, Lappish (10,000).* **Main exports:** *machinery and engineering products; pulp, paper, and other wood products; iron ore and steel; food products.*
Average temperatures: *17°C (63°F) July; −3°C (27°F) Jan. in Stockholm.* **Highest point:** *Mount Kebnekaise 2,117m (6,946ft).*

Sweden is a land of lakes, forests, and mountains. A sausage-shaped country, some 1,600 kilometres (1,000 miles) long, it ranges from the gentle, rolling south with its lakes, through the vast forests, to

the glacial mountains of the north. The 96,000 lakes make up 9 percent of the total area; over half the land is covered with forests; and a seventh lies within the Arctic Circle. Sweden is a highly industrialized nation, and enjoys a standard of living that ranks with that of North America.

Land and climate
The northern two-thirds of Sweden is sparsely populated. The Kölen Mountains form the northern boundary with Norway, and cutting a huge swathe through the country are the moss-carpeted forests and lichen-clad rocks. Swift rivers flow south-eastwards through this area to the Gulf of Bothnia, providing abundant hydroelectric power. Most of Sweden's people live in the southern lowlands, particularly in Skåne, the southernmost province.

Sweden has few fiords, but tens of thousands of tiny islands shelter the mainland. In winter, most of the northern coast freezes up from November to April, and in particularly severe winters nearly all the country is locked in ice. The south has comparatively mild winters, and the whole country has pleasant summers.

Economy
The economy of Sweden is based chiefly on engineering and industrial products. Natural resources include timber (pine, spruce, birch), iron ore, and water power. There is no coal, so the hydro-electric energy is supplemented by imported oil. As a result, there is little of the grime usually associated with such an industrial nation. Less than 6 percent of Sweden's work force is employed on the land.

Above: Fishermen's cottages crowd the water edge at Skärhämn, Bohuslan, Sweden. The west coast with its many islands is popular with summer visitors.

Right: Sweden's capital Stockholm is built on Saltsjön, an arm of the Baltic and Mälaren Lake. Skeppsbron Quay fronts the Old Town.

Sweden is the world's leading producer of iron ore, and this accounts for 6 percent of the country's exports. The engineering industry accounts for a third of Sweden's industrial production. Products include ships, motor-cars, and agricultural machinery. Sweden produces 10 percent of the world's wood pulp, and many other timber-based products, including paper, plywood, and furniture.

History and constitution
The Swedes enjoy one of the most advanced welfare systems in the world, with free education and medical treatment and generous pensions for the needy. Sweden is a constitutional monarchy, with a prime minister and a one-house parliament called the *Riksdag*. The constitution was adopted in 1809—only the United States has an older one. The Swedes call their country *Sverige*, 'land of the Svear'. The Roman historian Tacitus wrote about the Svear in AD 100. During the Viking period (8th–11th centuries), the Swedish Vikings went eastwards to trade and plunder. It was in the eleventh century that Christianity took hold in Sweden, which was developing on the lines of a feudal kingdom. Sweden was united with Denmark

and Norway in 1397. It broke away from the union in 1523 under Gustavus I, who encouraged Lutheranism, which became the state religion in about 1540. Sweden began to expand in the late 1500s, and won many victories in the Thirty Years' War (1618–48) and again under Charles XII (reigned 1697–1718), to become one of the greatest powers in Europe. But Swedish power soon declined, with defeat by Russia in the Battle of Poltava (1709). A period of parliamentary government followed the death of Charles XII.

During the Napoleonic Wars, Sweden lost Finland to Russia, but gained Norway from Denmark (Norway eventually became independent in 1905). The Industrial Revolution came late to Sweden, and there was such poverty that nearly half a million people emigrated to the United States between 1867 and 1886. But economic progress saw Sweden emerge as an important industrial nation by 1900. Sweden remained neutral in both world wars, and further rapid progress led to its present prosperity. During the last two decades it has had to bring in foreign workers, especially from Finland, to promote and maintain this prosperity. ■

Denmark

Area: 43,074km² (16,631sq.m.).
Population: 5,097,000. **Capital:** København or Copenhagen (1.4m.).
Language: Danish. **Ethnic groups:** Danish, German (30,000). **Main exports:** machinery, meat and meat products (especially bacon), chemicals, dairy products, fish. **Average temperatures:** 15°C (59°F) July; −1°C (30°F) Jan. in Copenhagen.
Highest point: Yding Skovhøj 173m (568ft).

A land of small farms, lakes, and islands, Denmark is one of the world's most prosperous countries. It is the oldest kingdom and one of the most efficient agricultural countries on earth. Its engineers are world famous and it has produced numerous Nobel prize winners in the sciences, including the atomic physicist Niels Bohr. Other great figures include the writer Hans Christian Andersen and the philosopher Søren Kierkegaard.

Land and climate
Denmark consists of a peninsula, Jylland (Jutland), and nearly 500 nearby islands, the largest of which is Sjaelland (Zealand). Denmark's capital, Copenhagen, lies on the east coast of Zealand, facing

Sweden across a narrow strait. Jutland borders West Germany to the south. The world's largest island, Greenland, discussed in the section on the Arctic, is a province of Denmark. It lies some 2,000km (1,250m.) from Denmark, and is about 50 times as large. The Faröes, a smaller group of islands in the North Atlantic, between Iceland and the British Isles, are also part of the kingdom of

Denmark.

Most of Denmark is low-lying, with undulating plains. The west coast of Jutland has extensive sandy beaches, closing off inlets. Fiords are a feature of the other coasts, forming natural harbours. Most of the land in eastern Jutland is covered by morainic material deposited in ancient times by melting glaciers. Being almost surrounded by water, Denmark has a mild, damp climate.

Economy
About three-quarters of the land is used for farming. Nearly half of Denmark's industry is situated in the Copenhagen area, where more than a quarter of the people live. The country is poor in natural resources, so metals and fuel have to be imported in large quantities. Manufacturing industries based on these raw materials, however, provide important exports, particularly steel and machinery. And the country is known for the quality and beauty of its manufactured goods such as furniture and silver. Although only 10 percent of the country's labour force is engaged in agriculture, fishing, and forestry, it is for its food products that Denmark is best known. The deep moraine soils of the islands provide the best farmland. The farms are small, but intensive and scientific methods have earned the Danes a reputation as outstanding farmers. The main occupation is the raising of pigs and cattle, and the chief products are butter, cheese, bacon, and ham. The chief crop is barley, of which Denmark is one of the world's leading producers.

The population of Denmark is almost entirely Scandinavian. The only minority

Above: This beautiful manor house at Egeskov is on Fyn, one of the islands in the archipelago of Eastern Denmark. It was built in 1550 by Marshal Frans Brockenhuus, who had oak piles driven into the lake bed so that they formed a natural moat around the sheer walls.

group, about 30,000 people of German descent, live in Jutland, along the border with Germany. The Danes have a reputation as a permissive people, and they are among the greatest beer drinkers and cigar smokers in the world.

History and constitution
Denmark is a constitutional monarchy, with a prime minister and a one-house parliament called the *Folketing*. The constitution of Denmark is founded on the charter of 1953.

The country was settled by the Danes, a Scandinavian branch of the Teutons, in the 6th century. The Danes took part in Viking raids on western Europe for some 300 years from the 8th century. They lived in small communities at first, but were united in about 950 by King Harald Bluetooth, who introduced Christianity to the country. Danish kings ruled England from 1013 to 1042, and when Denmark, Norway, and Sweden were united in 1397, Denmark was the centre of power. In the 17th and 18th centuries, however, Denmark lost much of its territory and power to Sweden in a series of wars. In 1814 it lost Norway to Sweden in the Napoleonic Wars.

During World War II, Denmark was occupied by the Germans, but there was widespread resistance to the Nazis. After the war, American aid helped rebuild the country's economy. Manufacturing gradually overtook farming as the leading industry. One of the original members of EFTA, in 1959, Denmark joined the European Economic Community in 1973. ■

Left: Neat farms at Mols Hills, Denmark, show the care that is characteristic of Danish agriculture. Although manufactured goods now lead farm exports, intensive cultivation is vital to Denmark's economy.

1 : 3 000 000

Projection: Conical with two standard parallels   East from Greenwich   COPYRIGHT GEORGE PHILIP & SON, LTD.

Asia and European Russia

Asia is the largest, most populous and physically most diverse of the world's continents. In geographic terms it extends from the Pacific to the Mediterranean and the Ural mountains of Russia. But here, South-West Asia is discussed separately while the whole of Russia is included in this section. Although most of Russia's population and industry lie west of the Urals in European Russia, its vast Siberian lands make up a third of the entire Asian continent. Russia was historically the only East-West route not impeded by natural barriers. And Russia today remains the only European power to have established a lasting physical presence in Asia.

Strictly speaking, Russia is only the major republic of the Union of Soviet Socialist Republics (USSR), the largest country in the world. Occupying a sixth of the earth's total land area, it is seven times larger than India. At its widest point, between eastern Europe and the Pacific, the USSR stretches across a distance of 8,000km (5,250 miles). Its climate ranges from some of the world's lowest temperatures in the Arctic north to the blistering heat of deserts in Central Asia. Its vast agricultural lands and mineral resources have made it a major economic power.

Politically however, Russia's potential dominance of Asia is challenged by the rise of the People's Republic of China. Between 1840 and 1945, China fell under the influence first of European powers and then of Japan. Today it is reasserting its historic position as the most influential nation of Asia. The physical contrasts between China's arid interior and the favoured eastern plains that support the bulk of its awesome population continue to present major economic problems. China's form of socialism also prescribes for its people a more rigorous way of life than most nations would willingly adopt.

China shares with much of south and south-east Asia a monsoonal weather pattern that is produced by atmospheric pressure changes in Central Asia and which brings alternating periods of heavy rain and drought. The dependence of farmers on this pattern of rainfall makes southern Asia particularly vulnerable to famine following poor harvests. It is therefore in India, Pakistan and Bangladesh that rising birthrates in recent years have put the greatest pressure on diminishing resources of land. Food is more abundant in South-East Asia with its rich rice-growing regions. There progress has sometimes been hampered less by rising populations than by the destructive impact of war. The end of the conflict in Indo-China may bring rapid development in Vietnam, paralleling the advances made in Korea since the 1950s.

Despite some highly developed areas, such as Singapore, Hong Kong, Taiwan, much of South-East Asia is poorly developed industrially. In general throughout Asia about two-thirds of the people are farmers. The notable exception is Japan, a country in many ways more Western than Asian. Although still tentative in taking any diplomatic initiatives within the region, Japan has become a major source of finance and expertise throughout much of South-East Asia during the past 15 years, as well as the major trading partner for many countries of the region.

Density of population: Asia

Inhabitants	per mile²	per km²
	under 2	under 1
	2 – 16	1 – 6
	16 – 32	6 – 12
	32 – 64	12 – 25
	64 – 128	25 – 50
	128 – 256	50 – 100
	256 – 512	100 – 200
	over 512	over 200

■ Towns of over 500 000 inhabitants

DENSITY OF POPULATION
1:80 000 000

Projection: Bonne   East from Greenwich

The Union of Soviet Socialist Republics

Area: *22,271,327km²
(8,599,300sq.m.).* **Population:**
257,000,000. **Capital:** *Moscow
(7,528,000).* **Language:** *Russian is
the native tongue of 60 percent of the
people; also Ukrainian, Byelorussian,
Lithuanian, Latvian, Estonian,
Moldavian, Yiddish, Georgian,
Armenian, Uzbek, Tatar, Kazakh,
Azerbaijani and 50 others.* **Ethnic
groups:** *Russian 55 percent,
Ukrainians 17 percent, Uzbeks 3.8
percent, Byelorussian 3.7 percent,
Tatars 2.5 percent, Kazakhs 2.2
percent.* **Main exports:** *oil, coal,
iron and manganese ore, paper, cotton,
engineering products, transport
equipment, watches.* **Average
temperatures:** *– 11°C (13°F) Jan.
18°C (64°F) July, in Moscow.
– 50°C (– 58°F) Jan. 14°C (57°F)
July in Siberia. 21°C (70°F) Jan.
30°C (86°F) July, in central Asia.*
Highest point: *Communism Peak
7,495m (24,590ft).*

The land

Russia's landscape consists broadly of a
large upland plateau in the east and two
vast plains separated by a range of
mountains extending from north to
south and rising to a moderate height.
Taller ranges rise along some of the
border areas.

The fertile East European Plain, where
nearly three-quarters of the Russian
people live, extends from the Polish
border in the west to the Ural Mountains
which are traditionally regarded as the
dividing line between Europe and Asia.
These mountains are rich in minerals and
reach their greatest height at 1,865m
(6,120ft).

The West Siberian Lowland, the
world's longest continuous plain, lies
east of the Urals. It is bounded by the
Arctic Ocean in the north and the Turan
Lowland in the south.

Much of the Turan Lowland is semi-
arid and the region contains two great
deserts: the Kara Kum and the Kyzyl
Kum.

The Central Siberian Uplands, which
have important mineral deposits, lie east
of the river Yenisei and rise to a height of
600m (2,000ft).

The Uplands continue into eastern
Siberia where some of the peaks rise to
more than 3,048m (10,000ft).

Russia's highest mountains are in the
Pamir Knot on the border with Afghanistan. Communism Peak, the country's
highest point, is in this range.

The Caucasus range in the southwest
between the Caspian and Black seas is
Russia's second-highest with some peaks
rising to 5,486m (18,000ft). Russia's
other mountainous regions are the Altai,
Tien Shan and Sayan ranges along the
border with China and Mongolia. These
mountains rise to more than 3,048m
(10,000ft) in places. The Kamchatka
peninsula in eastern Asia is mountainous
and volcanic.

Russia's lowest point is the Karagiye
depression near the Caspian Sea which is
132m (433ft) below sea level.

The Caspian, covering more than
422,153km² (163,000sq.m.) is the largest
body of inland water in the world.
Russia also has Europe's biggest lake,
Lake Ladoga near Leningrad which
covers 18,388km² (7,100sq.m.). Lake
Baykal in the central Siberian Uplands
is 1,737m (5,700ft) deep and the deepest
fresh-water lake in the world.

Among Russia's important rivers is
the Volga which flows 3,680km (2,300m.)
from the Valday Hills near Moscow into
the Caspian and is the longest river in
Europe. Canals link the Volga with the
Baltic in the north and with the River
Don near Volgograd, formerly Stalingrad. The Dnepr, or Dnieper, the third-
largest river in Europe, flows into the
Black Sea and is a major source of electrical energy. Siberia's main rivers—the
Yenisei, Lena and Ob—are each more

than 3,200km (2,000m.) long.

Climate

Russia is a land of climatic extremes. In
Verkhoyansk in eastern Siberia a temperature of −90°F (−68°C) has been
recorded while in central Asia January
temperatures can rise to 77°F (25°C).
In general, the summers are warm. But
long, cold winters are characteristic of
most of the country, with snow covering
the ground for several months. The
European Plain and the Pacific coast
receive the greatest precipitation both as
rain and snow with amounts ranging from
20 to 40 inches a year. The Arctic,
Siberia and the desert regions receive less
than 10 inches a year. Rainfall is generally
light to moderate in the east.

Natural resources

Russia's enormous natural wealth puts
it in the lead in the output of certain
minerals. Coal reserves are estimated at
7,800,000,000,000 metric tons and deposits are widespread although the
Donets and the Kuznets basins are the
main mining regions. Output rivals that
of the US.

Known oil reserves total 70 billion
metric tons, chiefly in the Volga and
Urals regions but with important deposits in the Caucasus. New fields are being
exploited in western Siberia and Kazakhstan. Unexploited petroleum deposits,
either under ground or water, are estimated at 300,000 billion metric tons.
Production of both oil and natural gas is
rising rapidly, supplying Russia with its
main energy source and also being exported to several East European allies.

About 40 percent of the world's reserves of iron ore are located in Russia
which leads the world in the production
of this metal. Ukraine and the Urals are
the chief sources. Russia also leads in the
production of manganese which is mined
in Ukraine and Georgia. There are big
copper deposits in the Urals, Uzbekistan,
Kazakhstan and Armenia and the Altai
region is rich in lead and zinc. Rarer
minerals, such as titanium, are produced
in Ukraine and the Urals and uranium in
Uzbekistan.

Russia is the world's second-largest
producer of gold after South Africa. It
is also a major source of precious minerals
such as diamonds, beryllium and mercury.

Timber resources are an estimated
80,000,000,000m³ (2,800,000,000,000ft³).
The chief forest areas are in Siberia and
the far east.

Economy: agriculture

There is no private ownership in industry
in Russia and only a limited form of it in
agriculture. All economic activity is
carried out either as a state enterprise or
as a collective or cooperative.

The economy is directed from the
centre by the State Planning Commission
(Gosplan) through five-year plans pre-
pared by various state committees spe-
cializing in different sectors of the
economy.

Self-employment is rare, being confined to such persons as craftsmen, highly
skilled artisans, authors, actors, composers
and performers of the arts.

The only significant free enterprise
sector is in agriculture. In the fruit and
vegetable markets of towns and cities
farmers sell produce from private plots
which they are allowed to cultivate under
the collective farming system Although
small, these plots supply nearly half the
total output of fruit and vegetables as
well as considerable quantities of meat
and dairy products.

Agriculture is predominantly socialized
however, with two types of farm: the

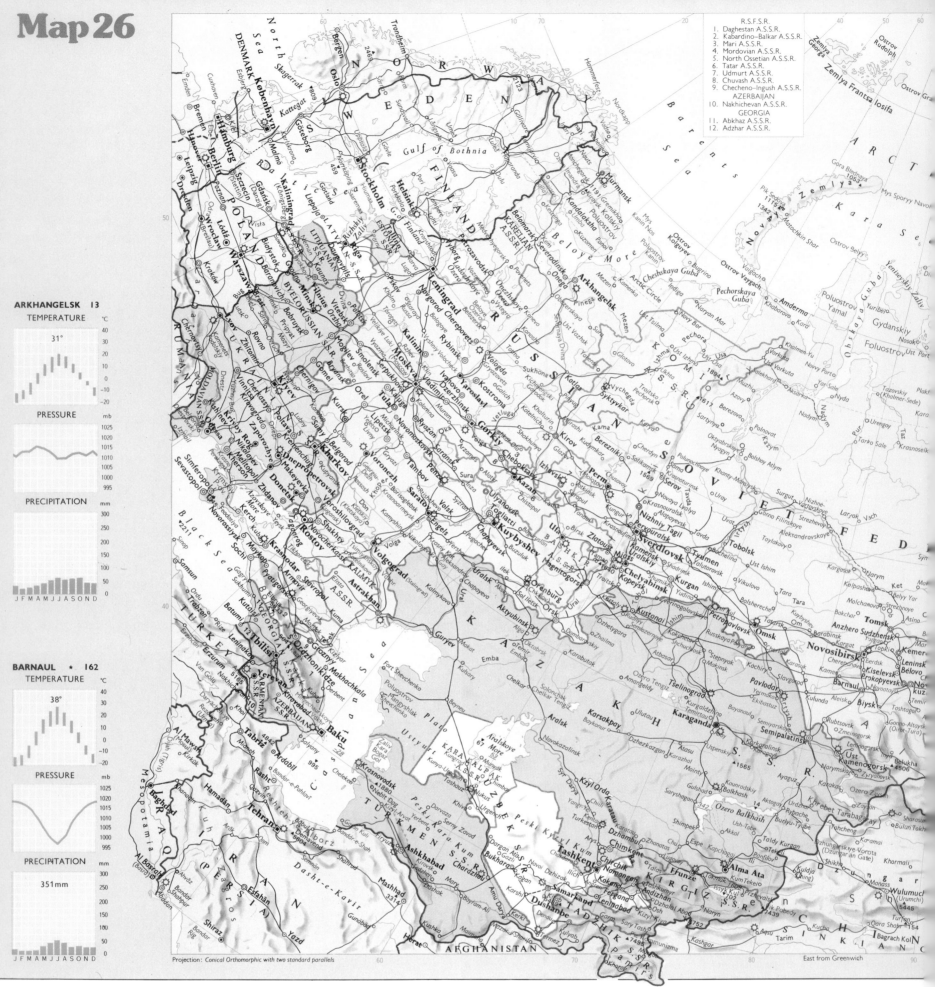

ARKHANGELSK 13
TEMPERATURE °C

PRESSURE mb

PRECIPITATION mm

BARNAUL ★ 162
TEMPERATURE °C

PRESSURE mb

PRECIPITATION mm

kolkhoz (collective farm) and the sovkhoz (state farm). Collective farms operate as a cooperative on a profit-sharing basis. Apart from certain delivery obligations to the government, they have freedom in planning and decision-making.

On state farms, where planning is under closer government control, employees are paid a wage. There are nearly 34,000 collective farms and about 15,000 state farms. The state farms are about twice as large as the collectives and average 6,000 hectares (15,000 acres). Such units might each carry 1,240 cattle, 1,600 sheep and goats and 880 pigs in mixed farming areas.

Chief crops are wheat, rye, maize, barley, oats, sugar beet, potatoes, sunflower seeds, tea and cotton. About 25 percent of the population works on the land.

Despite its tremendous potential, Russian agriculture has frequently suffered from inefficiency since it was socialized in the 1930s. This has been blamed partly on collective farmers spending more time on their small private plots and neglecting the wider needs of the collective. Weather conditions such as drought have been a periodic factor in crop failure. The 1975 grain harvest was greatly reduced and Russia was again forced to make major grain purchases from the United States.

Hardly more than a quarter of the total area of the USSR is farmed. The main farming region is in the European Plain, but during the 1950s the government began to develop the so-called virgin lands of central Asia. Special strains of cereal crops have also been evolved to grow in less clement climates, as in Siberia.

One of the problems facing Russian agriculture has been migration to the cities as the country transformed itself from a backward rural nation into an industrial power. More than half the population now live in urban areas. Demand for specialized foods such as meat has been rising and Russian farmers have found it difficult to meet. Livestock numbers are now increasing.

Industry and trade
As an industrial power Russia is second only to the United States. After the 1917 revolution all efforts were devoted to building up heavy industry. But the period up to the end of World War II brought little improvement in the availability of consumer goods for the Russian people despite significant advances in other sectors of the economy.

However, from the late 1950s the government began to pay more heed to the consumer sector. In the 1971–75 plan the growth rate for output of consumer goods was for the first time set at higher than that for heavy industry.

Industrial production still represents about 77 percent of the gross national product and half of industry is still geared to heavy engineering and non-consumer activity, such as metallurgy and chemicals. Chief products are machinery, heavy transport equipment, machine tools, plastics, synthetic fibres, chemicals and fertilizers.

In the consumer sector Russia has greatly increased output of domestic refrigerators, washing machines, radio and television sets, textiles, cameras, clocks and watches from the 1960s onward although output cannot match demand. During this period the country also began to build up a private motor car industry with the help of the Fiat motor company of Italy.

Russia's foreign trade is significant only within a restricted area of the world and most of it is with the countries of eastern Europe which are subject to considerable Soviet influence in their own trade policies through the planning organization COMECON (Council for Mutual Economic Aid) established in 1949. Some consumer goods are exported to developing countries in Africa and Asia. Trade with the west, although increasing, is mainly in raw materials such

Map 27

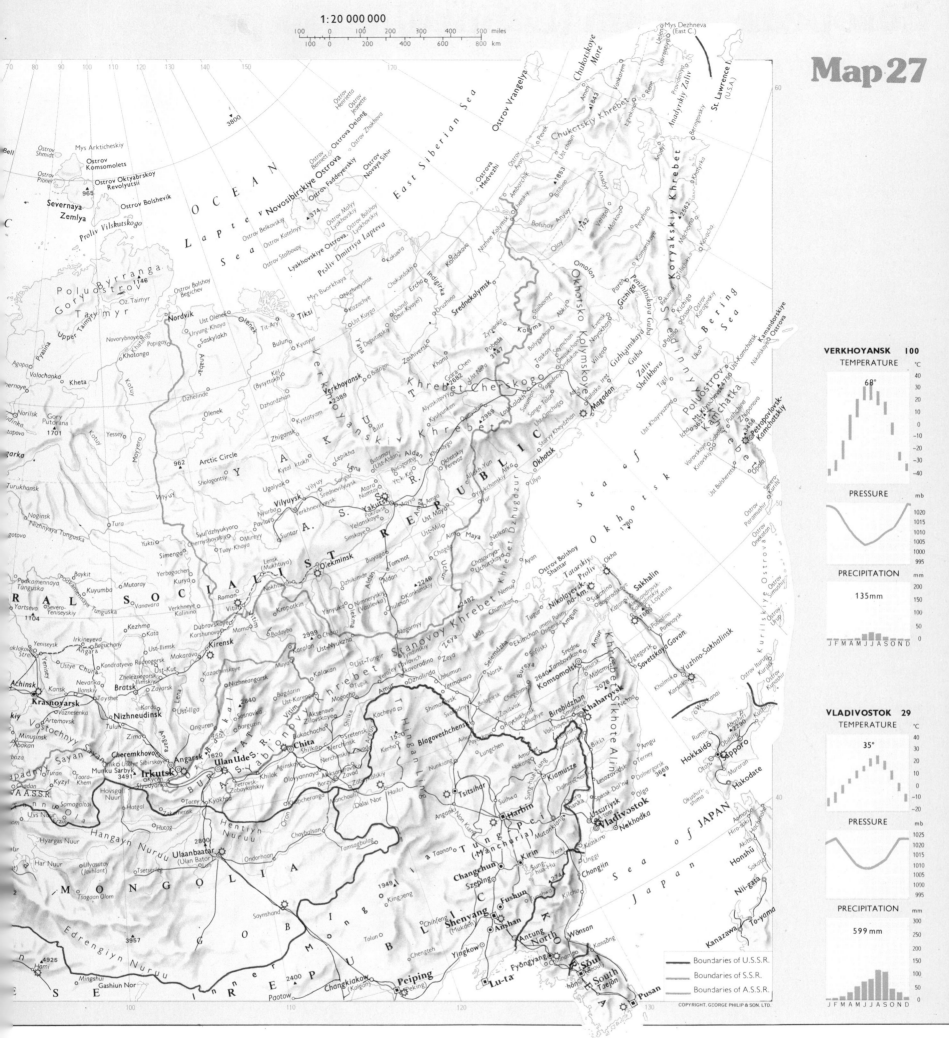

1:20 000 000

VERKHOYANSK 100
TEMPERATURE °C
68°
PRESSURE mb
PRECIPITATION mm
135mm
J F M A M J J A S O N D

VLADIVOSTOK 29
TEMPERATURE °C
35°
PRESSURE mb
PRECIPITATION mm
599 mm
J F M A M J J A S O N D

Boundaries of U.S.S.R.
Boundaries of S.S.R.
Boundaries of A.S.S.R.

COPYRIGHT. GEORGE PHILIP & SON. LTD.

as hides and skins, ores, petroleum and textile fibres.

Russia has approximately 560,000km (350,000m.) of roads. The main problem facing motor transport is the sheer size of the country and the climatic extremes which reduce vast zones to frozen wastes, bog or desert. Railways are an important means of transport and there is a network of 134,400km (84,000m.). Air transport also plays an important part, especially in communications with remote regions in Asia.

Russia's hydroelectric potential is twice that of the United States and about 11 percent of the world's total. Most of the power comes from large schemes on the rivers Volga and Dnepr but the Yenisei, Angara, Ob and Irtysh rivers also supply considerable energy.

The people
Scores of ethnic groups make up the Russian population, each group having its own distinctive language and cultural traditions.

The Slavs, comprising the Russians, Ukrainians and Byelorussians, form the largest single group although their languages differ slightly. The Turkic peoples of central Asia are second followed by the Tatars, the Ugro-Finnish of the Baltic, the Japhetics of the Caucasus and the Iranians of Azerbaijan, Armenia and parts of central Asia.

The government encourages the development of various languages and cultures but Russian still remains the most important tongue. In the Baltic regions and in some other areas where strong ethnic or cultural traditions were seen as threats to national unity, conscious efforts have been made to break up groups of peoples.

The Russian constitution guarantees freedom of worship but religion is firmly separated from the state. The traditional

Right: Lake Baikal eastern Siberia is the world's deepest lake (1,737m) holding a fifth of all fresh water.

LENINGRAD 4

TEMPERATURE °C
27°
40 30 20 10 0 -10 -20

PRESSURE mb
1025 1020 1015 1010 1005 1000 995

PRECIPITATION mm
603mm
300 250 200 150 100 50 0
J F M A M J J A S O N D

MOSKVA ★ 156

TEMPERATURE °C
31°
40 30 20 10 0 -10 -20

PRESSURE mb
1005 1000 995 990 985 980 975

PRECIPITATION mm
624mm
300 250 200 150 100 50 0
J F M A M J J A S O N D

Projection: Conical with two standard parallels

East: from Greenwich

faith of the Slavs is the Russian Orthodox Church. Lithuania is a Roman Catholic region while Estonia and Latvia are traditionally Lutheran. Most of the Turkic peoples are Muslims and there are some Buddhists in eastern Asia.

Sport and athletics are extremely popular and the government gives them considerable help and encouragement. Russian teams have distinguished themselves internationally in soccer, winter sports, especially ice hockey and rowing. At the Olympic Games, together with the United States, Russia usually takes the lion's share of gold medals.

The government also encourages cultural activities. Chess is a national pastime. Opera and ballet are greatly appreciated with celebrated companies such as the Bolshoi in Moscow and the Kirov in Leningrad.

Left: The Winter Palace, Leningrad, baroque home of the Tsars, was stormed by revolutionary forces in 1917.

Map 29

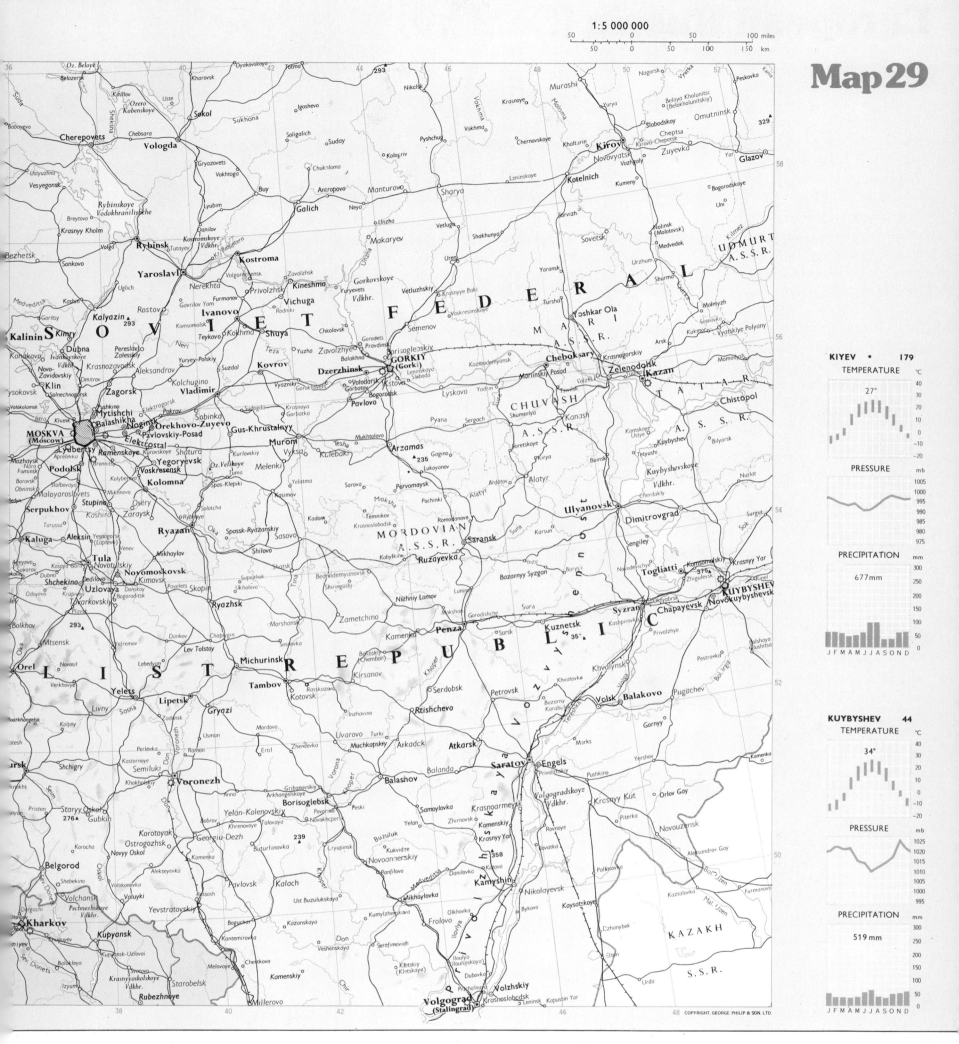

1:5 000 000

KIYEV * 179
TEMPERATURE °C
27°
PRESSURE mb
PRECIPITATION mm
677mm
J F M A M J J A S O N D

KUYBYSHEV 44
TEMPERATURE °C
34°
PRESSURE mb
PRECIPITATION mm
519 mm
J F M A M J J A S O N D

COPYRIGHT. GEORGE PHILIP & SON. LTD.

There is also a great literary tradition born from such great authors as Pushkin, Tolstoy, Dostoyevsky and Chekhov. Modern Russian literature however is expected by the government to devote itself mainly to subjects concerning the day-to-day life of the mass of the people and any departure from this to speculative philosophy or criticism of the political system is discouraged. Several outstanding writers such as Solzhenitsin and Pasternak have resisted this pressure to conform.

Government

Russia is a federation of 15 republics: Russian Federation, Armenia, Azerbaijan, Byelorussia, Estonia, Georgia, Kazakhstan, Kirgizia, Latvia, Lithuania, Moldavia, Tadzhikistan, Turkmenistan, Ukraine and Uzbekistan.

Each of the republics has its own legislature but the highest lawmaking body is the Supreme Soviet of the Soviet Union which meets in Moscow. This is a parliament which has two chambers: the Council of the Union and the Council of the Nationalities. The president of the presidium of the Supreme Soviet is also head of state.

Executive power is exercised by the Council of Ministers whose chairman is prime minister.

Effective power lies with the communist party and no other party is permitted. Party membership is granted to relatively few as a privilege and in recognition of unusual ability. The party shapes major policies which later receive the formal approval of the Supreme Soviet. The general secretary of the party's central committee is regarded as the most powerful official in Russia.

Apart from the republics, Russia has 20 autonomous republics, eight autonomous regions, 10 national districts and six territories to accommodate special ethnic groups such as Jews and German-speaking communities.

History

The Scythians were among the earliest inhabitants of Russia. In pre-Christian times they lived in the steppe region on the northern shores of the Black Sea. The Slavs, who later established their dominance, migrated from the northern forests and settled along the rivers Volga and Don. They founded the city of Novgorod about the 9th century AD and also the state of Kiev which soon emerged as the major power. Christianity was introduced through Kiev's trading contacts with Byzantium.

Kiev was vanquished by the Golden Horde of the Mongols in the 1200s and the new rulers set up their empire in what is now Volgograd.

Moscow emerged as the strongest state from the 1400s. It proceeded to unite the country by conquest and the campaign reached its culmination when Ivan IV, known as 'the Terrible', defeated the Tartars during the mid-1500s and made Kazan and Astrakhan part of Russia.

Russia fell into disarray after Ivan's death. The country was invaded by Poles. Cossacks in the Don region ceaselessly tried to overthrow the tsar and palace intrigues were fomented by the lordly boyars.

Peter the Great became tsar in 1696 determined to curb the boyars and modernize Russia. He built the country's first navy and wrested right of way through the Baltic after a 21-year war with Sweden. Peter also built St Petersburg, now Leningrad, as part of his aim of closer relationships with Europe.

Westernization continued under Catherine the Great who reigned from 1762 to 1796. Her successful campaigns against the Turks secured for Russia access to the Black Sea.

By this time Russia had become a major imperial power allied with Prussia, Austria and Britain against Napoleon. The French emperor invaded Russia but his armies were routed in 1812.

The later 1800s were a time of discontent and risings. The same period saw imperial expansion during which Russia

SIMFEROPOL 205
TEMPERATURE °C
23°
PRESSURE mb
PRECIPITATION mm
482 mm
J F M A M J J A S O N D

ODESSA 64
TEMPERATURE °C
25°
PRESSURE mb
PRECIPITATION mm
473 mm
J F M A M J J A S O N D

acquired Kazakhstan, Turkestan, Uzbekistan and other large territories in eastern Asia.

Rivalry led to war with Japan and in 1905 the Russian fleet was ignominiously sunk after sailing halfway round the world for the engagement.

The defeat accelerated the major discontent at home. In the same year there was an abortive revolution which, however, forced Tsar Nicholas II to promise a new constitution and reforms.

Meanwhile the Marxist Social Democrat Party split up into its two factions: the Bolsheviks and the Mensheviks. The Bolsheviks, led by Vladimir Ulyanov, later to call himself Lenin, were much more radical and better organized.

Russia entered World War I against Germany and Austria. The conflict sharpened the misery at home and in

Left: Borzhomi Gorge, Georgia, is in a densely populated region of intensive fruit and vegetable cultivation.

1917 the tsarist system collapsed and Lenin and his Bolsheviks came to power. The Tsar and his family were executed.

Civil war broke out but despite the intervention of British, French and American forces on the side of the counter-revolutionary 'white' Russians, the Red Army was victorious.

Lenin died in 1924. His place was soon taken by Joseph Stalin who had established himself by the late 1920s and ruthlessly eliminated his rivals.

The Russian people rallied to the defence of their motherland in World War II. After untold suffering they drove the German invader out and established a buffer zone in the east European states.

Postwar tension between Russia and the west led to a period of mutual suspicion and hostility known as the Cold War. However, after Stalin's death in 1953 the first signs of a thaw appeared and developed. At the same time Russia's relations with China deteriorated as the two major communist powers disagreed

Map 31

1:5 000 000

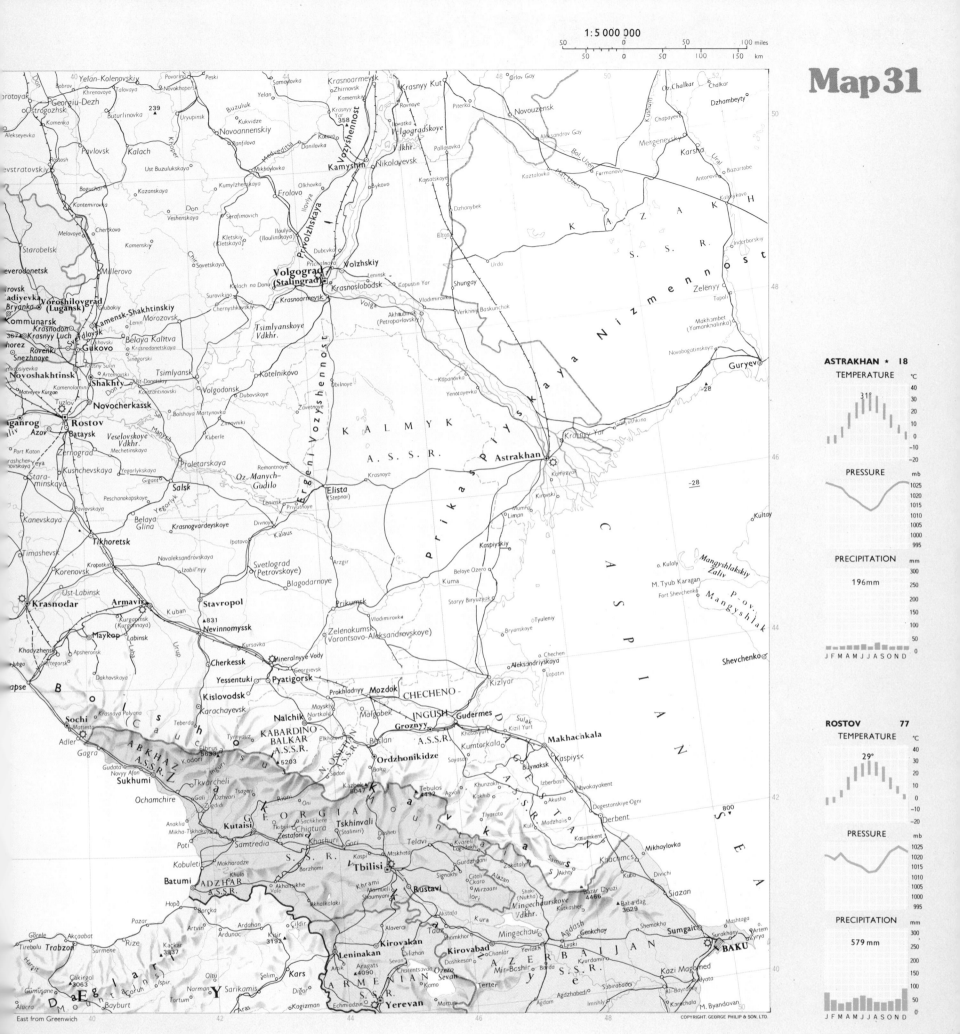

ASTRAKHAN ★ 18
TEMPERATURE ℃
311
PRESSURE mb
PRECIPITATION mm
196mm
J F M A M J J A S O N D

ROSTOV 77
TEMPERATURE ℃
29°
PRESSURE mb
PRECIPITATION mm
579 mm
J F M A M J J A S O N D

East from Greenwich COPYRIGHT. GEORGE PHILIP & SON. LTD.

---

on the application of Marxist principles.

In 1961 Russia launched the first manned space flight and followed it with spectacular achievements such as the first hard landing on the moon and the planet Venus.

By the 1970s Russia and the United States were reconciled enough to sign a preliminary agreement to limit strategic weapons and the two countries had collaborated in space exploration. ■

Mongolia

Mongolia is an independent republic in eastern Asia. It consists of a vast plateau part of which is in the Gobi desert.

Mongolia lies between Russia on the north and China in the south. The Altai Range rises 4,268m (14,000ft) in the north. The climate is extreme with severe winters and short summers. July temperatures reach 100°F (38°C) and fall to −54°F (−40°C) in January.

Three times larger than France,

Mongolia is the most thinly populated country in the world with a population of about 1,600,000 in an area of 1,535,810km² (593,000sq.m.). The capital, Ulan Bator, has about 280,000 inhabitants.

Outside the capital the Mongolian people are mainly nomadic herdsmen tending camel, sheep, goats and horses. The traditional religion is Buddhism. Chief exports are cattle, wool, hides and meat products. The country also has reserves of coal, gold, tungsten, uranium, petroleum and copper.

Dating from the great Mongol emperor Genghis Khan, Mongolia emerged from Russian and Chinese domination in 1924 as an independent republic with a communist system of government similar to that of its major ally and trading partner, Russia. ■

Right: In Turkmenia near the Afghanistan border of the USSR, herdsmen raise pedigree camels.

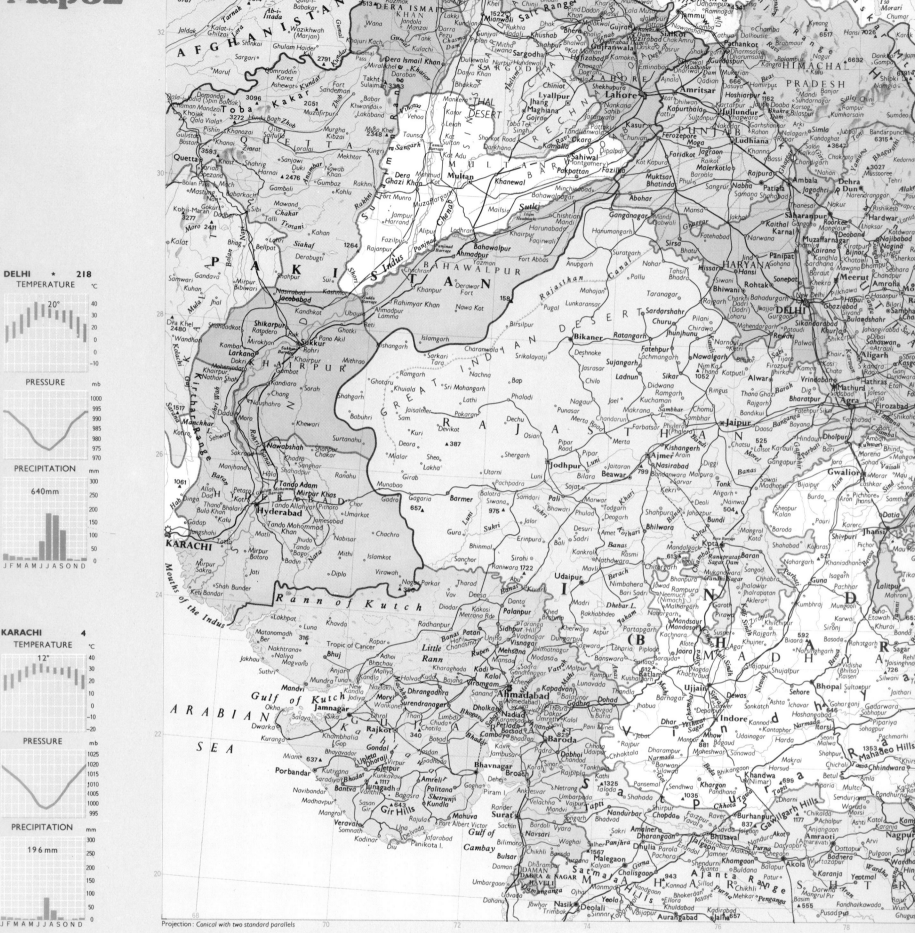

DELHI ★ 218
TEMPERATURE °C

PRESSURE mb

PRECIPITATION mm
640mm

KARACHI 4
TEMPERATURE °C

PRESSURE mb

PRECIPITATION mm
196mm

Projection: Conical with two standard parallels

Pakistan

Area: *803,943km² (310,404sq.m.)*
Population: *68 million.* **Capital:**
Islamabad (285,000). **Largest city:**
Karachi (3.5 million). **Languages:**
Punjabi, Urdu, English. **Ethnic
groups:** *Punjabis, Sindhis, Pathans.*
Main exports: *cotton and leather
goods, hides, skins, carpets.* **Average
temperatures:** *19°C (66°F) Jan.
30°C (86°F) June on central plain.*
Highest point: *Nanga Parbat
8,125m (26,660ft).*

The Islamic Republic of Pakistan was
established as a home for India's large
Moslem minority when British rule
ended in 1947. It consisted originally of
two sections 1,600km (1,000 miles) apart
but after civil war in 1971 the eastern
section gained independence as Bangladesh. A country of few and poorly-
developed resources with less than 20 per
cent of its population literate, Pakistan
faces formidable economic problems in
coping with its high birthrate.

Most of the population farm or herd
livestock in the eastern and central region
of the Punjab where the Indus and six
other rivers irrigate a wide alluvial plain.
North of the temperate upper Indus
region the land rises to the towering
wall of the Hindu Kush. Mountain
ranges extend southward to the arid
plateaus of Baluchistan to the west.

The monsoonal climate is characterized
by hot, dry summers with temperatures
above 40°C on the plain, ending in a
rainy season. In winter, from October to
March, a cold dry wind blows from the
northeast.

Wheat is the staple crop with cotton,
sugar cane, rice and tobacco also grown.
Rich fishing grounds provide vital protein. Energy resources include a huge
natural gas field at Sui, oil on the Potwar
plateau and considerable hydro-electric
potential. Low-grade coal seams are
worked and there are iron ore, salt and
limestone deposits.

The Islamic faith, followed by nearly
90 per cent of the population, is the main
cohesive force in a nation of diverse
cultures and languages. The government
has veered towards a socialist economy
since 1971 when rule by decree was
instituted and banks, main industries and
communications were nationalized. Pakistan controls some territory in the
Kashmir province. ∎

*Right: Silversmiths in Karachi
represent a tradition of handcrafting
that plays an important part in
Pakistan's economy at both urban and
village level. Karachi, the country's
chief port and largest city, was
founded in the 18th century and grew
into an important trading centre under
British rule in India. The centre of
Sind province, it has become Pakistan's
major industrial area.*

Map 33

1:6 000 000

50 0 50 100 150 miles
50 0 50 100 150 200 250 km

CHINESE REPUBLIC

TIBET

SOUTHERN ASIA
POLITICAL
1:40 000 000

AFGHANISTAN · KASHMIR · PAKISTAN · NEPAL · BHUTAN · BANGLA-DESH · BURMA · INDIA · SRI LANKA · Colombo

---

KABUL ★ 1815

TEMPERATURE °C
28°

PRESSURE mb

PRECIPITATION mm
338mm

J F M A M J J A S O N D

CALCUTTA ★ 6

TEMPERATURE °C
11°

PRESSURE mb

PRECIPITATION mm
1600mm

J F M A M J J A S O N D

East from Greenwich

COPYRIGHT. GEORGE PHILIP & SON. LTD.

BAY OF BENGAL

Mouths of the Ganga

Bangladesh

Area: *142,776km² (55,126sq.m.)*
Population: *81 million.* **Capital:**
Dacca (980,000). **Languages:**
Bengali, Urdu, Hindi. **Ethnic**
groups: *Bengalis, Biharis.* **Main**
exports: *Jute, skins, hides.* **Average**
temperature: *28°C (82°F).*
Highest point: *Mt Keokradong*
1,230 (4,034ft).

Bangladesh emerged as a new nation in
1971 when the Bengali majority in East
Pakistan asserted independence in a civil
war that left an already undernourished
population in widespread poverty. With
a birthrate averaging 3 percent a year
and a population density of 530 per square
kilometre, the country is forced to import grains, adding to the economic
burden of paying for vital imports of
fuel, fertilizers and machine goods.

Bangladesh occupies the largest delta
in the world, a flat, fertile plain crossed
by the Ganges, Brahmaputra and Meghna
rivers. The monsoonal climate is generally warm and humid with high temperatures in April and heavy rain between June and October. Floods, often
resulting from cyclones and tidal waves
funnelled up the Bay of Bengal menace
harvests and bring starvation, disease and
death.

The population is 80 percent Moslem
and overwhelmingly rural, mostly small
farmers living in stilt houses and using
ancient methods to produce the staple
food, rice. The major cash crop, jute,

Right: The Star Mosque at Dacca,
capital of Bangladesh, is the focus of
worship for the Moslem community
which makes up about 80 percent of the
country's population. Islam was the
main force holding together the former
eastern and western sections of Pakistan.

Above: The Hindu temples of India are centres of worship and focal points of crowded annual festivals.

Top: Rice is the major crop of the Vale of Kashmir whose mild climate and fertility make it the main farming area.

accounts for half the total world supply and jute processing is the only significant export earning industry. Fishing is important and tea is also grown. The military-backed government hopes to expand industry and exploit oil from the Bay of Bengal, but lack of capital is a formidable problem. ■

Nepal

Area: *140,797km² (54,362sq.m.).* **Population:** *11.9 million.* **Capital:** *Katmandu (333,000).* **Language:** *Nepali.* **Ethnic groups:** *Nepalis, Gurkhas, Sherpas.* **Main exports:** *cattle, hides, timber.* **Average temperatures:** *10°C (50°F) Jan. 26°C (78°F) July in Katmandu.* **Highest point:** *Mt Everest 8,848m (29,028ft).*

Nepal is an independent constitutional monarchy famed as the birthplace of

Gautama Buddha and the main point of access to the world's highest peak, Mt Everest. From the sub-arctic temperatures of the high Himalayas, the land falls through temperate mountain valleys to warm, swampy plains (Terai) near the Indian border.

Jute and sugar cane are grown in the Terai region and forests covering more than half the country provide timber. Most of the people are illiterate subsistence farmers growing rice, maize and millet on terraced slopes in the Nepal Valley. Tourism and small industries are developing. ■

Sikkim

The tiny mountain kingdom of Sikkim has been an associate state of India since September 1974. It has an area of 7,107km² (2,744sq.m.) and a population of 231,000 with a capital at Gangtok (12,000). Most of the people are Nepalese farmers growing cereals in the river valleys. Sikkim is the world's principal source of the spice cardamom. Its towering mountains include Mt Kanchenjunga, 8,585m (28,146ft). ■

Bhutan

The independent Buddhist kingdom of Bhutan is a constitutional monarchy

Above: This Buddhist temple is one of many in Katmandu, capital of Nepal, founded AD 723.

bordered by India (which controls its foreign affairs), Tibet and Sikkim. It has an area of 47,000km² (18,147sq.m.), a population of some 1 million and a capital at Thimbu (9,000). From the icy peaks of the Eastern Himalayas, the land falls to sub-tropical river valleys and plains near the Indian border. The people are mainly illiterate herdsmen and farmers growing barley, rice and wheat on terraced slopes. ■

Jammu and Kashmir

Kashmir is the subject of a territorial dispute between India, which controls two-thirds of the country through a governing assembly, and Pakistan, which holds the north-western remainder. A beautiful mountainous region, it has an area of 222,237km² (85,806sq.m.) and a population of 5.7 million, two-thirds Moslem, The capital is Srinagar (286,000) in summer and Jammu (103,000) in winter, when upland temperatures fall to freezing point. Most of the people grow rice, maize, wheat and fruit in the Vale of Kashmir or weave wool and silk in cottage industries. Mt Godwin Austen 8,611m (28,250ft) is the highest of many

peaks in the Himalaya and Karakoram ranges, which dominate the territory. ■

India

Area: *3,268,081km² (1,261,807sq.m.).* **Population:** *600 million.* **Capital:** *New Delhi (3,650,000).* **Largest city:** *Calcutta (8 million).* **Languages:** *Hindi and English most widely spoken of 10 major languages.* **Ethnic groups:** *Indo-Aryan, Dravidian, Mongoloid.* **Main exports:** *Tea, jute, coffee, cotton goods, hides and skins, iron ore.* **Average temperatures:** *29°C (85°F), June, 21°C (70°F) Jan. in Delhi.* **Highest point:** *Nanda Devi 7,817m (25,645ft).*

India, although only the seventh biggest country in the world in area, has the second highest population. Culturally the centre of Hinduism, it has been deeply influenced by the 200 years of British rule that preceded its independence in 1947. During this time the railway system (fourth largest in the world), bureaucracy, language and constitutional traditions of the British established patterns that remain embedded in Indian life.

Physically, India is shut off from central Asia by the great mountain wall of the Himalayas, with many peaks rising above 7,000 metres. South of this arc lies a wide plain irrigated by the three immense river systems of the Indus, Ganges and Brahmaputra. This mainly flat alluvial plain supports much of India's population. The Indian Peninsula is dominated by the Deccan Plateau which rises to the Western Ghats. A narrow coastal plain lies between these hills and the Arabian Sea. East of the Eastern Ghats, a broader plain is crossed by several major rivers. These coastal plains are also heavily populated.

Peninsular India lies within the Tropic of Cancer and throughout the subcontinent the climate is generally warm and humid with summer temperatures rising to 38°C (100°F) or higher in the Ganges plain. The dominant climatic influences are seasonal monsoons which bring rain from June to September, particularly heavy in Assam. A drier wind brings a cool season from December to February. Hot, dry weather from March to May precedes the return of heavy rain. The monsoon can mean life or death if it comes too late or is too torrential for crops to survive.

Agriculture and industry

The average per capita income in India is less than $US 100 a year and undernourishment affects millions. Although the country has some 180 million cattle and 50 million buffaloes, Hinduism forbids their slaughter for meat. The milk yield is low and agricultural methods are generally inefficient with little application of technology. The demand for food has led to the deforestation of much of the country and farm land covers about half the total area. But with nearly 70 percent of the population engaged in agriculture (many as sharecroppers), farm organization is inefficient and in spite of production improvements through the 'Green Revolution', staples such as rice and wheat have to be imported to bolster output. Much food is lost through ineffective storage. Nevertheless the production of tea, especially in Assam, peanuts, pepper and sugar cane is the largest in the world. Important strides are being made in extending irrigation of arid areas.

India has large reserves of coal in the northeast and some of the world's biggest and best-grade deposits of iron ore in the east and south of the Peninsula. It also leads the world in production of mica and is second in manganese output. Bauxite is among a wide range of other mineral resources. Oil output from the northern plains is rising, as is hydro-electricity capacity. The advance of nuclear technology led to the testing of a nuclear device in 1974.

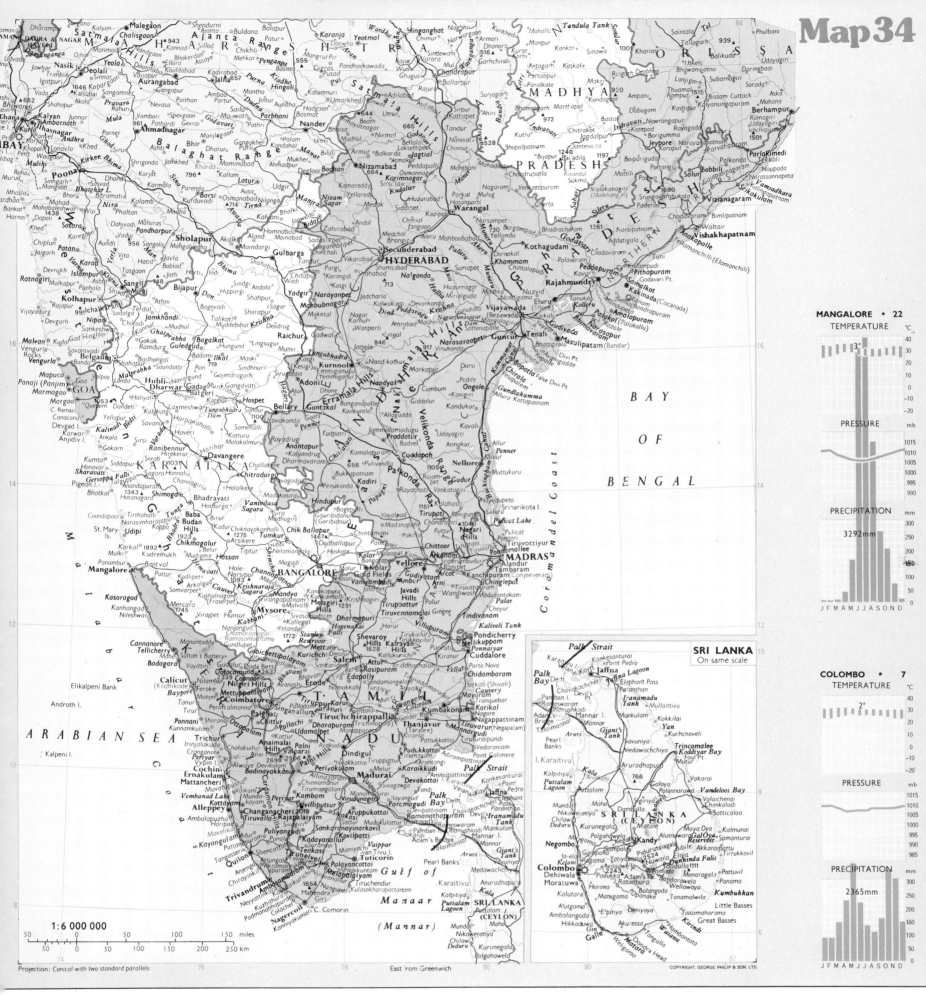

Industrial production is based on a series of five-year plans which have rapidly expanded the steel, engineering and electrical industries. About half the factory workforce is employed in the most successful industry, textiles. India is third in world production of cotton goods. Industry is concentrated mainly in the northeast, coastal west and south, with Bombay a major textiles area. Output of the privately owned textile factories is supplemented by a range of village handcrafts, including silk-weaving and carpet-making.

People, constitution and history
India is a democratic federal republic and member of the Commonwealth of Nations. Strongly centralized rule is exercised by the government in New Delhi, dominated since the first elections in 1952 by the Congress Party. Religion plays a crucial role in India. More than 83 percent of the population is Hindu and the laws of this faith influence both social and economic life. There are 3,000 castes, each imposing specific restrictions. Laws prohibiting unequal treatment because of caste, religion or sex are only slowly changing traditional attitudes. Despite free schooling to 14, literacy has risen to only 30 percent. With 845 languages and dialects spoken in India, the choice of Hindi as the official language (replacing English) in 1965 aroused tensions as access to the best jobs in industry and administration now depends on its mastery.

The Indian people descend from the intermarriage of dark Dravidians who settled the Indus valley about 3000 BC and Aryans who invaded it about 1500 BC. Muslim and Mongol invasions after the 11th century led to the Mogul empire which disintegrated before the inroads of European traders, culminating in the rule of the British East India Company in the mid-1800s. When the British withdrew in 1947 the sub-continent was partitioned into Muslim Pakistan and Hindu India after bloody riots. India's most severe economic problem continues to be her population growth, averaging 2.5 percent, 15 million, a year. ■

Sri Lanka

Area 65,610km² (25,332sq.m.). **Population:** 14 million. **Capital:** Colombo (570,000). **Languages:** Sinhala, English, Tamil. **Ethnic groups:** Sinhalese (75 percent), Tamils, Moors, Burghers. **Main exports:** Tea, rubber, coconut products, graphite. **Average temperature:** 27°C (80°F). **Highest point:** Pidurutalagala 2,524m (8,281ft).

Sri Lanka (Ceylon), a vivid tropical island 32 kilometres (20 miles) off the south-eastern coast of India, is an important shipping entrepot and producer of tea and rubber. Its main trading partner is Britain which colonized the island in 1802 and granted it independence in 1948. In 1960 Mrs Sirimavo Bandaranaike became the world's first woman prime minister and in 1972 she instituted a socialist republic. Buddhism is the major religion.

A low coastal plain, broad in the north, surrounds a mountainous interior and is irrigated by many narrow rivers. Sea breezes on the coast and altitude in the hills temper the tropical climate. There are dry zones in the north-east but rainfall is heavy in the south-west where most of the cash crops are grown. Ceylon is second only to India in tea production, but has to import much of its food.

Sri Lanka has the world's biggest output of high-quality graphite and there are gemstone deposits. Forests covering 40 percent of the island are rich in ebony and other hardwoods. The Government hopes to expand a wide range of industries based on hydro-electric power. A major problem is the lack of significant industrial mineral resources. ■

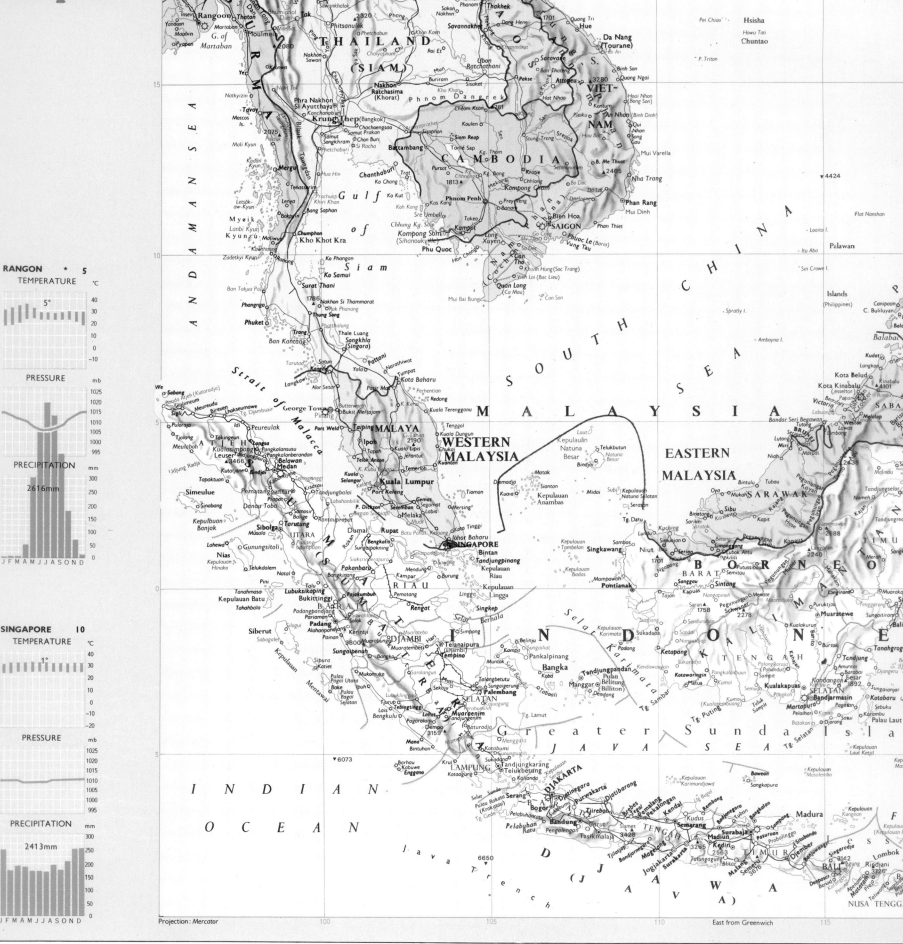

RANGON ★ 5
TEMPERATURE °C
5°
PRESSURE mb
PRECIPITATION
2616mm
J F M A M J J A S O N D

SINGAPORE 10
TEMPERATURE °C
1°
PRESSURE mb
PRECIPITATION
2413mm
J F M A M J J A S O N D

Projection: Mercator   East from Greenwich

The Philippines

Area: *299,404km² (115,600sq.m.).*
Population: *43 million.* **Capital:**
Quezon City (750,000). **Largest city:**
Manila (2 million). **Languages:**
Filipino (Tagalog), English, Spanish.
Ethnic groups: *Malayo-Polynesian
(90 percent), Chinese, Spanish,
American.* **Main exports:** *Timber,
copra, sugar, hemp, tobacco.* **Average
temperatures:** *24°C (75°F) Jan.;
28°C (82°F) June (coastal).* **Highest
point:** *Mt Apo, 2,954m (9,692ft).*

The only predominantly Christian nation
in Asia (80 percent Roman Catholic),
the Republic of the Philippines comprises 730 inhabited islands and thousands
of coral atolls forming a splintered
triangle between Taiwan to the north
and Borneo to the south. It is a country
of brilliant-hued flowers, dense rain-
forests, swift rivers, active volcanoes and
picturesque villages of raised bamboo or
rattan huts amidst rice, maize, sweet
potato and banana cultivations. The
climate is hot and wet with frequent
typhoons between June and November.
Monsoons between October and March
bring heavy rain to the eastern Philippines
and rainfall averages 200cm (80in) in
Manila.

More than half of the population live
by farming or fishing. The volcanic
mountain chain running the length of
the islands leaves only narrow coastal
plains in most areas but the Philippines
has achieved self-sufficiency in rice by
high-yield plantations on the main island
of Luzon.

Hydro-electric and geothermal power
is being developed and embryo manufacturing industries have been started
with the aid of the USA which is the
Republic's main trading partner. But
most of the workforce is engaged in
agricultural processing with 1.2 million
in coconut production. The Philippines
is the world's leading copra producer and
a major supplier of abaca (Malia hemp),
used in making rope. It has fine hardwoods, such as mahogany and is the
world's sixth biggest timber producer.

Independence, achieved in 1946, followed 350 years of Spanish and nearly
50 years of American control. Spanish–
American cultural influence is strong.
With sharp inequalities of wealth,
political democracy has been difficult to
sustain. In 1972, martial law was introduced with the president ruling by decree
in the face of insurrections in the north
and amongst Moslems on the large
southern island of Mindanao. ■

*Right: Bananas flourish in a valley of
western Java. Plant life is luxuriant
throughout Indonesia, although only
Java, Bali and parts of Sumatra have
soils of high quality and large
cultivated areas cleared of forests.
Wildlife is exceptionally rich.*

Map 36

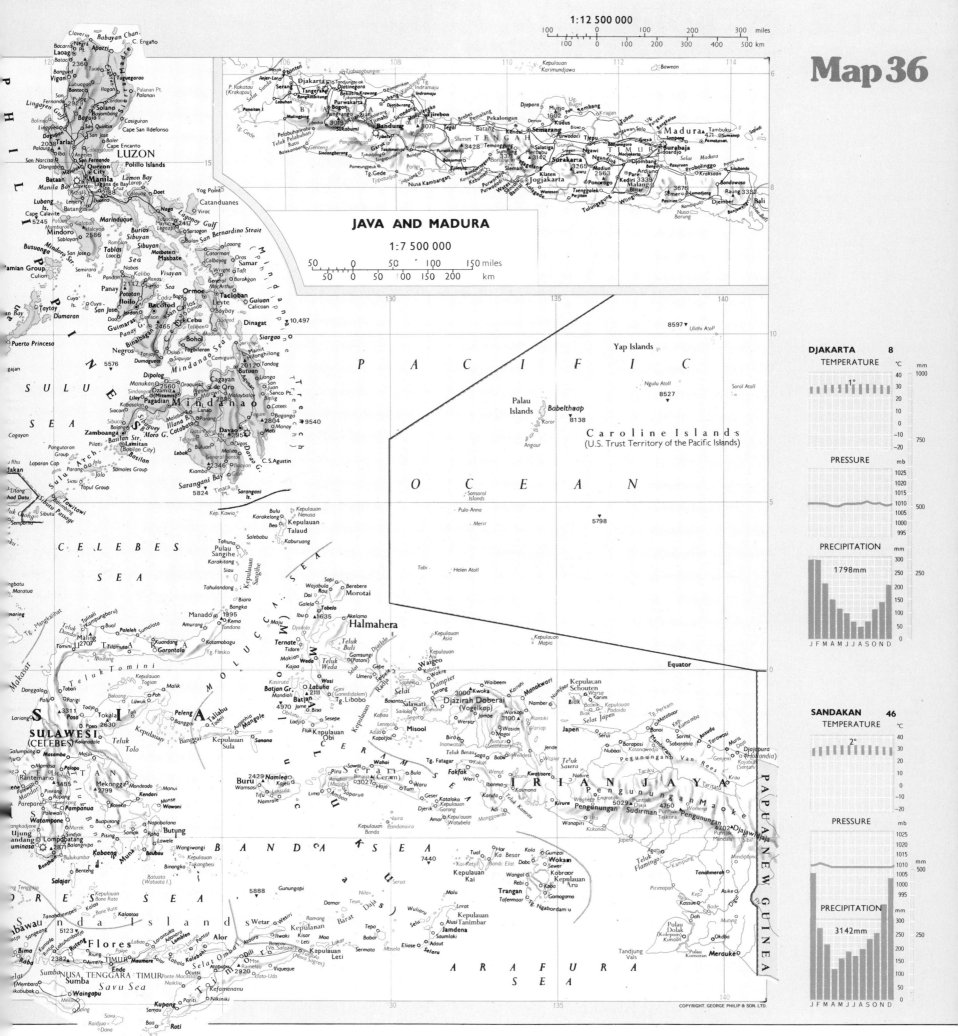

JAVA AND MADURA
1:7 500 000

1:12 500 000

Indonesia

Area: 1,904,342km² (735,267sq.m.). **Population:** 130 million. **Capital:** Djakarta (5 million). **Languages:** Bahasa Indonesian, Malayo-Polynesian dialects. **Ethnic groups:** Javanese (50 percent), Sudanese, Malay, Chinese. **Main exports:** Oil and petroleum products, timber, rubber, coffee, tin. **Average temperature:** 27°C (80°F). **Highest point:** Djaja Peak, 5,030m (16,503ft).

The Republic of Indonesia is the largest nation in South-East Asia and by population the fifth biggest in the world. Its gross national product is only about a twentieth of Japan's, however. An archipelago of more than 13,600 islands stretching from the Indian Ocean to the Pacific between the land masses of South-East Asia and Australia, it has a wet, tropical climate with a spectacular variety of wildlife. Most of the islands are mountainous, heavily forested and thinly populated. There are more than 400 volcanoes, 100 of them active. Though its population is mainly of Malay stock and is overwhelmingly Moslem, the Republic has three million Chinese who run much of its commercial life.

The three biggest islands, Kalimantan (Borneo), Sumatra and Irian Barat (formerly western New Guinea) make up nearly three-quarters of Indonesia's land area but nearly two-thirds of the population is crammed on the most fertile rice-growing island, Java. In addition to the capital, Djakarta, Java has the two next biggest cities, Surabaja (1.6 million) and Bandung (1.3 million). With little manufacturing industry, most of the population still depends on subsistence rice farming, though Indonesia is not yet self-sufficient in this staple crop.

Ample resources of oil, wood, coal, and hydro-electric power give Indonesia considerable industrial potential but there are transport and other difficulties in developing it. Sumatra, Kalimantan and Java have large oil fields and oil has already become the mainstay of trade with more than 400 million barrels exported annually. Tin, bauxite and nickel are important mineral products, with others yet to be developed. Production of rubber, formerly Indonesia's main export, is again rising, while teak is the most important wood in a timber industry of great potential.

After more than three centuries of Dutch control, Indonesia won independence in 1949. Since the failure of a communist coup in 1965, the country has established closer relations with the Western bloc, trading mainly with the USA, Japan and Singapore. With the consent of a People's Consultative Assembly, its president rules through an executive backed by the armed forces (330,000 strong). Literacy, now 70 percent, is being expanded rapidly. ■

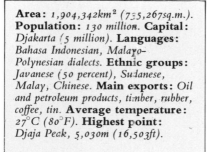

Mainland South-East Asia

Map 37

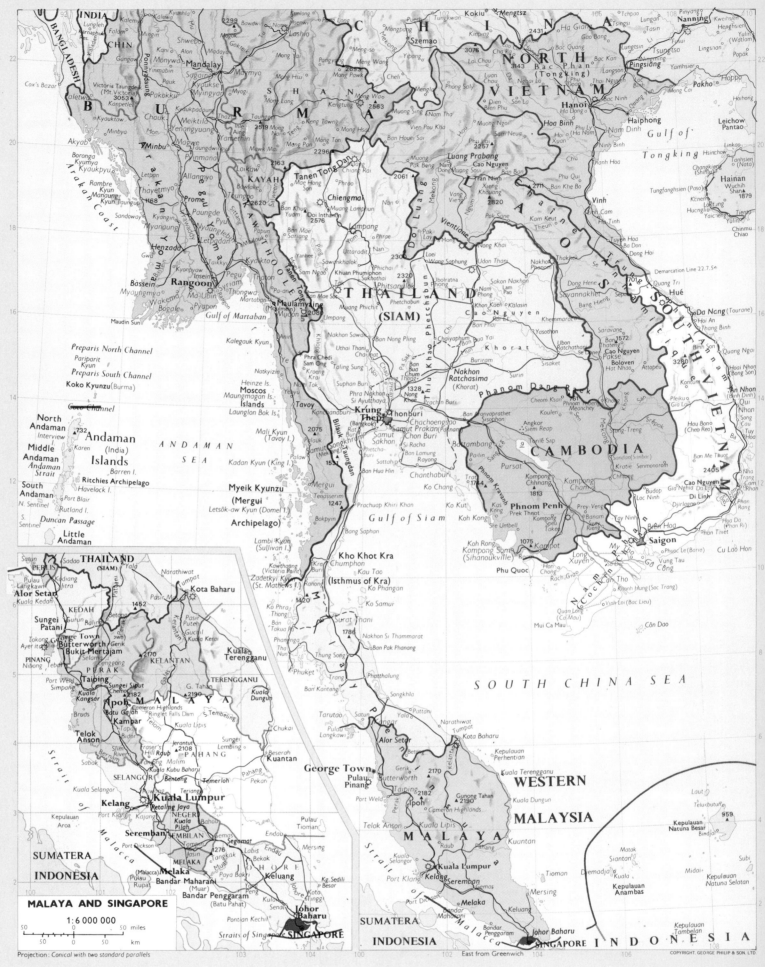

MANDALE ★ 77

TEMPERATURE °C

11°

PRESSURE mb

PRECIPITATION mm

828mm

J F M A M J J A S O N D

KRUNG THEP 2

TEMPERATURE °C

5°

PRESSURE mb

PRECIPITATION mm

1397mm

J F M A M J J A S O N D

MALAYA AND SINGAPORE

1:6 000 000

Projection: Conical with two standard parallels

Burma

Area: *678,033km² (261,790sq.m.).*
Population: *30.8 million.* **Capital:**
Rangoon (2m). **Languages:**
*Burmese and many Sino-Tibetan
tongues.* **Ethnic groups:** *Burmese,
Chinese (350,000), Indian (120,000).*
Main exports: *rice, teak, rubber, oil,
minerals.* **Average temperatures:**
*33°C (92°F) April, 21°C (70°F) Dec.
in Rangoon but much colder in high
country.* **Highest point:** *Hkakabo
Razi 5,881m (19,296ft).*

The Socialist Republic of the Union of
Burma has chosen a Buddhist way to
socialism and has succeeded in isolating
itself from political alignments in its
region. Settled originally from China
and Tibet, Burma became a British
province of India in 1885, won inde-

pendence in 1948 and has been a one-
party state since 1962. Little touched by
western technology, it is a vivid green
land of a myriad temples and pagodas,
the most famous of them the 2,500-year
old Shwe Dagon pagoda in Rangoon.

Upper Burma is mountainous and
thickly forested with major valleys
formed by rivers running to the Bay of
Bengal, the longest of which is the
Irrawaddy (2,012km or 1,250 miles).
This river system spreads out into a wide
delta west of Rangoon. In the south, a
narrow swampy coastal strip hemmed in
by mountains runs down into the Malay
Peninsula. Burma's hot, wet climate and
fertile rice-growing plains make it a rich
area and four-fifths of the annual crop is
exported. With tropical forests covering
half the country, Burma is the world's
leading supplier of teak and a major
producer of bamboo. The population is
80 percent rural and apart from crafts
there is little manufacturing. Oil in the
Irrawaddy valley supplies all local needs.

Fine jade and gemstones are among many
mineral resources. Burma trades mainly
with Britain, India, Indonesia and Japan.

Laos

Area: *236,800km² (91,429sq.m.).*
Population: *3.3 million.* **Capital:**
Vientiane (130,000). **Language:**
Lao. **Ethnic groups:** *Lao (50 percent),
Meo, Thai, Kha, Yao.* **Main
exports:** *opium, handicrafts.*
Average temperatures: *28°C
(82°F) July, 21°C (70°F) Jan.*
Highest point: *Mt Bia 2,817m
(9,242ft).*

Laos was once known as Lan Xang—
'land of a million elephants'. It is a
mountainous, humid, densely forested
country cut off from its neighbouring
states by the Annamese mountains in the
north and east and by the broad Mekong

River on the west. Laos has rich teak
forests and undeveloped reserves of gold,
gypsum, lead, silver, tin and zinc.

Along the Mekong which forms the
boundary with Thailand, fertile rice-
growing areas support most of the
population. Corn, tobacco and cotton
are grown in highland areas and the Meo
hill people harvest large crops of opium.
Thatched houses on bamboo stilts are
common in lower areas where heavy
monsoon rain between May and September brings flooding. Though China is
constructing a highway in the north,
most of the roads are passable only in
dry weather. There are no railways and
the Mekong and its tributaries provide
the main means of transport.

Buddhist Laos was part of French Indo-
China for 50 years until 1954 when it
became an independent constitutional
monarchy with a royal capital at Luang
Prabang. Efforts to form a neutral
government broke down in 1960 and a
war between Royal Lao forces, backed

by the United States, and the Pathet Lao, backed by North Vietnam, became a key part of the bigger conflict in Vietnam because of supply trails running through Laos. Two years after a ceasefire in 1973 the Pathet Lao took over the government and ended the monarchy. ■

Vietnam (North and South)

Area: *North, 158,750km²* (61,294sq.m.); South, 173,655km² (67,108sq.m.). **Population:** *North, 23.6 million; South 20.9 million.* **Capitals:** *Hanoi (400,000), Saigon (1.75 million).* **Languages:** *Vietnamese, Montagnard dialects, French, English.* **Ethnic groups:** *Vietnamese (90 percent) Montagnard (3.2 million), Chinese (800,000), Cambodian.* **Main exports:** *Coal (North), rubber, rice (South).* **Average temperatures:** *29°C (85°F) June, 17°C (63°F) Jan. in Hanoi but rarely below 26°C (79°F) in Saigon.* **Highest point:** *Fan Si Pan (North Vietnam) 3,143m (10,312ft).*

In the course of three bitter Indo-China wars between 1945 and 1975, Vietnam was divided in two, disrupting an economic balance between the coal-based industrial resources of the north and the rice-surpluses of the south. After the conflict ended in April, 1975, the Provisional Revolutionary Government in the south moved steadily towards unification with the socialist Democratic Republic of Vietnam in the north.

Physically, Vietnam consists of the deltas of the Red and Mekong rivers, linked by a narrow coastal plain with the Annamite mountain chain extending from the borders of China in the north down the western side of the country towards Saigon. The Red River drains rich, densely-populated farmland protected by dikes against summer floods. To the west, the country is mountainous jungle, inhabited mainly by Montagnard tribes. Rice is grown in the middle coastal lowlands but the most fertile areas lie in the broad southern delta of the Mekong.

Only 15 percent of the country in the north is farmed (mainly in collectives). But there are large coal deposits and other minerals including gold, iron, lead, phosphate, tin, tungsten and zinc. In the south, some manufacturing has been developed, mainly cement, paper and textiles, but energy resources are few. Rubber is now the main export, the war having cut back rice production. Despite urban development in the south, two-thirds of Vietnam's people are farmers. Literacy is high and international reconstruction aid is expected to produce rapid economic growth.

The Vietnamese people, predominantly Buddhists speaking an ancient monosyllabic language, originally expanded southward from China. France ruled the country from the late 1800s until it was forced out in 1954, leaving a communist regime in the north and an anti-communist one in the south where there is a large Roman Catholic minority. Despite massive American military intervention, the ensuing civil war was won by the north and its southern allies who opposed the Saigon government and sought sweeping land reforms. ■

Thailand

Area: *514,000km² (198,457sq.m.).* **Population:** *40 million.* **Capital:** *Bangkok (4 million).* **Languages:** *Thai, Chinese, Malay.* **Ethnic groups:** *Thai, Chinese (3 million), Malay, Vietnamese.* **Main exports:** *Rice, rubber, tin, maize, timber, jute.* **Average temperatures:** *33°C (92 F) April, 24°C (75°F) Nov. in Bangkok.* **Highest point:** *Inthanom Peak 2,595m (8,514ft).*

The fertile, densely-forested kingdom of Thailand is among the most prosperous nations of its region and the only one never colonized by Europeans. It has steep mountains in the northwest and the high, dry Khorat Plateau on the east. But most of its population is concentrated in the broad rice-growing valley formed by the Chao Phraya River which runs to the port capital of Bangkok, a crowded, cosmopolitan city built over canals. Southern Thailand is a narrow mountainous strip extending into the Malay Peninsula.

Three-quarters of the people are engaged in rice-growing and live in small villages grouped around Buddhist wats. Thailand exports a sixth of its 13 million tonnes annual rice crop. It is the world's third largest rubber producer, mainly from plantations in the south. Thailand is also an important supplier of tin and other varied mineral resources are underdeveloped. Its silk, lacquer and handicrafts are famous. With investment from the USA and Japan, manufacturing and hydroelectric power are being developed.

Thailand's climate is dominated by heavy monsoon rain between May and September. The rail and road system is still rudimentary and water transport and fishing are important in the economy. Forests, mainly of teak, cover nearly 60 percent of the land and teem with bird and animal life and elephants are used in the timber industry.

The slim, small-boned Thai people have a distinctive and colourful culture. A large Chinese minority is active in commercial life. The Thai state was founded about 1350. A constitutional monarchy with a civilian government but a recent tradition of military rule, Thailand was strongly pro-western in the 1950s when the South-East Asia Treaty Organization headquarters was established in Bangkok. A skilful diplomatic balance is maintained with Thailand's neighbours and some rural unrest, mainly in the north, has been contained. ■

Cambodia

Area: *181,035km² (69,898sq.m.).* **Population:** *7.3 million.* **Capital:** *Phnom Penh (formerly 600,000).* **Ethnic groups:** *Khmer, Chinese (300,000), Vietnamese (100,000).* **Languages:** *Khmer, French, Chinese.* **Main exports:** *formerly rubber, corn, rice.* **Average temperature:** *29°C (85°F).*

The Khmer Republic was once the centre of an empire controlling much of South-East Asia. Angkor Wat and other ancient Buddhist-Hindu ruins north of the Tonle Sap (Great Lake) bear witness to the greatness of its thousand-year monarchy. A French protectorate from 1863 to 1953, it was embroiled in the Vietnam conflict in 1970 when civil war followed the dissolution of the monarchy. The victorious National United Front of Cambodia (Khmers Rouges) inaugurated a Marxist state in April, 1975 and a swollen population in the capital, Phnom Penh, was dispersed as a first step in reorganizing the shattered economy.

Bordered by low mountains, the country is predominantly flat and wet. It is dominated by the Mekong River which rises under heavy monsoon rains (May–November) and reverses the Tonle Sap river, flooding a large area around the lake. This is a crucial feature of the subsistence rice-growing and internal fishing economy on which 90 percent of the population depends. Important rubber plantations near the Vietnam border were destroyed in the war and fledgling manufacturing industries around the modern city of Phnom Penh were also disrupted. ■

Right: Parasols, usually vividly coloured and often, as here, decorated by hand, express a love of bright hues that is found throughout South-East Asia. They are useful as well as beautiful, a shield against sun and rain.

Above: Characteristic Thai architecture in the Summer Palace, near Bangkok.

Above: The Emerald Buddha is housed in one of Bankok's massed temples.

Malaysia

Area: *330,435km² (127,581sq.m.).*
Population: *11.8 million.* **Capital:**
Kuala Lumpur (510,000). **Languages:**
Bahasa Malay, English, Chinese.
Ethnic groups: *Malay (45 percent),
Chinese (36 percent), Indian (10
percent).* **Main exports:** *Rubber,
timber, tin, palm oil, iron ore.*
Average temperatures: *27°C
(81°F) in West Malaysia; 31°C
(88°F) in East Malaysia.* **Highest
point:** *Mt Kinabalu (Sabah),
4,101m (13,455ft).*

The Federation of Malaysia is a constitutional monarchy within the Commonwealth made up of 13 states, nine of them
Moslem sultanates. Two of these states—
Sabah and Sarawak—are former British
protectorates in northern Borneo (East
Malaysia) and are separated from the
Malay peninsula by the South China Sea.
Apart from cool highland areas, Malaysia
is hot and damp with dense jungle covering much of the country, particularly in
East Malaysia. Sabah and Sarawak are
mountainous and the coastal plains of the
peninsula are also divided by central
ranges. Rainfall is heavy from November
to March.

Much of the population is concentrated
in coastal villages and illiteracy is high.
But efficient production of rubber, tin,
timber and other natural resources has
produced a relatively high standard of
living. Malaysia is the world's leading
rubber producer and supplies more than
a third of the world's tin concentrates.
There are oil fields off the east coast of the
peninsula as well as off Sabah and Sarawak
and refineries in Sarawak process oil from
the neighbouring state of Brunei.

The most multi-racial nation of the
region, Malaysia has coped well with
tensions between the rural Malay
majority and a predominantly urban,
high-skilled Chinese minority. It is a
parliamentary democracy with a coalition
Alliance Party ruling. Strong links are
retained with Britain which controlled
and developed the peninsula for a
century and granted it independence
after a long struggle against communist
insurgency. Japan is now a major in-
vestor and is Malaysia's main trading
partner. ∎

Singapore

Area: *584km² (225sq.m.).*
Population: *2.3 million.*
Languages: *Malay, Mandarin
Chinese, Tamil, English.* **Ethnic
groups:** *Chinese (74 percent),
Malay (14 percent), Indian (8 percent).*
Main exports: *Petroleum products
and oil, processed rubber, ships,
manufactured goods.*
Average temperature: *27°C (80°F).*

The tiny but dynamic island republic of
Singapore, separated from the Malay
peninsula by a causeway across the 1.2km-
wide Johore Strait, has the highest
standard of living in South-East Asia. Its
wealth is based largely on the skill with
which its Chinese majority has exploited
a fine harbour at the crossroads of Asian
sea lanes to become the world's fourth
biggest port and a major trading, ship-
building and processing entrepot.

A former British colony, Singapore
became independent within the Commonwealth in 1959. A brief political
marriage with Malaysia was broken off
in 1965 and the city state is a progressive
democracy governed since independence
by the People's Action Party.

The warm climate is tempered by sea
breezes. Annual rainfall averages 241cm
(95in). The low-lying, swampy terrain
is intensively cultivated but much of the
republic's food has to be imported. About
90 percent of the population lives in
the city where shipbuilding yards, petro-
chemical plants, oil refineries, engineering works, mills and factories are
concentrated. ∎

Brunei, Timor

Brunei is an oil-rich British protectorate
which did not join Malaysia. A sultanate
surrounded by Sarawak in northern
Borneo, it has an area of 5,765km²
(2,226sq.m.) and a population of 156,000,
mainly Malay and Chinese (25 percent).
The capital is Banda Seri Begawan
(pop. 37,000). Brunei has rich offshore
and onshore oil fields.

Timor, an overseas territory of Portugal
until an independence movement
emerged in 1975, occupies the eastern
part of Indonesian Timor. Its area is
14,925km² (5,763sq.m.), its capital is
Dili (pop. 20,000) and its people are
mainly Malay–Papuan, engaged almost
wholly in agriculture. ∎

*Right: This longhouse near Kuching,
East Malaysia, is shared by several
families of Dyaks.*

*Below: Barges jam one of Singapore's
busy docks. The free port handles a
huge volume of transit shipping.*

Below: Street markets with their pans of produce spilling over the pavement never seem to close in South-East Asia.

1:20 000 000

Projection: Bonne

East from Greenwich

COPYRIGHT GEORGE PHILIP & SON, LTD

The People's Republic of China

Area: 9,561,000km² (3,691,523sq.m.).
Population: 850 million. **Capital:** Peiping, or Peking (8.2m). **Largest city:** Shanghai (11.2m). **Languages:** Mandarin (official) and many other Chinese dialects, chiefly Wu, Cantonese, Fukien, Hakka. **Ethnic groups:** Sinitic, Mongoloid. **Main exports:** Agricultural products, silk and textiles, tin, molybdenum, tea. **Average temperatures:** −7°C (20°F) Jan. in north and central areas but warmer in south and −23°C (−10°F) in northwest and Tibet. 27°C (80°F) July, but hotter in deserts and cooler in the mountains. **Highest point:** Mt Everest 8,848m (29,028ft).

China has the biggest population of any country (about a fifth of the world total) and the third largest land area after Russia and Canada. Its Chinese name, Chung Kuo (Middle Kingdom) reflects its importance as the oldest independent nation, with a history stretching back more than 2,000 years. Its ancient civilization invented paper and printing, silk, porcelain, gunpowder and the compass. In addition to its heritage of art and literature it has been the centre of the Buddhist religion Confucianism and Taoism. Unified government emerged with the Shang dynasty about 1500 BC and under the Han dynasty (206 BC–AD 220) the Chinese empire rivalled that of Rome in extent. After a period of Mongol dominance in the 13th century, Chinese power was finally reasserted under the Chi'ing dynasty of the Manchus, who ruled from 1644 to 1911. A long period of deliberate isolation from western technology ended in the 19th century. The humiliating imposition of foreign spheres of influence gave way to the emergence of modern Chinese nationalism under Sun Yat-sen in 1921.

A bitter struggle with Japan from 1937 to 1945 was followed by a civil war that ended in the withdrawal of the Nationalist government of Chiang Kai-shek to Taiwan and the victory of the Chinese Communist Party under Mao Tse-tung in 1949. During the past 25 years China has been transformed from a backward agricultural nation into an increasingly industrial economy with a nuclear and space technology and an increasing capacity to exploit its vast mineral resources. Confrontation with the West, highlighted by the Korean War of 1950–53, and by tension over America's protection of Taiwan, followed by a sharp quarrel with Russia, has given way to a more flexible international stance and to increasing participation in international affairs. China was admitted to the United Nations in 1971.

The People's Republic of China comprises 21 provinces, five self-governing regions and three special cities, Peking, Shanghai and Tientsin. The autonomous regions include Tibet, which was independent from 1914 until 1950. The country is a one-party state, strongly

Left: The Great Wall of China, built to check incursions from the north 2,000 years ago, runs for 2,400km.

centralized on Peking and ruled by the Chinese Communist Party with 17 million members. Elected people's representatives vote for candidates nominated by the party for the National People's Congress. The State Council is headed by the premier and the Chairman of the Republic is Head of State.

People and social organization
For visitors to China, the most overwhelming impression is of its teeming population and the sense of purposeful organization and energy. More than 90 percent of China's 830 million people live in the eastern fifth of the country. There are about 30 cities with populations of more than a million, including Shanghai, the world's second biggest city. The rural population in the eastern sector is also dense, especially around the mouths of the Yangtze Kiang and Hwang Ho (Yellow) rivers as well as in the coastal valleys and plains and the north central plain. Although the government is encouraging late marriages and smaller families, the population is growing by about 14 million a year, putting continued pressure on social and economic resources.

Nearly a third of the people live in urban areas. Grain (rice in the south, wheat in the north) is the staple diet, supplemented with vegetables and fish. Literacy (only 50 percent in 1960) is being extended through adult education and by combining study with work in farms or factories. Private ownership has been abolished and the government directs both the type of work and the wages paid. The close-knit pattern of village life centred on the traditional Chinese extended family has been broken up to some degree and religion, especially Confucianism, is not officially encouraged. Large communities organized as cooperatives or communes have replaced individual land holdings, although some small plots are allowed. Housing ranges from modern apartments to houses of mud and straw or bamboo and clay, caves and, in Inner Mongolia, tents. Life in China is austere by western standards, with few consumer goods available and a social uniformity exemplified by the blue work clothes worn by millions. But by a massive redistribution of land to the peasants and by replacing the old reverence for academic scholarship with the sense of a common struggle to achieve national goals, the government has been able to mobilize the people behind its programmes. Paramilitary youth organizations have often been the spearhead of social action, backed by skilful techniques of mass political education. Revolutionary impetus has been maintained, sometimes at great economic cost, by convulsive radical movements such as the Cultural Revolution of the 1960s.

Land and climate
Nearly two-thirds of China's land surface is classed as highlands or plateaus. In general the land slopes from west to east, with the two major river systems of the Yangtze Kiang and Hwang Ho flowing in a similar direction. China can be divided into three main regions.

Western (or outer) China is cut off from the Indian sub-continent in the southwest by the Himalaya Mountains. North of this towering chain the vast Tibet Plateau extends in a series of bleak uplands, averaging 4,600m (15,000ft) in height. Most of the two million Tibetans live in the southern valleys. Beyond the Kunlun Mountains on the north of the plateau, the Takla Makan desert and Dzungarian Basin stretch westward through Sinkiang to the Tien Shan and Pamir mountains and north to the Altai mountains bordering Asian Russia and Mongolia. The Turfan Depression on the northern edge of the Takla Makan desert is 154m (505ft) below sea level. The Gobi Desert extends southward from Mongolia, making up part of a desert belt spreading from west to east across 3,860km (2,400 miles).

Northern China includes the rolling Manchurian Plain in the northeast and the broad North China Plain extending southward from Peking, crossed by the Hwang Ho River. The name Yellow River derives from the colour of its

waters, which carry silt from the Loess Highlands in the west where the river in its upper reaches cuts gorges in a region of fine, wind-blown soil. Both the Manchurian Plain and the North China Plain are fertile agricultural areas.

Southern China, lying east and south of the Tsin Ling mountains, is dominated in the north by the Yangtze Kiang River, 5,800km (3,600 miles) long—the world's longest river after the Nile and Amazon. Like the Hwang Ho, it rises in the Tibet Plateau and crosses a fertile plain. Its upper reaches, surrounded by mountains, cross another rich farming area, the Szechwan Basin. South of the Yangtze Plain, rugged hills and uplands with terraced farms extend to a smaller plain around Kwangchow (Canton).

The climate of Southern China is humid and subtropical but in the north and west harsh seasonal variations are produced by the movement of two dominant air masses. Cold, dry air moving eastward from Central Asia in winter brings temperatures as low as -34°C $(-30^\circ$F), freezing the northern rivers, including the Hwang Ho, for several months. Yet in summer, desert temperatures rise to more than 38°C $(100^\circ$F) as warm air blows inland from the sea, bringing eastern areas most of their annual rainfall, averaging 200cm (80in) in coastal areas. Little moisture reaches Mongolia and Sinkiang.

Agriculture, fishing and forestry
With at least two-thirds of its people engaged in agriculture, China is the third largest producer of food in the world. But because of its huge population it remains locked in a centuries-old struggle for self-sufficiency and wheat still has to be imported from countries such as Canada and Australia. Hardly more than a third of its land area can be farmed and flood, drought and erosion are constant dangers. With little modern machinery and fertilizers (apart from animal and human manure), methods of irrigation and cultivation rely heavily on muscle power. Yet China leads the world

in production of rice, is second in vegetables and third in wheat, cotton, maize and tea. It has the most pigs (nearly 200 million) and the third most sheep (100 million).

About a seventh of the land is under intensive cultivation, mainly in the east. The South China ricelands extend to the Yangtze plain. Cotton is also grown mainly in this plain and in the North China Plain and Loess Highlands. The wheat belt extends from the Loess Highlands and North China Plain to Manchuria and the corn belt from the Yunnan Plateau to Manchuria. The northwest is the major pastoral area, with many sheep and goats. Vegetables and fruit are grown widely in the east and tea and rubber in the south.

Fish are a major protein source and China's shallow coastal waters provide a rich variety, supplemented by inland fishing. Forests cover only a tenth of the land, mainly in border areas, and China has to import some timber.

After the redistribution of land to the peasants, a full-scale system of people's communes had been established by 1958 to pool resources. The communes are generally large, averaging 4,500 families. Most are commercial, industrial, social and paramilitary units as well as agricultural ones.

Minerals, industry and trade
Through a series of Five Year Plans since 1949, the government has sought to convert China into a leading industrial power, drawing on large mineral resources, many of which are still largely unexploited. With formidable transport problems, especially in the west where the road and rail system is limited, and with several organizational setbacks, this aim has only partially been achieved. Production of consumer goods is still low. But great strides have been made in heavy industry particularly in Manchuria. China now ranks seventh in world iron and steel production.

Nearly 90 percent of energy is supplied by coal, mined chiefly north of the

Yangtze in open-cast beds. China is third in world coal production and fifth in iron, mainly from low-grade deposits in the northeast. Oil production is increasing from apparently-large reserves in Sinkiang Kansu and elsewhere. South China has the most important deposits of other minerals, especially tungsten, antimony, tin and molybdenum, with lesser reserves of manganese, lead, copper and zinc. There is large but poorly-developed hydroelectric potential.

In spite of efforts to decentralize industry, it continues to be concentrated mainly in the east. The Szechwan Basin, Manchuria the area around Shanghai, and other large centres such as Peking, Tientsin, Chungking, Nanking and Hangchow are major industrial centres. A wide range of manufactures, from aircraft to chemicals, are produced with textiles the biggest light industry. Handicrafts are important, making up about a quarter of manufactured goods. Until the 1960s, China traded mainly with Russia but its most important trading partners now are Hong Kong, Japan and West Germany. The doctrine of self-sufficiency continues to produce a favourable trade balance.■

Taiwan

Area: *35,961km² (13,885sq.m.).*
Population: *16m.* **Capital:** *Taipei (1.9m).* **Languages:** *Mandarin and other Chinese dialects.* **Ethnic groups:** *Chinese, Malayo-Polynesian (150,000).* **Main exports:** *Textiles, electronic equipment, plywood, canned foods.* **Average temperatures:** *18°C (65°F) Jan. 27°C (80°F) July.*
Highest point: *Yu Shan 3,997m (13,113ft).*

Minerals and industry: China

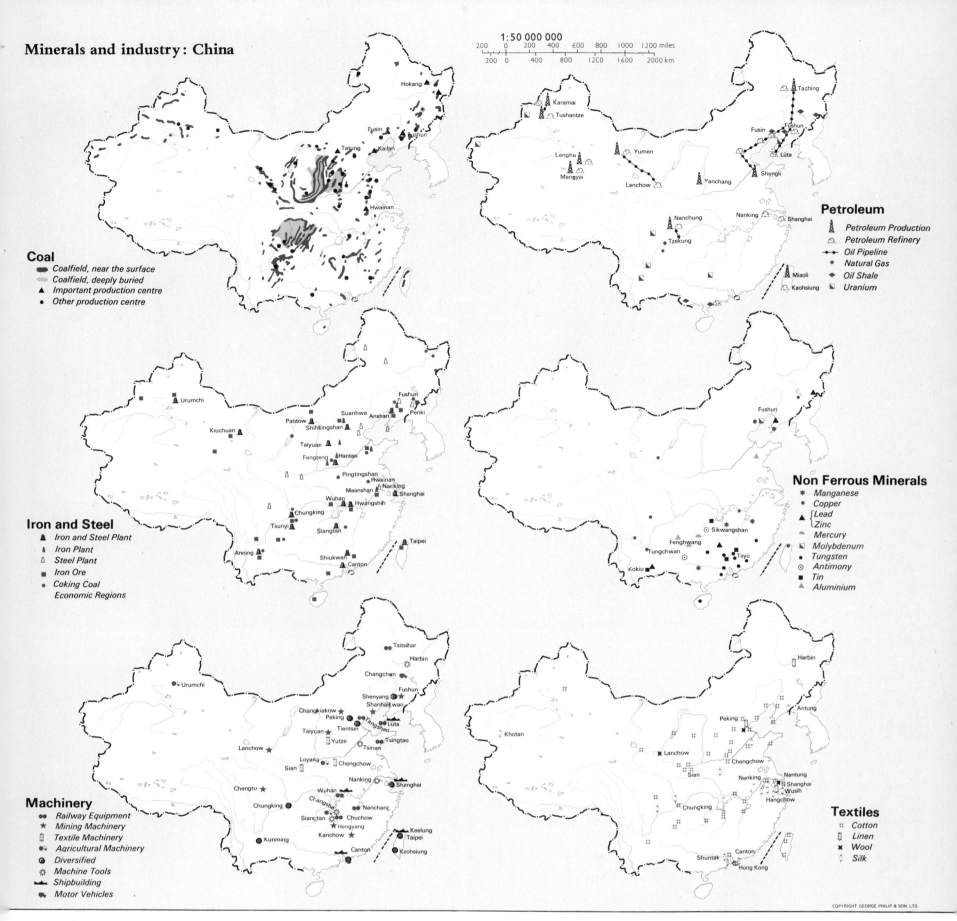

1 : 50 000 000

Coal
- ▬ Coalfield, near the surface
- ▬ Coalfield, deeply buried
- ▲ Important production centre
- ● Other production centre

Iron and Steel
- ▲ Iron and Steel Plant
- ▲ Iron Plant
- △ Steel Plant
- ■ Iron Ore
- ● Coking Coal
  Economic Regions

Machinery
- ●● Railway Equipment
- ★ Mining Machinery
- ◫ Textile Machinery
- ●◦ Agricultural Machinery
- ● Diversified
- ✷ Machine Tools
- ⚓ Shipbuilding
- ⬛ Motor Vehicles

Petroleum
- ▲ Petroleum Production
- ⌂ Petroleum Refinery
- •─• Oil Pipeline
- ● Natural Gas
- ◆ Oil Shale
- ▽ Uranium

Non Ferrous Minerals
- ✳ Manganese
- ● Copper
- ▲ Lead
- ⌐ Zinc
- ● Mercury
- ● Molybdenum
- ■ Tungsten
- ⊙ Antimony
- ● Tin
- ▲ Aluminium

Textiles
- ⊞ Cotton
- ◫ Linen
- ✖ Wool
- ◇ Silk

The Republic of Taiwan lies 140km (90 miles) off the coast of China. Also known as Formosa or Nationalist China, it includes the Pescadores islands in the Taiwan Strait and the island fortresses of Quemoy and Matsu a few kilometres off the Chinese coast. Its claim to represent the government of mainland China has lost credibility since 1971 when its seat at the United Nations was transferred to the People's Republic of China. But with one of the best-balanced economies in the region, it is a prosperous, well-armed nation that shows no sign yet of wishing to revert to its former status as a Chinese province.

China was forced to cede Taiwan to Japan in 1895 and regained the island only in 1945. In 1949 it became a refuge for the defeated regime of Chiang Kai-shek when about 1.5 million Chinese crossed from the mainland. Under the protection and with the economic aid of the US, its population doubled in 20 years and since 1958 China has made no effort to regain the island by force. The presidential constitution is still based on that of the mainland in 1945 and most political and economic power is held by the new Chinese settlers. Taiwanese Chinese are mainly in agriculture, which employs about half the workforce.

Most of the people live on the western coastal plain. Terraced hills rise to the dramatic Chungyang Range which is heavily forested and runs the length of the island, forming steep cliffs on the east. Swift rivers are apt to flood during the summer and winter monsoons while typhoons are common. The humid, sub-tropical climate suits crops such as rice, sugar cane, soyabeans, fruit and vegetables and although only a quarter of the land can be farmed, intensive cultivation produces two or three crops a year. Holdings average only 1.2 hectares (3 acres) but are now being consolidated. Fishing is an important industry.

There are valuable reserves of natural gas and some coal, copper and gold deposits. But the main natural resource is timber and forest products are a major export. The rapid development of manufacturing and processing industries has also made Taiwan a leading exporter of clothing, textiles, electrical equipment and a wide range of other finished goods. Literacy is high and about 13 percent of the workforce is now in manufacturing. Tourism is of growing importance. ∎

Korea (North and South)

The Korean peninsula extends southward from northeast China (Manchuria). Korea's long history as a unified kingdom, largely independent within China's sphere of influence, ended in 1910 when it was seized by Japan. Since Japan's defeat in 1945 the peninsula has been divided between the states now known as the Democratic People's Republic of Korea (North) and the Republic of Korea (South). As the north was primarily industrial and the south agricultural, the division was unfortunate. The communist regime in the north attacked the south in 1950, beginning a destructive war in which United Nations forces led by the US came to the aid of the south while Russia and China supported the north. The war reached a stalemate in 1953 and a Demilitarized Zone of 1,260km² (487sq.m.) now separates the two republics at about the 38th parallel. Peaceful reunification was accepted in principle in 1972 but little progress has yet been made towards it.

The peninsula divides the Sea of Japan on the east from the Yellow Sea on the west. It reaches its widest point of 515km (320 miles) near Pyongyang. The Korea Strait, 192km (120 miles) wide separates Korea from Japan and there are about 3,000 islands, the largest of which, Cheju, has South Korea's highest peak, Halla-San. Mountains and rugged hills are the most characteristic land features. Ranges, highest on the east, extend down the centre of the peninsula from the Chinese border, which is formed largely by the Yalu River. The climate is monsoonal with hot humid summers but cold, dry winters that are long and quite severe, particularly in the north. ∎

North Korea

Area: 120,538km² (46,540sq.m.). **Population:** 16m. **Capital:** Pyongyang (2.6m). **Language and ethnic group:** Korean. **Main exports:** Copper, iron ore, lead, tungsten, zinc. **Average temperatures:** −3°C (26°F) Jan. 21°C (70°F) July. **Highest point:** Paektu-San 2,744m (9,003ft).

The Democratic People's Republic of Korea is governed by the Korean Communist Party and has a large army (360,000) and militia (1 million). Apart from a small strip of coastal lowland in the northeast, the rolling northwestern plain around Pyongyang supports most of the population. Although the economy is predominantly industrial, grain output has risen rapidly under a programme of collective farming in units averaging about 300 families.

North Korea has some of the richest mineral deposits in Asia and is a leading producer of graphite, tungsten and magnesium. Coal, iron ore, lead, zinc and petroleum, together with hydro-electric power, are the basis of fast-growing industries in which most factories are government-owned. Trade is chiefly with Russia and China. ∎

South Korea

Area: *98,477km² (38,022sq.m.).*
Population: *35m.* **Capital:** *Soul, or Seoul (5.5m).* **Language and ethnic group:** *Korean.* **Main exports:** *Clothing, textiles, electrical equipment, fish, tungsten.* **Average temperatures:** *−2°C (28°F) Jan. 24°C (75°F) July.* **Highest point:** *Halla-San 1,950m (6,398ft).*

The Republic of Korea has a partly elective government but is under presidential rule and maintains a standing army of 540,000. As in North Korea, literacy is high. Successful efforts have been made to transform the primarily agricultural economy into a mixed one. Despite few mineral resources apart from tungsten, a strong manufacturing sector has been built up, chiefly in textiles, plywood, plastics, fertilizers, cement, electronics and, more recently, cars. This is concentrated chiefly in the Seoul area.

The rolling southwestern plain around Seoul is also an important agricultural area, as is the southern plain drained by the Naktong River. There are some 2.5 million farms, most of them covering less than a hectare (2½ acres). Rice is the main crop, followed by beans, barley and wheat. Fishing is also important. Trade is mainly with Japan and the US. ■

Hong Kong

Area: *1,044km² (403sq.m.).*
Population: *4,300,000.* **Capital:** *Victoria (700,000).* **Languages:** *English, Chinese.* **Ethnic groups:** *Chinese (98 percent), European.* **Main exports:** *Textiles, plastics, electronic equipment, ships.* **Average temperatures:** *15°C (59°F) Jan. 28°C (82°F) July.* **Highest point:** *Tai Mo Shan 958m (3,144ft).*

The British Crown colony of Hong Kong occupies a unique place in the world as the last toehold of 19th century European influence in China. Its political viability depends on its usefulness to China as a key point of contact with the west. Its economic prosperity is based on a highly-skilled manufacturing workforce, trade through its magnificent free port and heavy tourist traffic (1 million annually).

The colony, largely autonomous, lies near the Chu Chiang (Pearl) River on the south coast of China 145km (90m.) southeast of Canton. Together with some 240 small islands it comprises the island of Hong Kong with the business centre of Victoria on its northern slopes, the Kowloon Peninsula, which is the main industrial and shopping area, and a predominantly farming area north of this on the Chinese mainland known as the New Territories. Britain acquired Hong Kong in 1843, Kowloon in 1860 and a 99-year lease of the New Territories in 1898. The population has soared eightfold since 1945 and a major achievement has been the housing of hundreds of thousands of squatter refugees from China.

Hong Kong has a tropical monsoon climate, wet between June and September. The hilly terrain and limited land area mean that much food has to be imported to supplement fishing and fruit and vegetable farming. Ship-building is the main heavy industry but most of the workforce is in light industry, especially textiles, plastics and electronics. Hong Kong handles about half of China's external trade and exports 90 percent of its own manufactured products, mainly to the US and Britain.

Macau, or **Macao,** a Portuguese enclave at the mouth of the Pearl River, 64km (40m.) west of Hong Kong, is a tourist and gambling centre comprising the city of Macau and two small islands. It has an area of 16km² (6sq.m.) and a population of about 300,000, mainly Chinese. ■

Above: A junk spreads its sails—still a common sight along the China coast, although mainly restricted to local trade.
Below: Shoppers crowd one of Hong Kong's 'ladder' streets, traders' signs presenting a medley of colours above their heads.

1:12 000 000

50 0 50 100 150 200 250 miles
50 0 50 100 150 200 250 300 350 400 km

HONG KONG 33
TEMPERATURE °C
13°

PRESSURE mb

PRECIPITATION mm
2161mm
J F M A M J J A S O N D

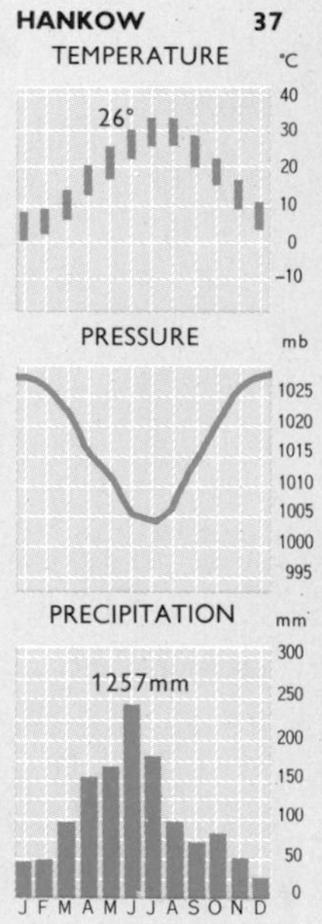

HANKOW 37
TEMPERATURE °C
26°

PRESSURE mb

PRECIPITATION mm
1257mm
J F M A M J J A S O N D

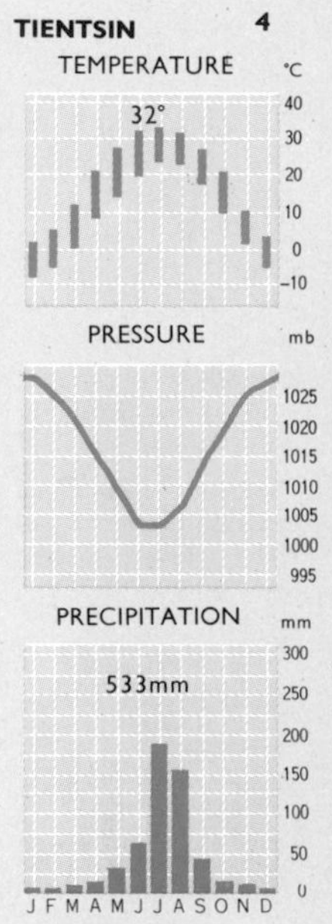

TIENTSIN 4
TEMPERATURE °C
32°

PRESSURE mb

PRECIPITATION mm
533mm
J F M A M J J A S O N D

U.S.S.R.

MONGOLIA

INNER MONGOLIAN AUTONOMOUS REGION

HEILUNGKIANG

HARBIN

KIRIN

Changchun

SHENYANG (Mukden)

NORTH KOREA

Pyongyang

SOUTH KOREA

Inchon

PUSAN

SEA OF JAPAN

JAPAN

NINGSIA HUI A.R.

THE GREAT WALL

PEIPING (Peking)

TIENTSIN

HOPEI

TAIYUAN

SHANSI

SHANTUNG

TSINGTAO

YELLOW SEA

SIAN

SHENSI

HONAN

KIANGSU

NANKING

SHANGHAI

EAST CHINA SEA

SZECHWAN

CHUNGKING

HUPEI

WUHAN

ANHWEI

Hangchow

CHEKIANG

Ningpo

KWEICHOW

HUNAN

Changsha

KIANGSI

Nanchang

FUKIEN

Foochow (Minhow)

TAIWAN (FORMOSA)

Taipei

Kaohsiung

Tropic of Cancer

KWANGSI-CHUANG A.D.

Nanning

KWANGTUNG

KWANGCHOW (Canton)

Shantow (Swatow)

Macau

HONGKONG (Br.)

Hainan

NORTH VIETNAM

Gulf of Tongking

SOUTH CHINA SEA

PHILIPPINES

PACIFIC OCEAN

RYUKYU-retto

East from Greenwich

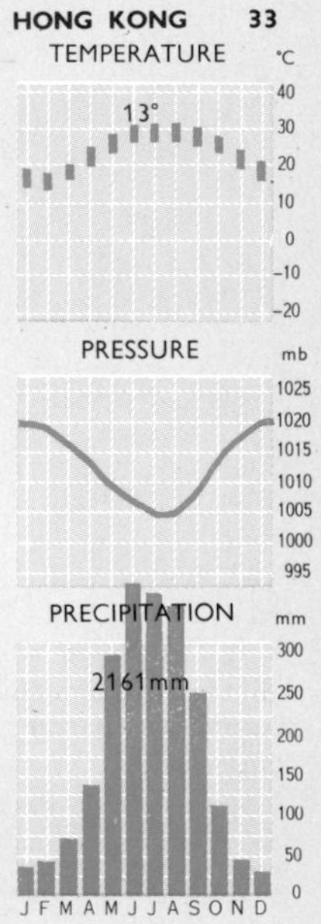

COPYRIGHT. GEORGE PHILIP & SON. LTD.

85

Above: Japan's flawless Mt Fuji is a central theme in Japanese mythology.

Japan

Area: *370,000km² (143,000sq.m.).*
Population: *112,627,000.*
Capital: *Tokyo (11.6 million).*
Language: *Japanese.* Ethnic
groups: *Japanese, Ainu (15,000).*
Main exports: *iron and steel, ships, motor-cars, electrical and other machinery and appliances, chemicals, textile products, canned fish.* Average
temperatures: *3°C (37°F) Jan. 26°C (78°F) Aug. in Tokyo.* Highest
point: *Mount Fuji 3,776m (12,388ft).*

A nation once symbolized by cherry blossom, the geisha, and an inscrutable isolationism, Japan now projects an image of highly efficient industrialization. Its products—cameras, hi-fi equipment, televisions, super-tankers — are familiar in most parts of the world. From a defeated, overcrowded, humiliated country at the end of World War II, it has transformed itself into one of the leading industrial nations of the world. With meagre natural resources, it has been able to do this only because of the tremendous energy and determination of its people.

Land and climate

Japan consists of four main islands and over 3,000 smaller ones. The four large islands—Hokkaido, Honshu, Shikoku, and Kyushu—are strung out along the coast of eastern Asia in a great arc. Honshu, the largest island, is about the same size as Great Britain. The islands are the upper part of a great mountain range that rises from the floor of the Pacific. As a result, Japan is a rugged country, with only 15 percent of its land level enough for cultivation. About 200 of Japan's mountains are volcanoes, of which nearly 60 are active.

About 75 percent of Japan's people live on Honshu, crowded into the cities and conurbations along the southern coast. Half of Japan's population lives on only 2 percent of its land area. Tokyo, with a population of 11.6 million, is the largest city in the world. Seven other Japanese cities have populations of more than a million. Honshu has several swift rivers

Left: Shinto, a largely Buddhist cult, has become for its followers, an expression of Japanese patriotism.

which supply hydroelectric power. Hot springs can be found throughout the island. The mountain sides are thickly forested.

Most of Japan has a moderate climate, although Hokkaido has cool summers and cold winters. Honshu has warm, humid summers, and mild winters in the south but is cold in the north. The two smaller islands have long hot summers and mild winters. All of Japan has a high rainfall. There are two seasons of heavy rain, following the pattern of the Asiatic monsoon. And in the western mountains, winter snow collects to such a depth that spring floods are extremely difficult to control. Together with typhoons and tidal waves, floods claim an average of 600 victims a year.

Water is Japan's only significant natural resource. By means of thousands of irrigation channels, it helps crops grow at a remarkable rate, making possible some of the highest agricultural yields in the world. It is harnessed to produce the abundant hydroelectric power that supplies Japan's huge cities and industrial complexes.

Japan has more earthquakes than anywhere else in the world—some 1,500 a year. Most of these are barely perceptible but there is one severe earthquake on average every 2½ years. Occasionally, these are disastrous. In 1923, half of Tokyo and all of Yokohama were destroyed by an earthquake and the resulting fires.

People and culture

Japan is characterized by an almost complete identity of race, people, and nation. The only minority group is the Ainu, a Caucasoid people whose ancestors were among the first occupants of the islands. Most of the remaining Ainu, some 15,000, live on Hokkaido. The Japanese resemble the Chinese. They have yellowish skin, high cheek bones, dark, oblique eyes, and straight black hair. They are, on average, shorter than the Chinese and Koreans.

There are two main religions in Japan, Shintoism and Buddhism, and many Japanese practise both. Buddhism, in particular, has played a great part in the development of art in Japan. Its best painting and sculpture shows a strong Buddhist influence. In the theatre, Japan

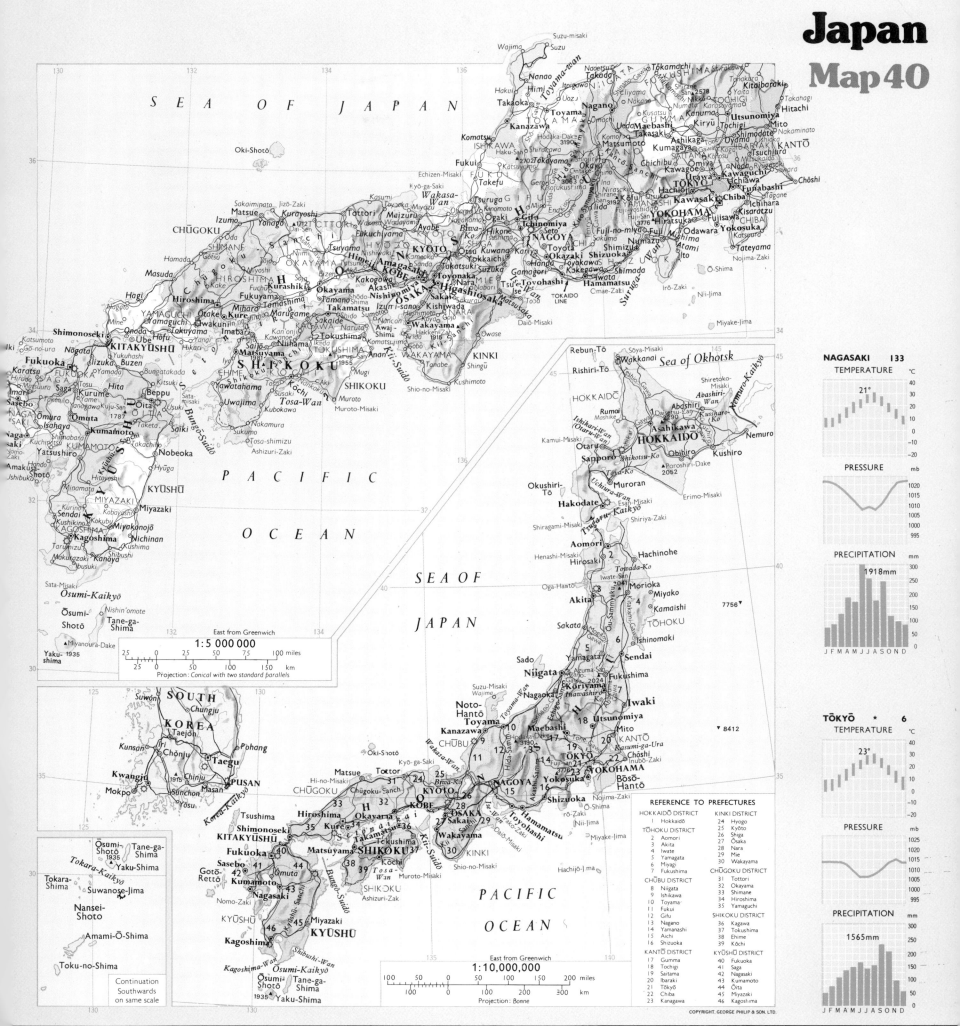

created two new forms of drama, noh and kabuki. It is known also for its colour printing, ceramics, silk embroidery, and flower arranging. The distinctive Japanese culture is also seen in clothing and cuisine, and particularly in domestic architecture.

In sport, the Japanese gave the world martial arts such as judo and karate, and they have their own highly ritualized form of wrestling, Sumo. They excel, too, at gymnastics and table tennis. Their most popular sport, however, is baseball.

Economy

Some 27 percent of the work force is engaged in modern manufacturing industry. Japan leads the world in shipbuilding, motorcycle manufacture, electronics, and the production of radios, cameras, and watches, and is second in the manufacture of motor-cars and television sets. Textiles and chemicals are also important industries.

About 18 percent of Japan's labour force is employed in agriculture, forestry and fishing. Despite the shortage of

arable land, Japan is self-sufficient in rice. Other important crops include potatoes, cabbage, sweet potatoes, fruit and wheat. The forests produce good-quality timber, but Japan has to import much wood for its manufacturing industries.

Japan is the leading fishing nation in the world. The fish caught in greatest quantities are cod, haddock, mackerel and shellfish, and other catches include whales, octopus, squid and eels.

Constitution and history

Japan's Diet has a House of Representatives and a House of Councillors. The government is based on the 1947 constitution, formulated after Japan's defeat in World War II. Under this, the emperor has no governmental powers, and Japan renounces its sovereign right to make war.

The present Imperial Family are direct descendants of the house of Yamato, which united Japan as a nation in about AD 200. Emperors ruled with varying degrees of authority until the mid-1100s. In about 1200, a new warrior class came

to power, called *shoguns* (great generals). Successive families of shoguns ruled for nearly 700 years, until the young Emperor Meiji was restored to imperial power in 1868.

For hundreds of years, Japan had followed a policy of complete seclusion from the rest of the world. It was the Americans who, in an attempt to gain power in the Pacific, forced the Japanese to open their ports to foreign ships. Commodore Matthew Perry was sent with warships in 1853 to open trade relations with Japan. He delivered a letter from the president of the United States, and returned in 1854 to sign a treaty with the reluctant Japanese.

Japan's imperialistic expansion began in the 1880s. Rivalry with China led to a war (1894–95) in which Japan gained from China Formosa and a sphere of influence in Korea. With further gains from a war with Russia (1904–5), Japan became a world power. As an ally of Britain in World War I, Japan was able to seize German territory in Asia and the

Pacific. But Japan followed a policy of peace until the early 1930s, when its military leaders began to take advantage of growing nationalism and anti-West feeling, provoked in part by the West's refusal to accept the Japanese as full equals. Japan seized Manchuria in 1931, and won control of other parts of China in the late 1930s. Anti-communist treaties were signed with Germany and Italy, and, with the military now in full control, the Japanese attacked American bases at Pearl Harbour in December 1941. After initial victories in World War II, Japan gradually slipped to complete defeat, but surrendered only after atom bombs had obliterated Hiroshima and Nagasaki in 1945.

American occupation forces under General Douglas MacArthur stayed until 1952, by which time Japan had a new constitution, was demilitarized, and had begun a programme of economic reform. Out of defeat, Japan grew from the mid-1950s, in less than two decades, into one of the world's major industrial powers. ∎

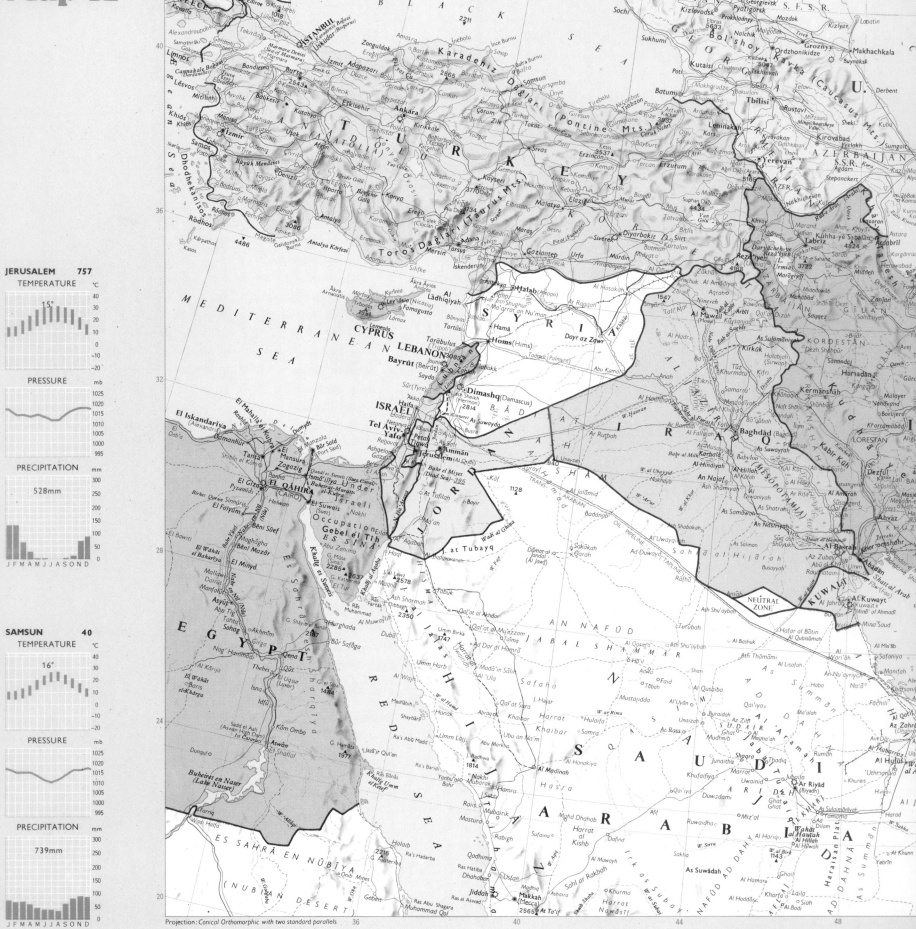

JERUSALEM 757
TEMPERATURE °C
15°

PRESSURE mb

PRECIPITATION mm
528mm
JFMAMJJASOND

SAMSUN 40
TEMPERATURE °C
16°

PRESSURE mb

PRECIPITATION mm
739mm
JFMAMJJASOND

Projection: Conical Orthomorphic with two standard parallels

South-West Asia

Until recent years South-West Asia was noted more for its historical context than for its natural resources. Today, the importance of Arabian oil has brought it to the forefront of world geopolitical affairs. But a parched environment remains a dominant feature of the region and although industry is developing in several countries the majority of the people are poor farmers.

The region stretches from Turkey in the north to the vast desert of the Arabian peninsular in the south and to the Hindu Kush in Afghanistan. Including Ethiopia, Afars and Issas and Somalia on the Horn of Africa, historically linked to Arabia, the area has a total population of some 150 million. With Egypt and Sudan (discussed in the section on Africa), it is sometimes called the Middle East. It has been the birthplace of the major world religions of Judaism, Christianity and Islam.

Arabs form the largest population group, together with Turks, Iranians, Jews, Armenians and Africans, and Arabic is the most widely-spoken language. Turkey was a major power in the Mediterranean regions until 1918 when the British and French moved in, only to give way to independence movements between the 1930s and the 1960s. Apart from Greek-Turkish tensions on Cyprus and recent Moslem-Christian conflict in Lebanon, the chief political problem in the region stems from the creation of Israel in 1948. The grievances of the Arabs has led to continual border clashes and to wars in 1948-49, 1956, 1967 and 1973.

By 1974 the region was producing a third of the world's petroleum and exporting most of it. Price rises in the 1970s imposed by the Organization of Petroleum Exporting Countries (Opec) have increased the revenues of such leading exporters as Saudi Arabia, Iran, Kuwait and Iraq. Other oil states include Abu Dhabi, Bahrain, Oman and Qatar.

Turkey

Area: 780,576km² (301,382sq.m.).
Population: 40 million. **Capital:**
Ankara (1.3m). **Largest city:**
Istanbul (2.6m). **Language:** Turkish.
Ethnic groups: Turks, Kurds (1.7m),
Arabs, Circassians, Armenians, Greeks.
Main exports: grains, cotton,
tobacco, chromium and minerals, dried
fruit and nuts, carpets. **Average
temperatures:** 4°C (40°F) Jan. 27°C
(80°F) July on coast but much colder
on plateau. **Highest point:** Mt
Ararat 5,185m (17,011ft).

Turkey is a large republic bridging Europe and Asia, with most if its territory forming the peninsula of Asia Minor. Its position, spanning the waterway between the Black Sea and the Mediterranean (the Straits), has given it strategic importance. Its rich cultural heritage is centred upon the famous city of Istanbul. As Constantinople, this city was the capital of the Byzantine Empire, bastion of Graeco-Roman civilization for a thousand years. As Istanbul, it was the centre of the Moslem world, mingling Arabic and Turkish traditions. The site of ancient Troy lies on Turkey's western shores while close to its eastern border rises Mt Ararat, the legendary-resting place of Noah's Ark. Since the 1920s, when Turkey adopted western social and economic ideas, much headway has been made in developing an industrial and manufacturing base in a nation that remains primarily agricultural.

People and constitution

The dark-skinned Turkish people are a mixture of Asiatic, Balkan and Mediterranean stocks. The Seljuk Turks took Asia Minor from the Byzantine Empire in the 11th century. After the fall of Constantinople to the Ottoman Turks in 1453, the Turkish Empire was extended

Map 42

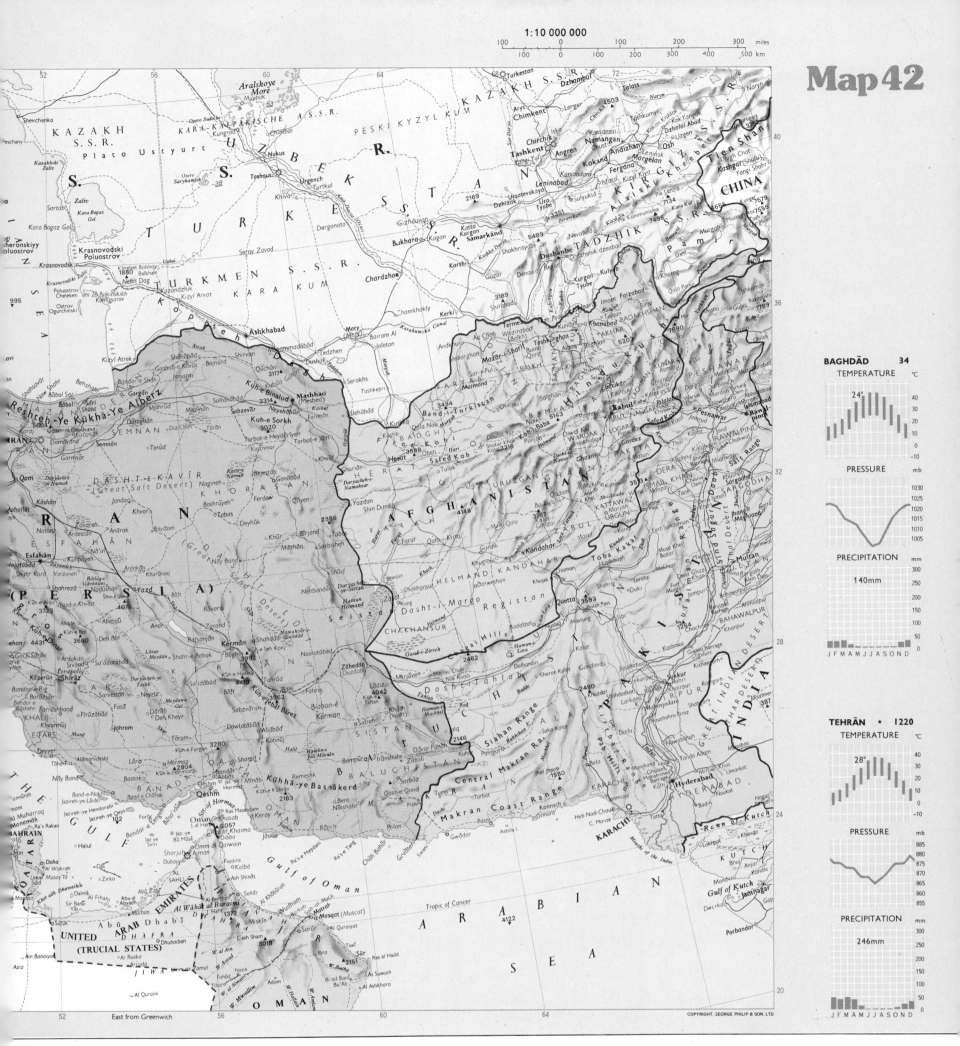

1:10 000 000

COPYRIGHT. GEORGE PHILIP & SON. LTD.

BAGHDĀD   34

TEMPERATURE   °C

PRESSURE   mb

PRECIPITATION   mm

140mm

J F M A M J J A S O N D

TEHRĀN ★ 1220

TEMPERATURE   °C

PRESSURE   mb

PRECIPITATION   mm

246mm

J F M A M J J A S O N D

---

to the Balkans, Central Europe, Persia and North Africa, reaching its height toward the end of the 16th century before the battle of Lepanto halted its spread into Europe. Territory was then lost steadily, although in the 19th century the European Powers propped Turkey up to hold Russia in check. The Young Turk movement pressed for modernization from 1908 and under Mustafa Kemal gained power in 1922, abolishing the sultanate in favour of a republic, reforming the legal and educational system and ending restrictions on women such as the veil and harem. In 1947, Turkey turned to America for aid against Russian pressure, becoming a Nato member in 1952. Today, Turkey is a presidential republic with a two-house elected legislature. Most of the people are Moslems. Literacy has risen to about 70 percent.

Land and climate

Thrace (European Turkey) has rolling plains extending to low mountains bordering Bulgaria. Anatolia (Asia Minor) is dominated by a rugged inland plateau 800–1,800m (2,600 to 6,000ft) high bordered on the north by the Pontic Mountains and on the south by the Taurus Mountains with a narrow coastal strip along the Mediterranean and a broader plain in the north. The plateau is dry with severe winters but the climate is mild and moist in coastal areas and in Thrace. Anatolia is prone to earthquakes.

Economy

Three-quarters of the workforce is employed in agriculture. Sheep and goats are raised on the plateau, which is also the main area for grains and sugar beet. Cotton and fruit are grown in coastal areas and tobacco in the north. Fishing is concentrated mainly in the Black Sea.

Although carpets provide Turkey's

Left: The temple of Hadrianus at Ephesus, Turkey, stands among the ruins of what was once the first city of Rome's Asian province.

only significant manufactured export apart from hand-crafted products, the manufacturing sector is expanding with government backing, particularly in textiles, chemicals, paper, cement and glass. With an iron and steel plant at Karabuk, heavy industry is also developing. Petroleum production from oil reserves in the southeast is rising. Turkey is also an important chromium producer and has some copper, iron, lead, zinc and silver. Its main energy source, however, is coal, mined chiefly at Zonguldak. In recent years Turkey has been a major source of migrant labour in Europe, especially West Germany. ∎

Cyprus

Area: *9,251km² (3,527sq.m.).* **Population:** *665,000.* **Capital:** *Nicosia (116,000).* **Languages:** *Greek, Turkish.* **Ethnic groups:** *Greek (77 percent), Turkish.* **Main exports:** *Wine, fruit, asbestos, copper and iron ores, olive oil.* **Average temperatures:** *13°C (55°F) Jan. 27°C (80°F) July.* **Highest point:** *Mt Olympus, 1,952m (6,403ft).*

The republic of Cyprus lies only 64km (40 miles) south of Turkey in the eastern Mediterranean and 97km (60 miles) west of Syria. It is an island of rugged beauty with a history of political turbulence both before and since 1960 when a struggle for *enosis* (union with Greece) led to Britain granting its former colony independence on the basis of equal rights for the Greek and Turkish communities. Tension between the Greek-speaking, Greek Orthodox majority and the Turkish Moslem minority finally erupted in civil war in 1974. A Turkish invasion to prevent a Greek takeover was followed by a UN-supervised ceasefire that left the northeastern sector of the island in Turkish hands, and by moves towards formal partition.

The three main land forms are the northern Kyrenia range, the Troodos Range, highest in the southwest, and the broad Mesaoria Plain between them. Although snow falls on the higher mountains winters are mild and the hot, dry summers are ideal for citrus fruits. The climate, the long coastline of rocky headlands and fine beaches and the wealth of historical sites makes tourism an important industry. About half the Cypriot people are small farmers and vine-growing is the chief industry. Mining is also carried on, mainly in the Troodos Range. ∎

Syria

Area: *185,180km² (71,498sq.m.).* **Population:** *6,728,000.* **Capital:** *Dimashq or Damascus (837,000).* **Languages:** *Arabic, Kurdish, Armenian, French.* **Ethnic groups:** *Arabs, Kurds, Armenians.* **Main exports:** *cotton, textiles, fruit, vegetables, tobacco.* **Average temperatures:** *0°C (32°F) Jan. 32°C (90°F) July.* **Highest point:** *J. ash Sheikh (Mt Hermon), 2,814m (9,232ft).*

Northern Syria is covered by rolling plains, with deserts rise in the south and west. High mountains rise above the coastal plain along the Mediterranean. The coast has a mild climate with ample rainfall. The arid interior has more extreme temperatures. Farming, especially fruit production, is the chief activity, with the help of irrigation.

The valley of the Euphrates was a cradle of civilization and Syria was the home of several ancient empires. It finally became a Roman province. Muslim Arabs conquered the area in AD 636, but Christian Crusaders ruled much of the country for two centuries. It was part of the Turkish empire until World War I. France then ruled the territory until 1946, when Syria became independent. In 1958, Syria united with

Above: This church fresco at Assinou, Cyprus, is in a tradition of Eastern Orthodox religion dating back to the Byzantine Empire. Under later Turkish occupation the bishops became political as well as religious leaders of the Greek community and were also active in the movement for independence.

Egypt in the United Arab Republic but became independent again in 1961.

A socialist republic, Syria fought in the wars against Israel. In 1967 Israel took some Syrian territory but part of this was returned in 1975. ∎

Iraq

Area: *438,446km² (169,284sq.m.).* **Population:** *8,587,000.* **Capital:** *Baghdad (3,167,000).* **Languages:** *Arabic, Kurdish.* **Ethnic groups:** *Arabs, Kurds, Persians, Turks.* **Main exports:** *petroleum, petroleum products, dates, hides, cement, wool.* **Average temperatures:** *9°C (48°F) Jan. 34°C (94°F) July.* **Highest point:** *Zagros mountains, over 3,048m (10,000ft).*

The Tigris-Euphrates region of Iraq (Mesopotamia) was a centre of ancient civilizations, including Babylonia and Assyria. Today most of Iraq is a dry, sandy plain, with swamps in the south, desert in the west and mountains in the northeast. The rainfall is low but the plains are well irrigated by the Euphrates and Tigris rivers. Most Iraqis are farmers, raising large numbers of livestock. Most farms are along the two main rivers. They produce cereals, fruit and tobacco. Iraq is one of the world's major petroleum producers.

Conquered by Muslim Arabs in the AD 600s, Iraq later became part of the Turkish empire. Britain ruled the country from 1918 until 1932, when Iraq became an independent monarchy. The army took control in 1958 and established a republic. A period of unrest followed and there were two more army revolts which led to changes in the leadership.

Fighting occurred in the 1960s and 1970s with the Kurdish minority in the north, but a peace agreement was signed in 1974. Iraq has fought against Israel in the Arab-Israeli wars since 1948. But, because they have no common frontiers, there have been no territorial changes. ∎

Lebanon

Area: *10,400km² (4,015sq.m.).* **Population:** *2,700,000.* **Capital:** *Beirut (700,000).* **Languages:** *Arabic, French.* **Ethnic groups:** *Arabs.* **Main exports:** *Banking services, vegetables, tobacco, textiles, machinery.* **Average temperatures:** *10°C (50°F) Jan. 27°C (80°F) July.* **Highest point:** *3,083m (10,115ft).*

Lebanon is made up of a narrow coastal plain, the Lebanon mountains which run throughout the country, and a fertile inland plain. The climate is temperate and most people are farmers, producing cereals and fruit. Manufactures include textiles, cement and processed foods. Because of the lack of minerals, commerce and trading are important.

France took an interest in the region from the 1860s because Lebanon had a Christian majority. France ruled Lebanon from 1918 until 1946, when it became an independent parliamentary republic. The government is divided on religious lines. The Muslims claim that the Christians dominate the country, while the Christians fear a Muslim takeover. In 1975 and 1976 serious fighting occurred between private armies of Christians and Muslims. Fears of intervention by Syria or Israel caused much tension. ∎

Israel

Area: *20,700km² (7,992sq.m.).* **Population:** *3,314,000.* **Capital:** *Jerusalem (304,000).* **Languages:** *Hebrew, Arabic.* **Ethnic groups:** *Jews, Arabs (400,000).* **Main exports:** *fruit, vegetables, textiles, engineering products, minerals, fertilizers.* **Average temperatures:** *7°C (45°F) Jan. 24°C (75°F) July.* **Highest point:** *Mt Meiron, 1,208m (3,963ft).*

Since Israel became an independent parliamentary democracy in 1948, Israelis have worked to develop their country and establish industries. Their achievements in land reclamation and irrigation have been outstanding. Many Israelis live and work in co-operative communities, such as kibbutzim, where the people collectively own all property. But the Israelis have also faced a continuing struggle with the Arab world. Israel has a

flourishing tourist industry, especially because of its Biblical sites.

The land is divided into four main regions. The coast, Galilee in the north, and the Emek, south of Galilee are fertile areas. The coast is a region of citrus fruit and vegetable production and mixed farming. Galilee's products include cereals, olives and tobacco. The Emek is a region of varied crops and it is notable for fish breeding.

The largest region, the Negev, is in the south. Formerly a barren desert, parts of the northern Negev have been irrigated. Sisal, groundnuts, cotton and flower bulbs are cultivated on the irrigated land. The Negev has petroleum and natural gas deposits. Other minerals, including potash, bromine and salt, are mined in the Dead Sea area.

The Arab-Israeli conflict

Some Jews have always lived in Palestine, but most Israelis are recent immigrants, who have been settling in the area since the 1880s. In 1948 the UN decided to partition Palestine into a Jewish and an Arab state. But this was unacceptable to the Arabs. Israel's neighbours attacked and, at the end of the conflict, Israel held all of Palestine except the central region of Samaria, part of Judea (including the Old City of Jerusalem) and the Gaza Strip along the Mediterranean coast. Since 1948, Jews have arrived from many countries. Jews from North Africa and the Middle East now form a slight majority of the population.

Palestinian Arab refugees formed guerrilla armies in Arab lands. War broke out in 1956 and Israel temporarily occupied the Sinai region of Egypt. In a third war in 1967, Israel took Sinai, Samaria, Jerusalem, Judea and the Golan Heights in Syria. Jewish settlements were set up in some of the occupied zones, but they were not permitted in Samaria. Religious Jews have made several attempts to colonize this area without success. In Sinai, Israel diverted the petroleum output for her own use.

Despite Arab advances in the war of 1973, Israel retained control of most of the territory it took in 1967. However, a 1975 agreement restored some of Sinai to Egypt and part of the Golan was returned to Syria. As part of the agreement, Israeli ships obtained freedom of passage through the Suez Canal, which was closed between 1967 and 1975. Palestinian guerrillas opposed the 1975 agreement and continued to demand the dissolution of the state of Israel. ∎

Jordan

> **Area:** *95,396km² (36,832sq.m.).*
> **Population:** *2.5m.* **Capital:**
> *Amman (500,000).* **Languages:**
> *Arabic, Circassian.* **Ethnic groups:**
> *Arabs, Circassians.* **Main exports:**
> *phosphates, fruit and vegetables, hides.*
> **Average temperatures:** *7°C (45°F)*
> *Jan. 24°C (75°F) July.* **Highest**
> **point:** *Jebel Ram, 1,754m (5,755ft).*

Most of Jordan consists of sandy desert and rocky plains, but uplands west of the River Jordan are fertile. This region produces most of Jordan's food. Because only a small part of Jordan can be farmed, many people work in commerce. Bedouin tribes in eastern and southern areas raise livestock. Potash, phosphates and manganese are found in the Dead Sea and in the southern region.

The state of Transjordan was set up by Britain after World War I. It became an independent constitutional monarchy in 1946. In 1948 Jordan fought Israel and conquered central Palestine and part of Jerusalem. It received 500,000 Palestinian refugees and Palestinians still form a major part of Jordan's population.

Israel occupied the west bank area of Jordan and Jordanian Jerusalem in 1967, depriving Jordan of its most fertile area. However, Arabs from the west bank can visit Jordan and vice versa. A dispute with Palestinian nationalists in Jordan led to heavy fighting in the 1960s. Finally, the guerrillas withdrew from Jordanian territory. ∎

Iran

> **Area:** *1,648,000km² (636,293sq.m.).*
> **Population:** *27,355,000.* **Capital:**
> *Tehran (2,720,000).* **Languages:**
> *Persian, Kurdish, Turki, Baluchi.*
> **Ethnic groups:** *Iranians, Kurds,*
> *Arabs, Turks.* **Main exports:**
> *petroleum, petroleum products, carpets,*
> *cotton, hides, fruit, minerals.* **Average**
> **temperatures:** *0°C (32°F) Jan.*
> *35°C (95°F) July.* **Highest point:**
> *Qolleh ye Demavand or Mt Demavend,*
> *5,604m (18,389ft).*

Iran (Persia) consists mainly of high plateaus almost surrounded by mountains, with narrow lowlands along the Caspian Sea and the Gulf. The highest mountains are in the west and north. Two vast deserts lie in the east.

Farming is the main occupation and cereals, vegetables, fruit, cotton and tobacco are important. The Khuzistan

Right: The oldest known map of the Holy Land is the Ma'daba mosaic, dating from the 6th century, found at Medeba, Jordan.

Below: The museum at Akko (formerly Acre), Israel, was once the bath-house of a Turkish governor.

lowlands in the southwest have Iran's richest petroleum deposits which make it the fourth leading world petroleum producer. Semi-nomadic tribes, such as the Baktiari, and settled groups of Kurds and Turcomans raise livestock.

Ancient Persia was powerful between 550 and 330 BC, but it fell to the armies of Alexander the Great. It was later ruled by the Parthians and the Persian Sassanid dynasty until it fell to the Muslim Arabs in the AD 600s. Later it was constantly attacked by Mongols, Turks and Russians.

Iran lost territory to Russia in the 1800s and Britain became the dominant power in the Gulf region. In 1925 the ruling dynasty was overthrown by the Pahlavi family. Mohammad Reza Pahlavi took office as Shah in 1941 after Britain and Russia had threatened to intervene. They each retained a force in the country until after World War II. Russian troops finally withdrew from Iranian territory in the late 1940s.

A left wing government took office in the 1950s and nationalized the petroleum industry. The Shah left the country but was restored to power after a short time. He began a reform programme in 1962, including the granting of ownership of land to peasant farmers. The Shah and

Empress were crowned in 1967 and the 2,000th anniversary of the empire was sumptuously celebrated in 1973. Economic development has been greatly aided by the revenue received for petroleum exports and a vigorous industrialization programme has been launched. ∎

Afghanistan

> **Area:** *649,831km² (250,900sq.m.).*
> **Population:** *19 million.* **Capital:**
> *Kabul (485,000).* **Languages:**
> *Pushtu, Persian.* **Ethnic groups:**
> *Pathans (55 percent), Tadshiks,*
> *Uzbeks.* **Main exports:** *Natural gas,*
> *lambskins, cotton, nuts, fruit, carpets.*
> **Average temperatures:** *−3°C*
> *(27°F) Jan. 25°C (77°F) July in*
> *Kabul.* **Highest point:** *7,620m*
> *(25,000ft) in the Hindu Kush.*

Afghanistan is a land-locked Moslem republic bordered by the USSR in the north, Iran in the west and Pakistan in the south and east, with a narrow corridor to China and Kashmir. Its position between Asia Minor and India made it an historic invasion route and in the 19th century the British in India regarded it as

Above: A drilling rig at Fahud, Oman, symbolizes the oil wealth that is transforming a desolate Arabian land.

a key buffer state against Russia. Britain recognized its independence as a constitutional monarchy in 1919. Following an army coup in 1973, a presidential republic was established.

Physically, Afghanistan is dominated by the towering ranges of the Hindu Kush which slope westward across much of the country to a high plateau, mainly of sandy desert in the southwest. Fertile plains lie to the north. Most of the population is concentrated in the four river valleys of the Kabul in the east, the Helmand in the southwest, the Hari Rud in the northwest and the Amu Darya in the north.

No part of the country is less than 609m (2,000ft) above sea level and a large area above 2,500m (8,000ft) has long, severe winters. There are sharp extremes of climate elsewhere and the mountains cut Afghanistan off from the rain-bearing Indian monsoons. Average rainfall is only 30cm (12in) a year.

Afghanistan is a land of striking beauty but scanty resources. As about three-quarters of the population live by farming the shortage of cultivated land means that the economy is precarious. Although the major crop is wheat, some grain has to be imported. Sheep, cattle and goats are mustered for their meat and wool and the black Karakul lambskins are an important export. The society is essentially conservative and village-orientated and educational facilities are so limited that only some 10 percent of the people are literate. There are large groups of nomadic tribesmen, particularly near the border with Pakistan.

Industry is concentrated mainly on textiles with some cement and sugar works. Natural gas from Shorbaghan is sent to Russia and Afghanistan has the world's largest deposits of the semi-precious stone lapis lazuli. Some coal, chromite and salt is mined but other potential resources of oil, sulphur, gold, silver, lead, copper and zinc are unexploited. Transport presents serious problems, even in developing the ample hydro-electric power resources. ■

United Arab Emirates, Qatar, Kuwait, Bahrain

Once extremely poor, the small east Arabian states are now among the world's major petroleum producers and oil revenues are bringing rapid development. Other products are fish, dates and camels. The people are Muslims and mostly Arabs, but there are Baluchi, Indian and Negro minorities. The special treaties these states once had with Britain are now ended and they are fully independent.

United Arab Emirates has an area of 82,877km² (32,000sq.m.) and 189,000 people. Its capital is Abu Dhabi (60,000).

Qatar has an area of 10,360km² (4,000 sq.m.) and 180,000 people. Its capital is Doha (130,000).

Kuwait has an area of 17,818km² (6,880sq.m.) and 826,000 people. Its capital is Kuwait (80,000).

Bahrain has an area of 583km² (225sq.m.) and a population of 217,000. Its capital is Manama (90,000). ■

Saudi Arabia

Area: *2,149,690km² (829,995sq.m.).* **Population:** *8,940,000.* **Capital:** *Ar Riyad or Riyadh (225,000).* **Language:** *Arabic.* **Ethnic groups:** *Arabs.* **Main exports:** *petroleum and petroleum products.* **Average temperatures:** *22°C (72°F) Jan. 30°C (86°F) July, with cooler winters in north.* **Highest point:** *Asir range, 3,048m (10,000ft).*

Saudi Arabia occupies most of the Arabian peninsula. It has a long Red Sea coastline in the west and a substantial Gulf coastal strip lying between Kuwait and the United Arab Emirates.

The west coast is low-lying, rising to mountains behind which is a rocky, sandy interior. This desert country extends across the peninsula to the Gulf coast. A vast sand desert, known as the Rub'al Khali (empty quarter) covers the southeast of the country.

The people are Muslims and two of its cities, Makkah (Mecca) and Al Madinah (Medina), are the holiest places of Islam. The former is the birthplace of the Prophet Muhammad and the religious capital of the kingdom. Thousands of pilgrims from all over the Islamic world visit Makkah every year.

Although the government has invested heavily in agricultural development, many Saudis are Bedouins who still lead nomadic lives. Farmers produce cereals, dates, fruit, hides, honey and wool, as well as raising camels, horses and sheep. Future development plans include irrigation, desert reclamation and the control of moving sands.

Petroleum, first discovered in 1938, is Saudi Arabia's most important resource and provides almost all of the country's foreign earnings. In 1975 Saudi Arabia was the third largest producer of petroleum after the US and the USSR. Crude oil is shipped abroad or to refineries on the Persian Gulf. A pipeline carries oil to the Lebanese Mediterranean port of Sayda.

Originally divided into several states, Saudi Arabia was under nominal Turkish control for several centuries. Its leaders fought with the Allies in World War I and gained full independence for their lands. In 1926 the ruler of Nejd (central Arabia) conquered the coastal states and founded the modern Saudi Arabian kingdom. Saudi Arabia has supported other Arab nations in their struggle against Israel. ■

South Yemen

Area: *336,858km² (130,066sq.m.).* **Population:** *1,667,000.* **Capital:** *Al 'Adan or Aden (264,000).* **Language:** *Arabic.* **Ethnic groups:** *Arabs.* **Main exports:** *cotton, oil products, ship bunkering, fish, fish products.* **Average temperatures:** *25°C (77°F) Jan. 35°C (95°F) July at Al 'Adan.* **Highest point:** *in Hadhramawt, 2,469m (8,100ft).*

The country called South Yemen was formerly named the Federation of South Arabia. It lies in the southeast of the Arabian peninsula and it has a long coast-line along the Gulf of Aden. It borders on Yemen, Saudi Arabia and Oman. South Yemen is a mountainous country with burning hot deserts along the frontier with Saudi Arabia.

The people are Muslims and most of them are farmers. The principal crops are millet, sesame and sorghum, but cotton is becoming increasingly important.

Fishing is the second most important activity. Al 'Adan was a thriving port of call for ships until the Suez Canal was closed in 1967. South Yemen plans to build up its commerce again following the reopening of the Canal in 1975.

Al 'Adan was a haunt of pirates until Britain took it over in 1839. The colony and the neighbouring protectorate became a federation in 1962 and, in 1967, National Liberation Front nationalists overran the sultanates and set up a republic. The country's official name is now the People's Democratic Republic of Yemen. ■

Ethiopia

Area: *1,221,900km² (471,776sq.m.).* **Population:** *27,076,000.* **Capital:** *Addis Ababa (644,000).* **Languages:** *Amharic, Galla.* **Ethnic groups:** *Semites (Amhara, Tigre), Cushites (Galla, Somali).* **Main exports:** *coffee, civet, hides, oil seeds, wax.* **Average temperature:** *17°C (63°F) on the highlands.* **Highest point:** *Ras Dashen, 4,620m (15,158ft).*

Ethiopia consists mainly of two plateaus, divided by the East African Rift Valley. The northern plateau contains mountain ranges and volcanic peaks, such as Ras Dashen. The capital Addis Ababa is on the plateau at about 2,438m (8,000ft) above sea level. The southern plateau is smaller. It descends to dry, semi-desert areas in the south-east. The plateaus are cool, well-watered and fertile and most people are farmers. The chief cash crop is coffee. Tropical forests occur in the southwest and an arid plain borders the Red Sea.

A uniquely isolated Coptic Christian state from the AD 300s, Ethiopia is the oldest independent nation in Africa. Italy occupied Ethiopia from 1936 until 1941, when it was liberated by British and Ethiopian troops. After the war, Emperor Haile Selassie's reforms were considered by many Ethiopians to be too limited and too slow. Finally, the country became a republic after army officers deposed the emperor in 1974. The army officers ruled through a committee called the Dergue, which announced in 1975 that it would pursue socialist policies. One of the Dergue's problems is a struggle for independence by the Muslim people of Eritrea province, where an armed uprising began in the early 1970s.

The Somali Republic Afars and Issas

The Somali Republic is mainly mountainous in the north. The south is semi-desert, with fertile areas along the Juba and Shebelle rivers. Livestock products are the chief exports, but crops are grown in the south. The republic consists of the former colonies of British and Italian Somaliland which were united after independence in 1960. Since 1969, the military government has declared that it is pursuing Marxist objectives. It receives arms from the USSR.

Most people in the French territory of Afars and Issas belong to Somali clans. There are some Arabs and Europeans. The territory is mostly desert. Its economy is based on livestock and on revenues from the port of Djibouti. At the end of 1975, France announced its intention to make the territory independent.

The **Somali Republic** has an area of 637,657km² (246,199sq.m.) and a population of 3,155,000. Its capital is Mogadiscio (200,000).

Afars and Issas has an area of 22,000km² (8,494sq.m.) and 105,000

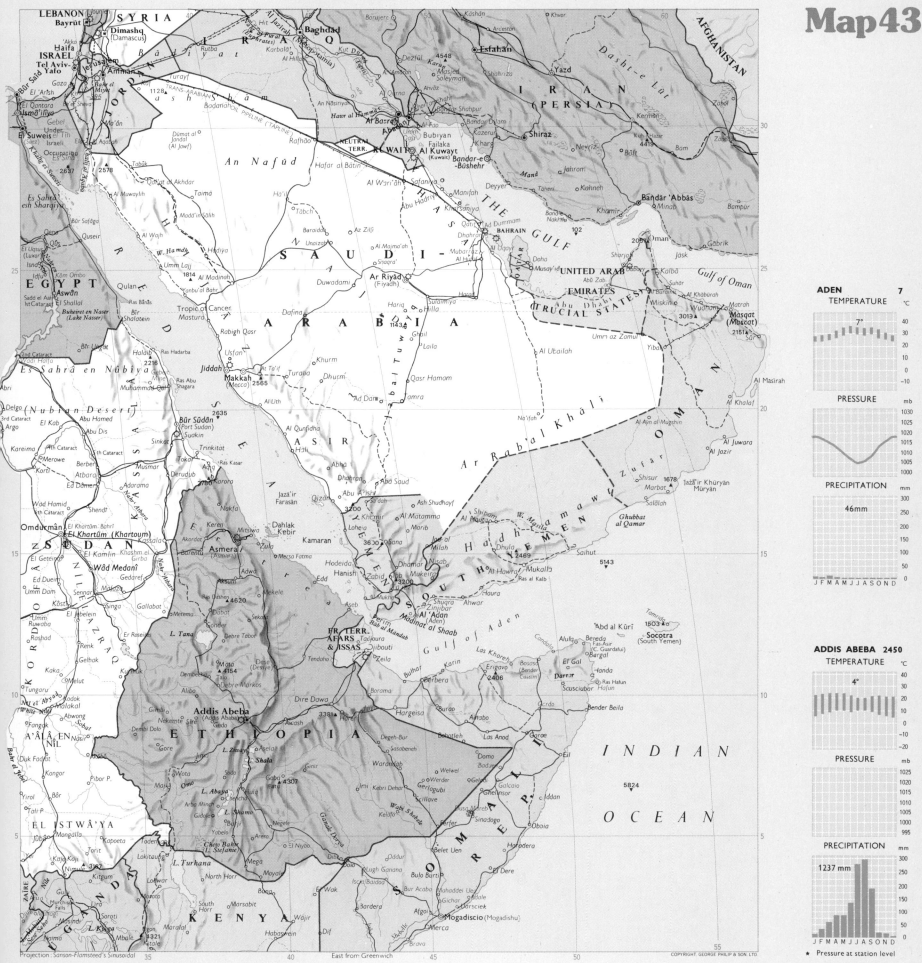

ADEN   7
TEMPERATURE   °C

PRESSURE   mb

PRECIPITATION   mm
46mm

J F M A M J J A S O N D

ADDIS ABEBA   2450
TEMPERATURE   °C

4°

PRESSURE

PRECIPITATION   mm
1237 mm

J F M A M J J A S O N D

★ Pressure at station level

Projection: Sanson-Flamsteed's Sinusoidal   East from Greenwich   COPYRIGHT. GEORGE PHILIP & SON. LTD.

---

people. Its capital is Djibouti (62,000). ∎

Oman

> **Area:** 212,380km² (82,000sq.m.).
> **Population:** 799,000. **Capital:**
> Muscat (50,000). **Language:**
> Arabic. **Ethnic groups:** Arabs with
> minorities of Baluchis, Indians and
> Negroes. **Main exports:** petroleum,
> dates, limes, fish, tobacco, fruit,
> vegetables. **Average temperature:**
> 31°C (88°F). **Highest point:** Jabal
> Ash Sham, 3,035m (9,957ft).

Oman is situated in southeast Arabia and
has a coastline extending 1,600km
(1,000m.) between the United Arab
Emirates and South Yemen. Inland,
Oman extends to the edge of the great
Rab' al Khali desert in Saudi Arabia. A
range of hills and a plateau lie behind the
narrow coastal plain. The northwestern
coastal plain is fertile with date gardens

stretching for more than 240km (150m),
but the rest of the coast is barren. In the
south lies the fertile province of Dhofar.
Dates are the chief export and little else
is grown except for subsistence crops.
Inland tribes breed many camels. Oil
production began in 1967 and new wells
are being developed. Oman will soon
become a major petroleum producer.

Oman was an independent state from
the 11th century but was harassed by
Persia for many years. The Portuguese
controlled Oman's ports for over 100
years but, by 1698, Oman was free. In
the 1700s, there were internal problems
but the present royal family took control.
A treaty was signed with Britain in 1748.
In the mid-1800s, Oman lost its overseas
possessions, including Zanzibar, which
established a sultanate under a member of
the royal house. In 1970, the new sultan,
who had deposed his father, began a programme of reform. The government now
controls the interior, although a rebel
group has been fighting government
forces for some years. In 1958 Oman

ceded the port and district of Gwadur in
Baluchistan to Pakistan and, in 1967, it
gained a group of islands off its coast
from Britain. ∎

Yemen

> **Area:** 200,000km² (77,220sq.m.).
> **Population:** 7,000,000. **Capital:**
> Sana (125,000). **Language:** Arabic.
> **Ethnic groups:** Arabs. **Main
> exports:** coffee, qat (narcotic shrub).
> **Average temperatures:** 16°C
> (60°F) Jan. 27°C (80°F) July.
> **Highest point:** in the Asir range,
> 3,048m (10,000ft).

Yemen, officially the Yemen Arab
Republic, lies in the southwest of the
Arabian peninsula. Saudi Arabia is to the
north and South Yemen to the south.
The Red Sea is Yemen's western
boundary. The land is mountainous with
a low-lying coastal belt. But Yemen is

more productive agriculturally than
other parts of the Arabian peninsula.

The Yemenis are Muslims and most of
them are farmers or fishermen. Millet is
the chief subsistence crop. Cotton is
grown along the coast and the famous
'Mokha' coffee is an important export.
Qat, a shrub whose leaves are narcotic,
is now the country's leading export. It
is used widely throughout the peninsula
and in adjacent parts of Africa. Yemen
has received aid from China, the United
States and the Soviet Union.

In ancient times, Yemen was a wealthy
and powerful state. It was ruled by religious leaders called Imams. In 1962
Imam Ahmad died. Army officers deposed his son and proclaimed the
country a republic. In the ensuing struggle
for power, the republican forces were
helped by Egypt and the royalists were
aided by Saudi Arabia. By 1967 the republicans were in control. In 1974, however, the constitution was suspended and
a nine-member Command Council took
over the government of the country. ∎

Africa

1 : 40 000 000

400   0   400   800   1200   1600 km

LUANDA   59

TEMPERATURE   °C

6°

PRESSURE   mb

PRECIPITATION   mm

323mm

J F M A M J J A S O N D

ACCRA   27

TEMPERATURE   °C

4°

PRESSURE   mb

PRECIPITATION   mm

724mm

J F M A M J J A S O N D

DENSITY OF POPULATION
1 : 80 000 000

Inhabitants

per mile²	per km²	per mile²	per km²
under 2	under 1	32- 64	12- 25
2- 8	1- 3	64-128	25- 50
8-16	3- 6	128-256	50-100
16-32	6-12	over 256	over100

■ Towns of over 250 000 inhabitants

Projection: Zenithal Equidistant

LES.   Lesotho
O.F.S.   Orange Free State
SWAZ.   Swaziland
T.A.I.   Territory of Afars & Issas

COPYRIGHT. GEORGE PHILIP & SON. LTD.

Africa

Africa today forms a large part of the developing world. The map of the region has changed greatly since 1945 with rapid transitions from colonial status to full independence, achieved in some cases only after bitter wars against former European rulers. Many place names, particularly those recalling colonialism, have been changed. For example, the Belgian Congo became Zaire and its capital, Leopoldville, was renamed Kinshasa.

Since independence, economic difficulties and inter-communal strife have led to the creation of many one-party states and military governments. South Africa, the continent's most prosperous country, has a government controlled by settlers of European origin who form only 17 percent of the population. An even smaller European minority (4.5 percent) seized independence in the British colony of Rhodesia in 1965 and have retained control despite international sanctions and the emer-gence of a guerilla opposition, sup-ported by neighbouring black African countries.

Africa contains vast tracts of burn-ing desert, large areas of unreliable rainfall and other areas of dense tropical forest. Because so much of the environment is hostile to man, the continent is thinly populated. But falling mortality rates have recently led to population rises that have added to economic problems.

Plantation agriculture is neverthe-less important and many African countries now depend for export revenue on cash crops. Ghana leads the world in cocoa production and Nigeria in palm oil exports. Other major agricultural exports include coffee, cotton and tobacco.

The main economic potential of Africa however lies in its vast mineral reserves. Nigeria and Libya are among leading oil exporters. South Africa produces about three-quarters of the non-communist world's gold. Zaire is the leading industrial diamond pro-ducer and Zambia is among the top copper exporters.

Morocco

Area: *446,550km² (172,413sq.m.).*
Population: *16,309,000.* **Capital:**
Rabat (703,000). **Language:** *Arabic.*
Ethnic groups: *Arabs, Berbers.*
Main exports: *phosphates, citrus
fruits, cork, fish, timber, wool.*
Average temperatures: *16°C
(60°F) Jan. 22°C (72°F) July on
coast.* **Highest point:** *Mt Toubkal,
4,165m (13,665ft).*

The lowlands and low plateaus facing the
Atlantic Ocean are the richest and most
populous parts of Morocco. The climate
is equable and moist, although summer
days are often hot. The largest city,
Casablanca (1.9m.), is on the coast.
Casablanca, Agadir, Essaouira and Safi
are centres of an important fishing industry. Beyond the coastlands, a dry
strip of land separates the fertile low
plateaus from the high plateaus and
ranges of the Atlas mountains. The
mountains have an extreme climate.
Summer temperatures often reach 37°C
(100°F), whereas in winter temperatures plummet to −10°C (14°F).

About 7 out of every 10 Moroccans
work in agriculture. Morocco's production of phosphates, the chief export, is
second only to that of the US. Manufacturing is increasing in importance, but
unemployment is high and has led to considerable emigration to Europe.

Most of Morocco was a French protectorate between 1912 and 1956, although
the north was Spanish. The country became independent in 1956 as a constitutional monarchy. The king now governs
with an elected chamber of 240 deputies.
The king appoints the prime minister and
other ministers and can dissolve the
assembly. In the 1970s, Morocco claimed
the territory of Spanish Sahara, which
has large phosphate deposits. The
Spaniards agreed to withdraw in early
1976, leaving Morocco occupying the

*Left: A Kuda bull and two does drink
from a water-hole in the Mkuze Game
Reserve, northern Zululand. Also on
the reserve are leopards and crocodiles.*

*Above: Fès, Morocco was once famous
for making the Islamic cap, the fez.*

*Above, right: Azemmour is one of
many port towns in Morocco.*

north and Mauritania the south. But
Saharan nationalists opposed both the
Moroccans and the Mauritanians. ■

Libya

Area: *1,759,540km² (679,358sq.m.).*
Population: *2,324,000.* **Capitals:**
*Banghāzi (321,000), Tarābulus or
Tripoli (376,000).* **Language:**
Arabic. **Ethnic groups:** *Arabs,
Berbers.* **Main export:** *petroleum.*
Average temperatures: *11°C
(52°F) Jan. 29°C (85°F) July on
coast.* **Highest point:** *Picco Bette,
2,286m (7,500ft).*

Most of Libya's fertile land is near the
coast, especially in the west between the
Tunisian border and Misratah. In places
behind the coast there is a dry plateau,
parts of which are fertile. The most fertile region in the east is the Al Marj
(Barce) plain. Libya's chief crops are
barley, groundnuts, olives, wheat and
other typical Mediterranean crops. In
the south, the low coastal plateaus merge
into the Sahara, where settlements occur
only around oases and petroleum fields.
Nearly nine-tenths of Libya is desert.
But it has the highest per capita income
in Africa because of its petroleum exports. To conserve its resources, Libya
reduced its petroleum production in the
1970s and in 1975 it was the second largest African producer.

Formerly Turkish, Libya came under
Italian rule in 1912, although the east
was not subdued until 1932. During
World War II, Libya was the scene of
several major battles. From 1943, Britain
controlled the north and France the
south. In 1951 Libya became an independent monarchy. Army officers deposed the monarch in 1969. They established a Revolutionary Command Council which has introduced an Islamic form
of socialism. ■

Commercial crops: Africa

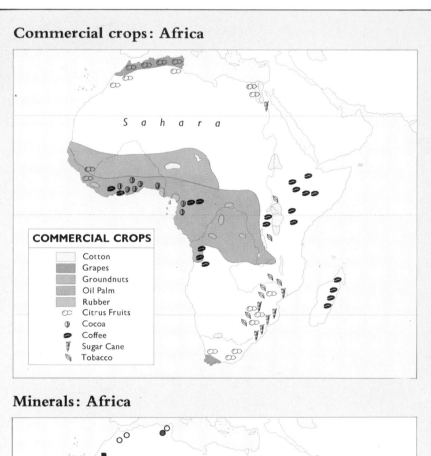

COMMERCIAL CROPS

- Cotton
- Grapes
- Groundnuts
- Oil Palm
- Rubber
- Citrus Fruits
- Cocoa
- Coffee
- Sugar Cane
- Tobacco

Minerals: Africa

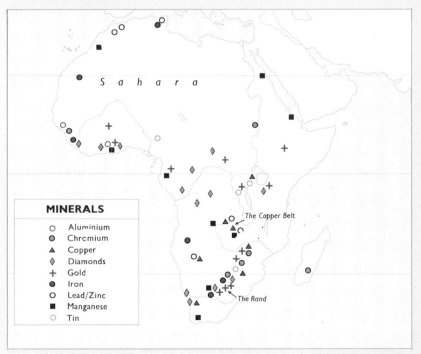

MINERALS

- ○ Aluminium
- ◉ Chromium
- ▲ Copper
- ◆ Diamonds
- ✛ Gold
- ● Iron
- ○ Lead/Zinc
- ■ Manganese
- ○ Tin

The Copper Belt

The Rand

Tunisia

Area: *163,610km² (63,170sq.m.).*
Population: *5,777,000.* **Capital:**
Tunis (944,000). **Languages:**
Arabic, French. **Ethnic groups:**
Arabs, Berbers. **Main exports:**
*phosphates, agricultural products,
esparto grass.* **Average temperatures:**
*10°C (50°F) Jan. 27°C (80°F) July
on coast.* **Highest point:** *Djebel
Chambi, 1,566m (5,138ft).*

Lying at the eastern end of the Atlas
mountains, Tunisia is a sunny country
with an increasing tourist trade. Its relief
is varied and the rainfall decreases from
north to south—the south being desert.
Tunisia's most valuable industry is
mining, especially phosphates, which
form 35 percent of the exports. But most
people are farmers, although farming
contributes only one-fifth of the national
income. Crops include barley, dates,
figs, grapes, maize, oats, olives, oranges,
sorghum and wheat.

Tunisia won independence as a monarchy in 1956, but became a single-party
presidential republic in 1957. In 1974
Tunisia and Libya announced that they
planned to merge as one nation in the
future. ∎

Algeria

Area *2,381,741km² (919,590sq.m.).*
Population: *16,798,000.* **Capital:**
Alger or Algiers (1.2m.).
Language: *Arabic, French.* **Ethnic
groups:** *Arabs, Berbers.* **Main
exports:** *barley, dates, fruits, iron ore,
olives, petroleum and natural gas,
phosphates, wine.* **Average
temperatures:** *16°C (60°F) Jan.
22°C (75°F) July, on the coast.*
Highest point: *Mt Tahat, 2,918m
(9,573ft).*

Although it is Africa's third largest
petroleum producer and a leading producer of natural gas, Algeria is mainly a
farming country. Farming is mostly confined to the Mediterranean zone and vines
are the chief commercial crop. Cereals,
citrus fruits and olives are also important.
The inland steppes of the High Atlas are
used as pasture. The thinly-populated
Sahara, where petroleum and natural gas
are extracted, covers most of the country.

Algeria, a Muslim nation, was a
French territory from 1848 to 1962.
Between 1954 and 1962, the Algerian
National Liberation Front (FLN) fought
with French forces. Most French settlers,
who numbered about one million, returned to France in 1961–1962. Algeria
has had a military government since
1965. This government has established
close links with the Soviet Union.
Algeria is a one-party state. The FLN
nominates the president and candidates
for the Assembly. The country's high
birth-rate and high unemployment rate
make emigration, especially to France, a
necessary safety valve. ∎

Egypt

Area: *1,001,449km² (386,659sq.m.).*
Population: *37,100,00.* **Capital:** *El
Qâhira or Cairo (5m.).* **Language:**
Arabic. **Ethnic groups:** *Arabs and
some people of European and Turkish
descent.* **Main exports:** *cotton textiles
and raw cotton, iron and steel,
machinery, fertilizers, chemicals.*
Average temperatures: *13°C (55°F)
Jan. 32°C (90°F) July.* **Highest
point:** *Jabal Katrinah, 2,637m
(8,652ft).*

Egyptians are mostly of Arab or Turkish
descent, but there are Berber and Euro-
pean minorities. Most people are Sunni
Muslims, although there is a Coptic
Christian minority. Egypt has been an
Arabic-speaking state since AD 640.
More than 95 percent of all Egyptians

Above: El-Kantra bridge spans a deep gorge at Constantin, Algeria. The city's rocky site made it an historic fortress.
Below: The stone Colossi of Memnon near Thebes, Egypt, were built under the pharaoh Amenhotep III about 1400 BC.

live in the Nile valley and farming occupies three-fifths of the people. Around the Nile delta are two of Africa's largest cities, El Qâhira or Cairo and El Iskandarîya or Alexandria (1.9m.).

Ancient Egypt, one of the world's greatest civilizations, grew up in the Nile valley. Alexander the Great conquered Egypt in 332 BC and the area later became part of the Roman empire. Christianity was introduced and Egypt became the centre of the Coptic Church in AD 395. But after the Arab conquest of AD 640, Egypt adopted Islam and the Arabic language.

From 1517, Egypt was a province of the Ottoman empire. France ruled Egypt briefly between 1798 and 1801, when British and Turkish forces helped to expel them. In 1805, Mohammed Ali Pasha was appointed governor by the Turks. He began to modernize the country and, in 1841, he defeated the Ottomans. After his death, Egypt's prosperity declined, although the Suez Canal was opened in 1869. In 1882, Britain occupied the country and held it as a protectorate between 1914 and 1922, when it became a monarchy. By 1936, British troops occupied only the Canal zone.

Conflict with Israel
In 1948–1949 Egyptian forces fought against the establishment of the state of Israel. In Egypt, nationalism increased and, under Colonel Nasser, Egypt was declared a republic in 1953. Britain agreed to withdraw its troops by 1956, but in that year Nasser nationalized the Suez Canal. An abortive British–French invasion aimed at holding the Canal Zone ended after a few months.

Conflict with Israel has hampered Egypt's economic progress. Israel still holds most of the Sinai peninsula which it conquered in 1967. During the short war, the Suez Canal was blocked. Further hostilities occurred in 1973. In 1975, an agreement was reached creating a UN buffer zone in Sinai. The Suez Canal was reopened and Israeli ships were allowed to pass through it.

Officially called the Arab Republic of Egypt (AER), Egypt is a one-party socialist state. The elected 620-member People's Assembly nominates the president, who is supreme commander of the armed forces.

Physical features and climate
Most of Egypt is desert and nearly all the people live in the fertile Nile valley, which covers only three percent of the land. The upper Nile valley is narrow and lined by cliffs in places. The lower Nile valley includes the broad, thickly-populated Nile delta.

To the west of the Nile, the wind-swept desert contains the Qattara Depression, which is 133m (436ft) below sea level. To the east, highlands border the Red Sea. Egypt's highest mountains are in the Sinai peninsula, now occupied by the Israelis. The climate of Egypt is hot and dry. The rainfall decreases from north to south between 254 and 25 millimetres (10 to 1 inches).

Minerals and industry
Egypt has important petroleum deposits. It also produces phosphates and some iron ore.

In Africa, Egypt is second only to South Africa in industrial output. Industries located in the main cities are varied, including cigarettes, cotton textiles, fertilizers, iron and steel, machinery, paper, shoes and sugar refining. Much of Egypt's power comes from the Aswan High Dam. The unblocked Suez Canal is expected to be a major source of revenue. In Egypt, the Nile is used for transport and the country has 4,510km (2,800m.) of railways and 13,890km (8,630m.) of highways

Agriculture
Most Egyptians are farmers, who irrigate their small farms along the Nile. The chief commercial crop is cotton. Other crops include barley, beans, fruits, lentils, maize, millet, onions, rice, sugar-cane and wheat. Egypt has large numbers of cattle and sheep.

Trade and foreign relations
Egypt trades with both western and communist countries. The USSR has

supplied arms to Egypt, but Egypt has avoided political commitments to either east or west. The chief aim of its foreign policy is Arab unity, although attempts at mergers with other Arab countries have been unsuccessful. ∎

Mauritania
Western Sahara

These two largely desert or semi-desert countries face the Atlantic Ocean. Mauritania, an independent republic since 1960, has important iron ore reserves.

In 1975, Spain agreed to withdraw from Spanish (or Western) Sahara, letting Morocco take the north, which has large deposits of phosphates, and Mauritania the south. However, an Algerian-backed Saharan nationalist group resisted Moroccan and Mauritanian occupation and claimed full independence.

Mauritania has an area of 1,030,700km² (397,953sq.m.) and 1,326,000 people. The capital is Nouakchott (70,000).

Spanish Sahara was called **Western Sahara** after the Spaniards withdrew in early 1976. The territory covers 266,000km² (102,703sq.m.) and has about 100,000 people. The capital is El Aaiún (24,000).

Mali, Niger,
Chad, Upper Volta

These landlocked nations became independent from France in 1960. Each territory has subsequently become a military republic. In Mali, Niger and Chad, the Sahara covers the north and savanna occurs in the south. Upper Volta has a higher average annual rainfall than elsewhere but rainfall is generally unreliable. All four countries depend on agriculture and migration of many workers to the south.

Mali has been a republic governed by a National Liberation Committee since an army coup in 1968. It has an area of

Above: Camels are vital in Tunisia.

1,240,000km² (478,764sq.m.) and 5,604,000 people. The capital is Bamako (170,000).

Niger, a military republic since 1974, has an area of 1,267,000km² (489,189 sq.m.) and 4,504,000 people. The capital is Niamey (102,000).

Chad has an area of 1,284,000km² (495,752sq.m.) and 4,024,000 people. The capital is N'Djamena (102,000). An army coup took place in 1975.

Upper Volta became a military republic in 1966. In 1971 partial civilian rule was restored, but another military coup occurred in 1974 and the National Assembly was dissolved. Upper Volta has an area of 274,200km² (105,869sq.m.) and 5,980,000 people. The capital is Ouagadougou (125,000).

Sudan

Area: *2,505,813km² (967,494sq.m.).*
Population: *17,757,000.* **Capital:**
El Khartum or Khartoum (855,000).
Language: *Arabic.* **Ethnic groups:**
Arabs and Nubians in the north, Black Africans in the south. **Main exports:**
cotton, dates, groundnuts, gum arabic, hides and skins, livestock. **Average temperatures:** *16°C (60°F) Jan. 35°C (95°F) July.* **Highest point:**
Mt Kinyeti, 3,187m (10,456ft).

Sudan is the largest African country. Much of the north is desert, which merges into grassland, savanna and forest in the south. Sudan is divided ethnically into the Muslim, Arabic-speaking north and the Black African south, where over 100 languages are used. This division resulted in a civil war (1964–1972) which ended when the south was granted considerable autonomy. Farming is Sudan's chief activity and cotton grown under irrigation, is the main crop. Industrialization has advanced since the 1960s. Sudan, a military republic, became independent in 1956.

NORTH ATLANTIC

OCEAN

ALGER 59

TEMPERATURE ℃

13°

PRESSURE mb

PRECIPITATION mm

762mm

J F M A M J J A S O N D

TOMBOUCTOU 301

TEMPERATURE ℃

13°

PRECIPITATION mm

231mm

J F M A M J J A S O N D

Projection: Sanson Flamsteed's Sinusoidal

West from Greenwich   East from Greenwich

Left: Sardines from the Atlantic are unloaded at Dakar, capital of Senegal and the most westerly city in Africa.

Senegal, Gambia

Senegal, a former French territory which became independent in 1960, encloses the small former British territory of Gambia which became independent in 1965. Groundnuts are the chief exports of both countries.

Most Senegalese are Muslims and the official language is French. Senegal is a one-party republic. Massive reserves of iron ore have been discovered recently and Senegal could become one of Africa's chief producers.

Most Gambians are Muslims and the official language is English. Gambia became a republic with an elected house of representatives.

Senegal has an area of 196,192km² (75,750sq.m.) and 4,441,000 people. The capital is Dakar (581,000).

Gambia has an area of 11,295km² (4,361sq.m.) and 493,000 people. The capital is Banjul, or Bathurst (43,000). ■

Guinea, Guinea-Bissau

Guinea, a former French territory, became an independent republic in 1958. Most people are Muslims and the official language is French. Before 1958, Guinea was an agricultural country. Today minerals, including bauxite, diamonds and iron ore, are the chief exports. Guinea has been greatly assisted by communist countries, including the USSR.

Neighbouring Guinea-Bissau, which has an economy based on farming, won independence from Portugal in 1974. This followed a long war of liberation which began in 1962. Most people are Muslims.

Guinea has an area of 245,957km² (94,964sq.m.) and 4,412,000 people. The capital is Conakry (172,000).

Guinea-Bissau has an area of

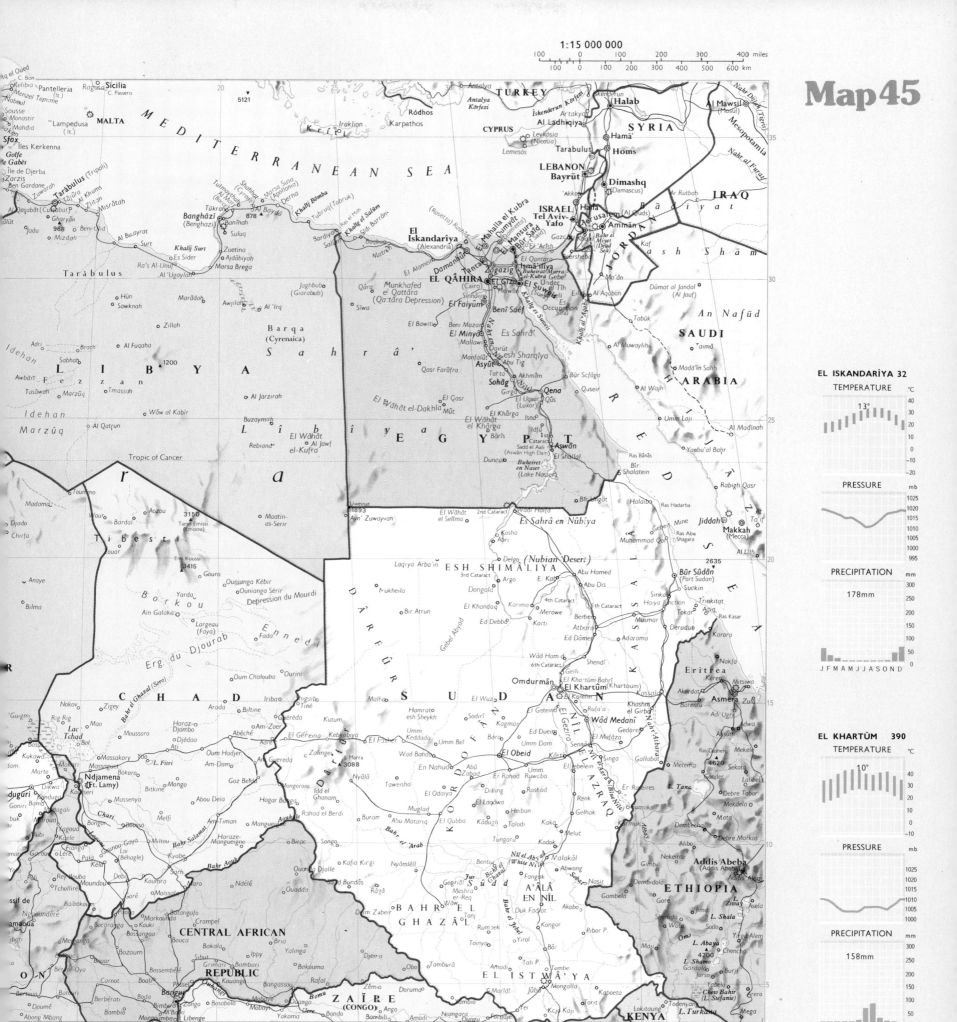

Map 45

1:15 000 000

36,125km² (13,948sq.m.) and 509,000 people. The capital is Bissau (6,000). ■

Sierra Leone, Liberia

The history of both of these states is linked with the slave trade. Freetown, capital of Sierra Leone, was founded in 1788 as a home for freed slaves. The modern descendants of these slaves form an important group called Creoles. Sierra Leone was a British colony from 1808 to 1961. In 1971, it became a republic.

Free Afro-American slaves founded Monrovia in 1822. Liberia became independent in 1847, but it has remained under US influence. Its constitution is modelled on the US constitution. There is a senate and a house of representatives.

Sierra Leone's chief exports are minerals, including diamonds and iron ore. Tropical crops are grown by the farmers, who make up more than 80 percent of the population.

In the last 20 years, iron ore has overtaken rubber as Liberia's chief export. Liberia's large shipping fleet includes mainly foreign ships, which fly Liberia's flag. The ship owners take advantage of the low rates of taxation charged by Liberia.

Sierra Leone has an area of 71,740km² (27,699sq.m.) and 2,861,000 people. The capital is Freetown (148,000).

Liberia has an area of 111,369km² (43,000sq.m.) and 1,747,000 people. The capital is Monrovia (100 000). ■

Ivory Coast, Ghana, Togo, Benin

These four countries extend northwards from the Gulf of Guinea. They have similar climates and vegetation. The southern forests are important for their timber and for tropical crop plantations. The northern savanna is used for grazing and for the cultivation of such crops as cotton and millet.

Ivory Coast has an area of 322,463km² (124,503sq.m.) and a population of 4,876,000. The capital is Abidjan (500,000). A former French territory, Ivory Coast became independent in 1960 and later a one-party state. Coffee, cocoa and cotton are the chief exports. Industries in Abidjan process farm products, cement, paper, timber and other products. Power comes from the hydro-electric project on the Bia River.

Ghana has an area of 238,537km² (92,099sq.m.) and a population of 9,867,000. The capital is Accra (758,000). Formerly the British colony of Gold Coast, Ghana became independent in 1957, incorporating part of neighbouring Togoland. Ghana became a republic in 1960, but the government was overthrown by a military group in 1966. In 1969 Ghana returned to civilian rule, but a second military coup in 1972 re-established army rule through the National Redemption Council.

Ghana is the world's largest producer of cocoa and timber is another important export. The Volta River hydro-electric scheme provides power for aluminium smelting and other industries. Some gold and diamonds are also exported.

Togo has an area of 56,000km² (21,622sq.m.) and 2,220,000 people. The capital is Lome (148,000). Part of former Togoland was incorporated into Ghana in 1957. The rest was ruled by France until it became independent in 1960. After two coups, Togo became a military republic. Togo's chief exports are cocoa, coffee, palm oil and phosphates.

Benin was called Dahomey until November 1975, when the name change was announced. Benin has an area of 112,622km² (43,483sq.m.) and a population of 3,071,000. The capital is Porto Novo (74,000). The country became independent from France in 1960. Between 1960 and 1972, Benin suffered five coups. It is now a military republic. The economy is based on farming and palm oil is the chief export. ■

Nigeria

Area: *923,768km² (356,667sq.m.).*
Population: *62,869,000.* **Capital:**
Lagos (875,000). **Languages:** *Hausa,
Ibo, Yoruba.* **Ethnic groups:** *about
250, including Hausa, Kanuri, Fulani,
Ibo, Yoruba.* **Main exports:**
*petroleum, cocoa, cotton, groundnuts,
palm kernels and oil, hides and skins,
rubber, timber, tin and alloys.* **Average:
temperatures:** *27°C (80°F) in the
south.* **Highest point:** *nearly 2,130m
(7,000ft) on Cameroon border.*

Nigeria has a larger population than any
other African country, although 13
African countries cover a larger area.
About 84 out of every 100 Nigerians live
in rural areas. But Nigeria is unusual in
Africa in having many well-developed
large towns, including Lagos, Ibadan,
Ogbomosho, Kano and Oshogbo.

Nigerians are divided into about 250
groups, each of which has its own language or dialect. The chief groups in
the Muslim north are the Fulani, Hausa
and Kanuri. Muslims make up 47 percent
of the population. The people in the
south are mainly Christians (35 percent of
the total population) or they practise
traditional religions (18 percent). The
largest groups in the south are the Ibo
in the southeast and the Yoruba in the
west. Nigeria's ethnic diversity has
created many problems, including the
civil war of 1967–1970.

History and constitution
Knowledge of Nigeria's early history is
fragmentary. However, archaeologists
have discovered impressive artistic cultures, such as Nok (1000 BC–AD 2000),
Ife (after AD 1200) and Benin, which was
flourishing in the late 1400s, when the
Portuguese visited the area. Early
Nigerian sculpture is unusual because
figures have more or less classical proportions, which is rare in African art.

Britain occupied Lagos in 1861 and,
gradually, British influence spread inland.
In 1900 the British colony of Southern
Nigeria was established, followed by the
creation of a protectorate over Northern
Nigeria in 1906. The North and South
were merged in 1914 to form modern
Nigeria.

Britain applied a policy of indirect
federal rule. After 1945, Nigeria was
divided into three regions, North, East
and West. A central council co-ordinated
the regional governments. Nigeria became independent in 1960 as a federation
and in 1963 it became a republic.

Ethnic differences caused tensions, and
two army coups occurred in 1966. Fighting also broke out between Hausas and
Ibos who lived in the north. To reduce
tensions, the military government split
Nigeria into 12 regions, but the former
Eastern Region broke away and set up a
rebel republic called Biafra. A bitter war
ended with Biafra's defeat in 1970. Since
then, the military government has tried
to rebuild the economy and create
racial harmony. It has benefited from
the large revenues obtained from petroleum exports.

A supreme military council, presided
over by the head of state, now forms the
federal government of Nigeria, and each
of the regions has a military governor.

Physical features and climate
Nigeria is mostly a land of low plateau
and plains. Mangrove swamps border
much of the coast, which includes the
delta of the great Niger River. Inland,
tropical forests merge into savanna in the
centre of the country. The hot, wet coast
has average temperatures of about 27°C
(80°F) all the year round. In the north,
temperatures vary from season to season.
Summer temperatures sometimes reach
46°C (115°F).

Minerals and industry
Nigeria possesses major petroleum deposits, which were first discovered in 1956.
By 1975 Nigeria was Africa's largest
petroleum producer. The revenue was
used to launch major development
plans in 1970–1974 and 1975–1980. Other
minerals include tin and coal.

Nigeria has varied industries, producing metal and engineering products as

well as processing farm and forest products. The country has more than
4,180km (2,600m.) of railways and
88,500km (55,000m.) of maintained
roads.

Agriculture, forestry and fishing
Most Nigerians work on farms. Groundnuts, palm oil, cocoa and rubber are important exports. Food crops include
bananas, cassava, maize, millet, rice and
yams. Large herds of cows, sheep and
goats are also important.

Nigeria exports hardwoods from the
southern forests, which cover about
31,000km² (12,000sq.m.). Fishing is carried on in and around the Niger delta
and fish are a useful source of extra
protein.

Trade and foreign relations
Britain remains the chief trading partner
of Nigeria, although the US, the West
Indies, the Netherlands and France are
also important buyers of Nigerian
petroleum. Since the end of the civil
war, Nigeria has played an increasingly
active role in African affairs. ■

Central African Republic
Congo, Gabon

With Chad, these three territories formed
part of French Equatorial Africa from
1910 to 1960, when they became separate
independent states. Central African
Republic and Congo were politically
unstable and were taken over by military
governments. Gabon has been stable, but
it became a one-party state in 1967.

Central African Republic, one of the
poorest nations in Africa, has an area of
622,984km² (240,534sq.m.) and a population of 1,612,000. The capital is Bangui

(pop. 302,000). Most of the people are
subsistence farmers.

Congo has an area of 342,000km²
(132,046sq.m.) and 1,053,000 people. Its
capital is Brazzaville (pop. 250,000), and
its chief export is timber, with some
diamonds.

Gabon has an area of 267,667km²
(103,346sq.m.) and 526,000 people. The
capital is Libreville (pop. 106,000). A
fairly prosperous African country, Gabon
has large mineral resources, which form
the basis of its exports, including iron
ore, manganese, petroleum and uranium,
and also has valuable stands of timber.
Gabon retains close links with France. ■

Cameroon
Equatorial Guinea

These neighbouring states nestle in
northwestern equatorial Africa. Cameroon was created in 1961 when the
southern part of the former British
Cameroons joined French Cameroon
(independent 1960) to form one nation.
Equatorial Guinea was Spanish until
1968. It consists of the territory of Rio
Muni on the mainland and the island of
Macias Nguema Biyoga (formerly Fernando Póo). Both Cameroon and
Equatorial Guinea export cocoa and
coffee.

Cameroon covers 475,442km²
(183,568sq.m.) and has 6,404,000 people.
Its capital is Yaoundé (pop. 178,000)
although the largest city is Douala
(300,000). Its highest point, Mt Cameroon
is 4,070m (13,354ft) high and is the
wettest place in Africa with 10,160mm
(400in) of rain per year. Cameroon has
many ethnic groups, some numbering
only 50 persons. One of the larger groups,
the Fang, form the majority in Rio Muni.

*Above: Mokwa, scene of this street
market, is in the western region of
Nigeria. Nearly 90 per cent of Nigeria's
large population lives in rural villages.
Building materials are usually simple,
ranging from mud to bamboo.*

Equatorial Guinea has an area of
28,051km² (10,830sq.m.), with a population of 307,000. Its capital is Bata (pop.
3,500). ■

Zambia

Area: *752,614km² (290,584sq.m.).*
Population: *4,965,000.* **Capital:**
Lusaka (347,000). **Languages:**
Bemba, Nyanja, English. **Ethnic
groups:** *Tonga, Lozi, Bemba,
Ngoni.* **Main exports:** *copper, zinc,
lead, tobacco.* **Average temperatures:**
21°–35°C (70°–95°F). **Highest
point:** *Muchinga Mts, 2,130m
(7,000ft).*

Land-locked Zambia stands on a savanna-
covered plateau. Zambia has more than
70 ethnic groups. Most are farmers and
many are at subsistence level. Zambia's
wealth lies in mining. Copper accounts
for 90 percent of the exports. The
Copperbelt region on the Zaïre border
is Zambia's most densely-populated
area, with centres at Kitwe, Mufulira and
Ndola. The Kariba Dam in the south
supplies power for copper smelting.
Other minerals include cadmium, cobalt,
lead and zinc.

Formerly the British protectorate of
Northern Rhodesia, the country became
independent as Zambia in 1964. It became a one-party state in 1972. ■

Above: A bush village near Ibadan, Nigeria shows poor crops.

Right: Victoria Falls carry the waters of the Zambezi River thundering over a vast precipice.

Zaïre

Area: *2,345,409km² (905,562sq.m.).* **Population:** *24,901,000.* **Capital:** *Kinshasa (1.4m.).* **Languages:** *French, Swahili, Lingala.* **Ethnic groups:** *Bakongo, Baluba, Balunda, Bamongo.* **Main exports:** *copper, zinc, cobalt, cassiterite, industrial diamonds, oil palm products, coffee, cotton.* **Average temperature:** *27°C (80°F) in low-lying areas.* **Highest point** *Ruwenzori on Ugandan border 5,109m (16,761ft).*

Formerly named Congo, Zaïre is the second largest African country, more than 1½ times as large as the combined area of the European Economic Community. Most of Zaïre lies in the depression of the Zaïre (formerly Congo) River and its tributaries. Mountains rise in the east and south. Tropical forest covers the Zaïre basin, which is hot and wet, with savanna in the drier north and south. Grassland covers parts of the higher eastern region.

Zaïre has a few pygmies, but most of the population consists of Bantu-speaking peoples. About 75 percent of the people work on farms. But the nation's wealth is based on minerals, especially copper from Shaba province. Zaïre is also the world's leading industrial diamond producer. The explorer Henry Morton

Above: As dusk falls over the Kenya savanna, an elephant heads for water.

Above, right: Coconuts are the main cash crop on the island of Zanzibar.

Stanley established the potential of Zaïre in the 1870s. From 1884, Zaïre was the personal property of King Léopold II of Belgium. After reports of ill-treatment of the people by Europeans, the Belgian government took control in 1908.

Zaïre became independent in 1960. Civil disorder and fighting broke out. From 1965, order was restored and, by the 1970s, the country was stable. Recent development of its massive hydro-electricity potential has included the construction of Inga Dam, near Matadi, which will eventually be the largest hydro-electric complex in the world. ■

Kenya

Area: *582,646km² (224,960sq.m.).*
Population: *13,360,000.* **Capital:** *Nairobi (540,000).* **Languages:** *Swahili, English.* **Ethnic groups:** *Kikuyu, Luo, Luhya.* **Main exports:** *coffee, tea, petroleum products.* **Average temperatures:** *27°C (80°F) on the coast, 10°–21°C (50°–70°F) on the plateau.* **Highest point:** *Mt Kenya 5,199m (17,058ft).*

Rich in wildlife and superb scenery, Kenya has a fast-expanding tourist industry, which is second only to coffee as a source of revenue. Nearly half of Kenya is a high plateau. The plateau is divided by the East African Rift Valley which, in places, is flanked by walls more than 900m (3,000ft) high. Volcanic masses, such as Mt Kenya, rise above the plateau. To the north-east, the country becomes arid.

Farming is the main occupation. The pleasant, fertile southwest plateau attracted many European settlers when Kenya became a British colony in 1920. The presence of European and Asian immigrants aggravated a land shortage among Kenya's largest ethnic group, the Kikuyu, and in 1952 the Kikuyu launched an uprising called Mau Mau. Although the rebellion was put down, Kenya became independent in 1963. A one-party state, Kenya has pursued a policy of land redistribution, Africanization and economic development. Nairobi is rapidly expanding, as is the industrial area around its port, Mombasa. ■

Uganda

Area: *236,036km² (91,133sq.m.).*
Population: *11,535,000.* **Capital:** *Kampala (332,000).* **Languages:** *English, Swahili.* **Ethnic groups:** *Baganda, Banyoro, Batoro.* **Main exports:** *coffee, cotton.* **Average temperatures:** *15°–29°C (59°–84°F).* **Highest point:** *Mt Elgon 4,321m (14,176ft) on Kenya border; Ruwenzori border with Zaïre 5,109m (16,761ft).*

Water, including part of Lake Victoria, covers about one-seventh of Uganda and fish are an important source of protein. The economy, however, is based on farming and the rich soils support food and cash crop farming especially coffee and cotton. Local processing industries get power from the Jinja hydro-electric plant. Most of Uganda is between 900 and 1,500m (3,000–5,000ft) above sea level and the climate is milder than normal for equatorial areas.

More than 40 ethnic groups live in Uganda. The largest group, the Baganda, lives in Buganda province, the richest farming region. From 1893 to 1962, Britain ruled Uganda. After independence, unrest was caused by conflict between the Baganda and the central government. The present military government has pursued a policy of Africanization, which has included the expulsion of 50,000 Ugandan Asians, formerly the largest minority. ■

Malawi

Area: *126,338km² (48,779sq.m.).*
Population: *5,043,000.* **Capital:** *Lilongwe (20,000).* **Largest city:** *Blantyre (150,000).* **Languages:** *English, Nyanja/Chewa.* **Ethnic groups:** *Nyanja/Chewa, Tumbuka, Yao, Lomwe.* **Main exports:** *tea, tobacco.* **Average temperatures:** *23°C (74°F) on plains, 21°C (69°F) in highlands.* **Highest point:** *Mt Mlanje, 3,000m (9,843ft).*

Malawi is a densely-populated, land-locked country. Lake Malawi (Nyasa) is in the Rift Valley in the east. The west is a tableland. Farming is the chief activity. The chief cash crops are tea and tobacco. Because of the dense population, many workers migrate to Rhodesia, South Africa and Zambia. Formerly the British protectorate of Nyasaland, Malawi, a one-party republic, became independent in 1963. ■

Tanzania

Area: *945,087km² (364,898sq.m.).*
Population: *15,164,000.* **Capital:** *Dar es Salaam (344,000).* **Languages:** *English, Swahili.* **Ethnic groups:** *Sukuma, Nyamwezi, Ha, Makonde, Gogo.* **Main exports:** *Sisal, coffee, cotton, pyrethrum, cloves, sugar.* **Average temperatures:** *26°C (78°F) on coast, 17°C (63°F) on plateau.* **Highest point:** *Mt Kilimanjaro 5,895m (19,340ft).*

Tanzania consists of mainland Tanganyika and the small offshore island territory of Zanzibar. These territories united in 1964. The mainland has a tropical coastal belt and a cooler, drier inland plateau. Africa's highest mountain, Kilimanjaro, is in the north-east.

More than 120 ethnic groups live in Tanzania and there are small European, Asian and Arab minorities. Tanzania has a farming economy, mostly subsistence, but cash crops form the bulk of the exports. A one-party state, Tanzania has implemented a self-help policy called *Ujamaa*, whereby people are brought together to work in co-operative villages. Tanzania was a German colony from the 1880s to 1918, when Britain took over. Tanganyika became independent in 1961 and Zanzibar in 1963. Two of the country's main problems are unreliable rainfall in the interior and a poorly-developed communication system, which has been improved by the recent completion of the Tanzania–Zambia railway.

Rwanda, Burundi

Rwanda and Burundi are small, densely-populated states in the heart of equatorial Africa. Most of the people are subsistence cultivators. Their chief export is coffee. There is a Bantu Hutu majority, with the minority Tutsi (9 percent in Rwanda and less than 15 percent in Burundi) and a few Twa (pygmies).

Called Ruanda-Urundi, the area was colonized by Germany in the late 1800s. After World War II, Belgium was mandated to govern the area until 1962, when it split into two independent nations. The Tutsi minority were feudal rulers over the Hutu. In the last 20 years, much Tutsi-Hutu conflict has occurred. The Hutu removed the Tutsi leadership of Rwanda in 1959. In Burundi, many Hutu were massacred by the Tutsi in the 1970s.

Rwanda has an area of 26,338km² (10,169sq.m.) and 4,202,000 people. Its capital is Kigali (pop. 25,000).

Burundi has an area of 27,834km² (10,747sq.m.) and 3,600,000 people. Its capital is Bujumbura (pop. 100,000). ■

1:18 000 000

100   0   100   200   300   400 miles
100   0   100 200 300 400 500 600 km

Major countries and regions labelled on the map:

NIGER · CHAD · NIGERIA · CAMEROON · CENTRAL AFRICAN REPUBLIC · SUDAN · EQUATORIAL GUINEA · GABON · CONGO · ZAIRE (CONGO) · ETHIOPIA · UGANDA · KENYA · RWANDA · BURUNDI · TANZANIA · ANGOLA · ZAMBIA · MALAWI · MOZAMBIQUE · RHODESIA · BOTSWANA · SOUTH WEST AFRICA (NAMIBIA) · SOUTH AFRICA · CAPE PROVINCE · TRANSVAAL · ORANJE-VRYSTAAT (O.V.S.) · NATAL · LESOTHO · SWAZILAND · TRANSKEI · CABINDA · MALAGASY REPUBLIC

ATLANTIC OCEAN · INDIAN OCEAN

Tropic of Capricorn

Selected cities: Lagos, Douala, Libreville, Brazzaville, Kinshasa (Léopoldville), Luanda, Lubumbashi, Lusaka, Salisbury, Bulawayo, Windhoek, Johannesburg, Pretoria, Cape Town (Kaapstad), Port Elizabeth, East London, Durban, Bloemfontein, Kimberley, Nairobi, Mombasa, Dar-es-Salaam, Addis Abeba, El Khartûm, Omdurmân, Antananarivo (Tananarive)

Climate charts

NAIROBI ★ 1820
- TEMPERATURE °C — 4°
- PRESSURE mb — 825 / 820 / 815 / 810
- PRECIPITATION mm — 958mm — J F M A M J J A S O N D

MOMBASA ★ 16
- TEMPERATURE °C — 4°
- PRESSURE mb — 1025 / 1020 / 1015 / 1010 / 1005 / 1000 / 995
- PRECIPITATION mm — 1201mm — J F M A M J J A S O N D

ENTEBBE ★ 1182
- TEMPERATURE °C — 2°
- PRESSURE mb — 890 / 885 / 880 / 875 / 870 / 865
- PRECIPITATION mm — 1506mm — J F M A M J J A S O N D

MALAGASY REPUBLIC — On same scale as General Map

Projection: Sanson Flamsteed's Sinusoidal

East from Greenwich

COPYRIGHT GEORGE PHILIP & SON LTD.

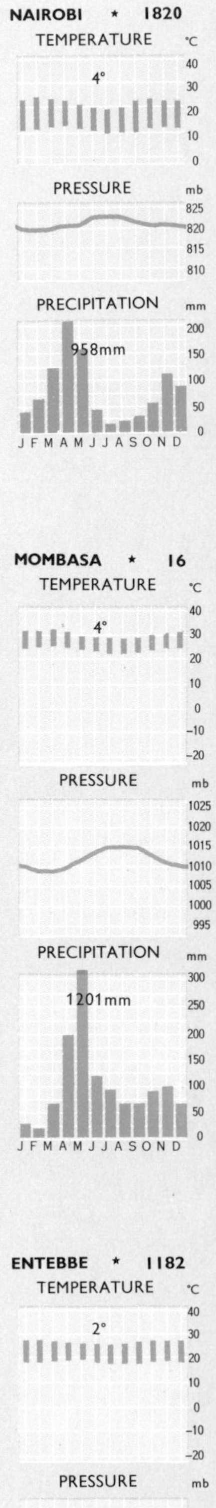

103

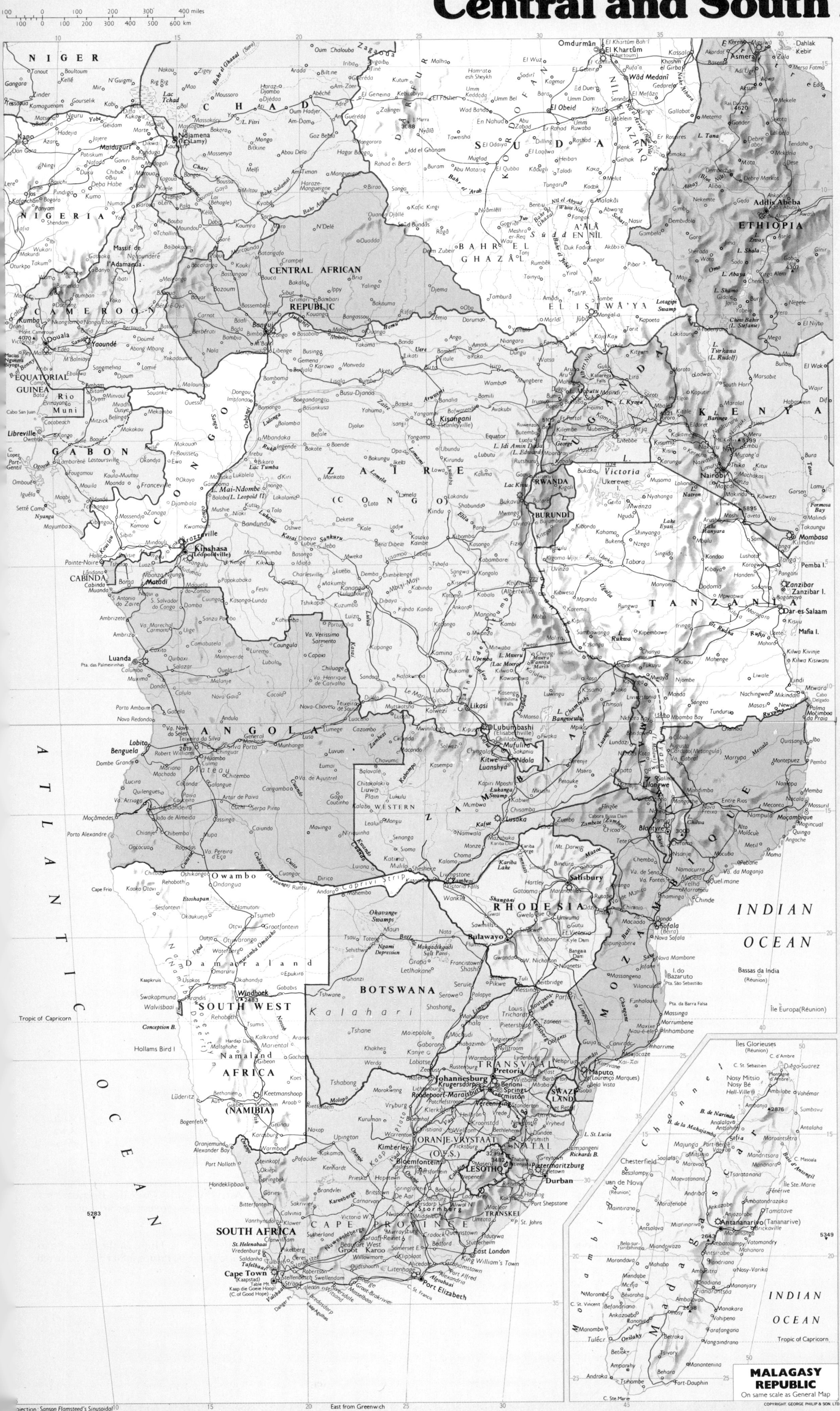

Angola, Mozambique

These former Portuguese territories became independent in 1975, following several years of guerilla activity. The cost of the colonial wars weakened Portugal's economy and was one reason for the 1974 coup in Portugal which brought left-wing groups to power. Civil war in Angola erupted after the Portuguese withdrawal.

Coffee is Angola's chief crop, but diamonds, iron ore, petroleum and other minerals are produced. Mozambique's economy is based on farming especially cashew nuts, copra, cotton, sisal, sugar and tea. The new Cabora Bassa dam is a major source of power. Mozambique also derives income from its migrant labourers and from its ports and transport facilities.

Angola has an area of 1,246,700km² (481,351sq.m.), with 5,673,000 people. Its capital is Luanda (500,000).

Mozambique has an area of 783,030km² (302,328sq.m.), with 8,823,000 people. The capital is Lourenço Marques (250,000).

Namibia (South-West Africa)

Area: *824,292km² (318,259sq.m.).* **Population:** *702,000.* **Capital:** *Windhoek (64,700).* **Languages:** *Afrikaans, English.* **Ethnic groups:** *Ovambos, Whites, Damaras.* **Main exports:** *diamonds, base metals, fish products, meat.* **Average temperature:** *19°C (66°F) in the highlands.* **Highest point:** *2,483m (8,146ft).*

This huge, arid and sparsely-inhabited territory contains the coastal Namib desert and part of the Kalahari semi-desert. Most people live in the central

Above: The cheetah, whose skin was once prized for chieftain's robes, is today one of Africa's threatened species. It is protected on many wildlife reserves set up throughout eastern and southern Africa.

Right: Grapes harvested on the dry tablelands of Cape Province are the basis of a flourishing South African wine industry notable for its sherry, much of it exported to Britain. Some of the best vineyards lie in the Paarl-Stellenbosch area.

highlands where livestock raising is important. But the country's mineral resources, especially diamonds, are most important. South Africa was mandated to rule this former German territory in 1919 and has refused to accept UN rulings that it should now become the independent country of Namibia. In 1971 the World Court of Justice declared continuing South African rule of the territory to be illegal.

Botswana, Lesotho, Swaziland

These territories were formerly ruled by Britain. Botswana (formerly Bechuanaland) and Lesotho (Basutoland) became independent in 1966 and Swaziland in 1968. These nations are closely linked with South Africa, to which they supply many migrant labourers. Much of Botswana is semi-desert. Beef cattle raising is the chief economic activity. Livestock are important in mountainous Lesotho, but mining is becoming increasingly significant in Swaziland.

Botswana has an area of 600,372km² (231,804sq.m.) and 695,000 people. The capital is Gaborone (27,000).

Lesotho has an area of 30,355km² (11,720sq.m.) and 1,038,000 people. Its capital is Maseru (20,000).

Swaziland has an area of 17,363km² (6,704sq.m.) and 504,000 people. Its capital is Mbabane (18,000). ■

Rhodesia

Area: *390,580km² (150,803sq.m.).*
Population: *6,332,000.* **Capital:**
Salisbury (513,000). **Languages:**
English, Ndebele, Shona. **Ethnic
groups:** *Bantu-speaking groups,
including Ndebele, Shona; about
273,000 Europeans; 29,000 Asians and
Coloureds.* **Main exports:** *tobacco,
asbestos, copper, meat, clothing,
chrome ore.* **Average temperatures:**
*Salisbury, 14°C (57°F) June, 21°C
(70°F) Nov.* **Highest point:** *near
Mozambique border, more than
2,440m (8,000ft).*

Most of Rhodesia has a mild climate
which is attractive to Europeans, who
form a powerful minority. In 1965 the
European-dominated government of
Rhodesia unilaterally declared their
country independent. Britain declared
this act illegal and Rhodesia remains,
technically, a British colony.

People
Most Rhodesians are Bantu-speaking
Africans. The largest groups are the
Ndebele (Matabele) in the south and the
Shona (Mashona) in the north. About
60 percent of the Bantu people live in
reserved African areas. Most of the others
work for Europeans in the towns, mines
and on European-owned farms.

History and constitution
From 1898 Rhodesia was governed by a
British High Commissioner in South
Africa, but the British settlers secured
internal self-government in 1923. Between 1953 and 1963, Rhodesia was part
of a federation with Malawi and Zambia.
After the federation was dissolved,
Rhodesia failed to agree on an independence settlement with Britain that
would allow early progress toward
majority rule. On November 11, 1965,
the Rhodesian government declared the
country independent. Britain and other
countries imposed economic sanctions

*Above: Baobab trees, native to tropical
Africa, are a feature of Messina in the
Transvaal, where they are protected.*

against Rhodesia, but failed to bring
down the government. In 1970 Rhodesia
declared itself a republic with a Senate
and House of Assembly, dominated by
Europeans.

Physical features and climate
Rhodesia consists mostly of a plateau,
called the *high veld*, averaging about
1,400m (4,593ft) above sea level. Lower
areas, the *low veld*, include the Zambezi
trough in the north and the Limpopo
lowlands in the south.

The tropical climate is moderated by
the altitude. Most areas have between
700 and 900mm (28–35 inches) of rain
per year, although the eastern highlands
are much wetter. Woodland savanna
covers much of Rhodesia.

Minerals
Mining contributes 6 percent of the gross
domestic product. The most valuable
mineral is asbestos. Coal, copper, chrome
and gold are also mined.

Industry and communications
Hydro-electricity from the Kariba Dam
is now the chief source of power for
manufacturing, which contributes 23
percent of the GDP. The chief manufacturing centres are Bulawayo and
Salisbury.

The chief artery of communications is
the Bulawayo-Salisbury railway. In 1976
Mozambique closed its railways and
ports to Rhodesia, leaving the country
with only two rail links to the sea. One
line runs through Botswana into South
Africa. The other line, opened in 1974,
runs directly into South Africa.

Agriculture
Agriculture accounts for 17 percent of
the GDP. Tobacco is the chief cash crop
and maize the main African subsistence
crop. Other products include citrus
fruits, sugar-cane and tea. Cattle farming
is also important. The country is divided
into African reserved areas (45.6 percent),
European reserved areas (45.6 percent)
and protected wildlife areas (8.8 percent).

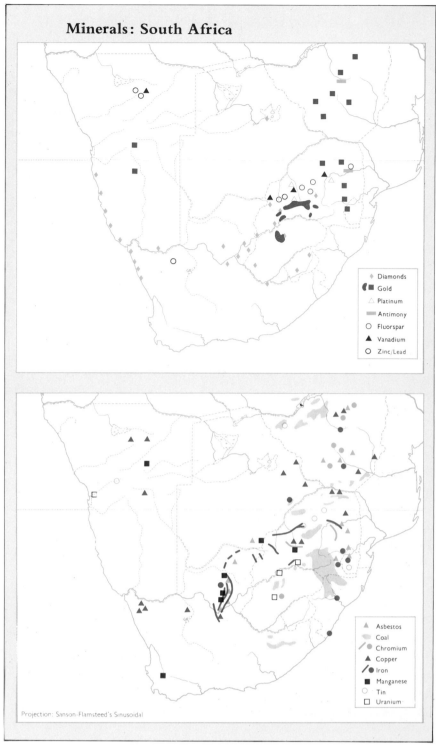

Minerals: South Africa

Diamonds
Gold
Platinum
Antimony
Fluorspar
Vanadium
Zinc/Lead

Asbestos
Coal
Chromium
Copper
Iron
Manganese
Tin
Uranium

Projection: Sanson-Flamsteed's Sinusoidal

South Africa

Area: *1,221,037km² (471,442sq.m.).*
Population: *25,071,000.* **Capitals:**
*Cape Town (1.1m.), Pretoria
(562,000).* **Largest city:**
Johannesburg (1.4m.). **Languages:**
*Afrikaans, English, Bantu and Asian
languages.* **Ethnic groups:** *Black
Africans, including Zulu and Xhosa
(70.2 percent), Europeans (17.5
percent), Coloureds (9.4 percent),
Asians (2.9 percent).* **Main exports:**
*cereals, diamonds, fissionable materials,
fruits, gold and other metals, iron and
steel, machinery and vehicles, maize,
textiles.* **Average temperatures:**
*Cape Town 13°C (55°C) July, 22°C
(71°F) Feb.; Johannesburg 10°C
(51°F) June, 21°C (69°F) Jan.*
Highest point: *Mont aux Sources
on Lesotho border, 3,299m (10,823ft).*

South Africa is the most developed and
industrialized nation in Africa. Its wealth
is based on its rich mineral resources and
its efficient farming. It produces uranium,
coal, gem diamonds, asbestos, copper
and about two-thirds of the world's new
gold.

People
Europeans account for 17.5 percent of the
population, but they control the government and the economy. About 65 percent
speak Afrikaans—a language derived
from Dutch. Most other Europeans
speak English.

The largest groups of Bantu-speaking
Black Africans are the Zulu (26.7 percent
of the total population) and the Xhosa
(25.9 percent). Under the policy of
separate development, formerly called
apartheid, the government has established
eight homelands, or Bantustans, for the
Bantu people. It intends to make these
homelands, which cover 13 percent of

South Africa, independent states by 1979.
But less than half of the Bantu people
live in the homelands. The rest work in
European areas.

Coloureds, people of mixed origin,
live mainly in Cape Province. Most are
unskilled labourers. Their interests are
represented by the Coloured Peoples'
Representative Council. The Asians live
mainly in Natal, where they are farmers,
traders or factory workers. The South
African Indian Council represents them.

History and constitution
The Dutch established the first European
settlement on the site of Cape Town in
1652. Gradually, settlers called *Boers*
(farmers) spread inland. From 1781 they
fought a series of wars against the Bantu
people.

Between 1795 and 1803, and again in
1806, the British ruled the Cape. Many
Afrikaners opposed British rule and, in
1835, they began the Great Trek which
led to the founding of Orange Free State
and the South African Republic (now the
Transvaal). The British and Afrikaners
fought wars in 1880–1881 and 1899–
1902, which Britain won. In 1910 the
Orange Free State, Transvaal, Cape
Province and Natal united to form the
Union of South Africa.

After World War I, South Africa was
mandated to govern German South-West
Africa (Namibia). From 1948 the
Afrikaner National party has formed the
government. Its racial policies have been
criticized by many countries. Under
pressure, South Africa withdrew from
the British Commonwealth in 1961 and
became a republic.

South Africa has a Senate and a House
of Assembly, all of whose members are
whites. The State President is elected for
seven-year terms.

Physical features and climate
South Africa consists mainly of a
plateau, more than 1,220m. (4,000ft)
above sea level, bordered by steep escarp-

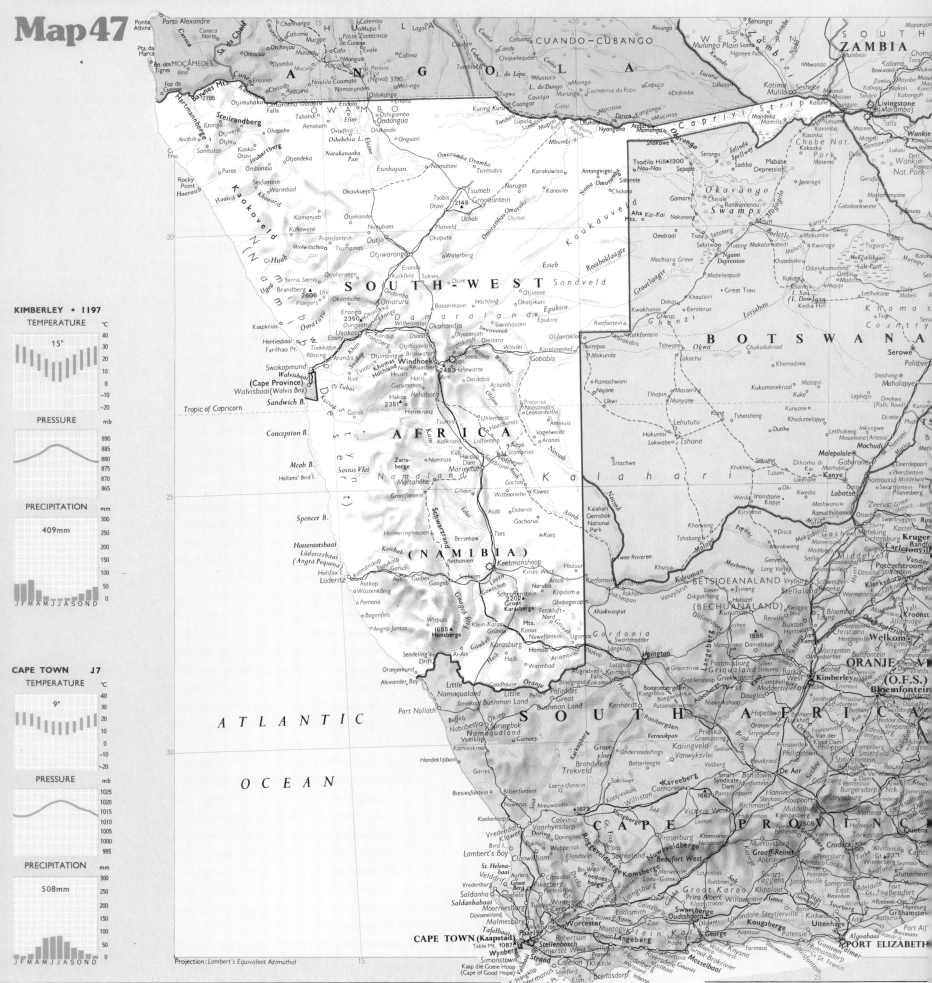

KIMBERLEY ★ 1197
TEMPERATURE °C
15°
PRESSURE mb
PRECIPITATION mm
409mm
J F M A M J J A S O N D

CAPE TOWN J7
TEMPERATURE °C
9°
PRESSURE mb
PRECIPITATION mm
508mm
J F M A M J J A S O N D

Projection: Lambert's Equivalent Azimuthal

ments, including the lofty Drakensberg. The chief rivers draining the plateau are the Orange and Limpopo systems. Around the plateau are mountain ranges and lower plateau.

The climate is mostly sub-tropical, but the altitude moderates temperatures. Parts of the interior suffer from frosts. Most of the country has less than 762mm. (30in.) of rain per year and half of South Africa is arid or semi-arid. The south-west Cape has a pleasant Mediterranean climate. Most African savanna animals flourish in protected areas, especially in the Kruger National Park.

Minerals
Gold, South Africa's most valuable mineral, is mined around Johannesburg and in Orange Free State. South Africa produces many other metals and diamonds. Important coal mines are in the Witwatersrand and in Natal.

Industry and communications
Manufacturing is the most valuable sector of the economy. The chief in-

dustrial centres are south Transvaal and the ports of Cape Town, Durban and Port Elizabeth.

Agriculture, forestry and fishing
Agriculture, forestry and fishing employ about 28 percent of the people. Pastoral farming, especially sheep and cattle, is extremely important. Arable farms cover only 5 percent of the land. Maize is the chief African subsistence crop. Cotton, fruits, groundnuts, sugar, tobacco and wines are major cash crops. Only about 1 percent of the land is forested, but forestry supplies most domestic requirements. Fishing is important off the west coast.

Trade and foreign relations
Despite political problems, South Africa is an important trading nation. Major trading partners include Britain and other EEC countries, the US and Japan. In the mid-1970s, South Africa was seeking détente with black Africa and it participated in attempts to solve the problem of Rhodesia. ■

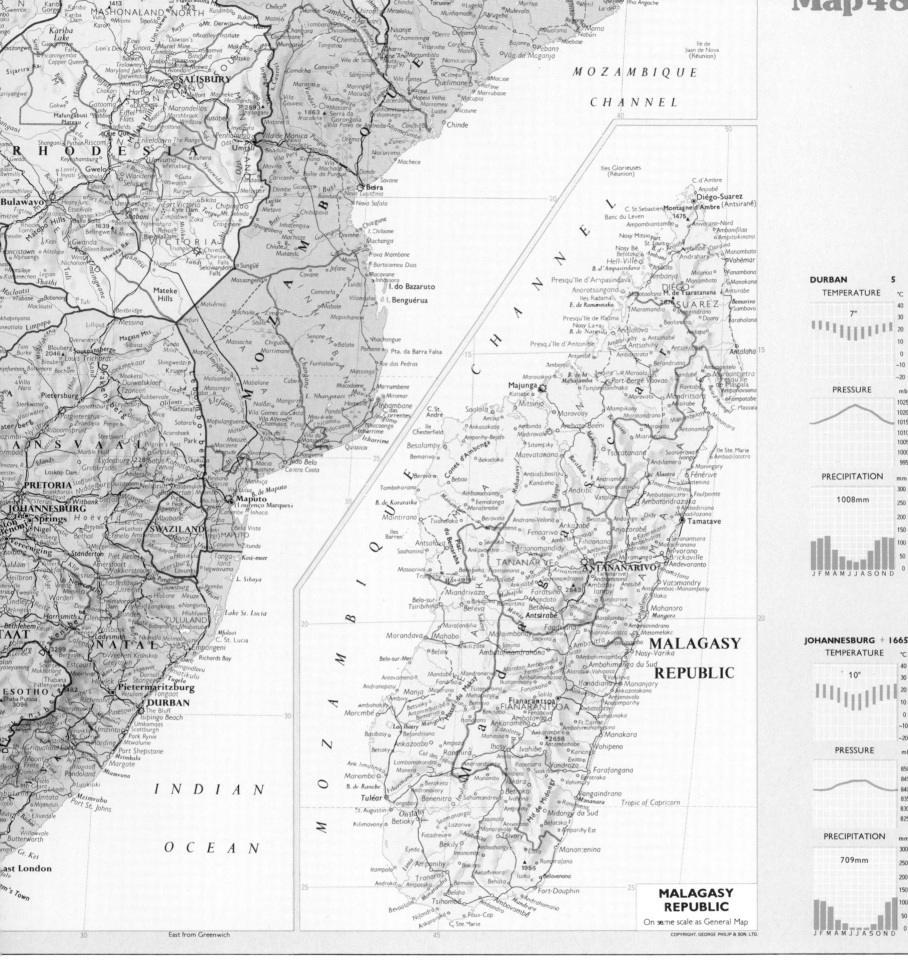

Map 48

Far left: Mine heaps outside Johannesburg recall the discovery of gold on the high Rand in 1886.

Left: Packing manioc or cassava roots in baskets, in Madagascar.

Malagasy Republic

Area: 587,041km² (226,657sq.m.). **Population:** 6,750,000. **Capital:** Tananarive (342,000). **Languages:** Malagasy, French. **Ethnic groups:** about 20, of which the Merina are the largest. **Main exports:** cloves, coffee, vanilla, sugar. **Average temperature:** 29°C (85°F) on coast, cooler highlands. **Highest point:** Mt Maromokotro, 2,876m (9,436ft).

The Malagasy Republic consists of Madagascar, the world's fourth largest island and some small islands. The central plateau of Madagascar divides the eastern forests from the western plains. The southwest is semi-arid. The country's economy is based on farming, but only four percent of the land is cultivated. Coffee is the chief cash crop.

People from Indonesia settled in Madagascar about 1,000 years ago. They mixed with people from mainland Africa and Arabs. The country was ruled by France between 1885 and 1960, when it became independent as a military republic. ∎

Mauritius

Mauritius, lying 800km (500 miles) east of Madagascar is a densely populated island republic within the Commonwealth with an area of 1,865km² (720sq.m.) and a population of 835,000, mainly Indian. Its warm, damp climate and volcanic soil are suited to sugar cane on which its economy is almost wholly dependent. ∎

107

Australia

Map 49

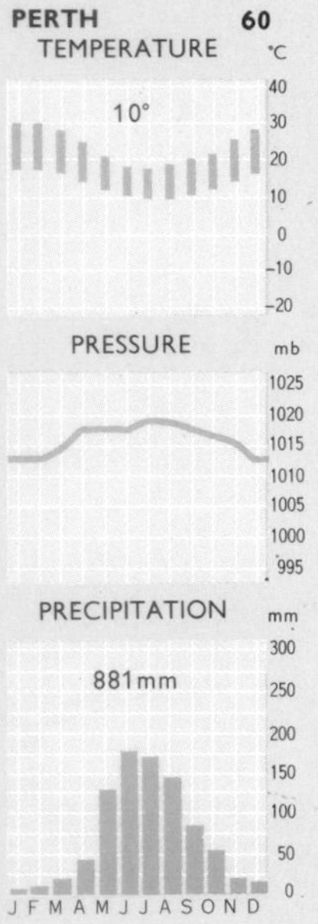

(Map of Western Australia and the Northern Territory with numerous place names, physical features, and two climate data panels for Perth and Darwin shown at left.)

PERTH **60**
TEMPERATURE °C
10°
PRESSURE mb
PRECIPITATION mm
881mm
J F M A M J J A S O N D

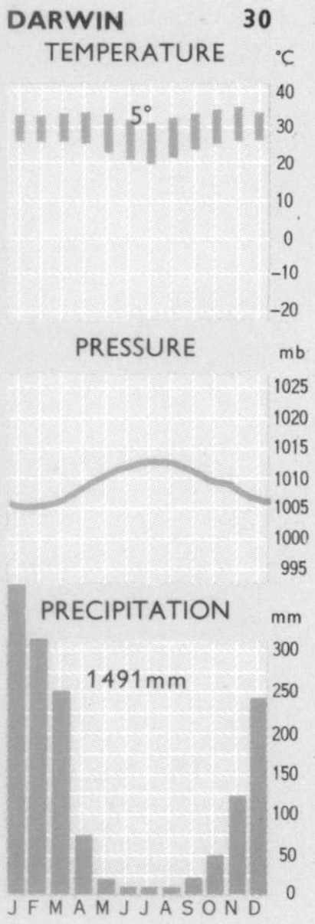

DARWIN **30**
TEMPERATURE °C
5°
PRESSURE mb
PRECIPITATION mm
1491mm
J F M A M J J A S O N D

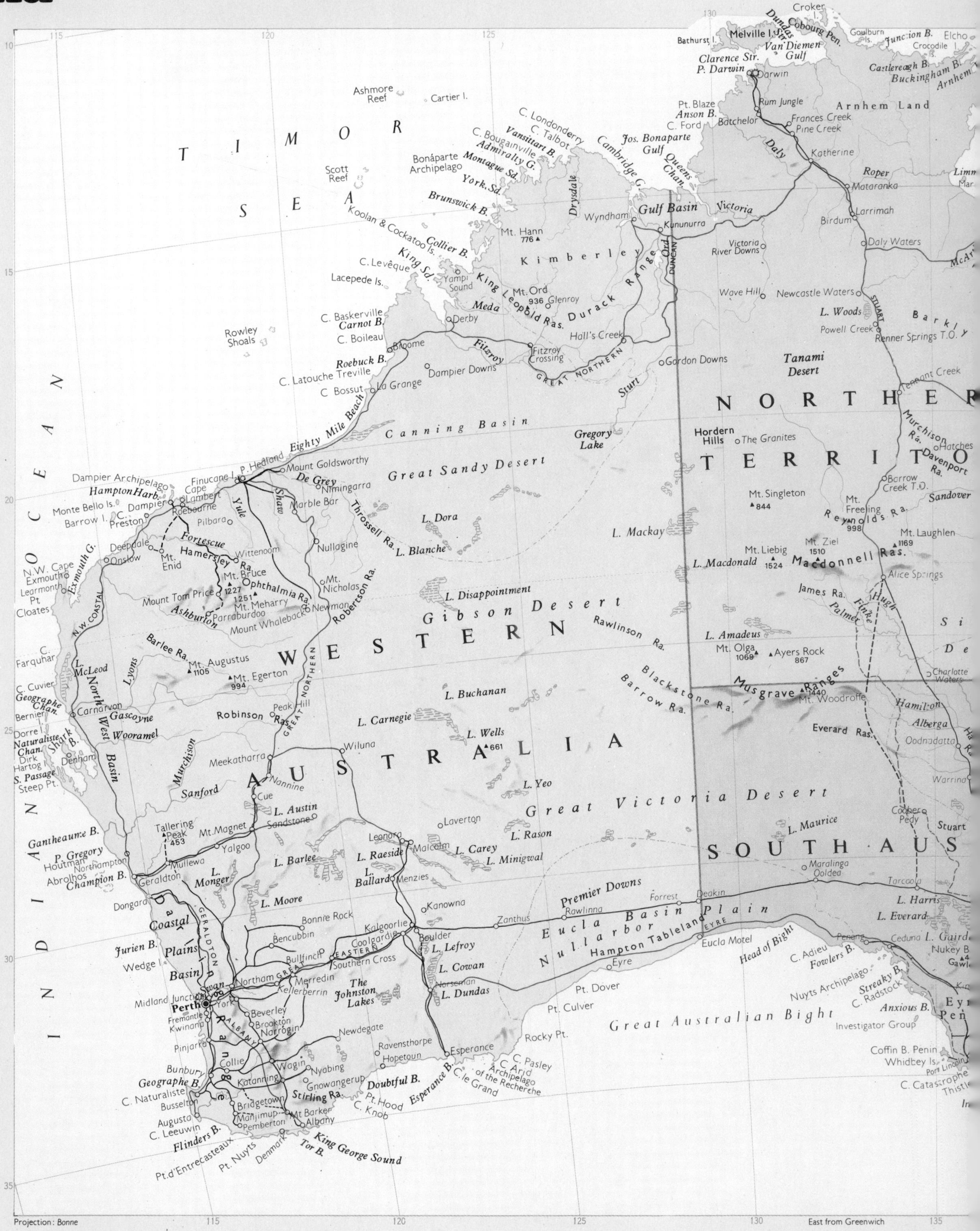

Projection: Bonne

East from Greenwich

Australia

Australia, the sixth biggest continental land mass in the world, is the driest and flattest of all and the only one occupied by a single nation. From the air, much of the interior looks like a featureless red shield, burnished by sun. Only a third of the land has adequate rainfall for agriculture, but with the help of irrigation and artesian bores, two-thirds of it is farmed. Australia is also rich in minerals.

The continent is ancient in formation. Physically, it is dominated by the arid Western Plateau. Broken by several major ranges in the west and centre, this plateau rises from the Indian Ocean to an average height of 300 metres (1,000ft) and slopes gradually eastward across two-thirds of the continent to the Central Lowlands which stretch from the Gulf of Carpentaria in the north to the Great Australian Bight in the south. From the sheep, cattle and wheat-growing country in the basin formed by the Murray River and its tributaries, the Eastern Highlands rise to the Great Dividing Range. Relatively low in Queensland, this long mountain chain reaches its greatest height in the Australian Alps and runs through Victoria to the southern island of Tasmania. East of the Great Dividing Range is a warm, moist, coastal strip.

Spanning 33 degrees of latitude (the equivalent of the distance from Panama to Montreal), Australia has a wide climatic range with temperatures as low as −23°C (−8°F) on record. But in the south the summers are generally warm and sunny, the winters mild and damp. In the tropical north, the summer brings heavy monsoon rains. Tasmania also has high rainfall. But two-thirds of the continent receives less than 50cm (20in) of rain annually and evaporation is rapid. Apart from desert and small areas of rain forest in the north, the characteristic vegetation is scrub, mainly eucalyptus (gum) and acacia (wattle) trees and grasses is adapted to dry conditions.

The Commonwealth of Australia

Area: 7,686,848km² (2,967,909sq.m.). **Population:** 13,780,000. **Capital:** Canberra (170,000). **Largest city:** Sydney (2.9 million). **Language:** English. **Ethnic groups:** British (80 percent), Italian, Greek, Aboriginal. **Main exports:** Iron ore, coal and other minerals, wool, beef, wheat, sugar, dairy products. **Average temperatures:** 26°C (78°F) Jan.; 16°C (62°F) July in Sydney; 32°C (90°F) Jan., 23°C (74°F) July in Darwin. **Highest point:** Mt Kosciusko 2,228m (7,310ft).

In the harsh, bright landscape of Australia, a predominantly Anglo-Saxon people have created in the past 200 years a nation with a sense of expansive destiny. Their country is as big as the entire Indian subcontinent but its wealth is shared by fewer than 14 million people. Like Americans in the nineteenth century, they are characteristically energetic, brashly optimistic and youthful. Half the population is aged under 25. Since 1945 rapid immigration (more than 3 million) and development of mineral resources have produced an affluent society.

Though half its immigrants still come from Britain the flavour of Australian life has been changed by an influx of large minorities from Italy, Greece, Central Europe, Holland, Poland and Turkey. There are about 140,000 Aborigines, most of them of mixed blood, but despite small numbers of Asians, Australia is overwhelmingly white. The outback (known as the 'bush') with its isolated farming stations linked by efficient airways and radio and television services and its dusty country towns with quiet verandahs has left an enduring mark of Australia's self-image.

Map 50

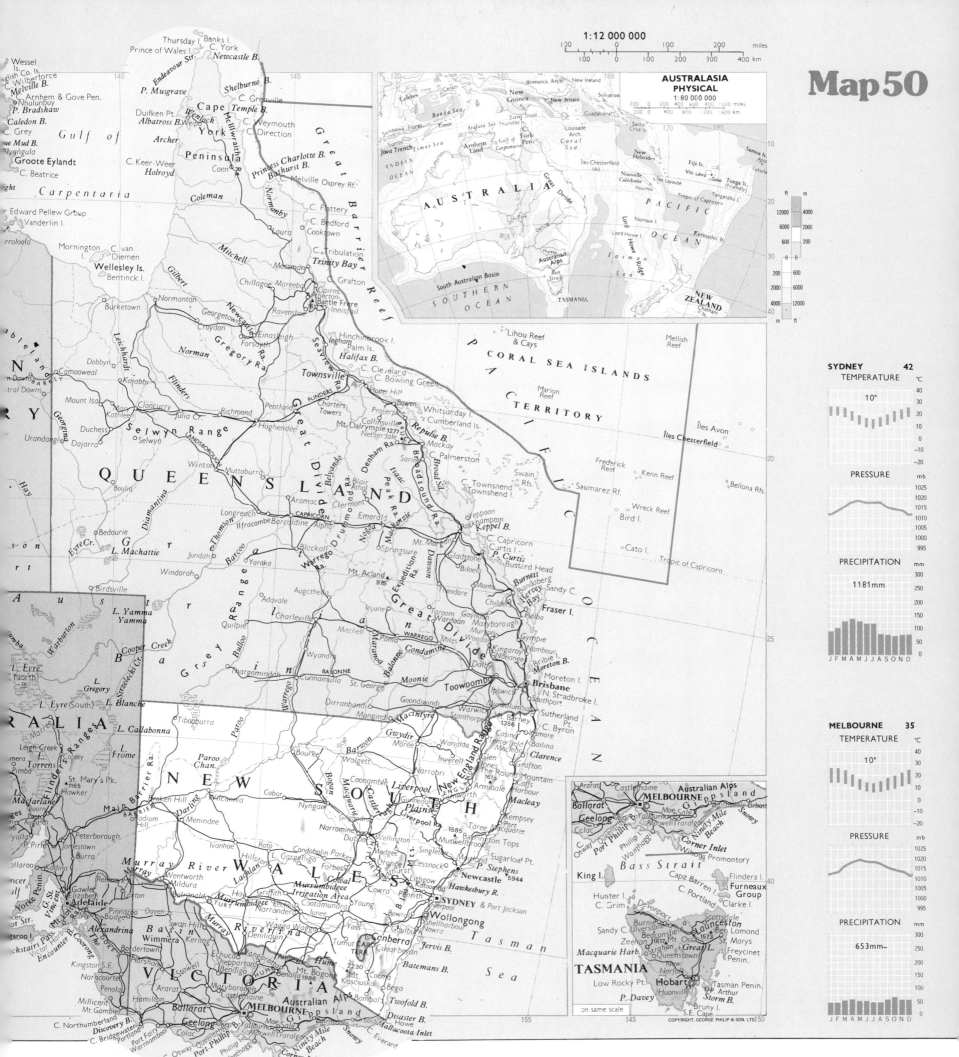

1:12 000 000

AUSTRALASIA PHYSICAL
1:80 000 000

SYDNEY 42
TEMPERATURE °C
PRESSURE mb
PRECIPITATION mm
1181mm
J F M A M J J A S O N D

MELBOURNE 35
TEMPERATURE °C
PRESSURE mb
PRECIPITATION mm
653mm
J F M A M J J A S O N D

But today most Australians live in cities with sprawling suburban bungalows of brick, wood and 'fibro' surrounding sophisticated urban centres.

Passionately addicted to horse-racing and the outdoor life, Australians are among the world's best athletes, excelling in swimming, tennis, sailing, cricket and a wide range of other sports. Despite a somewhat anti-intellectual ethos they have produced outstanding writers, painters, performing artists and scientists and have a well-developed education system, increasingly orientated towards technology. They are an informal, blunt, strongly egalitarian people with a rough-and-tumble tradition of political democracy.

History and constitution
The Commonwealth of Australia is a federation of six states and two territories. Until the late eighteenth century it was inhabited by mainly nomadic Aborigines who occupied it for several thousand years but developed no urban settlements. They numbered about 300,000 in 1770 when Captain James Cook claimed the island continent for Britain. A penal colony was established on the inhospitable shores of Port Jackson, near Sydney, in 1778 and free settlers from Britain began arriving also. From outposts in the south-west, settlement spread out slowly as explorers crossed the Great Dividing Range and penetrated the hinterland.

The discovery of gold in New South Wales and Victoria in the 1850s brought a wave of immigration. By 1859 there were six separate colonies including Queensland, South Australia, Western Australia and the island of Tasmania. Transport advances and the development of a strong pastoral economy based on

Right: Derwent Bridge, completed in 1965, spans the Derwent River which links Hobart with the sea.

the export of wool and meat to Britain led to the uniting of the six colonies in the independent Commonwealth of Australia in 1901.

In 1927, the capital was moved from Melbourne to Canberra where an administrative centre modelled on Washington D.C. was established on an empty plain midway between the rival cities of Melbourne and Sydney. The Federal Government administers both Australian Capital Territory (the Canberra area) and the huge but sparsely-settled Northern territory. A House of Representatives with 125 members and a 60-member Senate make up the Federal Parliament. The British monarch is the formal Head of State, represented by a Governor-General.

States and territories
Population is heavily concentrated in the south-east with about 40 percent of Australians living in Sydney and Melbourne. Estimated population distribution in 1975 was: New South Wales (4.9 million), Victoria (3.7 million), Queensland (1.9 million), South Australia (1.3 million), Western Australia (1.2 million), Tasmania (400,000), Australian Capital Territory (171,000), Northern Territory (80,000).

Sydney, capital of New South Wales, is a vibrant city built around a beautiful harbour set off by skyscrapers, the gleaming shells of its radically-designed Opera House and a steel suspension bridge 503 metres (1,650ft) long. It is the country's chief port and commercial centre as well as the focus of an industrial complex that includes the neighbouring cities of Newcastle and Woolongong. Victoria's capital, Melbourne (2.6 million) is a more urbane industrial city and the financial hub of the country. Australia's third largest city, Brisbane (920,000), capital of the holiday state of Queensland, is another major industrial city, as is Adelaide (875,000), capital of South Australia, a state that produces much of Australia's fine wine.

The biggest state is Western Australia with an area of 2,527,621km² (975,920sq. m.). But until the development of its vast mineral reserves in the 1960s it supported only a small population in the south-west corner. Its capital, Perth (750,000) with its adjoining port of Freemantle has two thirds of its population. An updated

Above: Ayers Rock is the main tourist attraction of Australia's 'Red Centre'.

single-gauge rail link to Sydney across a distance of nearly 4,000 kilometres was completed in 1970.

The smallest state, Tasmania, is an important fruit and horticultural and mineral-producing area with its capital in the port city of Hobart (159,000). The Northern Territory's administrative centre, Darwin (40,000) was devastated by a cyclone on Christmas Day, 1974. The service centre for its barren interior is the trim settlement of Alice Springs (11,500). Near it, at the geographical centre of the continent rise two remarkable sandstone outcrops, the monolith of Ayers Rock and the domes of Mt Olga.

Climate and water resources
Most areas of Australia have an average of eight hours of sunshine a day. Summer temperatures often climb to 38°C (100°F) in the hottest months which are January–February in the south and November–December in the north. Torrential rain falls in the tropical north in January–March, a season known as 'the Wet'. South of the Tropic of Capricorn, rain is relatively infrequent in summer. In Sydney, heat waves caused by hot, dry winds blowing off the land are periodically relieved by cooler winds blowing up the east coast from the south. Winters are mild and dry in the tropical north but depressions moving up from the south of the continent bring winter rain to most of Australia's cities and temperatures in Victoria and New South Wales fall to 10°C (50°F) or considerably lower in upland areas such as Canberra.

Some areas of Queensland and Tasmania get up to 450cm (180in) of rain a year but two-thirds of the continent must depend on irrigation or artesian water supplies. Though the plains bloom and creeks flow after rain, most of the rivers in the interior are usually dry. A feature of the interior is dry salt-encrusted lakes called playas such as Lake Eyre which covers a million square kilometres and is below sea level. Fortunately, Australia has the most extensive artesian reserves in the world. About a third of the continent is supplied by bores, 18,000 of them in the Great Artesian Basin which stretches from

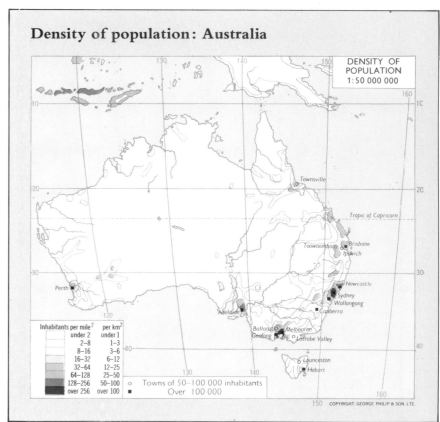

Density of population: Australia

DENSITY OF POPULATION 1:50 000 000

Inhabitants per mile²	per km²
under 2	under 1
2–8	1–3
8–16	3–6
16–32	6–12
32–64	12–25
64–128	25–50
128–256	50–100
over 256	over 100

o Towns of 50–100 000 inhabitants
■ Over 100 000

COPYRIGHT. GEORGE PHILIP & SON. LTD.

north central Queensland to South Australia.

Australia's main river system is the Murray and its major tributaries, the Darling and Murrumbidgie. The Murray rises in the Alps and flows to Encounter Bay near Adelaide. Its system is the basis of vast irrigation schemes in New South Wales, Victoria and South Australia. The Snowy Mountains Scheme, completed in 1972 at a cost of $A800 million, irrigates some 2,300km² and provides a hydro-electric generating capacity of nearly 4,000 megawatts. In Western Australia, the Ord River scheme in the Kimberleys will double the state's irrigated area.

Farming, forestry and fishing
Fewer than 20 percent of Australians live outside towns but it is the farms and farmers of the outback that give the nation its most distinctive character.

Scattered across the face of the continent are a quarter of a million farms and their production has always been the major source of the country's export earnings. Australia has about 165 million sheep producing a third of the world's wool. Its next most important product is wheat, two-thirds of it exported. Australia is also one of the world's leading exporters of beef and veal, exporting half its annual production. It has about 20 million beef cattle. Another four million dairy cattle produce half a million tonnes of dairy products. Some 8,000 sugar cane plantations in eastern Queensland and northern New South Wales produce 2.5 million tonnes of raw sugar a year. Fruit production ranges from the main crop, apples (23 million bushels) to a wide range of tropical fruits.

Most of Australia's farms are between 200 and 2,000 hectares (500 and 5,000

acres), but about 25,000 of them are bigger than this. In the Northern Territory, some cattle stations spread over immense areas of 400,000 hectares (1 million acres), carrying about 10,000 cattle. Outback sheep stations are also vast, averaging 20,000 hectares (50,000 acres) and each running about 6,000 sheep. Australia's hardy Merino breed with long fine wool makes up three quarters of the nation's flock.

The pastoral zone, which has most of Australia's big sheep and cattle stations, runs through central Queensland and New South Wales to South Australia. East and south of this is a wheat-sheep zone, with a similar zone in the western part of Western Australia. The high rainfall zone which carries most of Australia's dairy and mixed farms is found in Victoria and Tasmania, the eastern part of New South Wales and South Australia and the south-west of Western Australia.

Queensland is the main cattle state and New South Wales the chief wool state, followed by Western Australia. Much of the Western Plateau is too dry for farming. Outback farmers maintain a tenacious struggle against the ever-present threat of drought and the bush fires that often accompany it. Government support for farming is strong, with direct subsidies to dairy farmers and aid to other sectors.

Forestry is confined mainly to wetter areas of the east and south of the continent and Tasmania. Species of eucalyptus provide most of the country's needs for hardwood and paper but softwoods have to be imported. Radiata pine is being planted to overcome this. The fishing industry is confined mainly to meeting local needs with the biggest catch taken off Western Australia. In tropical waters, cultured pearls are grown.

Minerals and energy resources
The past 20 years have seen a major shift in Australia from a mainly pastoral economy to rapid industrial development. Iron ore and coal are the chief mineral exports. Australia is also the world's leading exporter of bauxite, fourth in production of lead and zinc and an important supplier of copper, nickel, manganese, tin and silver. Oil fields, mainly offshore, already produce three-quarters of the country's crude oil needs and iron and coal resources are the basis

Above: The soaring shells of the Sydney Opera House echo the many sails of the city's yachting fleet.

Right: Timber milling is an industry in some areas of the Australian bush, typically dominated by eucalyptus.

of a significant steel industry. Investment capital for the development of these resources has come mainly from the United States, Britain and Japan but Australia has recently adopted a policy of greater self-sufficiency, while continuing to offer tax concessions and other incentives for exploration.

Many of the most dramatic mineral finds of the past two decades have been made in Western Australia. Though Kalgoorlie has been a famous gold-producing centre since the discovery of its 'Golden Mile' in 1891, this state was for many years the least developed in the Commonwealth. Today it is the biggest exporter of iron ore (mainly to Japan) from vast deposits in the Hammersley and Ophthalmia ranges in the north-west of the state, feeding ports at Dampier and Port Hedland. Other important deposits are at Yampi Sound and Koolyanobbing. Iron is also mined in the Middleback Ranges in South Australia, Mt Bundy and Frances Creek in the Northern Territory and in north-west Tasmania around the Savage River. Two hectic booms in Australian mining shares during the late 1960s were set off by discoveries of nickel at Kambalda and elsewhere in central Western Australia.

Mining is also a major activity in the Northern Territory. Uranium deposits are being worked at Rum Jungle near Darwin and further north on the Gove peninsula, bauxite reserves are being opened up. Australia's vast bauxite deposits, notably at Weipa on Cape York Peninsula in Queensland and also in the Darling Ranges, Western Australia, supply an aluminium refinery at Gladstone and smelters at Kurri Kurri, Point Henry and Bell Bay (Tasmania) as well as a smelter at Bluff, New Zealand.

The most important copper deposits

Right: The Great Barrier Reef extends for about 2,000 kilometres along the north-eastern coast of Australia. This island is in the Capricorn group.

Natural vegetation: Australia

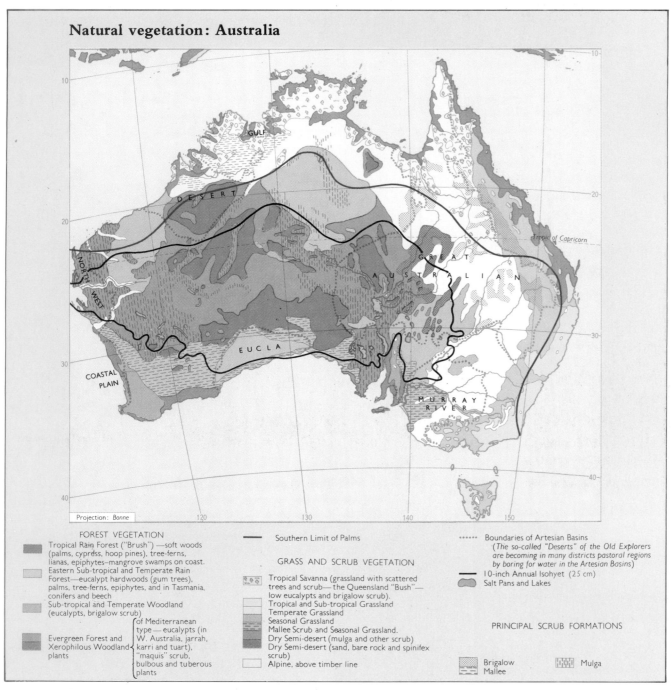

Projection: Bonne

FOREST VEGETATION

■ Tropical Rain Forest ("Brush")—soft woods (palms, cypress, hoop pines), tree-ferns, lianas, epiphytes–mangrove swamps on coast.

Eastern Sub-tropical and Temperate Rain Forest—eucalypt hardwoods (gum trees), palms, tree-ferns, epiphytes, and in Tasmania, conifers and beech

Sub-tropical and Temperate Woodland (eucalypts, brigalow scrub)

Evergreen Forest and Xerophilous Woodland plants {of Mediterranean type — eucalypts (in W. Australia, jarrah, karri and tuart), "maquis" scrub, bulbous and tuberous plants

—— Southern Limit of Palms

GRASS AND SCRUB VEGETATION

Tropical Savanna (grassland with scattered trees and scrub— the Queensland "Bush"— low eucalypts and brigalow scrub).

Tropical and Sub-tropical Grassland

Temperate Grassland

Seasonal Grassland

Mallee Scrub and Seasonal Grassland.

Dry Semi-desert (mulga and other scrub)

Dry Semi-desert (sand, bare rock and spinifex scrub)

Alpine, above timber line

•••••• Boundaries of Artesian Basins
(The so-called "Deserts" of the Old Explorers are becoming in many districts pastoral regions by boring for water in the Artesian Basins)

—— 10-inch Annual Isohyet (25 cm)

Salt Pans and Lakes

PRINCIPAL SCRUB FORMATIONS

Brigalow Mallee   Mulga

---

are at Mt Isa and Mt Morgan in Queensland and Cobar, New South Wales. Mt Isa is also a major producer of lead and zinc, together with the long-established mining centre of Broken Hill in the west of New South Wales, which also produces silver.

Though Western Australia is developing oil and natural gas fields at Barrow Island and Dongara, Australia's major energy resources lie in the east. Queensland's Moonie field was opened in 1961 and natural gas from the same sedimentary basin is piped to Brisbane. Adelaide is supplied with natural gas

from fields at Moomba and Gidgealpa. The most significant reserves of oil are offshore in the Bass Straight south of Victoria which processes the oil at Dutson. Most of Australia's power comes from coal-based thermal plants, though hydro-electricity is being developed, especially in Tasmania and New South Wales where a nuclear energy station has also been built.

Industry and trade
Australia has become a highly industrialized country with about a quarter of its work force engaged in manufacturing. Disruption of normal trade during World

War II stimulated rapid expansion of manufacturing and there are now nearly 40,000 factories. Industrial development has been based mainly on the coal deposits of the east. Victoria recovers brown coal by open-cast methods in the Latrobe Valley while both New South Wales and Queensland have large reserves of black coal. These, together with iron ores supply a steel industry managed by the Broken Hill Proprietary Company and its subsidiaries. A thriving automobile industry, largely overseas-owned produces upwards of 350,000 vehicles a year, including well-known Australian

models such as the Holden. This and a growing ship-building industry are supplied by steelworks at Port Kembla and Newcastle near Sydney, Whyalla in South Australia and Kwinana near Freemantle. Chemical, petro-chemical and textile industries are also based on local resources. Other important industries are engineering, foodstuffs and paper.

Exports of manufactured goods make up only a quarter of overseas earnings, however. Australia has the twelfth biggest volume of trade in the world. Until the early 1970s, farm products, chiefly wool, wheat and meat, accounted for more than half its export income But by 1975 with huge contracts for supplying iron ore and coking coal, exports of ores and refined metals were becoming increasingly significant earners. Australia's main customers are Japan for minerals and wool, the United States for meat and Britain for a wide range of products.

Australia's main imports are heavy machinery, transport equipment and textiles. The United States is the main supplier, followed by Britain, Japan, West Germany and Canada. Many home industries are protected by high tariffs. Trade with New Zealand is facilitated by the Australia–New Zealand Free Trade Agreement (Nafta). New Zealand is an important market for Australian cars and other manufactures and in return sells Australia pulp and paper.

External relations and territories
Australia is a member of the Commonwealth and its traditional links with Britain remain strong. But since 1945 it has turned increasingly towards the United States, its major ally in the 1951 ANZUS defence treaty. It is active diplomatically in the Pacific and South-East Asia, maintaining close relations with its largest neighbour, Indonesia and with its major trading partner, Japan. Australia governs several islands in the Indian Ocean: Christmas Island, which supplies phosphate, Cocos (Keeling) Island and the Heard and McDonald islands. Two Australian islands in the Tasman Sea are mainly tourist resorts: Norfolk Island (pop. 2,400) a former penal colony later settled by descendants of the Bounty mutineers, and coral ringed Lord Howe Island. Australia also administered Papua New Guinea until its independence in 1975. ■

Papua New Guinea

Area: 475,300km² (183,450sq.m.).
Population: 2.5 million. **Capital:** Port Moresby (67,000). **Languages:** English, pidgin, 700 tribal dialects.
Ethnic groups: Melanesian, Papuan, Negrito, Asian, European. **Main exports:** Copper, copra, coffee, cocoa, timber, rubber, gold. **Average temperature:** 27°C (80°F) in lowlands. **Highest point:** Mt Wilhelm 4,500m (14,762ft).

The new nation of Papua New Guinea, independent since 1975, comprises the eastern half of the large island of New Guinea, the major islands of New Britain in the Bismarck Archipelago and Bougainville in the Solomons and several smaller volcanic or coral islands. Formerly administered by Australia, the parliamentary government has resisted secession moves by Bougainville whose copper mine at Panguna is becoming the major revenue earner.

Predominantly hot, humid and wet, with mangrove swamps and coastal plains rising to tropical forests in the jagged Bismarck and Owen Stanley ranges, the main island of New Guinea has areas that were explored only recently and remnants of Stone Age head-hunting tribal cultures exist. Outside of the European-run cash crop plantations, mainly in the south-east and on New Britain, most of the people subsist on crops such as sago, yams and taro with pigs and poultry.

Left: Rugged terrain, here in the Eastern Highlands of Papua New Guinea, has led to cultural diversity.

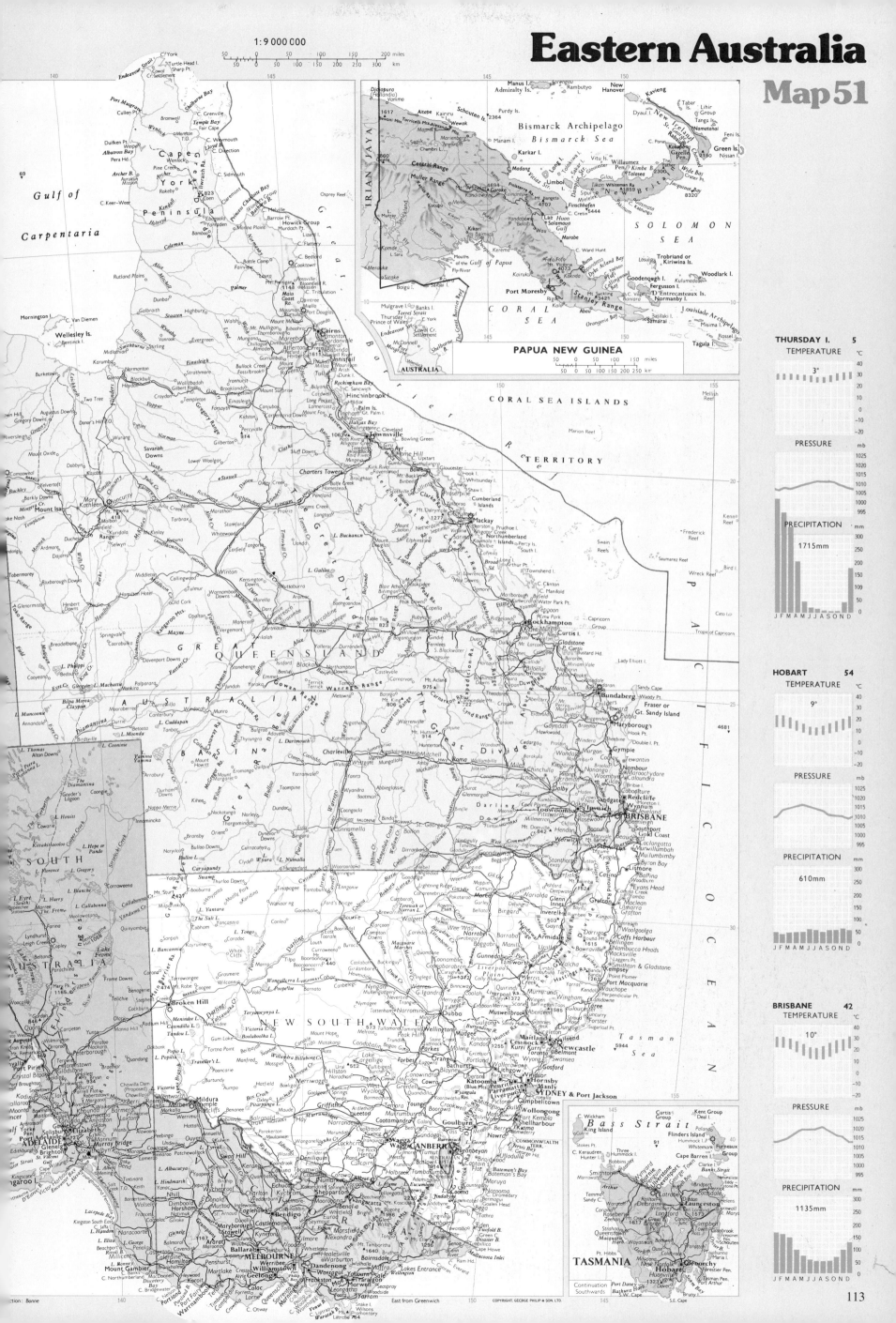

1 : 9 000 000

PAPUA NEW GUINEA

AUSTRALIA

TASMANIA

THURSDAY I.   5
TEMPERATURE   °C
3°
PRESSURE   mb
PRECIPITATION   mm
1715mm
J F M A M J J A S O N D

HOBART   54
TEMPERATURE   °C
9°
PRESSURE   mb
PRECIPITATION   mm
610mm
J F M A M J J A S O N D

BRISBANE   42
TEMPERATURE   °C
10°
PRESSURE   mb
PRECIPITATION   mm
1135mm
J F M A M J J A S O N D

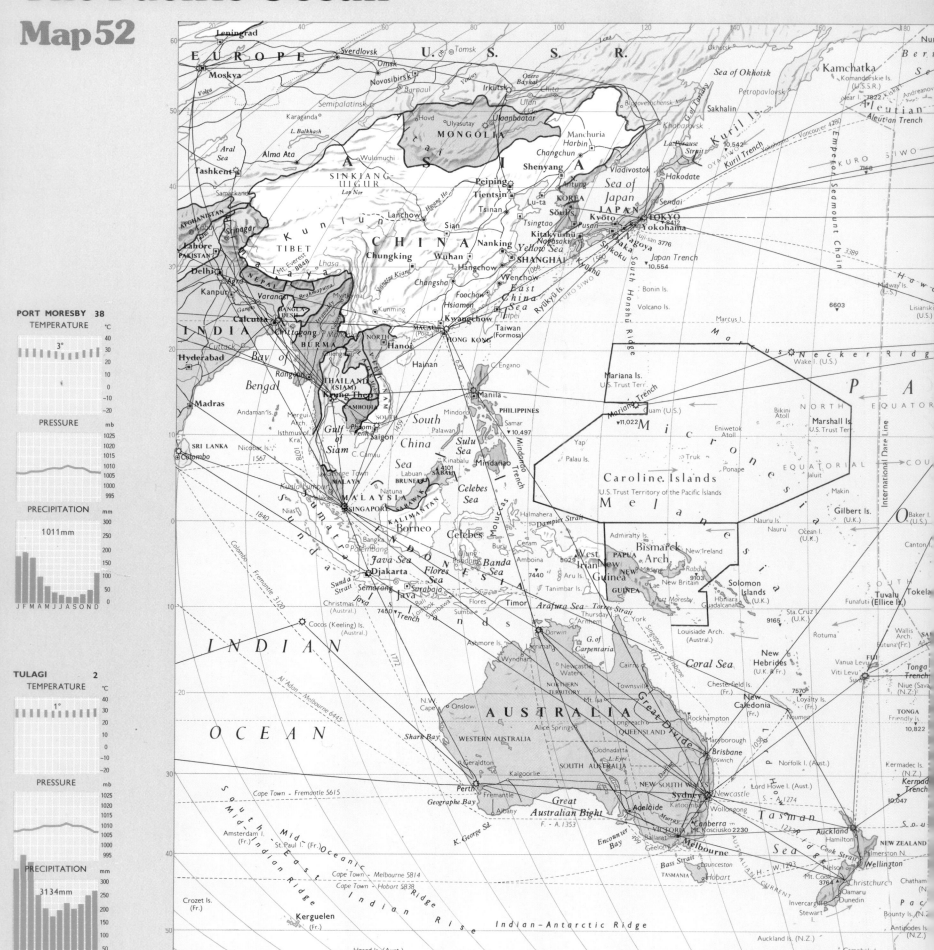

The Pacific Ocean

The Pacific has upwards of 20,000 islands but only two groups with substantial land areas and populations—New Zealand and the newly independent nation of Papua New Guinea (discussed in the section on Australia). Some 3.5 million people are distributed through the other islands of Polynesia, stretching up to the US state of Hawaii, Melanesia (from New Guinea to Fiji) and Micronesia in the western Pacific. Oceania was explored in detail only in the 18th century.

The Pacific is the greatest of the world's oceans, with an area vast enough to accommodate all the oceans. It can belie its name with devastating winds. In the sub-tropics, westerlies prevail, while in the tropics steadier trade winds blow from the east, cooling both sides of the equator. Many coral-fringed atolls may be remnants of off-shore reefs built up around volcanic islands.

Polynesia, Melanesia and Micronesia

Ever since Cook and other mariners charted them, the tropical islands of Polynesia, Melanesia and Micronesia have been romanticized by Europeans enchanted by their palm-fringed beaches and simple village-based societies. Tourism is now an important local industry, especially in Polynesia. Although much of the Pacific is part of the developing world with increasing migration to towns, the economics of most islands are still based on fishing and the farming of root crops, fruit, corn, coconuts, pigs and chickens.

The peoples of Oceania probably originated in Asia. They speak a variety of Malayo–Polynesian tongues, although English is the common language (simplified to Pidgin in Melanesia) and French is spoken in the New Hebrides, New Caledonia and French Polynesia. The Polynesians are taller and lighter skinned than Micronesians, who have some Asian features. Melanesians are shorter (except in Fiji) and darker, with more Negroid characteristics.

In the tropics, average temperatures on the islands range between 21–27°C (70–80°F). There is a wet season from December to March in Polynesia and Melanesia. The bigger islands are of a high volcanic type but most are low-lying atolls with coral reefs.

Hawaii, with an area of 16,705km² (6,450sq.m.) has the biggest population (828,000) and capital, Honolulu (600,000). A tourist and food-processing centre, it became the 50th state of the United States in 1959, is a major defence base and has ship-building and oil processing industries. The population is a mixture of American (40 percent), Japanese (30 percent), Polynesian (15 percent), Filipino and Chinese and is concentrated on Oahu. Hawaii itself is the largest of 132 islands in the group and has a famous active volcano, Mauna Loa 4,170m (13,680ft).

The US also administers **American Samoa** (34,000), **Guam** (100,000), the most important of several strategic island bases, and the **UN Trust Territory of the Pacific,** comprising the Micronesian groups of the Carolines, Marshalls and Marianas.

Fiji, with an area of 18,272km² (7,055sq.m.) and a population of 580,000, is the only Pacific nation with an Indian majority. A British colony until 1970, it is now an independent democracy with a capital at Suva (63,000). Fiji is an important producer of sugar and copra and has a gold mine at Vatukoula and lesser deposits of manganese, silver and copper. Land ownership is mainly in the hands of the Fijians who are slightly outnumbered by the Indian community.

The **New Hebrides** (population 98,000), with a port at Vila (12,000) are ruled jointly by Britain and France.

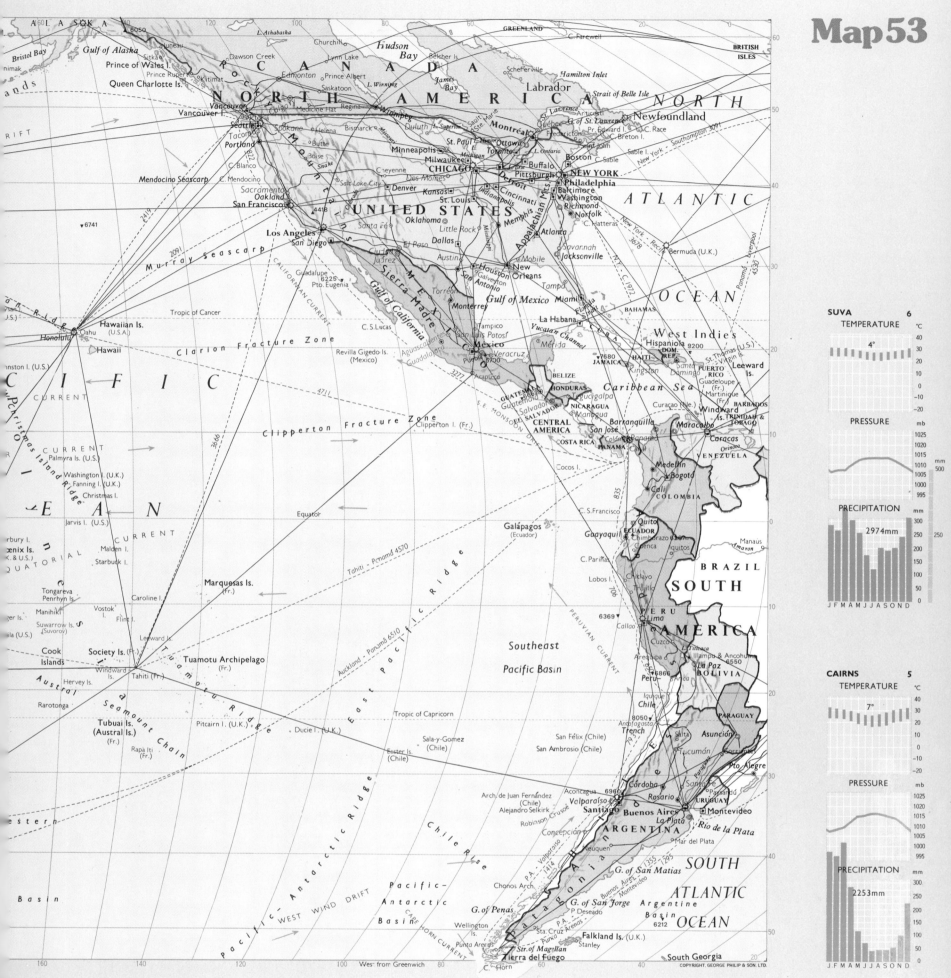

Britain also administers the **British Solomons** protectorate (181,000), the **Gilbert and Ellice Islands** (64,000), now moving towards independence, and the tiny colony of **Pitcairn,** famous as the hiding place of the Bounty mutineers. Southeast of Pitcairn lies **Easter Island,** an isolated Chilean dependency whose massive statues carved in volcanic rock are an archaeological mystery.

New Caledonia has significant mineral deposits, chiefly nickel, chrome and iron. An overseas territory of France, it has an area of 18,997km² (7,335sq.m.) and a population of 120,000 with a capital at Noumea (51,000). About half the population is Melanesian.

The tourist hub and centre of French influence in the Pacific is Papeete (80,000), capital of Tahiti in **French Polynesia** (120,000) which comprises the Society, Marquesas and Tubai Islands

Right: Surf breaks on a distant reef beyond a calm lagoon in Tahiti.

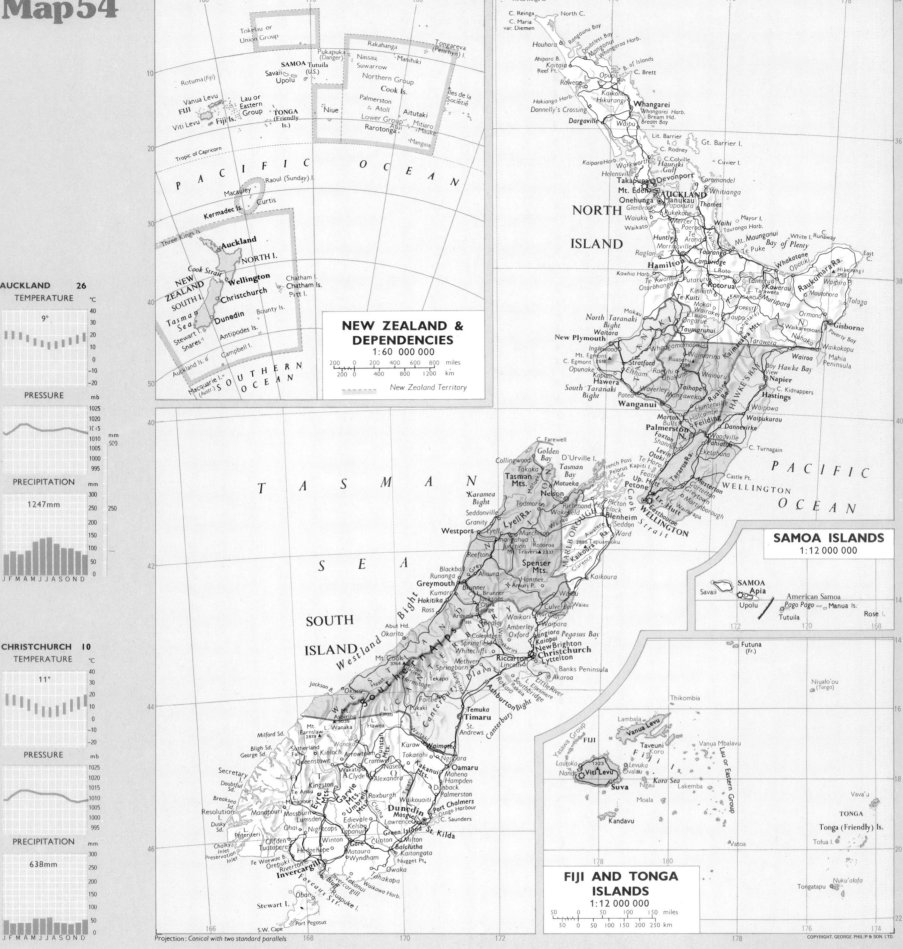

1:6 000 000

NEW ZEALAND & DEPENDENCIES
1:60 000 000
New Zealand Territory

SAMOA ISLANDS
1:12 000 000

FIJI AND TONGA ISLANDS
1:12 000 000

Projection: Conical with two standard parallels

COPYRIGHT. GEORGE PHILIP & SON. LTD.

AUCKLAND 26
TEMPERATURE °C
9°
PRESSURE mb
PRECIPITATION mm
1247mm

CHRISTCHURCH 10
TEMPERATURE °C
11°
PRESSURE mb
PRECIPITATION mm
638mm

and the Tuamotu Archipelago. Like the **Wallis and Futuna Islands,** this is also an overseas territory of France and French atomic tests are carried out in the Tuamotu group.

Western Samoa (160,000), with a capital at Apia, became the first independent Polynesian democracy in 1962 under the guidance of New Zealand which held a UN Trusteeship. It exports copra, bananas and cacao.

Tonga (103,000), a former British protectorate, is an independent Polynesian kingdom which exports copra and bananas.

Nauru (8,000), a tiny independent Micronesian island, has become rich through vast deposits of phosphate, also mined on Ocean Island, and shipped for fertilizer to Australia, New Zealand and Japan. ■

Right: New Zealand's capital, Wellington, is built on steep hills enclosing a fine harbour.

New Zealand

Area: *268,676km² (103,736sq.m.)*
Population: *3.1 million.* **Capital:**
Wellington (347,000). **Largest city:**
Auckland (780,000). **Languages:**
English, Maori. **Ethnic groups:**
British, Polynesian (250,000). **Main
exports:** *Dairy produce, wool, meat,
forest products.* **Average
temperatures:** *23°C (73°F) Jan.
8°C (46°F) July in Auckland but
cooler in south.* **Highest point:** *Mt
Cook 3,764m (12,349ft).*

New Zealand is the largest and most
prosperous island nation in the South
Pacific. Its people are predominantly
British but there is a high rate of intermarriage with a Maori minority, now
approaching 10 percent of the population.
A temperate climate and the application
of scientific farming methods to some of
the world's best grasslands have produced
a strong agricultural economy supported
by a wide range of manufacturing
industries and an expanding industrial
sector. In spite of its remoteness from its
major markets, New Zealand manages
to maintain full employment and a high
standard of living.. With a land area
slightly bigger than the United Kingdom's, but with a population of barely
three million, it also provides its people
with an unmatched opportunity to enjoy
landscapes and seascapes of striking
beauty.

History, constitution and people
New Zealand is one of the world's
youngest countries, historically as well as
geologically. Polynesian mariners covering immense distances in open canoes
reached the 'Land of the Long White
Cloud' from the Society Islands about
the tenth century and settled it by purposeful migration in the thirteenth
century. They found a land of forests
and birds whose only mammals were
two species of bats. European discovery
by Abel Tasman in 1642 was not followed
up until after Captain James Cook
charted the coasts in 1769. Settlement by
whalers, sealers and missionaries was
followed by Maori acceptance of British
sovereignty in the Treaty of Waitangi,
1840.

Largely self-governing from the 1860s,
New Zealand pioneered much social
legislation, including the earliest votes for
women in 1893. The country became an
independent dominion in 1907 and is a
unicameral parliamentary democracy
within the Commonwealth of Nations.
The British monarch is the nominal Head
of State represented by a Governor-
General. Close cultural and trade links
are retained with Britain, which remains
the major source of immigration. Including Pacific Islanders, the Polynesian
population numbers about 250,000, is
strongly concentrated in Auckland and is
well integrated into a multi-racial society.
There are minorities of Yugoslav, Dutch,
Chinese and Indian origin. Influenced by
their isolation, New Zealanders tend to
be undemonstrative, self-reliant and
egalitarian, proud of their sporting record
and their excellent health, educational
and social services.

Physical features and climate
New Zealand lies 1,930 kilometres
(1,200 miles) east of Australia. Its two
main islands are divided by the narrow
Cook Strait and are predominantly hilly
in the north and mountainous in the
south. The furthest inland point is only
130km (80 miles) from the sea.

In the North Island, the rolling
northern peninsula widens south of
Auckland into the Waikato basin. Both
regions carry hill and lowland farms,
orchards and forests. In the centre of the
island a denuded pumice plateau with
thermal springs surrounds several active
volcanoes, the highest Mt Ruapehu
2,797m (9,175ft). The eastern ranges
extend to the capital, Wellington, with
mainly sheep country on the east and
dairying predominating on the west.

The larger South Island is dominated
by the Southern Alps which soar to
permanent snowfields in the centre of

Above: The lonely grandeur of this scene is typical of long stretches of coastline on the West Coast of the South Island.

Above: Wairakei geothermal power station (second in the world) taps high-pressure steam from a thermal area near Lake Taupo.

the island, feeding a series of deep lakes
and major rivers including the Rakaia,
Waitaki and Clutha. Dense forests on the
west extend into the granite mountains
and deeply indented coastline of Fiord-
land. To the east lie the sheeplands and
grain-growing region of the Canterbury
Plains. South of this, the rolling Otago
Plateau extends to another rich pastoral
area in Southland. Stewart Island with a
small fishing settlement lies across
Foveaux Strait.

The climate is generally mild and
moist. Except inland, where summers are
hot and dry and the winters frosty, most
areas are tempered by sea breezes. These
become blustery around Wellington.
Pressure ridges move usually from east to
west, bringing high rainfall to some
southwestern areas but moderate falls
elsewhere.

The vegetation is mainly evergreen,
with beech and native fern in upland
areas. In addition to its beaches and
national parks, scenic grandeurs such as

the 580m (1,904ft) Sutherland Falls and
remnants of giant kauri forests, New
Zealand's introduced wildlife, including
deer, pigs, trout and salmon, make it
attractive to sporting tourists.

Agriculture, forestry and fishing
New Zealand's prosperity is based on its
earnings from grasslands which are often
fertilized by aerial top-dressing and
which carry nearly 60 million sheep and
nine million cattle. Although only a third
of the land is farmed, sheep flocks produce more than 300 million tonnes of
wool a year and provide a dual income
through the production of fat lambs and
mutton. The best sheep country is in
Canterbury and Southland in the South
Island and in Manawatu, Hawkes Bay
and South Auckland in the North Island.
Some high country sheep farms in Otago
and Canterbury cover 20,000 hectares
(50,000 acres) each, but the average is
about 450 hectares (1,125 acres).

A highly efficient dairy industry,
organized on cooperative lines, produces

export earnings that rival those of meat.
Butter and cheese head a wide range of
products. The richest dairy farms are in
the North Island, particularly Taranaki,
the Waikato, the Hauraki Plains and the
Bay of Plenty. There are four million
dairy cattle and another five million beef
cattle. Wheat, barley, corn and sugar beet
are grown, chiefly in the South Island.
Fruit production is also important, with
apples and pears from Nelson and
Hawkes Bay providing the main export
crops. Central Otago, Gisborne and
Northland are other fruit-growing areas.
New Zealand's improving white wines
come mainly from Auckland and Hawkes
Bay.

A third of the country is forested and
large plantations of exotic radiata pine,
chiefly in the Rotorua–Bay of Plenty
area, are the basis of a pulp and paper
industry that provides New Zealand's
only major manufactured exports. More
than 1.7 million cubic metres of timber
are cut annually. Fishing is under-

developed but a range of seafood delicacies include crayfish tails packed for export.

Minerals, industry, trade and territories

Despite their agricultural economy, most New Zealanders live in towns and work in secondary or service industries. Under import and tariff protection, a range of small-scale manufacturing has been fostered with strong electrical, transport, woodworking, machinery, textiles, chemicals and plastics sectors in addition to the major freezing and food-processing sector. Industry is heavily concentrated around Auckland with its fine gulf port. Christchurch, with a port at Lyttleton and Lower Hutt with a port at Wellington are also important. There are specialist ports, at Tauranga and Whangarei.

Mineral resources are scarce, apart from several coal deposits, mainly in the Waikato and Westland, natural gas at Kapuni and an offshore field in Taranaki. But an iron and steel industry at Glenbrook near Auckland is based on rich ironsands on the west coast of the North Island. Cheap hydro-electricity from the

Above: In the North Island, many sheep farms have been improved by skilful spreading of fertilizer by air.

Right: Ferns proliferate in the magnificent New Zealand bush and the silver fern, is a national emblem.

southern lakes provides power for an aluminium smelter at Bluff using Australian bauxite. Hydro-electricity from the Waikato, Clutha and Waitaki rivers is the main source of energy. There is a geothermal field at Wairakei.

New Zealand's trade in agricultural products, sold mainly to Britain and the US, earns nearly 90 percent of export income. Major imports are heavy machinery and transport equipment, metals, fuels, chemicals and textiles. Air New Zealand flies the Pacific and there is an extensive network of internal airways. New Zealand administers Niue and the Tokelau islands and handles defence and foreign affairs for the Cook Islands, a self-governing territory with a population of 29,000 which, like New Zealand itself, is rapidly expanding its tourist industry. ■

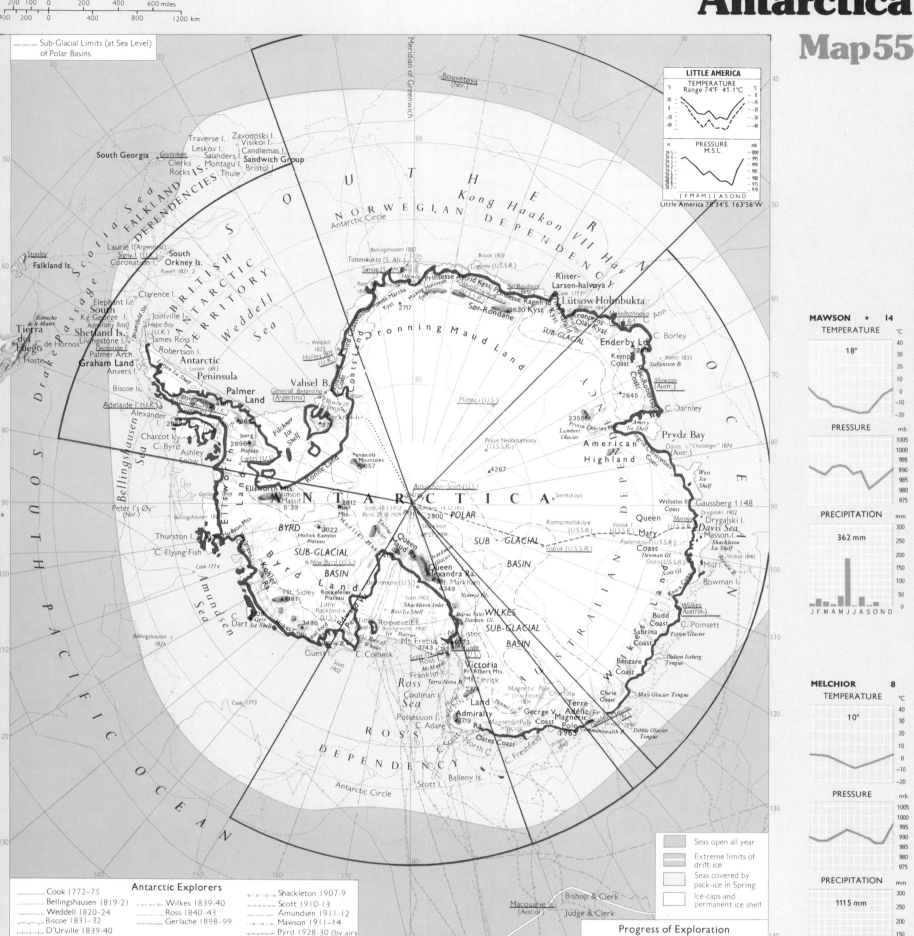

Scale 1:35 000 000

Sub-Glacial Limits (at Sea Level) of Polar Basins

LITTLE AMERICA
TEMPERATURE Range 74°F 41.1°C
PRESSURE M.S.L.
J F M A M J J A S O N D
Little America 78°34'S. 163°56'W

MAWSON ★ 14
TEMPERATURE 18°
PRESSURE
PRECIPITATION 362 mm
J F M A M J J A S O N D

MELCHIOR 8
TEMPERATURE 10°
PRESSURE
PRECIPITATION 1115 mm
J F M A M J J A S O N D

Seas open all year
Extreme limits of drift-ice
Seas covered by pack-ice in Spring
Ice-caps and permanent ice shelf

Antarctic Explorers
Cook 1772–75
Bellingshausen 1819–21
Weddell 1820–24
Biscoe 1831–32
D'Urville 1839–40
Byrd (U.S. Antarctic Service) 1939–41,1946–47(bases, Stonington I. & Little America)
Trans-Antarctic Route 1958
Wilkes 1839–40
Ross 1840–43
Gerlache 1898–99
Shackleton 1907–9
Scott 1910–13
Amundsen 1911–12
Mawson 1911–14
Byrd 1928–30 (by air)
Soviet Expedition 1959
Scott (N.Z.) Permanent Bases

Progress of Exploration
Coasts explored between 1800 & 1850
" " since 1900
+ Byrd 1926 Highest latitudes reached by explorers with date

COPYRIGHT. GEORGE PHILIP & SON. LTD.

Antarctica

Antarctica is the fifth largest continent in the world and the coldest and bleakest of all the land masses. Its area of 13,200,000km² (5,100,000sq.m.) is extended in midwinter (June) by pack ice stretching out for several hundred kilometres. A temperature of −88.3°C (−126.9°F) was registered near the South Pole—the lowest ever recorded. Although fossil plants indicate that vegetation once grew, the continent is now a desolate land, locked in ice and swept by freezing winds. Coastal areas warm up in summer but temperatures remain below freezing point.

Glaciers grind down long valleys from the Transantarctic Mountains which divide the continent into East Antarctica, facing the Indian Ocean and Africa, and West Antarctica, facing the Pacific. These mountains extend along the Antarctic Peninsula and rise to a high point of 5,140m (16,846ft) in the Vinson Massif.

Much of East Antarctica is a high plateau, more than 1,800m (6,000ft) above sea level, consisting of ancient rock covered by ice up to 2,700m (9,000ft) thick. In West Antarctica the icecap is even thicker —up to 4,270m (14,000ft) and there are two immense bays, the Ross Sea and the Weddell Sea.

The coasts are rich in sea life and the region's only significant, but declining, industry is whaling, carried on by Norway, Japan and other nations. East Antarctica has coal deposits and possibly oil and gas. Territorial claims to parts of Antarctica by Argentina, Australia, Britain, Chile, France, Norway and New Zealand have been deferred until 1989. Russia and the US are also active in the region and the US maintains four permanent stations in Operation Deep Freeze (supplied from Christchurch, New Zealand). At McMurdo Sound near the active volcano Mt Erebus 3,749m (12,448ft), nuclear energy provides comfortable living quarters alongside a 2,400m (8,000ft) runway.

Once called Terra Incognita Australis, Antarctica was visited by whalers from 1821 and exploration began in 1838. Roald Amundsen and four other Norwegians reached the South Pole on December 14, 1911, followed 35 days later by a British team, under Robert F. Scott, which perished on its return journey. The American Richard E. Byrd carried out extensive exploration from the 1920s and permanent bases were set up when an extensive joint research programme was carried out in 1958. ∎

Right: Penguins, such as this 'Chinstrap' species, come ashore to nest in huge colonies among the rocks and ice of Antarctica. Although flightless, the penguin is an agile swimmer and finds an ample supply of fish in Antarctic waters.

Above: The Statue of Liberty symbolizes freedom

The United States of America

State	Area Sq km	Area sq m	Population (1970 census)	Capital	Joined Union
Alabama	133,667	51,609	3,400,000	Montgomery	1819
Alaska	1,500,000	586,412	302,173	Juneau	1959
Arizona	295,023	113,909	1,700,000	Phoenix	1912
Arkansas	137,539	53,104	1,900,000	Little Rock	1836
California	411,013	158,693	19,900,000	Sacramento	1850
Colorado	269,998	104,247	2,200,000	Denver	1876
Connecticut	12,973	5,009	3,000,000	Hartford	1788
Delaware	5,328	2,057	548,104	Dover	1787
Florida	151,670	58,560	6,800,000	Tallahassee	1845
Georgia	152,488	58,876	4,600,000	Atlanta	1788
Hawaii	16,705	6,450	769,913	Honolulu	1959
Idaho	216,412	83,557	713,008	Boise	1890
Illinois	146,075	56,400	11,100,000	Springfield	1818
Indiana	93,993	36,291	5,200,000	Indianapolis	1816
Iowa	145,790	56,290	2,800,000	Des Moines	1846
Kansas	213,063	82,264	2,200,000	Topeka	1861
Kentucky	104,623	40,395	3,200,000	Frankfort	1792
Louisiana	125,674	48,523	3,600,000	Baton Rouge	1812
Maine	86,026	33,215	993,663	Augusta	1820
Maryland	27,394	10,577	3,900,000	Annapolis	1788
Massachusetts	21,385	8,257	5,700,000	Boston	1788
Michigan	150,779	58,216	8,800,000	Lansing	1837
Minnesota	217,735	84,068	3,800,000	St Paul	1858
Mississippi	123,584	47,716	2,200,000	Jackson	1817
Missouri	180,486	69,686	4,700,000	Jefferson City	1821
Montana	381,086	147,138	694,409	Helena	1889
Nebraska	200,017	77,227	1,500,000	Lincoln	1867
Nevada	286,297	110,540	488,738	Carson City	1864
New Hampshire	24,097	9,304	737,681	Concord	1788
New Jersey	20,295	7,836	7,200,000	Trenton	1787
New Mexico	315,113	121,666	1,000,000	Santa Fe	1912
New York	128,401	49,576	18,200,000	Albany	1788
North Carolina	136,197	52,586	5,100,000	Raleigh	1789
North Dakota	183,021	70,665	617,761	Bismarck	1889
Ohio	106,764	41,222	10,600,000	Columbus	1803
Oklahoma	181,089	69,919	2,500,000	Oklahoma City	1907
Oregon	251,180	96,981	2,100,000	Salem	1859
Pennsylvania	117,412	45,333	11,800,000	Harrisburg	1787
Rhode Island	3,144	1,214	949,723	Providence	1790
South Carolina	80,432	31,055	2,600,000	Columbia	1788
South Dakota	199,551	77,047	666,257	Pierre	1889
Tennessee	109,411	42,244	3,900,000	Nashville	1796
Texas	692,402	267,338	11,200,000	Austin	1845
Utah	219,931	84,916	1,000,000	Salt Lake City	1896
Vermont	24,887	9,609	444,732	Montpelier	1791
Virginia	105,716	40,817	4,600,000	Richmond	1788
Washington	176,616	68,192	3,400,000	Olympia	1889
West Virginia	62,628	24,181	1,700,000	Charleston	1863
Wisconsin	145,438	56,154	4,400,000	Madison	1848
Wyoming	253,596	97,914	332,416	Cheyenne	1890

Density of population: North America

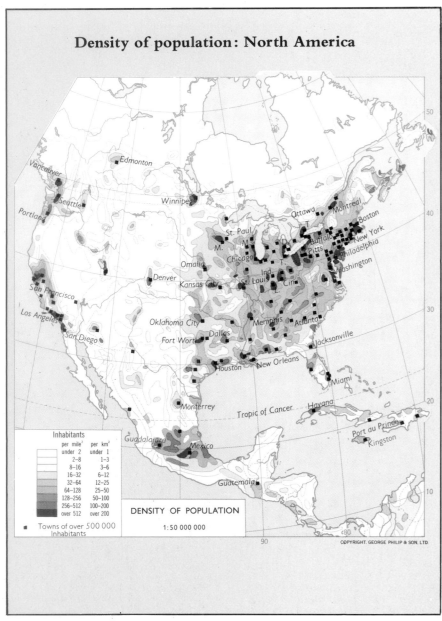

Inhabitants

per mile²	per km²
under 2	under 1
2–8	1–3
8–16	3–6
16–32	6–12
32–64	12–25
64–128	25–50
128–256	50–100
256–512	100–200
over 512	over 200

■ Towns of over 500 000 Inhabitants

DENSITY OF POPULATION

1:50 000 000

COPYRIGHT. GEORGE PHILIP & SON. LTD.

The Outlying Regions

Region	Status	Date Acquired
Howland, Baker, and Jarvis Islands	Unincorporated territory	1857
Johnston Island and Sand Island	Unincorporated territory	1858
Midway Islands	Unincorporated territory	1867
Guam	Organized unincorporated territory	1898
Palmyra Island	Unincorporated territory	1898
Puerto Rico	Commonwealth	1898
Wake Island	Unincorporated territory	1898
American Samoa	Organized unincorporated territory	1900
Canal Zone	Panama territory under US jurisdiction	1903
Virgin Islands of the US	Organized unincorporated territory	1917
Kingman Reef	Unincorporated territory	1922
Canton and Enderbury Islands	Administered with Britain	1939
Trust Territory of the Pacific Islands	UN trust territory under US administration	1947

North America

North America, including Canada, the United States, Mexico, Alaska, and Greenland, but excluding Central America and the West Indies, is the third largest continent after Asia and Africa. It has an area of more than 23.4km (9m sq.miles) and an esti- mated population of nearly 300m.

The continent is shaped roughly like an inverted triangle, with its broad base spanning the frozen wastes of the Arctic in the north and its apex dipping into the tropical waters of the Gulf of Mexico in the south-east. From north to south the greatest distance is about 6,400km (4,000 miles), and from east to west

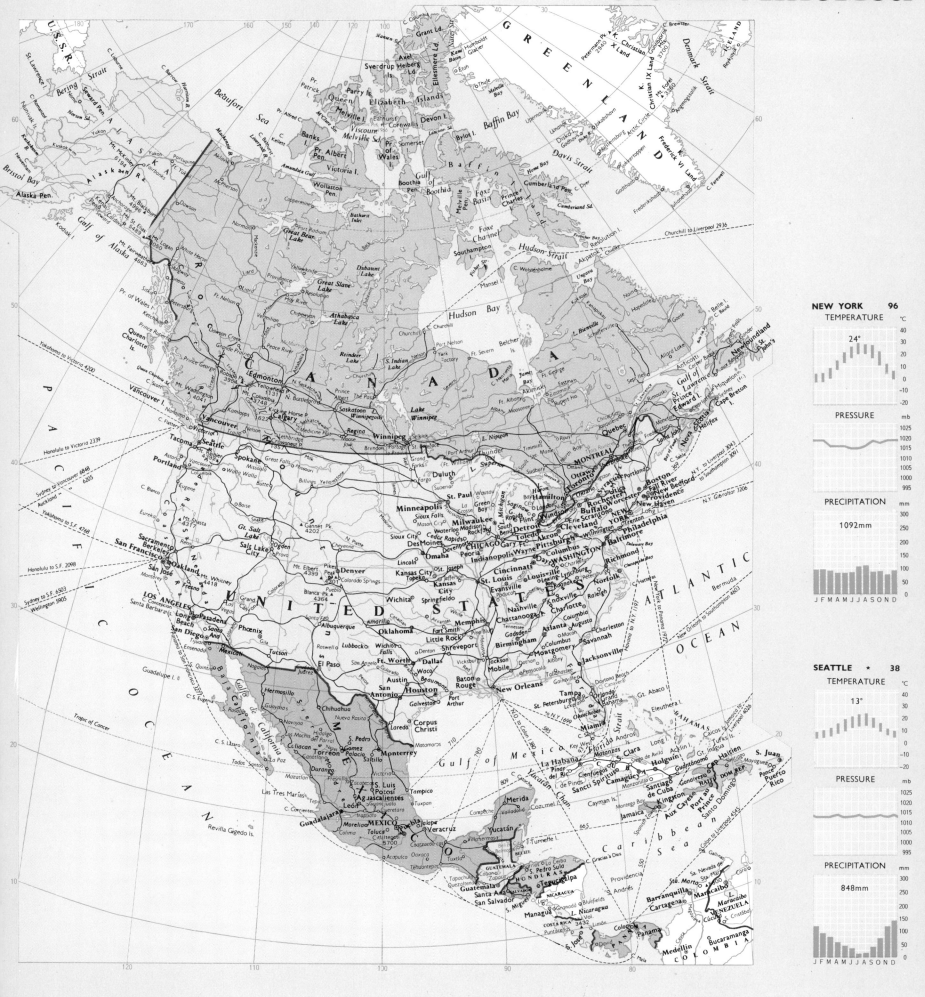

about 7,900km (4,900 miles). It is flanked on the west by the Pacific Ocean, on the east by the Atlantic and the Gulf of Mexico, on the north by the Arctic Ocean, and on the south it borders British Honduras and Guatemala in Central America.

North America's terrain exhibits almost every kind of surface from permanently ice-covered wastelands and scorching deserts to magnificent forests and lush, grass-covered plains. High mountains, huge rivers, lakes, and waterfalls, and incalculable deposits of mineral wealth all form part of the varied scene and add to the abundant natural resources of the continent.

There are three major regions distinguished by their widely differing landforms. The Western Highlands or Cordillera runs down the Pacific coast from Alaska through Mexico. The system is made up of the Rocky Mountains, the Alaska Range, the St Elias Mountains, the Cascade Range, the Sierra Nevada, and the Sierra

Madre. The Rockies extend for more than 4,800km (3,000 miles), and their high ridge, known as the Continental Divide, separates the river systems that flow to opposite sides of North America. Most of the mountains are high and rugged, with many peaks exceeding 4,270m (14,000ft).

The second major landform rises in the east of the continent, and is known as the Appalachian Highlands. This is made up of several mountain ranges and broad plateaus that are nowhere as high as the Western Highlands. The Laurentian, Adirondack, and northern ranges of the Appalachian Mountains make up the northern part of the system. The Appalachians continue southwards through the eastern United States.

The third landform covers the middle of the continent in the form of an immense plain that is 2,400km (1,500 miles) wide in places, and is drained by several large river systems. Among these are the Mississippi-Missouri in the south, the Great

Lakes—St Lawrence in the centre, and the Mackenzie, and the Red-Nelson-Saskatchewan in the north.

Temperatures vary widely over this huge land mass, and often reach extremes. A temperature of 57°C (134°F) has been recorded in Death Valley, in California. At the other end of the scale, the air temperature in the upper Yukon once fell to −63°C (−82°F). On the east, the temperature is influenced by the Gulf Stream and the Labrador Current. Rainfall generally is heavy on the coasts and often meagre in the interior of the continent.

Vegetation varies widely with climate and soil. In the far north trees are unknown, but moss, lichens, and a few stunted, hardy plants grow here and there during the brief summer weeks. Farther south, huge forests cover great parts of Canada and eastern and western regions of the United States. More than 1,000 kinds of trees have been counted, including the giant redwoods of Cali-

fornia, some of which grow more than 91m (300ft) high and are more than 3,000 years old. Tropical and desert vegetation is found in parts of the south.

About 30,000 years ago it seems likely that nomadic peoples from Asia crossed a land bridge that existed at that time between Siberia and Alaska. They were the ancestors of the North American Indians. The Eskimos arrived much later, again possibly from Asia, probably about 6,000 years ago. After Christopher Columbus alerted Europeans to the existence of North America in 1492, the continent was invaded at various times, mainly by Spanish, English, and French explorers. As settlements expanded, warfare broke out between the three nationalities, while the original inhabitants, the Indians, were steadily eliminated by all three.

Hawaii, the 50th state of the United States, is described in the article on Oceania. Mexico and Greenland are also described separately.

Canada

Map 56

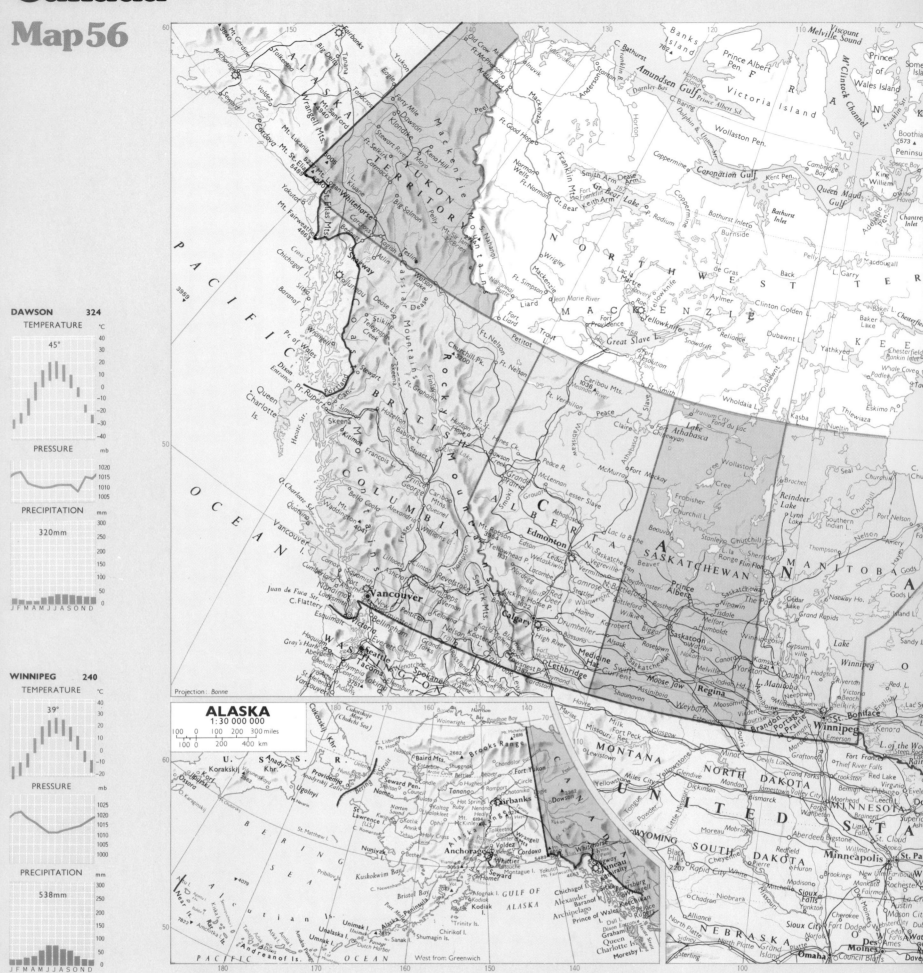

DAWSON 324

TEMPERATURE °C

45°

PRESSURE mb

PRECIPITATION mm

320mm

WINNIPEG 240

TEMPERATURE °C

39°

PRESSURE mb

PRECIPITATION mm

538mm

Projection: Bonne

ALASKA
1:30 000 000
100 0   100 200 300 miles
100 0   200 400 km

Canada

Area: 9,976,139km² (3,851,809sq.m.).
Population: 22,916,000. **Capital:**
Ottawa (602,510). **Largest city:**
Montreal (2.7m.). **Languages:**
English, French. **Ethnic groups:**
British, French, Amerindian, Eskimo.
Main exports: *lumber, paper,
metals, machinery, aluminium, wood
pulp, petroleum.* **Average
temperatures:** −18°C (0°F) Jan.
18°C (65°F) July in Winnipeg, but
considerably less severe winters in
coastal states, especially in the
southwest.
Highest point: *Mt Logan (Yukon
Territory)* 6,050m (19,850ft).

Canada, a land of long, harsh winters and
mild summers, is the largest country in
area in the Western Hemisphere and the
second largest in the world after the
USSR. Most of its great potential wealth

still lies untapped in its huge forests and
river systems and in mineral deposits
deep under ground. The people of this
young nation (which was only 100 years
old in 1967) are scattered patchily over
the vast land, but most of them live within 320km (200m.) of the United States
border in the south. Huge stretches in
the north are completely uninhabited.

The predominant cultures are British
(about 45 percent) and French (about
30 percent) in origin. Other Europeans
make up about 20 percent and the remainder of the people are Amerindians
and Eskimos.

French-speaking Canadians have to a
great extent retained their traditional
customs, Roman Catholic religion, and
culture, as well as their language. The
culture of the English-speaking communities is less definite because by no
means all their members are of English
stock.

All parliamentary business is carried
on in both English and French. The

federal courts also use both languages,
and stamps and banknotes are printed in
English and French. But in Quebec, the
official language has been French since
1974.

Most Canadian Indians live on government reserves. They include members of
the Algonkian, Huron, Iroquois, and
Salish groups, and by the mid-1970s
numbered about 296,000, with a steadily
increasing population.

Canada's 17,500 Eskimos, who live in
the far north between Alaska and Greenland, are also increasing in numbers.
Traditionally they have hunted and fished
in the frozen wastelands. But, particularly from the late 1960s onwards, many
have found well-paid jobs with mining,
transport, and petroleum companies.

Canadians as a whole are cheerful,
energetic, and self-reliant, with a pas-
sionate love of the outdoors. Hunting is a
favourite recreation. The Canadian outdoor image has been reinforced by the
colourful Royal Canadian Mounted

Police (the 'Mounties'), the country's
national law enforcement department.

History and constitution
The first recorded landing by a European
on Canadian soil was made in 1497 by
John Cabot, an Italian-born explorer
sailing in the service of King Henry VII
of England. Some 37 years later, the
French explorer Jacques Cartier landed on
the Gaspé Peninsula and sailed up the
St Lawrence River, naming his discovery
New France. Soon an intense rivalry
developed between the French and the
English.

In the early 1600s another French explorer, Samuel de Champlain, arrived in
the St Lawrence region and founded
Quebec, the first permanent settlement
in Canada. He also greatly extended the
area and influence of New France.

Fighting between the French and
English dragged on sporadically until the

*Right: A farm in New Brunswick, one
of Canada's Atlantic provinces.*

Map 57

1:15 000 000

MONTRÉAL 57

TEMPERATURE °C

31°

PRESSURE mb

PRECIPITATION mm

1036mm

J F M A M J J A S O N D

CHURCHILL 13

TEMPERATURE °C

40°

PRESSURE mb

PRECIPITATION mm

406mm

J F M A M J J A S O N D

COPYRIGHT. GEORGE PHILIP & SON. LTD.

fall of Quebec in 1759, when French Canada finally came under British rule. In 1867, the British North America Act established the Dominion of Canada.

Today, Canada is an independent, self-governing, constitutional monarchy, and a member of the Commonwealth of Nations. Its nominal head of state is the British monarch, who is represented by a governor general. The nation consists of a federation of 10 provinces and two territories. The provinces are: Alberta, British Columbia, Manitoba, New Brunswick, Newfoundland, Nova Scotia, Ontario, Prince Edward Island, Quebec, and Saskatchewan; and the territories are Northwest Territories and Yukon Territory.

Each province is self-governing, and the territories have some self-government. Parliament, which meets in Ottawa, is made up of 102 members of the Senate, appointed by the governor general, and 264 members of the House of Commons, elected by the people. The head of government is the prime minister, who is the leader of the majority party in the House of Commons. Voters in national elections must be Canadian citizens at least 18 years old.

Land and climate

Canada covers the whole of the northern half of North America except for Greenland and Alaska. It stretches 4,627km (2,875m.) from north to south, and 5,187km (3,223m.) from east to west.

The land falls into seven major natural regions: the Appalachian Highlands, an ancient system of low mountains that covers Newfoundland, the Gaspé Peninsula of Quebec, New Brunswick, Prince Edward Island, and Nova Scotia; the Great Lakes—St Lawrence Lowland, which is the most heavily populated and industrialized region in Canada; the Canadian Shield, beneath whose ancient rocks lies a vast storehouse of mineral wealth; the Hudson Bay Lowland, a low-lying, swampy region on the southwestern shore of Hudson Bay; the

Above: Lonely lakes and thick forests characterize the vast Canadian Shield.

Interior Plains, which cover much of the Prairie Provinces (Manitoba, Alberta, Saskatchewan) and part of north-eastern British Columbia, where Canada's great wheat belt is located; the Western Mountain region or Cordillera, which consists of two major mountain ranges—the Rockies and the Coast Mountains; and the Arctic Islands, almost all of which lie within the Arctic Circle.

Canada is abundantly supplied with rivers and lakes, and holds about one-third of all the fresh water on earth. The principal rivers are the Mackenzie, the St Lawrence, and the Fraser, although large areas of the country are also drained by the Columbia and the Yukon, parts of whose courses flow through the United States. Canada shares four of the Great Lakes (Ontario, Erie, Huron, and Superior) with the United States.

Canada has a continental climate that ranges from freezing cold to blistering heat. Northern Canada has long, cold winters and relatively short, cool summers with the warmest region in south-western Ontario.

Provinces and cities

The two largest and most heavily populated provinces are Ontario and Quebec. Ontario (8m) contains the main industrial centres. Its capital, Toronto (2.6m), is a busy port on Lake Ontario and the second largest city in Canada. Ottawa (602,510), the federal capital, is also in Ontario. Quebec Province (6m) is the centre of French-speaking Canada and is another leading industrial region. Its capital, Quebec, or Quebec City (480,502) is the unofficial capital of French Canada. Montreal (2.7m) is the province's largest city and the largest city in Canada. Located on the St Lawrence Seaway about 1,600km (1,000m.) from the Atlantic, it is one of the world's largest inland ports.

British Columbia (2.4m) is the third largest province, and includes Vancouver Island on which its capital city, Victoria (195,800), stands. Vancouver (1.1m) on the mainland, is the largest city and port. The province boasts spectacular mountain and coastal scenery, and is strongly British in character.

The Prairie Provinces form a huge wheat belt that helps to feed not only Canada but also much of the rest of the world, and large petroleum reserves are another asset in these provinces.

Farming, fishing and forestry

About nine-tenths of Canada's farm produce comes from the Great Lakes—St Lawrence Lowland and the Interior Plains. Grain crops, especially wheat, predominate. Livestock—dairy and beef cattle, poultry, pigs, and sheep—are a valuable source of farm income. Beef cattle ranches are found mainly in Alberta, whereas dairy herds are grazed mainly in the Great Lakes—St Lawrence Lowlands and parts of British Columbia. Vegetables and fruit flourish in the sunshine of British Columbia and on the Ontario peninsula, but they are also grown in a multitude of small-holdings in Prince Edward Island.

Canada has two of the world's greatest fishing grounds. These are the Grand Banks (cod, haddock, mackerel, herring, lobster) off the north-eastern shores of Newfoundland and Nova Scotia, and the coastal waters that fringe the shores of British Columbia (salmon, halibut, shellfish). Canada's many rivers and lakes also yield huge quantities of salmon, trout, perch, sturgeon, pike, and other species.

About half of Canada's land surface is forested. The softwood trees such as tamarack, balsam fir, and spruce supply wood pulp that is manufactured into more than half the world's newsprint. In addition, wood products of all kinds are made from these and other species.

Minerals and energy resources

Canada is the world's largest producer of asbestos, which comes mainly from eastern Quebec. It is also a leading producer of uranium, found chiefly in Ontario and northern Saskatchewan. The Western Interior Plains are particularly rich in oil, natural gas, bituminous sands, coal, gypsum, and potash. Iron ore comes from parts of Ontario, Newfoundland, Quebec, and British Columbia. The Canadian Shield is known to hold important deposits of gold, silver, copper, lead, iron, zinc, uranium, platinum, and nickel.

Canada's immense water resources have encouraged the building of hydro-electric plants that today make the nation one of the world's leading producers of hydro-electric power. About 66 percent of this power is generated in Ontario and Quebec. Newfoundland's Churchill Falls project is the largest single project in the Western Hemisphere, with a claimed capacity of more than 5 million kilowatts.

Industry and trade

Manufacturing is Canada's most important activity. More than 66 percent of the country's products are manufactured. The major products are processed food, transport equipment and machinery. Other important industries include the manufacture of paper and paper products and the processing of primary metals, chemical products and wood products.

Trade and foreign relations

Canada's principal trade partners (imports and exports) in order of importance are the United States, Britain, Japan and West Germany. Canada exports about 40 percent of its products and imports about the same proportion of the goods it needs. Two-thirds of its exports go to the United States. They include cars and parts, lumber, petroleum, aluminium, newsprint and whisky. It imports from the United States slightly more than it exports, including chemicals, plastics, iron and steel, computers, and cars and parts. To Britain, Canada exports wheat and tobacco as well as manufactured items. The opening of the St Lawrence Seaway (shared by Canada and the United States) in 1959 enabled ocean-going ships to reach the Great Lakes ports and brought a boom in Canadian trade, especially with Europe.

Under the premiership of Pierre Trudeau in the early and mid-1970s Canada began to loosen its traditional trading ties with the United States, Britain and other European countries and established commercial links with China, the Soviet Union, and various South American nations. ∎

The United States of America

Area: *9,363,123km² (3,615,122sq.m.).* **Population:** *215 million.* **Capital:** *Washington, D.C. (2.9m).* **Largest city:** *New York City (9.9m).* **Language:** *English.* **Ethnic groups:** *British, Continental Europeans, Negroes, Amerindians, Orientals.* **Main exports:** *transport equipment and machinery, food, live animals, raw materials, chemicals.* **Average temperatures:** *−2°C (29°F) Jan. 22°C (72°F) July in Boston, Mass; 19°C (67°F) Jan. 28°C (83°F) July in Miami, Florida.* **Highest point:** *Mt McKinley (Alaska) 6,194m (20,320ft).*

People and culture

The United States (often shortened to USA or US) is the fourth largest country in the world. This huge and varied land is one of the richest and most powerful nations and the majority of its peoples

Above: The World Trade Center dominates this view of New York.

enjoy the highest standards of living on earth.

Only the Soviet Union, Canada, and China are larger in area, and only China, India, and the Soviet Union have larger populations. Of the estimated 215.2 million people living in the United States in 1975, more than 22 million were blacks, about 6 million were of Spanish (Mexican) origin, and about 80,000 were Amerindians.

The nation today is a melting pot of dozens of different races. The Indians and Eskimos had already been living there for thousands of years when the first English settlers arrived in the 1600s and proceeded to colonize Virginia and New England, which today is made up of the states of Connecticut, Massachusetts, Rhode Island, Vermont, New Hampshire, and Maine.

The English were followed by others: Spaniards who went to what is now California and Florida, Dutch to New York, Germans to Pennsylvania, and French to Louisiana. Later, hundreds of thousands of Negroes were shipped from Africa to work as slaves on the plantations of the southern states. Rapid European immigration during the 19th century reached a peak in 1900–10.

After World War II there was another great influx of people, most of them homeless Jews and other European refugees. Today, the largest immigrant groups, in order of size, are Italians, Germans, Poles, and Russians. Almost all of them are well integrated into American life but they still retain a degree of individuality and culture in matters of worship, food, and traditional festivals.

There is complete freedom of worship in the United States. The majority of the people are Christians and about 5 percent Jews. There are also minority Islamic groups and followers of eastern religions. There are more Protestants than any other Christians, but Roman Catholics form the largest single Christian denomination.

Education is compulsory up to about the age of 16. Public schools are free, and run by state and local authorities. Churches and private individuals and agencies run a number of private educational establishments. The educational system is divided into primary (elementary), secondary (high school), and higher education. The latter includes colleges, technical schools, and universities. More than 99 percent of American adults can read and write. In 1954 the Supreme Court ruled that racial segregation in the public schools was unconstitutional, and since that time there has been a gradual but steady integration of black and white schoolchildren throughout the country, in spite of some violent opposition initially.

Americans in general are prosperous, optimistic, and extrovert. Although family ties are strong, they have a tradition based on the equality of men and the feeling of independence associated with this conviction. This may account in part for the energetic and restless nature of the typical American, who works and plays hard and has a passion for novelty. Among favourite outdoor activities are hunting, fishing, golf, baseball, and football.

History and constitution

The first white settlements in what is now the United States were established by the Spaniards in Florida in 1565. The first permanent English settlement was made at Jamestown, Virginia, in 1607. Thirteen years later, the Pilgrim Fathers travelled across the Atlantic in the *Mayflower* and landed at Plymouth, Massachusetts. They were Separatist Puritans who fled from religious persecution in England.

In 1682 English Quakers founded Pennsylvania, named after their leader,

Above: America's largest catch of lobster comes from the rugged coasts of Maine in the north-eastern corner of the USA.

William Penn. By 1760, 13 colonies had been established, stretching from Georgia in the south to Massachusetts in the north. The one-and-a-half million British subjects who lived in them were mainly of English, Scottish, German, Dutch, and Swedish extraction. For many years they were threatened by the French, who pushed southwards from the Great Lakes region of Canada as far as Louisiana. But by the end of the Seven Years War in 1763, the French had been permanently defeated and British rule established.

In the 1770s, the colonists began to rebel against British rule, rejecting 'taxation without representation'. The first fighting in what became known as the War of American Independence (called by Americans the War of the Revolution) broke out near Boston in 1775. In 1776 the colonies (New Hampshire, Massachusetts, Rhode Island, Connecticut, New York, New Jersey,

125

Pennsylvania, Delaware, Virginia, North Carolina, South Carolina, Maryland, and Georgia) declared themselves 'free and independent states'. Under the brilliant leadership of George Washington they defeated the British armies. Britain recognized the newly independent states by the Treaty of Paris in 1783.

The constitution was drawn up in 1787 and Washington was elected the first president of the new republic in 1789. In 1803 Louisiana was purchased from the French, and in 1819 Florida was bought from Spain. War broke out with Britain again in 1812 but lasted only two years. As a result of a war with Mexico (1846–48), the United States gained present-day Texas, California, Utah, and New Mexico.

In 1861 the Civil War began between 11 of the southern states (the Confederates) and the northern states (the Union). The war was fought mainly over the rights of the southern states to own and employ Negro slaves and to secede from the Union. The Confederate president was Jefferson Davis; the Union was led by Abraham Lincoln.

The war ended in 1865 with the defeat of the Confederates, the end of slavery, and a deep-rooted bitterness between the North and the South that lingered for generations.

American intervention in World War I in 1917 proved decisive for eventual victory but was followed by post-war isolationism in the United States. The Great Depression, which began in 1929, hit the United States hard. President Franklin D. Roosevelt, elected in 1933, finally led his country out of its crisis with his dynamic New Deal policies.

The United States entered World War II in December 1941, shouldering almost the whole burden of the war in the Pacific, and assuming a major role in the conflict against Germany and Italy. The Axis powers collapsed in 1945, Japan surrendering only after the Americans had dropped atomic bombs on Hiroshima and Nagasaki. Further military involvement in Korea (1950–53) and Vietnam (1964–73) left most Americans war-weary and disillusioned.

A milestone in space technology was achieved with the lunar landing of two

Below: Part of the distinctive charm of the six New England states lies in well-preserved wooden buildings like this gabled farmhouse.

American astronauts in 1969, followed by more ambitious explorations of the Moon. But these triumphs were soon to be overshadowed by the Watergate scandal of 1974 when President Richard Nixon resigned rather than face possible impeachment for alleged political improprieties. He was succeeded by his Vice-President, Gerald Ford.

The United States today is a federal republic of 50 states and the District of Columbia. This is an area of 179km² (69sq.m.) making up Washington, the nation's capital.

Government is exercised on three levels: national, state, and local. The national or federal government has three main branches—executive, legislative, and judicial. Each branch is usually independent of the other two and can exercise certain checks and balances. The chief executive is the president. He is elected for a four-year term and cannot serve more than two terms. The legislative branch is the Congress, which is made up of the Senate and the House of Representatives. The Senate consists of 100 members (two from each state) who are elected for six-year terms. The House of Representatives has 435 members, who are elected for two years. The numbers from each state vary according to their respective populations.

The judicial branch consists of the Supreme Court, made up of a chief justice and eight associate justices; some 90 federal district courts; and 11 courts of appeal.

At the state level, each state also has its own executive (the governor), legislative, and judicial branches. The states create and control all local governments, which operate in counties, boroughs, cities, towns, and some special districts.

The two main political parties are the Democrats and the Republicans. Distinctions between the two are not always clear-cut, but the Democratic party tends to be the party of the 'small man', with popular support in the South. The Republican Party tends to favour 'big business', with corresponding support in the North.

Land and climate

The United States occupies the central portion of the North American continent. It is bordered by Canada on the north, the Pacific Ocean on the west, Mexico on the southwest, the Caribbean Sea on the south, and the Atlantic Ocean on the east. The land extends 2,575km (1,598m.) from the Canadian border to

the Gulf of Mexico, and more than 4,800km (nearly 3,000m.) from the Atlantic to the Pacific. The state of Alaska, lying northwest of Canada, the island state of Hawaii, and various outlying regions add further to the nation's immense size.

There are three main physical regions: the western mountains, the eastern highlands, and the vast plains in between. Fringing the Pacific Ocean in the west is the Pacific Mountain System. The westernmost part of the system is known as the Pacific Coastal Region—a chain of low mountains and deep valleys. Eastward of this is the rugged Cascade Range running from Canada to northern California, and its southern continuation, the Sierra Nevada.

Inwards from the Pacific Mountain System are the Intermountain Plateaus. These are, for the most part, dry upland regions sometimes carved up by deep gorges. The magnificent Rocky Mountains rise to the east of the Intermountain Plateaus. They are high, rugged, and in

Above: The dome of the Capitol rises near the centre of Washington, D.C. The building houses the US Congress.

many places heavily forested. They are also rich in minerals.

In the extreme east of the country, the Coastal Plain extends from Massachusetts to the Gulf of Mexico, along the Atlantic coast. Low and often swampy, the plain varies between 120km (75m.) and 480km (300m.) in width. Inland from the Coastal Plain are the Appalachian Highlands, which extend from the Gulf of St Lawrence to Alabama. These highlands consist of very ancient, worn rocks whose highest peaks do not quite reach 2,400m (7,000ft).

Two contiguous regions—the Central Lowland, which stretches westwards from the Appalachians, and the Great Plains, which lie to the west of the Central Lowlands—cover the central part of the country. These two enormous regions jointly make up about half the area of the United States, and stretch from the Great Lakes to the Gulf of Mexico. They include some of the most fertile agricultural land in the world.

Fresh water is generally abundant in the United States except for a few desert regions in parts of the west and southwest. The largest drainage system is that of the Mississippi-Missouri-Ohio. These rivers, with their tributaries, flow southwards through the central plains and empty into the Gulf of Mexico. The Columbia in the north of the country, and the Colorado in the south, are the two most important rivers that empty into the Pacific. During its course, the Colorado has carved out a huge gash in the earth's surface more than 1.6km (1m) deep; the Grand Canyon, as it is called, is one of the wonders of the world.

Most of the short, swift rivers that flow into the Atlantic rise in the Appalachians; they include the Hudson, Delaware, and Potomac. Many rivers have been harnessed to provide hydroelectric power, water for irrigation, and waterways for transport.

The Great Lakes lie on the Canadian border. Only one of them—Lake Michigan—lies wholly within the United States; the other four are shared with Canada. On the border, too, are the famous and picturesque Niagara Falls. One of the two falls is American, the other Canadian. Their enormous water power has been harnessed for industrial and domestic use.

The country's climate varies widely according to latitude and physical features. Parts of the plateaus and mountains in the southwest are almost completely rainless, yet other regions fringing the Gulf of Mexico receive more than

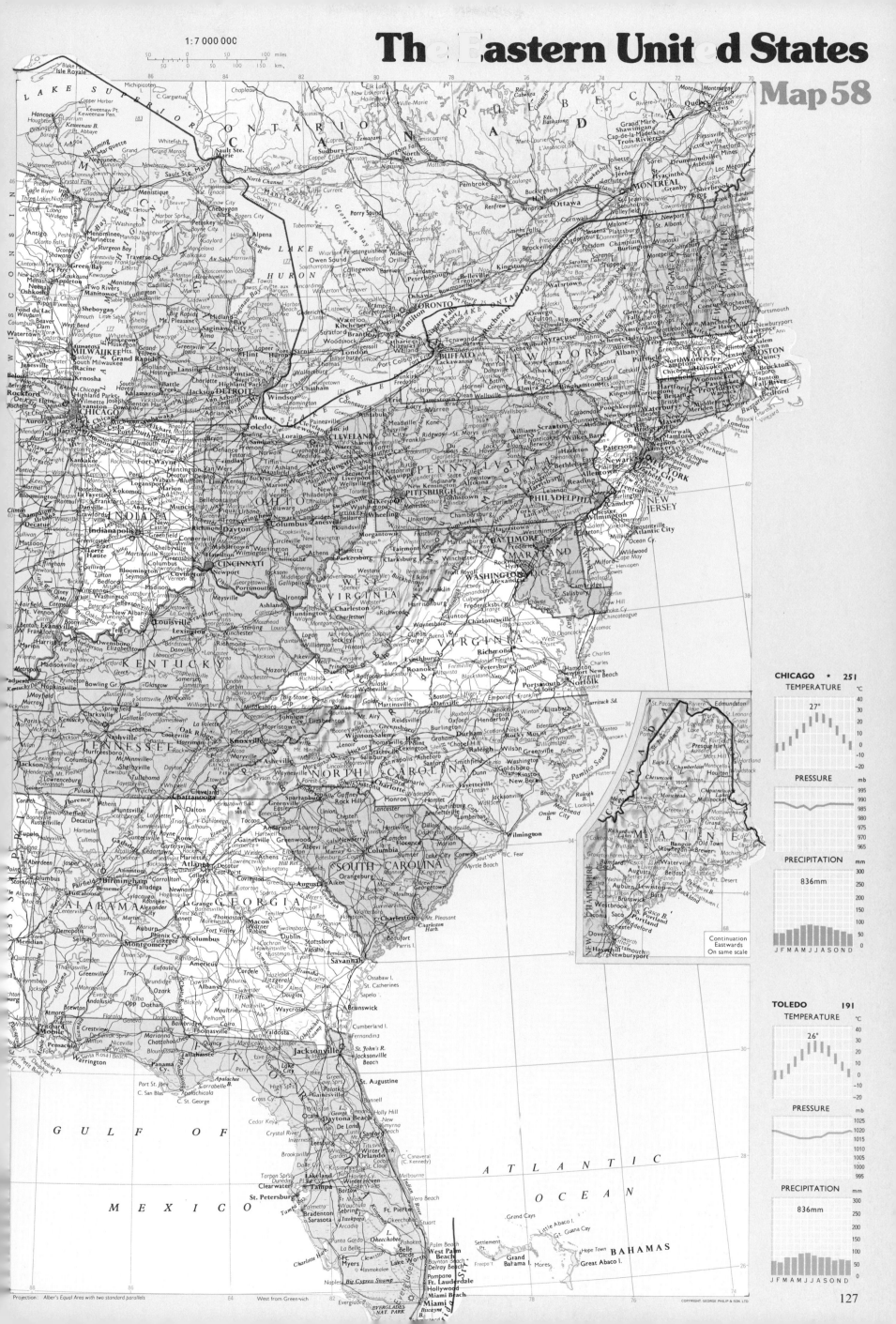

1:7 000 000

Projection: Alber's Equal Area with two standard parallels

West from Greenwich

COPYRIGHT GEORGE PHILIP & SON LTD.

Continuation
Eastwards
On same scale

CHICAGO ★ 251

TEMPERATURE °C

27°

PRESSURE mb

PRECIPITATION mm

836mm

J F M A M J J A S O N D

TOLEDO 191

TEMPERATURE °C

26°

PRESSURE mb

PRECIPITATION mm

836mm

J F M A M J J A S O N D

1 : 7 000 000

ST. LOUIS ★ 173
TEMPERATURE °C
26°
PRESSURE mb
PRECIPITATION mm
1001mm
J F M A M J J A S O N D

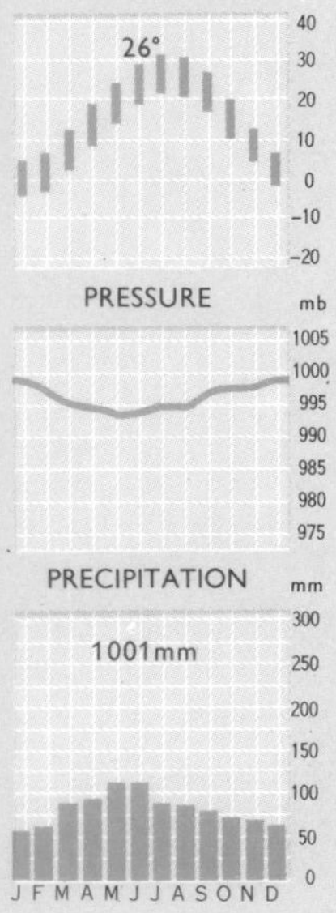

NEW ORLEANS ★ 2
TEMPERATURE °C
16°
PRESSURE mb
PRECIPITATION mm
1458mm
J F M A M J J A S O N D

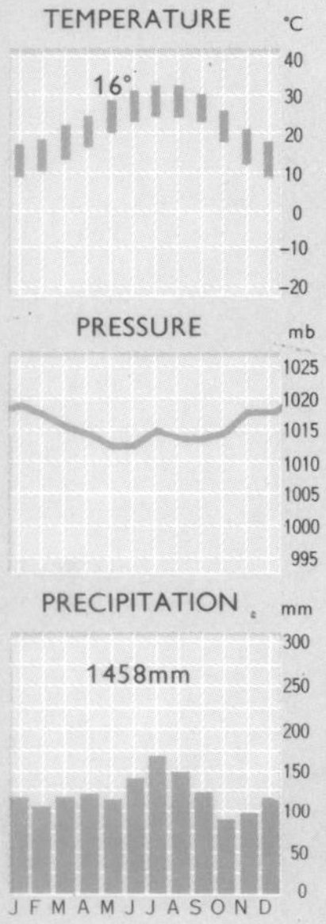

DENVER ★ 1610
TEMPERATURE °C
23°
PRESSURE mb
PRECIPITATION mm
358mm
J F M A M J J A S O N D

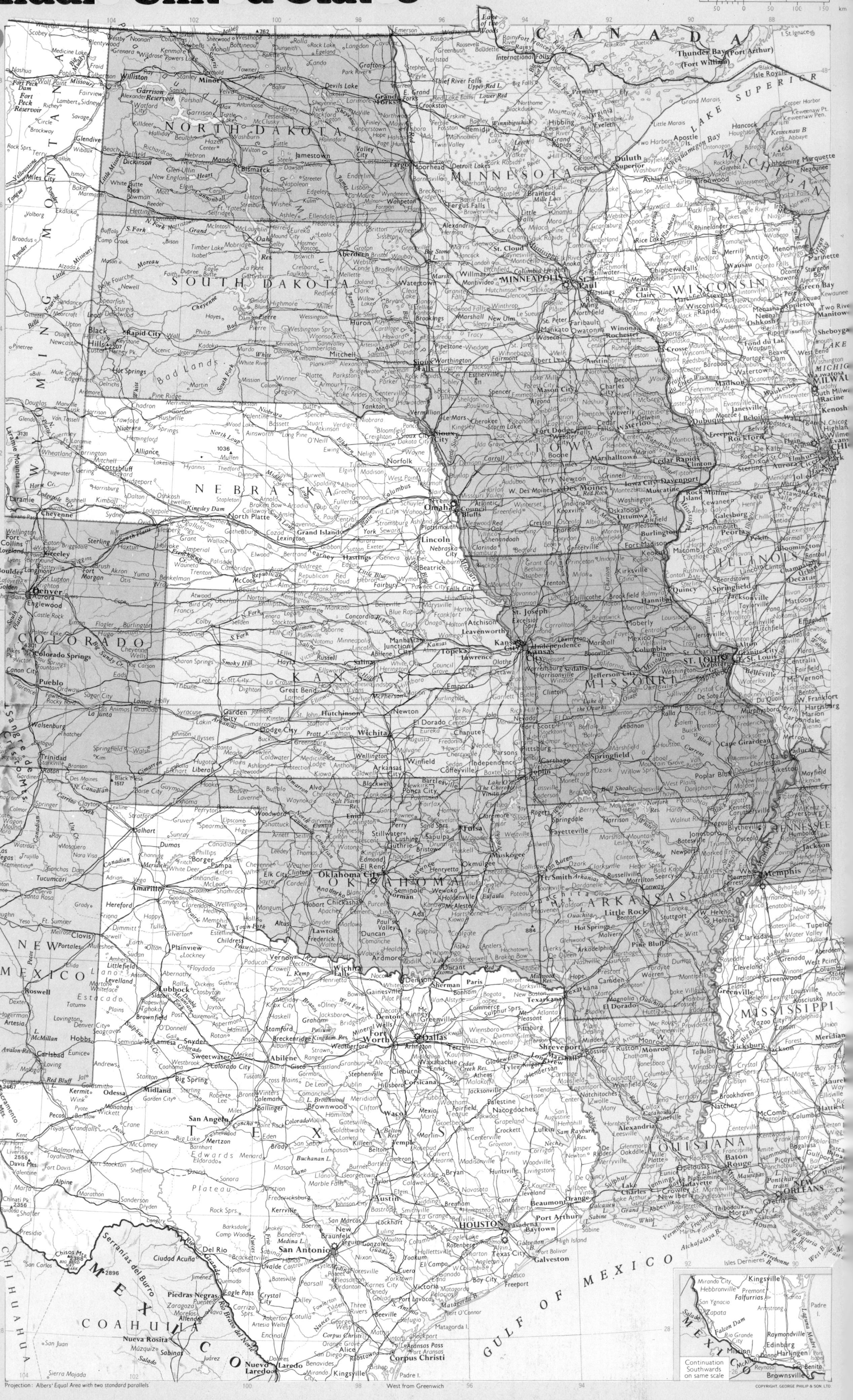

CANADA

MONTANA

NORTH DAKOTA

SOUTH DAKOTA

MINNESOTA

WISCONSIN

MICHIGAN

LAKE SUPERIOR

WYOMING

NEBRASKA

IOWA

ILLINOIS

COLORADO

KANSAS

MISSOURI

ST. LOUIS

OKLAHOMA

ARKANSAS

TENNESSEE

NEW MEXICO

TEXAS

LOUISIANA

MISSISSIPPI

CHIHUAHUA

COAHUILA

MEXICO

GULF OF MEXICO

Continuation Southwards on same scale

Projection: Albers' Equal Area with two standard parallels

West from Greenwich

COPYRIGHT GEORGE PHILIP & SON, LTD.

128

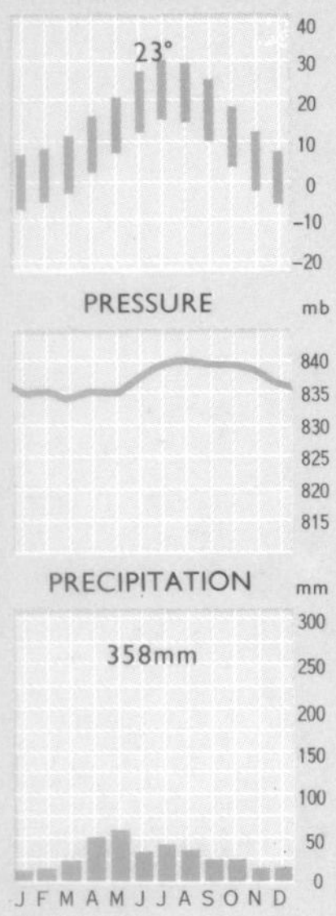

150cm (60in) of rain a year, as do the coasts of northern California, Washington, and Oregon. Permanent snow lies on some parts of the Rockies and in Alaska, while southern California, Florida, and Hawaii bask in a subtropical climate. The New England states have very cold winters and hot summers. In the Central Lowland plains, the absence of mountain barriers leaves the wind unobstructed, and unpredictable air currents can change the weather with great suddenness. Parts of the south are also subject to hurricanes, which cut destructive swathes inland from the Caribbean.

States and cities
The United States has traditionally been divided into ten great political and economic and social regions. The oldest, in terms of settlement and history, is New England, where much of the nation's industry is located. A region renowned for its wealth and density of population is New York, the 'Empire State'. New York City is by far the largest city in the country and is a centre of banking, trade, shipping, and transport. A third region is made up of Pennsylvania, New Jersey, and Delaware—the so-called Middle Atlantic States. This is a region that has valuable agricultural land, as well as immense deposits of iron and coal. It includes the cities of Pittsburg, with its great steelworks, and Philadelphia, a centre that blends tradition with industries such as chemicals and textiles.

The Middle West includes Ohio, Indiana, Illinois, Michigan, and Wisconsin. The iron ore of Michigan lies at the heart of its vast industry, although farming is also important. The nation's second largest city, Chicago, stands at the crossroads of major land, air, and sea routes and is one of North America's great grain and stock markets. Also in this region is Detroit, the motor vehicle manufacturing capital of the country and the world.

Minnesota, Iowa, North and South Dakota, Nebraska, and Kansas are known collectively as the Prairie States. They are the country's granary, producing enough maize and wheat to feed not only America but much of the rest of the world too. The Mountain States of Montana, Wyoming, Colorado, New Mexico, Utah, Nevada, Arizona, and Idaho are a mixture of pastureland, mining areas, and stretches of desert.

California, Oregon, Washington, Alaska, and Hawaii are known as the Pacific States. California is a noted holiday and tourist region, boasting the film capital of the world in Los Angeles. The city is the nation's third largest and is a major centre of oil production and refining, and of aircraft manufacture. Alaska and Hawaii were the 49th and 50th states respectively to join the Union, both in 1959. Alaska, easily the

largest of all the states, was purchased from Russia for $7.2m in 1867—less than 2 cents an acre.

The South is made up of the states of Virginia, North and South Carolina, Alabama, Georgia, Mississippi, Louisiana, and Florida. Subtropical produce such as tobacco, cotton, and rice are the staple crops. Texas, the richest and second biggest state, where everything seems larger than life-size, and Oklahoma, make up the South-West. This is the legendary home of the American cowboy. But today the region's incalculable wealth is derived mainly from oil. The Border States make up the last major division. It comprises the remaining states—Arkansas, Kentucky, Maryland, Missouri, Tennessee, and West Virginia —that stand between and divide the great economic areas. Kentucky's 'blue grass' feeds some of the country's finest bloodstock, while Nashville in Tennessee is the home of 'country music', a major pillar of the recording business.

Farming, forestry and fishing
There are some three million farms in the United States, averaging about 400 acres each. Together they make the nation the largest single agricultural producer in the world. After supplying domestic needs, American farmers have a large surplus for export.

Corn (maize) is grown in the so-called 'corn belt' of the Mid-West, where the fertile soil and equable climate are ideal. The United States grows nearly half the world's total corn crop.

Wheat grows in all areas except those with extremes of climate. Kansas (for winter wheat), North and South Dakota, Minnesota, and Montana produce the main harvests.

The 'cotton belt' of the South is the largest cotton-producing region in the world. Dairy farming is carried on mainly along parts of the North Pacific coast and in the northeast of the country. Fruit of various kinds is grown in many regions. California, Florida, and southwestern Arizona are the principal citrus crop areas; apples come from New York, Washington, and California; and sheltered mountain slopes in many areas produce grapes, plums, pears, peaches and cherries.

Livestock rearing is confined mainly to the western and south-western states such as Texas, Arizona, and New Mexico.

Above, right: The 192m (630ft) high Gateway Arch is a landmark of St Louis on the Mississippi River.

Right: Riverside Geyser in Yellowstone National Park, Wyoming.

Below: Lacework balconies in New Orleans recall French settlement.

Above: Desert winds have carved rocks in Bryce Canyon National Park, Utah, into richly-coloured formations.

There, cattle, sheep, and horses graze on millions of acres of range land.

More than half the United States was once covered with huge forests. But for many generations lumberjacks have been felling more trees than foresters have been planting. As a result, the lumber industry has moved steadily westwards from the Atlantic coast until today it is centred on the Pacific coast forests.

Fish forms an important part of the American diet. The two oceans, together with the Gulf of Mexico and the Great Lakes, yield an average of about three million tons of fish and other seafood a year.

Minerals and energy resources

The United States produces more crude petroleum than any other country—it amounts to about one-fifth of the world's entire output, and is easily the most valuable of the nation's minerals. The search for new oilfields never ceases, and in the late 1960s a major strike was made in the north of Alaska, but transport problems in that inhospitable terrain are immense. Natural gas, most of it from Texas, is the next most important mineral.

Coal is another valuable mineral—the United States is the second largest producer after the Soviet Union. Although the nation's largest deposits lie in Alaska, Illinois, and Montana, almost all the coal that is actually mined comes from the nine states east of the Mississippi, with Kentucky and West Virginia leading the others.

The country is also rich in iron ore (Michigan, Minnesota, and Wisconsin), copper (most of which comes from Arizona), and has substantial deposits of gold and silver. Promising strikes led to famous gold rushes—in California in 1849, Alaska at the turn of the century, and in other parts of the country at various times.

A resource that has helped to make the United States one of the richest nations on earth is its fertile soil. The different varieties give ample evidence of their fertility, from the rich, dark brown soil of the prairies to the alluvial deposits of the great Mississippi Valley. These soils support an almost endless variety of food crops, decorative plants, and forest trees.

The United States was a pioneer in the development of nuclear energy for use in wartime. But the nation is also well advanced in the building of nuclear power plants for peaceful uses—as potential large-scale producers of electrical power.

Industry and trade

The United States is the world's leading manufacturing nation. Most of its industry is located north of the Ohio River and east of the Mississippi. Food processing is the most valuable industry, followed by transport equipment, chemicals, machinery, and metal products. California, Wisconsin, Michigan, New Jersey, and New York lead in the food processing and packaging industries.

More iron and steel is produced in the United States than anywhere else on earth. Pennsylvania leads among the states, with a work force running into hundreds of thousands. Paper manufacture is another industry in which the United States has a clear lead over the rest of the world. The states that have the most timber for this industry are Oregon, Washington, Maine, and Wisconsin.

There is also a flourishing American textile industry. Carpets come mainly from Philadelphia; woollen goods from Massachusetts, Rhode Island, and Pennsylvania; and cotton goods are produced principally by Alabama, Georgia, and North and South Carolina.

Most Americans firmly believe that the great growth and wealth of their manufacturing industry stems from the lively spirit of competition inherent in free enterprise allied to a minimum of government interference.

The chief exports of the United States are listed at the beginning of the article. Imports are mainly basic raw materials such as tin, manganese, nickel, bauxite, and crude oil. In spite of the nation's enormous wealth, its share of world trade declined perceptibly in the late 1960s and early 1970s. In 1974 it stood at

Above: One of San Francisco's famous cable cars makes its way up from Fisherman's Wharf. Out in the bay is the former Federal prison of Alcatraz.

about 15 percent of the world total, although this still meant that it carried on a greater volume of international trade than any other single country. Canada is the main trading partner, followed by Japan, West Germany and Great Britain.

External relations and territories

In the mid-1970s, inflation and rising unemployment had hit the United States hard. But in spite of this, financial and material aid was poured out to various strategically located developing countries. In the United Nations, the United States found itself out-talked and out-manoeuvred by delegates from the Third World. But relations with China and the Soviet Union gradually improved. Outright collaboration with the Soviet Union, which had looked promising in space projects, received a setback with the eruption of civil war in Angola in 1976 and accusations of Russian and Cuban intervention there. The United States is prominent in seeking a peaceful accommodation between Israel and the Arab states and continues to be the mainstay of NATO in Europe.

The United States owns a number of islands, most of them in the Caribbean and the Pacific. The two most important territories are the Panama Canal Zone and the island of Puerto Rico. The Panama Canal Zone is a strip of land that encloses the Panama Canal and runs across the Republic of Panama. The United States pays Panama $1,930,000 a year for the use of the zone. Puerto Rico is an island that lies about 1,600km (1,000m) southeast of Florida. It is a commonwealth of the United States. Its people are classed as United States citizens with local self-government. Puerto Ricans are represented in the United States Congress but have no vote there nor do they pay federal taxes. ∎

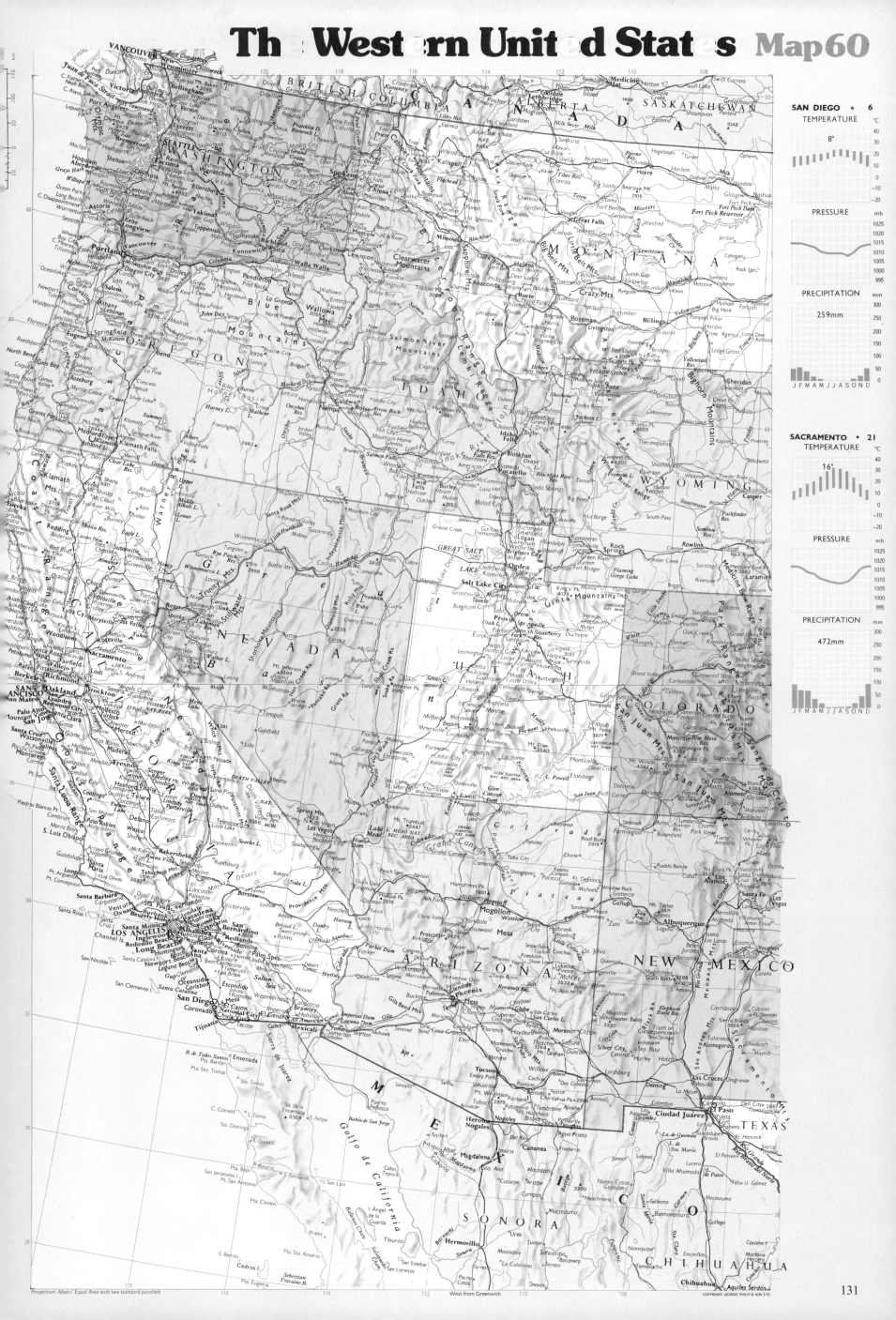

Central America

In 1492, Christopher Columbus was convinced he had reached India by sailing westwards round the globe. As a result, he gave the name West Indies to the lush green islands that dotted the warm Caribbean Sea where he made his landfall. He had actually touched the fringe of a vast New World that stretched almost from pole to pole.

In the wake of Columbus came the conquistadores, Spanish conquerors who quickly established themselves on the mainland that formed a mountainous barrier between the Caribbean and the Pacific Ocean. That region, lying between the southwestern United States in the north and South America, is today made up of Mexico and Central America. Mexico is properly part of North America, whereas Central America forms a narrow land bridge linking

Left: Chichén Itzá, Yucatan, was built by the Mayan civilization about 1100.

Below: Large cacti abound in the dry areas of Mexico, though in the rainy season they seem out of place in a green landscape.

Bottom: Butterfly nets and dugout canoes are still used by Tarascan Indian fishermen at Lake Pátzcuaro, Mexico.

North and South America.

This bridge extends more than 1,600 kilometres (1,000 miles) from Mexico to Colombia. Most of the countries that make up the region have coastlines on both the Pacific in the west and the Caribbean Sea, part of the Atlantic, in the east.

In 1823, Guatemala, El Salvador, Honduras, Nicaragua and Costa Rica broke free from Spanish rule to form the United Provinces. This federation lasted only 15 years but those five countries, together with Belize, Panama and the Panama Canal Zone comprise the region now known as Central America.

The Caribbean coastal plains are generally hot, humid and heavily forested. Behind them rise the central highlands. These in turn slope down to the Pacific coastal plains, which are usually rather narrow with less rainfall than on the east. Earthquakes, volcanic eruptions and hurricanes blowing in from the Caribbean sometimes devastate large areas. The climate is tropical and varies more with altitude than with the seasons.

The most valuable resources of Central America are forests of fine hardwood trees, rich volcanic soil and potential mineral wealth. Most of the people work on farms and plantations where bananas, coffee and cacao are the main crops.

The people themselves are largely a mixture of Indians (the original inhabitants) and Europeans, mainly Spaniards. Spanish is the official language except in Belize, where English is spoken.

English is also widely spoken in the West Indies—a loose term for the scattered string of islands in the Caribbean Sea. These form a 3,200-kilometre (2,000-mile) crescent stretching almost from the tip of Florida to the waters off the Venezuelan coast. The islands are usually classified in three main groups: the Bahamas in the north, the Greater Antilles near the centre and the Lesser Antilles in the southeast. The Greater Antilles include the large islands of Cuba, Puerto Rico, Jamaica and Hispaniola (Haiti and the Dominican Republic). The Lesser Antilles comprise the Windward Islands, Leeward Islands, Barbados, Trinidad and Tobago, and the Netherlands Antilles.

The Bahamas, Cuba, Haiti, the Dominican Republic, Jamaica, Grenada, Barbados and Trinidad and Tobago are independent nations. The remainder are either colonies or are linked in other ways to Britain, the United States, France or the Netherlands.

Originally colonized by European powers, several of the larger islands, such as Cuba and the island shared by Haiti and the Dominican Republic, later gained their independence. In 1967, four island states—Antigua, Dominica, St Christopher (St Kitts)-Nevis–Anguilla, and St Lucia—became associated with Britain instead of being colonies, and called themselves the West Indies Associated States. St Vincent joined them in 1969.

Mexico

Area: *1,972,547km² (761,605sq.m.).*
Population: *58,363,000.*
Capital: *Mexico City (9,856,700).*
Languages: *Spanish, Indian languages.* **Ethnic groups:** *mestizo (mixed white and Indian parentage) 75 percent, Amerindian 15 percent, European 10 percent.* **Main exports:** *cotton, sugar, coffee, sulphur, silver, shrimps.* **Average temperatures:** *24°C (75°F) lowlands, 18°C (64°F) central plateau, 15°C (59°F) mountains.* **Highest point:** *Mt Orizaba (Citlaltepetl), 5,700m (18,700ft).*

The United Mexican States, to give the country its official name, is a Latin American republic that shares a 2,491-kilometre (1,549-mile) border in the north with the United States. Mexico's western shores are washed by the Pacific, while its eastern coast lies on the Gulf of Mexico and the Caribbean Sea. On the southeast it borders Guatemala and Belize.

Mexico is a vast, rugged land of bold and striking contrasts. From the air, it

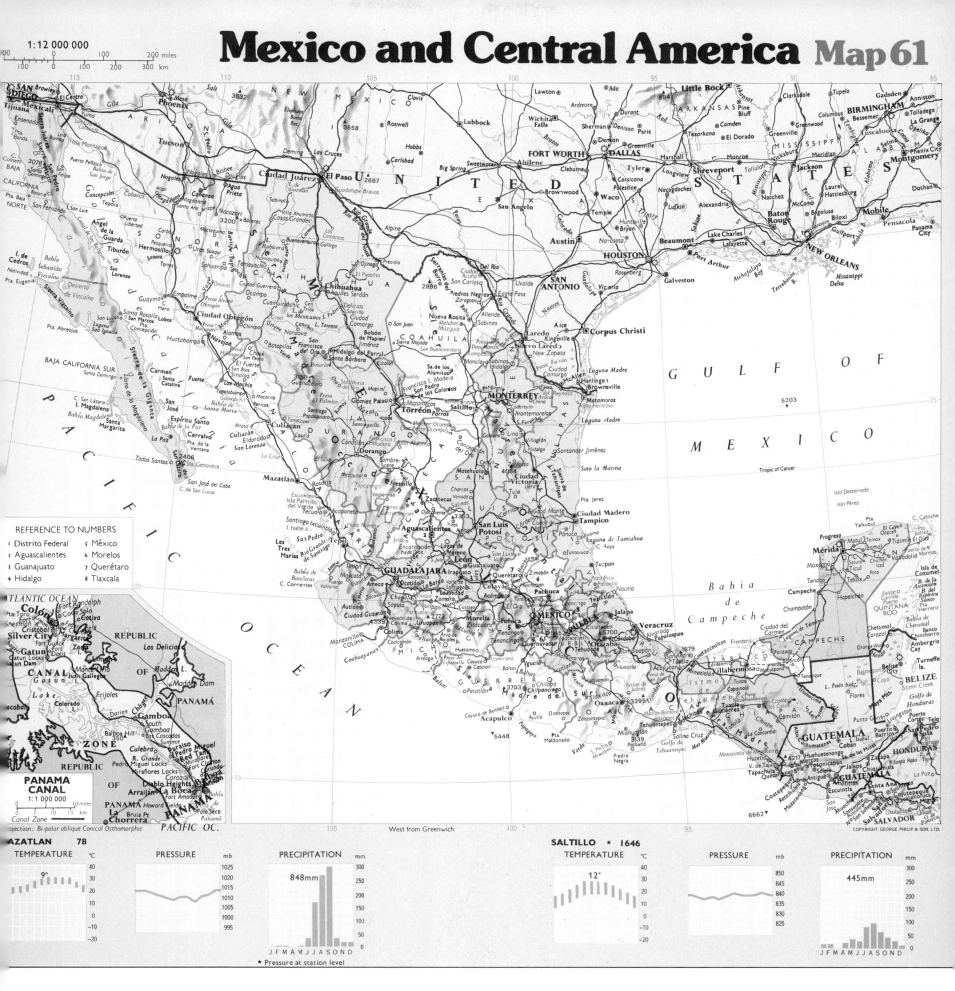

MAZATLAN   78

TEMPERATURE °C	PRESSURE mb	PRECIPITATION mm

848mm

SALTILLO ★ 1646

TEMPERATURE °C	PRESSURE mb	PRECIPITATION mm

445mm

* Pressure at station level

---

looks like a lump of badly crumpled parchment.

Lower (Baja) California is a narrow peninsula, 1,223 kilometres (760 miles) long, separated for most of its length from the Mexican mainland by the Gulf of California. It is a sparsely populated region of mountains and deserts.

Mexico's mountains are made up mostly of two ranges. In the west, the Sierra Madre Occidental runs northwards to the US border. In the east, the Sierra Madre Oriental skirts the shores of the Gulf of Mexico. The two ranges unite near the middle of the country to form a spectacular jumble of towering peaks and countless volcanoes.

Between the two Sierra Madre ranges lies the central plateau. The southern part of this region is fertile and temperate. As a result, two-thirds of the people live there. The tropical peninsula of Yucatán, in the southeast, is a limestone plain whose surface features range from steaming swamps to forested hills.

More than half the population is engaged in farming, fishing, breeding livestock, and forestry. The birthrate is high but the country is self-sufficient in cereals, vegetables, and fruit. Though still the largest producer of silver in the world,

Mexico's main minerals are copper, mercury, zinc, lead, iron and sulphur. Another important source of income is tourism. Mexico's pre-Columbian archaeological treasures attract more than two million visitors a year.

The first Spaniards arrived in the land that is now Mexico in 1517, when the Aztecs were the leading civilization in the region. By the mid-1500s, the invaders under Hernán Cortés had conquered the whole country. Mexico was unable to free itself from Spanish rule until 1821. It remains a predominantly Roman Catholic nation.

Today, Mexico is a one-party federal democracy under the rule of a strong president. In spite of a vigorous economy, rapid industrial development based on local oil resources and increasing prosperity in urban areas, there is still ground to be made up, economically and socially.

Guatemala

Guatemala is the most northerly of the Central American republics, and the third largest. On the east it is bordered by Belize, the Caribbean Sea, Honduras, and El Salvador; on the north and west by Mexico; and on the south by the Pacific

Ocean. It has an area of 108,889km² (42,042sq.m.) and a population of 6,173,000. The capital and largest city is Guatemala City, with 730,991 inhabitants.

Guatemala has more pure-blooded Indians, descendants of the Mayas, than any other Central American nation. They form the largest and poorest section of the community. A smaller section is made up of wealthy landowners who live on huge estates very much in the old colonial style. Most of the country's wealth has traditionally been based on coffee, sugar and cotton. Political changes have been generally violent. ∎

Belize

Belize, formerly British Honduras, is the odd man out among the Central American nations because it is a self-governing British colony. It lies on the east coast of the region, bordered on the north by Mexico, on the west and south by Guatemala, and on the east by the Caribbean Sea. Its area is 22,965km² (8,867sq.m.), and its population is 142,000. The capital, built inland in 1970 to protect it from frequent hurricanes, is Belmopan (3,000). The former capital and largest city is Belize City (39,332). ∎

Honduras

Honduras is a sparsely populated land of mountains and forests. It is the second largest of the Central American republics, and the world's third largest producer of bananas. It is bordered on the north and north-east by the Caribbean Sea, on the west by El Salvador and the Pacific, and on the south and southeast by Nicaragua. Its area is 112,088km² (43,277sq.m.) and it has a population of 2,948,000. The capital and largest city is Tegucigalpa (170,535). Honduras is in dispute with Britain over Belize, which it claims as its own. ∎

El Salvador

El Salvador is the smallest of the Central American republics, and one of the most densely populated. It is the only country that has no coastline on the Caribbean. On the north and east it is bordered by Honduras, on the west by Guatemala, and on the south by the Pacific. Its area is 21,393km² (8,260sq.m.) and it has a population of 4,193,000. The capital and largest city is San Salvador (337,171). The nation's economy is based mainly on coffee and cotton. ∎

Nicaragua

Nicaragua, the largest of the Central American nations, stretches from the Pacific to the Caribbean, which flank it west and east, respectively. Honduras lies to the north and Costa Rica to the south. Its area is 130,000km² (50,193sq. m.), and it has 2,374,000 inhabitants. The capital and largest city is Managua (262,047), which was ravaged in 1931 and 1972 by earthquakes. A feature of the land is Lake Nicaragua, one of the largest lakes in the Americas, and the only freshwater inland lake in the world containing sharks. Cotton, bananas, timber and sugar are the main exports. ■

Costa Rica

Costa Rica is unusual on several counts. It has the highest literacy rate in Latin America, a high per capita income, the most democratic government, and no standing armed forces. Nicaragua lies to the north and Panama to the south. A climber on the summit of Irazú volcano can see both the Pacific coast in the west and the Caribbean in the east. Costa Rica has an area of 50,700km² (19,575sq. m.) and a population of 2,022,000. The capital and largest city is San José (382,961). Costa Rican coffee is world famous. ■

Panama

Panama is a narrow, snake-like strip of land linking Central and South America. It has an area of 75,650km² (29,209sq.m.) and a population of 1,661,000. The capital and largest city is Panama City (419,000).

Panama exports bananas, shrimps and cacao, but its main income by far comes from the Panama Canal Zone, a narrow strip flanking the Panama Canal, one of the world's most important waterways. This it leases to the United States for $2,100,000 a year. But Panama is seeking return of the Canal Zone to its jurisdiction. ■

Cuba

Area: *114,524km² (44,218sq.m.).*
Population: *9,286,000.* **Capital:** *Havana (1.7 million).* **Languages:** *Spanish.* **Ethnic groups:** *European 73 percent, Negro and mestizo 27 percent.* **Main exports:** *sugar, nickel, tobacco, shrimps.* **Average temperature:** *Nov.–April 21°C (70°F), May–Oct. 27°C (81°F).* **Highest point:** *Pico Turquino, 2,132m (6,500ft).* ■

Cuba is the largest island in the Caribbean. It has several low mountain ranges, but mostly it is a land of fertile plains, valleys, and gentle hills. It has two principal river systems, one flowing north and west, the other flowing south.

Cuba is the world's second-biggest producer and the leading exporter of sugar and sugarcane. Another highly important crop is tobacco, and Cuban cigars are world famous.

In 1959, a young revolutionary lawyer, Fidel Castro, overthrew the harsh, dictatorial regime of Fulgencio Batista. Castro then turned Cuba into a socialist state modelled on the Soviet Union. The United States severed diplomatic relations with Cuba, which now depends heavily on its Soviet ally for assistance. ■

Puerto Rico

Puerto Rico is a commonwealth of the United States with internal self-government but without federal representation. Its area is only 8,897km² (3,435sq.m.), but it has a population of 2,929,400. The capital and largest city is San Juan (455,500). English and Spanish are the official languages. Most of the people are mestizos (Negro–Spanish descent). The mountainous, dry, but fertile island is a favourite with US holidaymakers. Before World War II, Puerto Rico was an impoverished island with many of its inhabitants emigrating to New York City in search of work. But a postwar programme of economic expansion labelled 'Operation Bootstrap' has increased manufacturing and sugar processing, which ranks second to tourism as the main dollar earning industry. ■

The Bahamas

The Bahamas are an archipelago of 700 islands and about 2,000 rocks and cays, but fewer than 30 of the islands are inhabited. They cover a land area of 13,935km² (5,380sq.m.), and have a population of 216,000. Nassau (100,000), on New Providence Island, is the capital and largest city. Tourism is the main industry. ■

Jamaica

Jamaica is a wildly beautiful, mountainous, densely crowded island that relies heavily on tourism for its income. Its area is 10,962km² (4,232sq.m.) and it has 2,002,000 inhabitants mainly of Negro descent. Kingston (507,000) is the capital and largest city. Although primarily an agricultural country growing sugar, bananas, cocoa, coffee and fruits, Jamaica is one of the world's largest producers of bauxite. British influence remains strong and Jamaica is the largest Carribean member of the Commonwealth. ■

Haiti

Haiti forms the western part of the island of Hispaniola, which it shares with the Dominican Republic. It has an area of 27,750km² (10,714sq.m.) and has 5,380,000 inhabitants. Port-au-Prince (341,000) is the capital and largest city. Most of the people are descended from African slaves whose rebellions against France established the first Negro republic in the early 1800s. The official language is French but most people speak Creole or one of several African dialects. With a history of despotic government and voodoo practice, the economy and social life are primitive and overcrowding reduces agriculture to subsistence level. ■

The Dominican Republic

The Dominican Republic occupies the eastern and much larger portion of the island of Hispaniola, with Haiti on its western frontier. It has an area of 48,734km² (18,816sq.m.) and a population of 4,699,000. The capital and largest city is Santo Domingo (700,000). Spanish is the official language. Most of the people are of mixed Spanish and Negro descent. Sugar and coffee are the chief exports. Until 1966 the Dominican Republic had a depressing history of violence and revolution. ■

The Leeward Islands

These comprise the Virgin Islands (US), the British Virgin Islands, St Kitts-Nevis-Anguilla, Antigua, Barbuda, Redonda,

Above: Dazzling sand and translucent bays are the mainstay of the economy of the Bahamas with its 700 low-lying islands.

Above: Sugar cane, here being harvested, is Jamaica's major cash crop, providing exports of sugar, rum and molasses.

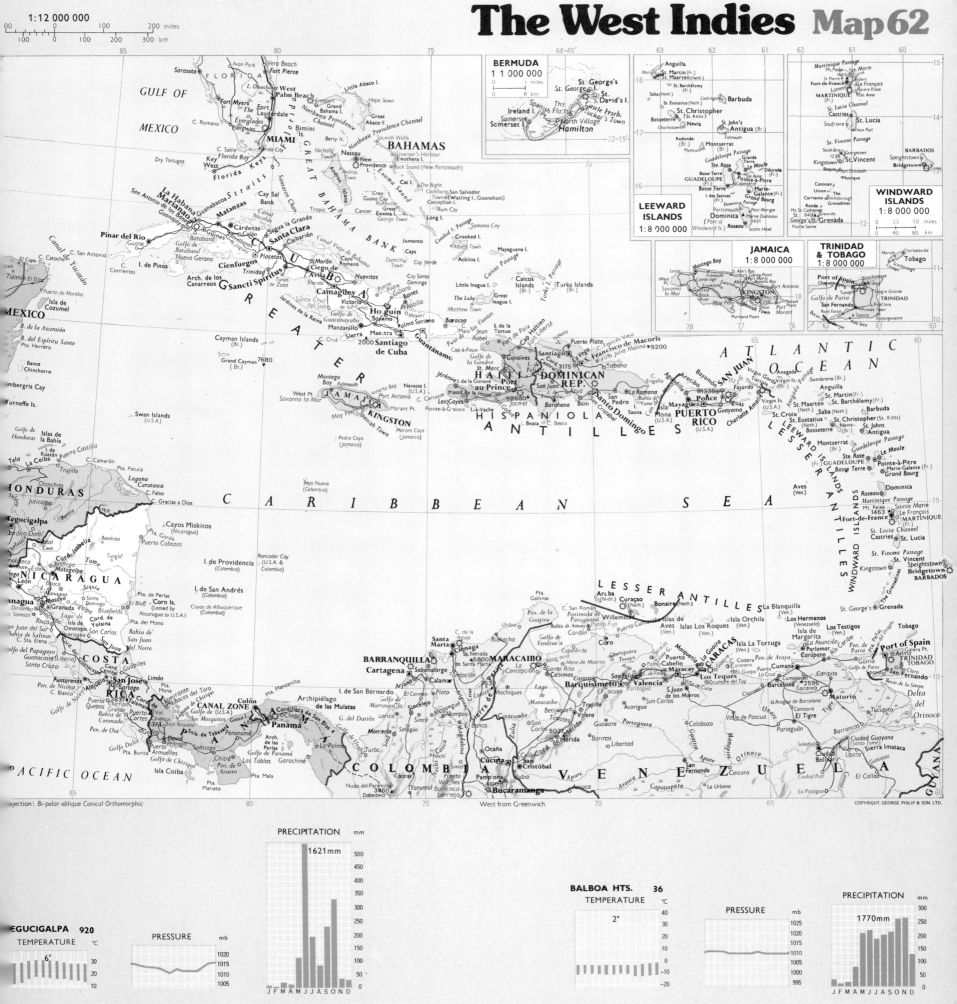

Montserrat, and Dominica (British); Guadeloupe, Marie-Galante, St Barthelemy, Les Saintes, Desirade, and the northern part of St Martin (French); and the Netherlands Antilles, made up of St Eustatius, Saba, and the southern part of St Martin. ∎

The Windward Islands

These are made up of St Lucia and St Vincent, Grenada (independent), Martinique (French), and 600 islets and reefs between Grenada and St Vincent called the Grenadines. ∎

Barbados

Barbados, the most easterly of the Caribbean islands, is a coral island. Since being granted independence by Britain in 1966, it has greatly expanded its tourist industry. It has an area of 431km² (166sq.m.) and a population of 240,000.

The capital and only large town is Bridgetown (105,000). ∎

Trinidad and Tobago

Trinidad and Tobago consists of the large island of Trinidad and the smaller island of Tobago lying 11 kilometres (7 miles) northeast of the Venezuelan coast. Its area is 5,128km² (1,980sq.m.) and its population is 1,084,000. Port-of-Spain (125,000) is the capital and largest city. The population is mostly Negro, but there is a large East Indian minority. The official language is English. Trinidad has a pitch lake that makes the country the largest producer of natural asphalt in the world. But its main revenue comes from petroleum. ∎

Right: Dense bush covers much of the mountainous north of Tobago, while the southern part of this tropical island has superb beaches and coral reefs.

South America

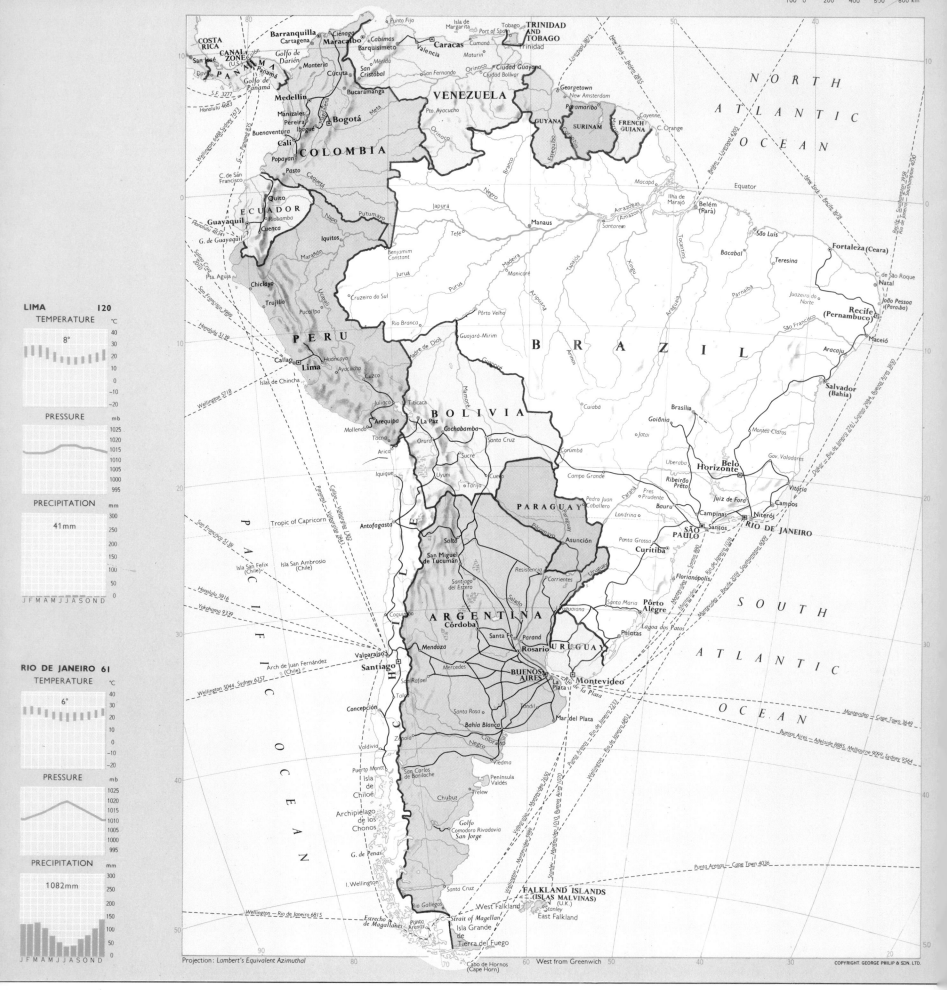

Projection: Lambert's Equivalent Azimuthal

1:30 000 000

COPYRIGHT. GEORGE PHILIP & SON. LTD.

LIMA   120
TEMPERATURE   °C
8°
PRESSURE   mb
PRECIPITATION   mm
41mm
J F M A M J J A S O N D

RIO DE JANEIRO 61
TEMPERATURE   °C
6°
PRESSURE   mb
PRECIPITATION   mm
1082mm
J F M A M J J A S O N D

South America

South America is the fourth largest of the continents. Because of its length and topography it experiences a great range of climatic conditions and has a greater variety of peoples and cultures than any other continent. In the case of many Amerindian tribes, life is little removed from that of the Stone Age. Yet in some of the large cities such as Buenos Aires, Rio de Janeiro, and São Paulo, culture is as sophisticated as anywhere in the world.

South America can be conveniently divided into three main areas: the young Andes Mountains in the west, the ancient, weathered Brazilian and Guiana Highlands in the east, and the immense interior lowland lying between them.

The Andes are so high and rugged that, until the advent of air travel, they proved to be an almost impassable barrier between east and west and seriously hindered the develop-

ment of the continent. A series of parallel ranges run all the way from northern Colombia to the southern tip of Tierra del Fuego. They are at their widest in Bolivia, where they spread out for about 640 kilometres (400 miles). Many of the peaks are active volcanoes.

The Brazilian Highlands make up the oldest part of South America. They extend eastwards into the "bulge" of Brazil, and southwards from the Amazon basin to the borders of Uruguay. For the most part they are gentle, well-watered hills whose fertile soil encourages the growth of coffee and cotton in favoured locations. The Guiana Highlands run across southeastern Venezuela, skirt the southern region of the Guianas, and enter north-eastern Brazil. The dense forests that grow there, interrupted by occasional clearings of tropical grassland, are still largely unexplored.

The interior lowland stretches from the Amazon basin to the Rio de la Plata. It includes the tropical rain

forests of the Amazon, the llanos or grassy plains of the lower Orinoco, and the plains of southern Bolivia, Paraguay and Argentina. These last plains, in their northern parts, are inhospitable and wild, and are known as the Gran Chaco; but farther south they merge with the Argentine Pampa, one of the most fertile regions of the continent. The three great river systems are those of the Orinoco, which flows northeastwards through Venezuela into the Atlantic; the Amazon which starts about 160 kilometres (100 miles) from the Pacific and flows for 6,400 kilometres (4,000 miles) before emptying into the Atlantic; and the system of the Rio de la Plata which with its tributaries drains parts of Bolivia, Brazil, Paraguay, and Uruguay and is the most important inland waterway system in South America.

Although South America experiences almost every kind of climate, there are few extremes as are found in North America or Asia, for example.

The highest temperatures are reached in northern Argentina, and the coldest in Tierra del Fuego, which faces Antarctica. The Peru or "Humboldt" current has a cooling effect on the Pacific coast, while the Brazil Current warms most of the Atlantic coast. Westerly winds from Antarctica bring cold air to much of the southern part of the continent.

Colombia

Area: *1,138,914km² (439,737sq.m.).*
Population: *24.7 million.* **Capital:** *Bogotá (2.8 million).* **Languages:** *Spanish.* **Ethnic groups:** *mixed Negro, Indian, and European stock.*
Main exports: *coffee, petroleum, emeralds, agricultural products.*
Average temperature: *varies with altitude, from subtropical heat to permanent snow.* **Highest point:** *Pico Cristóbal Colón, 5,775m (18,947ft).*

Above: Zipaquira, with its salt mines (foreground) stands at 2,800m (9,000ft) near Bogota, capital of Colombia.

Colombia is the fourth largest country in South America and the only one with a coastline on both sides of the continent. The Pacific Ocean lies on the west, the Isthmus of Panama on the northwest, and the Caribbean Sea on the north. To the south are Peru and Ecuador, to the southeast Brazil, and Venezuela lies to the northeast.

From the border with Ecuador almost to the shores of the Caribbean Sea, four great mountain ranges run parallel across the country between Bogota and the Pacific. Most people live in the high, narrow, fertile valleys that divide the mountain ranges. These mountains have traditionally formed a serious barrier to transport and communications and, as a result, the country's internal development and unification have been slow. Today, air transport forms a vital link between isolated communities.

Huge grassy plains, called *llanos*, cover parts of the south and east of the country. These eventually give way to the steaming equatorial rain forests of the Amazon basin. Colombia's largest river is the Magdalena which flows northwards for 1,600km (1,000 miles) to empty into the Caribbean. The valley of the Cauca, its main tributary, is a fertile farming region.

Colombia's main products are crude petroleum, coffee, bananas, gold, and emeralds. It supplies nearly all the world's emeralds. Although most people are of mixed ancestry, there are also about 400 tribes of Amerindians.

The nation is a presidential democracy. After a period of anarchy and bitter civil war from 1948 to 1958, the country entered an era of relative stability. But by the early 1970s, it was faced with grave inflation, unemployment, and a staggering population growth of 600,000 a year. ∎

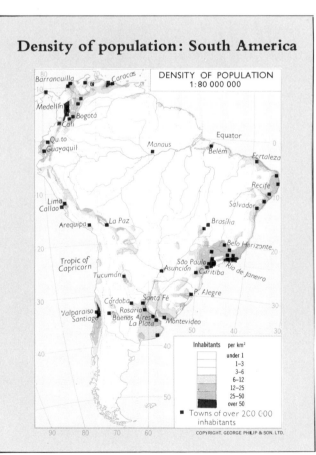

Density of population: South America

DENSITY OF POPULATION
1:80 000 000

Inhabitants per km²
under 1
1–3
3–6
6–12
12–25
25–50
over 50
■ Towns of over 200 000 inhabitants

COPYRIGHT, GEORGE PHILIP & SON. LTD.

Venezuela

Area: *912,050km² (352,145sq.m.).* **Population:** *12.1 million.* **Capital:** *Caracas (2.4 million).* **Languages:** *Spanish.* **Ethnic groups:** *mestizo (65 percent), European (21 percent), Negro (7 percent), Amerindian (2 percent).* **Main exports:** *petroleum and petroleum products, iron ore.* **Average temperature:** *varies with altitude, 21°C (69°F) at 900m (3,000ft).* **Highest point:** *Pico Bolívar, 1,877m (6,000ft).*

Venezuela lies on the northern coast of South America, with the Caribbean Sea forming its northern border. Colombia lies to the west, Brazil to the south, and Guyana to the east.

As a result of its petroleum deposits, Venezuela is the richest country in South America. Its name means 'Little Venice' in Spanish. The Spanish explorers who first set foot in the region in 1499 called it this after finding an Indian village on stilts in the middle of Lake Maracaibo that reminded them of Venice.

Venezuela can be divided into four main regions. The Andean or Venezuelan Highlands, a spur of the Andes, run

Above: The twin towers of Simon Bolivar Center, house government ministries in Caracas, Venezuela.

across the northwestern corner of the country. The second region is made up of the Maracaibo lowlands—a hot, humid region surrounding Lake Maracaibo. This is a huge, shallow, freshwater lake that is open to the sea. The nation's life-giving petroleum is taken from the lake's bed and shores. A third region, called the Guyana Highlands, rises to the south of the River Orinoco. It is a wild, sparsely populated area that covers more than half the country. Finally, the *llanos*

137

Projection: Sanson-Flamsteed's Sinusoidal

LA PAZ ★ 3658
TEMPERATURE °C
4°
PRESSURE mb
PRECIPITATION mm
574mm

QUITO ★ 2850
TEMPERATURE °C
1°
PRESSURE mb
PRECIPITATION mm
1123mm

(grassy plains) of the Orinoco occupy a vast central plain.

The Orinoco itself, 2,560km (1,600 miles) long, is the eighth longest river in the world. Venezuela also claims the highest waterfall in the world, Angel Falls, with a drop of 979m (3,212ft).

Venezuela's major resource is petroleum, and it exports more oil than any other country in Latin America. But supplies are expected to run out by the end of this century, so Venezuelans are rapidly developing new resources. These include especially iron, but also bauxite, asbestos, asphalt, and nickel. Cattle are reared on the *llanos,* but most farmers produce only enough food for themselves and their families.

After gaining its independence from Spain in 1811, Venezuela endured more than 100 years of violence and dictatorships. But following agrarian reform and a new constitution adopted in 1961, general elections of the late 1960s and early 1970s have been more democratic.

Guyana

Area: *214,969km² (83,000sq.m.).* **Population:** *803,000.* **Capital:** *Georgetown (195,000).* **Languages:** *English.* **Ethnic groups:** *E. Indian (47 percent), Negro (33 percent), mixed (12 percent), Amerindian (5 percent).* **Main exports:** *sugar, bauxite, alumina, manganese, rice.* **Average temperature:** *27°C (80°F).* **Highest point:** *Mt Roraima, 2,810m (9,219ft).*

Guyana, formerly British Guiana, is located on the northeast coast of South America. It is bordered by the Atlantic Ocean, Venezuela, Brazil, and Surinam. More than three-quarters of the land area is made up of equatorial rain forest. To the west and south of this region is a belt of grassy plains where a few cattle are reared. The third section is a strip of coastland on the Atlantic. Almost all the

138

Map 64

1:16 000 000

CARACAS 1042
TEMPERATURE °C
3°
PRESSURE mb
PRECIPITATION mm
833mm
J F M A M J J A S O N D

BOGOTA ★ 2645
TEMPERATURE °C
1°
PRESSURE mb
PRECIPITATION mm
1059mm
J F M A M J J A S O N D

COPYRIGHT. GEORGE PHILIP & SON, LTD.

Left: The falls at Kaieteur, Guyana, are the most spectacular in the whole of South America. On reaching the edge of the Guyana Plateau, the Potaro river falls a sheer 248m (741ft) before continuing its journey to the coast. Unlike most such high falls, the river is more than 100 metres wide as it reaches the cliff. Kaieteur is a notable tourist spot reached from Georgetown'. Guyana is drained by several larger rivers.

people live in this coastal strip, in spite of its humid climate and flat, swampy terrain.

Guyana is the fourth largest producer of bauxite in the world. It gained its independence from Britain in 1966 and became a republic in 1970. The country was initially developed as a sugar growing colony and sugar cane, with rice, continues to be the main crop. Relations between the large East Indian and Negro communities have often been strained. ∎

Surinam

Surinam, formerly Dutch Guiana, is one of the three small states on the north-east coast of South America known collectively as the Guianas. It is flanked by Guyana on the west and French Guiana on the east. To the north lies the Atlantic Ocean, and to the south is Brazil. The country has an area of 163,265km² (63,037sq.m.) and a population of 460,000. The capital and largest city is Paramaribo (150,000).

Surinam was an autonomous part of the Netherlands until 1975. Like the other Guianas, it is a tropical country with a low, flat, swampy plain on the coast. Inland there are dense forests, plateaus, and low mountains. Very little of the land is cultivated, but there are large, high grade deposits of bauxite which is the main export. Almost half the people are Negroes, but there are substantial minorities of East Indians and Chinese. Dutch is the official language,

but English, Chinese, and local dialects are widely spoken. ∎

French Guiana

French Guiana is the smallest and most sparsely populated of the Guianas. It is located on the northeast coast of South America and bordered on the north by the Atlantic Ocean, on the west by Surinam, and on the south and east by Brazil. It has an area of 91,000km² (35,135sq.m.), and a population of 69,000. The capital and largest city is Cayenne (24,581).

French Guiana is an overseas department of France. Most of the people are Negroes who live in the coastal lowlands. The land is hardly developed at all, and the few exports are mainly made up of timber, with some rum and sugar also.

The French penal colony of Devil's Island, an island off the coast of French Guiana, was notorious for its brutality. It was closed in 1944. ∎

Ecuador

Area: 283,561km² (109,484sq.m.). **Population:** 7.2 million. **Capital:** Quito (462,863). **Largest city:** Guayaquil (680,209). **Languages:** Spanish, Quechua. **Ethnic groups:** Indian (40 percent), mestizo (40 percent), European (10 percent), Negro (10 percent). **Main exports:** bananas, sugar cane, coffee, cocoa. **Average temperature:** varies with altitude, from tropical lowlands to snow-capped peaks. **Highest point:** Mt Chimborazo, 6,272m (20,577ft).

Ecuador is one of the smallest countries in South America. It is located on the northwestern coast of the continent. It gets its name (which means. 'Equator' in Spanish), from the fact that the country straddles the equator. Its neighbours are Colombia on the north and Peru on the east and south. The Pacific Ocean lies on the west.

Ecuador is a mountainous country, with two main ranges of the Andes running from northeast to southwest for about 680 kilometres (425 miles). Most of the inhabitants live in the fertile central valley that divides the ranges. There are more than 30 volcanoes, a number of them active. Among them is Cotopaxi, 5,896 metres (19,344ft) high, the highest active volcano in the world.

The Galápagos Islands, an offshore group, some 960 kilometres (600 miles) from the mainland, are also part of Ecuador.

Some of the rivers flow westwards down the mountain slopes into the Pacific, while the rest flow eastwards to form part of the Amazon system. A narrow, low-lying swampy plain fringes the Pacific Ocean in the west. To the east of the mountains is another sparsely populated stretch of lowlands, but these are densely forested.

The main products are bananas, coffee, cocoa, sugar, oil, and straw ('Panama') hats. Ecuador is the largest exporter of bananas in the world, but oil exports are increasing and may soon provide the country's main income.

Ecuador has potential wealth, based on its mineral resources. But internal divisions resulting from political differences, social inequalities, and geographical obstacles have kept the country largely undeveloped. ∎

Peru

Area *1,285,216km² (496,225sq.m.).* **Population:** *15.8 million.* **Capital:** *Lima (3.8 million).* **Languages:** *Spanish, Quechua, Aymara.* **Ethnic groups:** *Indian (46 percent), mestizo (43 percent), European (11 percent).* **Main exports:** *copper, fishmeal, silver, iron.* **Average temperature:** *coast, 25°C (77°F), elsewhere dependent on altitude.* **Highest point:** *Mt Huascarán, 6,767m (22,205ft).*

Peru, a land of deserts, mountains, and jungles, is the third largest country in South America. It lies on the west coast of the continent and is bordered on the northwest by Ecuador, on the northeast by Colombia, on the east by Brazil, on the southeast by Bolivia, on the south by Chile, and on the west by the Pacific Ocean.

Peru has a 2,253-kilometre (1,400-mile) coastline on the Pacific. Between the sea and the Andes in the hinterland is a long, narrow, desert coastal stretch with fertile oasis areas. Several ranges of the Andes running north and south form the backbone of the country. These are divided by deep valleys. The eastern slopes of the mountains descend into jungle-clad plains, a region in some parts little explored.

Peru's two longest rivers, the Marañón and Ucayali flow from the eastern side of the Andes to form the headwaters of the Amazon. On the west, more than 50 short rivers tumble down the mountains across the coastal plains and into the ocean.

The climate is almost tropical in many of the valleys, but it grows colder with altitude. The Humboldt current cools the Peruvian shores as it sweeps northwards and also brings rich fishing resources. With an annual catch exceeding 10 million tonnes, Peru has become one of the world's leading fishing nations.

Peru also has great mineral wealth. Among the most important minerals are antimony, copper, bismuth, gold, zinc, silver, and lead. The chemical industry and the processing of fertilizers are also important. Agricultural products include sugar, cotton, wool, and coffee and irrigation is important on the coastal plain.

Most of Peru's wealth is in the hands of the *criollos,* a small group who are the descendants of the original Spanish settlers. Although Spanish is the official language, Quechua, the language of the defeated Incas, is still widely spoken. ∎

Above: Macchu Picchu, the 'lost city' of the Incas in Peru, was excavated in 1911, revealing a citadel and several temples.
Below: Stone and thatch houses on the altiplano, Peru, shelter Indian farmers from the bleak winds of the high plateau.

Brazil

Area: *8,511,965km² (3,286,488sq.m.).*
Population: *107.7 million.* **Capital:**
Brasilia (710,900). **Largest city:** *Sao
Paulo (7.2 million).* **Languages:**
Portuguese. **Ethnic groups:**
*European (62 percent), mulatto (26
percent), Negro (11 percent).* **Main
exports:** *coffee, soya beans, cotton,
timber, iron ore.* **Average
temperatures:** *vary with latitude and
altitude; NE Brazil, 38°C (100°F);
Belo Horizonte (lat. 20°S), 20°C
(68°F).* **Highest point:** *Pico da
Bandeira, 2,890m (9,482ft).*

Brazil is a country of superlatives. It is the
largest country in South America, both in
area and population, and the fifth largest
country in the world. It covers almost
half of South America, and much of it
has remained unexplored until recently.
It possesses the world's greatest river
system—that of the Amazon—and some
of the world's largest forests. It grows
more coffee than any other country, and
its countless varieties of flora and fauna
have never been fully catalogued. The
capital, Brasilia, which superseded Rio
de Janeiro in 1960, is one of the world's
architectural showpieces.
Brazil sprawls over the northeastern
and much of the central part of South
America. It is bordered by French
Guiana, Surinam, Guyana, and Venezuela
on the north, Colombia on the northwest, Peru, Bolivia, Paraguay, and
Argentina on the west, Uruguay on the
south, and the Atlantic Ocean on the
east and northeast.
The land falls naturally into three main
regions. The northern part is made up of
the hot, humid, heavily forested region
of the Amazon basin and the Brazilian
Highlands, near the border with Venezuela. Strenuous government efforts are
being made to open up Amazonia. In
the northeast there is an extremely hot
region of scrubland where catastrophic
droughts are common. A series of
plateaus criss-crossed by fertile river
valleys make up the central and southern
parts of the country. About 50 percent
of the people, 75 percent of the agriculture, and 80 percent of the mining and
manufacturing industries are located in
this pleasant and healthy part of the
country.
Brazil can justifiably claim some of the
world's greatest rivers. The Amazon,
which is navigable for its entire length
within Brazil (3,158km, 1,962 miles),
discharges more water than any river
on earth. Other great waterways are the
Negro, Madeira, São Francisco,
Tocantíns, and Panama.
Most of Brazil's vast mineral wealth
remains untapped, but it already supplies
much of the world's quartz crystal, sheet
mica, beryl, columbium, manganese,
and iron ore. The country also has
valuable deposits of gold, diamonds,
nickel, and oil.
Brazil was originally claimed for
Portugal in 1500. Some 300 years later
it became a monarchy independent of
Portugal, and finally became a republic
in 1889. In 1964 the civilian government
was overthrown by a military junta. In
1975 there were signs of greater political
freedom in the offing. ∎

Bolivia

Area: *1,098,581km² (424,565sq.m.).*
Population: *5.6 million.* **Capital:**
*(actual) La Paz (562,000), (legal).
Sucre (85,000).* **Languages:** *Spanish,
Quechua, Aymara, and other
Amerindian dialects.* **Ethnic groups:**
*Amerindian (63 percent), mestizo
(22 percent), European (15 percent).*
Main exports: *silver, tin, petroleum,
tungsten.* **Average temperatures:**
*varies mainly between night and day;
at La Paz (annual) 9°C (47°F).*
Highest point: *Mt Tocorpuri
6,754m (22,162ft).*

Bolivia is a large landlocked country in
the heart of the continent. It is bordered
by Brazil on the north and east, by
Paraguay and Argentina on the south,
and by Peru and Chile on the west.
Bolivia straddles the Andes Mountains
where some of the highest peaks in the

*Above: The unforgettable bay of Rio de
Janiero with its Sugar Loaf mountain
has made Brazil's major port the most
renowned city in all of South America.*

whole system are found. Between two
parallel ranges in the west, lies the
Altiplano, a huge, high, bleak plateau
that forms the main physical feature of
the country, and where most of the
people live. Forested lowlands stretch
across the northern and eastern parts of
the country, and these merge with scrub
and desert farther south.
Lake Titicaca, the highest navigable
inland body of water in the world, lies
on the border with Peru at a height of
3,810 metres (12,507ft).
The climate is hot in western regions
and generally cooler in the east. The
rainy season lasts from December to
February.
Bolivia, in spite of huge deposits of tin
and silver, is the poorest nation in South
America. This is largely a result of a
drastic fall in tin exports in the face of
lower-cost production elsewhere, and
the many labour problems that have
occurred in the mines. Most of the
labour force is made up of Quechua and
Aymara Indians, who live a harsh and
monotonous life. In 1974 there were
peasants' revolts sparked off by food
shortages and official price rises. Bolivia's
main hope now is the development of
the huge petroleum resources discovered
in the eastern lowlands. ∎

Above: Chile is shaken by minor earthquakes almost daily and major ones are frequent. Here, Villarrica volcano in the central highlands erupts.

Chile

Area: *756,945km² (229,258sq.m.).* Population: *9.5 million.* Capital: *Santiago (2.6 million).* Languages: *Spanish.* Ethnic groups: *mestizo (68 percent), European (30 percent), Indian (2 percent).* Main exports: *copper, fertilizer, iron ore, molybdenum, silver, pulp and paper.* Average temperatures: *vary according to zone—central zone 20°C (68°F) January, 5°C (41°F) August.* Highest point: *Mt Ojos del Salado, 6,870m (22,539ft).*

Chile runs down the west coast of South America, a long, narrow ribbon of land that stretches about 4,500 kilometres (2,800 miles) from the borders of Peru nearly to the Antarctic. The land is sandwiched between the Andes in the east and the Pacific in the west, and is never more than 400 kilometres (250 miles) wide at any point. Peru lies to the north, and Chile's eastern neighbours are Bolivia and Argentina.

Chile's extreme length covers many geographical zones, and each has its own climate. The far south is made up of desolate forests, fiords, islands, and glaciers, ending at Cape Horn, the stormy tip of South America. To the north of this region is a wonderland of immense lakes, forests, mountains, and rivers that is the nation's favourite holiday resort. In the centre of the country is Chile's heartland, where most of the people live. This is a fertile region, warmed by summer sun and watered by winter rains. The basis of its prosperity however, is industrial. Still farther north most of the vegetation peters out in semi-desert. And in the extreme north true desert takes over, but that is where Chile's valuable copper and nitrate deposits are found.

The 150,000 pure-blooded Araucanian Indians who live in the south of the country are the descendants of the only large group of Amerindians who were never completely conquered, either by the Incas or the Spaniards.

In spite of possessing the world's largest reserves of copper, and being the leading producer of iodine, Chile suffered catastrophic inflation in the late 1960s. In 1970, Salvador Allende became the first Marxist to be elected president in South America. But three years later he died when a military junta overthrew the government. ■

Paraguay

Area: *406,752km² (157,048sq.m.).* Population: *2.8 million.* Capital: *Asunción (440,000).* Languages: *Spanish, Guaraní.* Ethnic groups: *mestizo (95 percent), European (5 percent).* Main exports: *meat products, quebracho extract, yerba mate (Paraguayan tea), cotton.* Average temperature: *24°C (74°F) throughout the year.* Highest point: *Paraná plateau, 600m (1,968ft).*

Paraguay, completely landlocked in the heart of the continent, is surrounded by Argentina, Bolivia, and Brazil. The land is cut in two by the River Paraguay, which, with the Paraná, forms two great arteries to the sea by way of the estuary of the Río de la Plata.

To the west of the River Paraguay is the Chaco, an inhospitable region of scrub, jungle, and swamps. To the east are gently rolling grasslands that rise to a forested plateau. Almost all the inhabitants live in this latter region. There they enjoy a subtropical climate with mild, fairly dry winters.

Paraguay, a military dictatorship, has fought and lost two disastrous wars against her neighbours during the last 100 years. Resources are few and most of the inhabitants are extremely poor. Most of the exports are agricultural products, including the extract of quebracho ('axe-breaker'), an extremely hard wood, used in tanning.

Although Spanish is the official language, the country is virtually bilingual, for most people also speak Guaraní, the language of the conquered Amerindians. Cattle ranching is the only major industry. ■

Argentina

Area: *2,776,889km² (1,072,163sq.m.).* Population: *25 million.* Capital: *Buenos Aires (9 million).* Languages: *Spanish.* Ethnic groups: *European (97 percent).* Main exports: *grain, meat, wool, hides.* Average temperatures: *(the Pampa) 21°C (70°F) January, 10°C (50°F) July.* Highest point: *Mt Aconcagua, 6,960m (22,835ft).*

Argentina is the second largest country in South America, after Brazil, both in area and population. It covers most of the southern and southeastern part of the continent, stretching from the tropics in the north almost to ice-bound Antarctica in the south.

The country is bordered on the north by Paraguay and Bolivia, on the northeast by Uruguay and Brazil, on the east and south by the South Atlantic, and on the west by Chile. Argentina shares the large island of Tierra del Fuego in the extreme south with Chile. Argentina, in common with other nations, also claims territory in the Antarctic. She bitterly disputes Britain's possession of the Falkland Islands, which Argentinians call *las Islas Malvinas.*

The Gran Chaco, a region of wooded plains, lies in the north of the country. To the south and southwest of Buenos Aires (the largest city in the southern hemisphere) is the prosperous heart of Argentina, the *Pampa.* This vast, almost treeless expanse of fertile grasslands is where millions of head of cattle and sheep are reared. In the Andean region to the west of the Pampa, orchards of citrus fruits and vineyards flourish in the shadow of the mountains. Argentina's mines are also located there. Patagonia, a bleak, windy plateau, lies to the south. There the main occupations are sheep farming and drilling for oil.

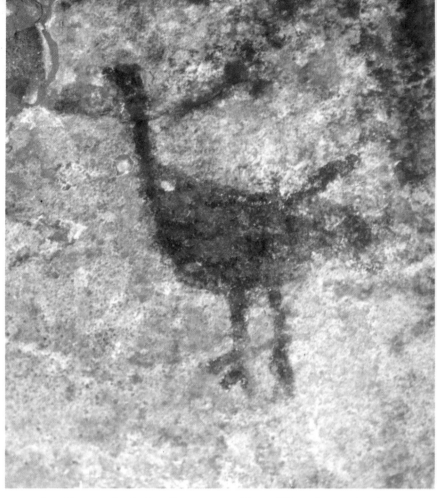

Above: This painting of a rhea (South American ostrich) was found in a shallow cave at Jujuy, north-western Argentina, in the foothills of the Andes.

Aconcagua, Argentina's highest point, is also the highest peak in the western hemisphere. The two most important rivers are the Paraná and Uruguay. They flow into the broad estuary of the Río de la Plata, on whose banks stand two imposing capital cities—Buenos Aires and Montevideo (Uruguay).

The climate varies with the zone. In the north, the winters are mild but the summers are humid and hot. Large areas of the extreme northwest are semi-desert. In the central region, the weather is mild all the year round, while in Patagonia winters are cold and summers are hot.

Besides exporting more beef than any other country, Argentina is one of the leading exporters of sheep and wool. Other important agricultural products include wheat, cotton, rye, barley, alfalfa, oats, linseed, fruit, sugar, and cotton. Mining produces quantities of coal, zinc, lead, copper, iron, silver, and gold, while oil production is on the increase. Meat processing and canning is the principal export industry.

There are almost no descendants of the original Amerindian inhabitants. Most of the people are of Spanish or Italian ancestry, and about a third of the country's population lives in Buenos Aires and its suburbs.

Argentina's post-World War II history has been one of political turmoil. In 1946 Juan Domingo Perón became president, but nine years later was overthrown and exiled to Spain. After a number of governments, both civilian and military, had risen and fallen, Perón returned in 1973, only to die the following year. His widow succeeded him and inherited a country torn by strife, with kidnappings and political murders occuring almost daily, and inflation reaching serious proportions. ■

Uruguay

Area: *177,508km² (66,536sq.m.).* Population: *3 million.* Capital: *Montevideo (1.3 million).* Languages: *Spanish.* Ethnic groups: *European (90 percent), mestizo and mulatto (10 percent).* Main exports: *wool, meat, hides.* Average temperatures: *23°C (74°F) January, 10°C (50°F) June.* Highest point: *Cuchilla Grande range, 600m (2,000ft).*

Uruguay, one of the smallest republics in South America, lies on the southeast

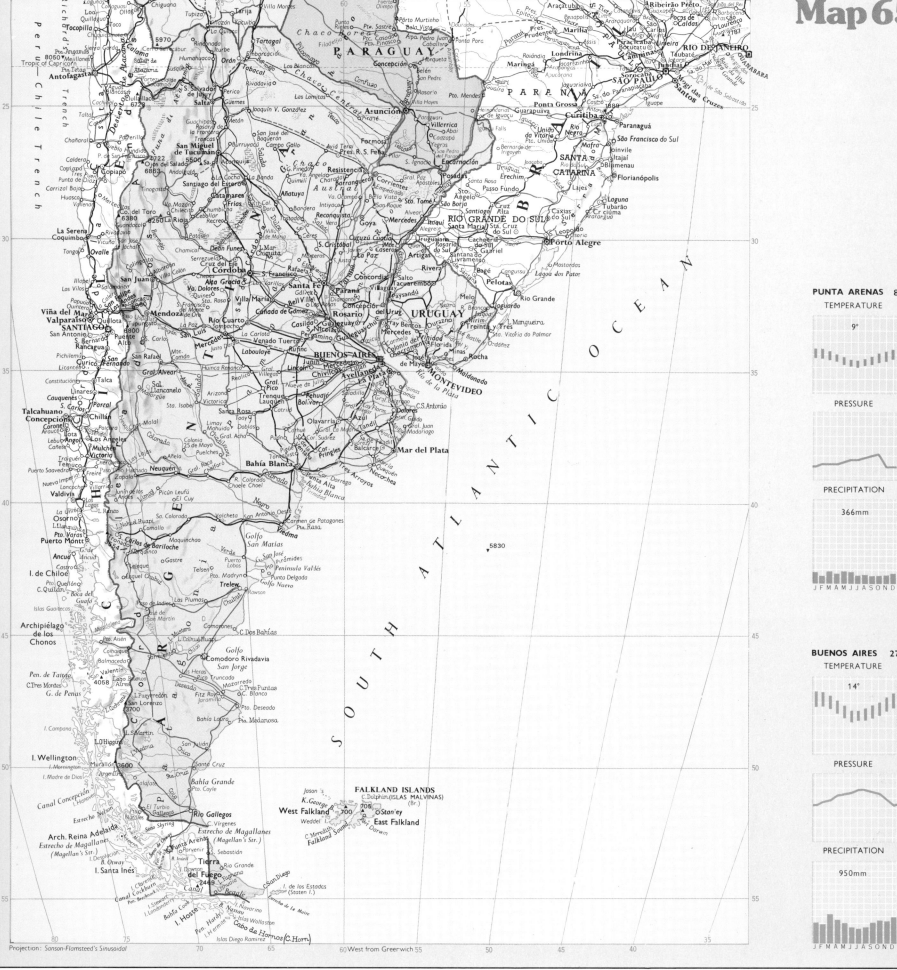

PUNTA ARENAS 8
TEMPERATURE °C
9°
PRESSURE mb
PRECIPITATION mm
366mm
J F M A M J J A S O N D

BUENOS AIRES 27
TEMPERATURE °C
14°
PRESSURE mb
PRECIPITATION mm
950mm
J F M A M J J A S O N D

Projection: Sanson-Flamsteed's Sinusoidal

coast of the continent. It is bordered by Argentina on the south and west, and by Brazil on the north and northeast. The Atlantic Ocean washes its southeastern shores.

Uruguay is a land of rolling, grassy hills, broad plains, and numerous streams. A unique feature of the country is that there is no great physical contrast between one part and another, and that virtually the whole of the land is populated. The River Uruguay and the Río de la Plata separate the country from Argentina. The Negro, flowing through the middle of the country, is another important river. The pleasant, healthy climate, with ample, well distributed rainfall, resembles that of the Mediterranean region.

Uruguay's excellent climate and its fertile soil are its main resources. The principal industry is agriculture, and there are more cattle and sheep in Uruguay than people. The rearing of livestock takes up 90 percent of the land.

Cattle are herded by colourful cowboys called *gauchos*.

Almost all the people are of European descent, mainly Spanish and Italian, and Montevideo, the capital, is the only large town.

Uruguay pioneered social democracy in South America and before World War II was regarded as the most stable of all Latin American republics. But in the 1960s and 1970s the overburdened social system began to break down. Widespread strikes and urban terrorism brought a government reaction of censorship and a general curtailment of some civil liberties.

Right: The gaucho is the folk hero of both Uruguay and Argentina, in the same way as is the cowboy in the USA. The term was originally applied to the nomadic mestizos of the pampas who were hired to round up vast herds of half-wild cattle in the 19th century. Modern cowhands continue to wear the traditional poncho and waistband.

Index to principal countries

Index to text

146

Index to maps

The number in bold type which follows each name in the index refers to the number of the plate where that feature or place will be found.

The geographical co-ordinates which follow the plate number are sometimes only approximate but are close enough for the place name to be located.

An open square □ signifies that the name refers to an administrative division of a country while a solid square ■ follows the name of a country.

Rivers have been indexed to their mouth or to their confluence.

The alphabetical order of names composed of two or more words is governed primarily by the first word and then by the second. This is an example of the rule:

> East Sussex
> East Siberian Sea
> Eastbourne
> Eastern Ghats
> Eastern Malaysia
> Eastleigh

Names composed of a proper name (Gibraltar) and a description (Strait of) are positioned alphabetically by the proper name. All river names are followed by R. If the same word occurs in the name of a town and a geographical feature, the town name is listed first followed by the name or names of the geographical features.

Names beginning with M', Mc are all indexed as if they were spelled Mac.

If the same place name occurs two or more times in the index and all are in the same country, each is followed by the name of the administrative subdivision in which it is located. The names are placed in the alphabetical order of the subdivisions. For example:

> Avon, R., Avon
> Avon, R., Hants
> Avon, R., Warwick

If the same place name occurs twice or more in the index and the places are in different countries they will be followed by the country names and the latter in alphabetical order.

> Athens, Greece
> Athens, U.S.A.

If there is a mixture of these situations, the primary order is fixed by the alphabetical sequence of the countries and the secondary order by that of the country subdivisions. In the latter case the country names are omitted.

> Augusta, Australia
> Augusta, Italy
> Augusta, Ga.   (U.S.A.) are omitted from
> Augusta, Me.   (U.S.A.) the index

A.S.S.R. – Autonomous Soviet Socialist Republic
Ala. – Alabama
Alas. – Alaska
Ang. – Angola
Arch. – Archipelago
Arg. – Argentina
Ariz. – Arizona
Ark. – Arkansas
B. – Baie, Bahía, Bay, Bucht, Bugt
B.C. – British Columbia
Br. – British
C. – Cabo, Cap, Cape
C.A.R. – Central African Republic
C. Prov. – Cape Province
Calif. – California
Chan. – Channel
Col. – Colombia
Colo. – Colorado
Conn. – Connecticut
Cord. – Cordillera
Cr. – Creek
D.C. – District of Columbia
Del. – Delaware
Dep. – Dependency
Des. – Desert
Dist. – District
Dom. Rep. – Dominican Republic
E. – East
Eng. – England

Fd. – Fjord
Fed. – Federal, Federation
Fla. – Florida
Fr. – France, French
G. – Golfe, Golfo, Gulf, Guba
Ga. – Georgia
Gt. – Great
Hants. – Hampshire
Hd. – Head
Hts. – Heights
I. – île, Ilha, Insel, Isla, Island
Id. – Idaho
Ill. – Illinois
Ind. – Indiana
K. – Kap, Kapp
Kans. – Kansas
Ky. – Kentucky
L. – Lac, Lacul, Lago, Lagoa, Lake, Limni, Loch, Lough
La. – Louisana
Ld. – Land
Man. – Manitoba
Mass. – Massachusetts
Md. – Maryland
Me. – Maine
Mich. – Michigan
Minn. – Minnesota
Miss. – Mississippi
Mo. – Missouri
Mont. – Montana
Mt. – Mont, Monte, Monti, Montaña, Mountain

Mys. – Mysore
N. – North, Northern
N.B. – New Brunswick
N.C. – North Carolina
N.D. – North Dakota
N.H. – New Hampshire
N. Ire. – Northern Ireland
N.J. – New Jersey
N. Mex. – New Mexico
N.S.W. – New South Wales
N.Y. – New York
N.Z. – New Zealand
Nat. Park – National Park
Nebr. – Nebraska
Nev. – Nevada
Newf. – Newfoundland
Nic. – Nicaragua
Nig. – Nigeria
O.F.S. – Orange Free State
Okla. – Oklahoma
Ont. – Ontario
Oreg. – Oregon
Os. – Ostrov
P. – Pass, Passo, Pasul
P.N.G. – Papua New Guinea
Pa. – Pennsylvania
Pak. – Pakistan
Pass. – Passage
Pen. – Peninsula
Pk. – Peak
Plat. – Plateau
Port. – Portugal, Portuguese

Prov. – Province, Provincial
Pt. – Point
Pta. – Ponta, Punta
Pte. – Pointe
Que. – Quebec
Queens. – Queensland
R. – Rio, River
R.S.F.S.R. – Russian Soviet Federal Socialist Republic
Ra.(s) – Range(s)
Reg. – Region
Rep. – Republic
Res. – Reserve, Reservoir
S. – South
S. Africa – South Africa
S. Austral. – South Australia
S.D. – South Dakota
S. Leone – Sierra Leone
S.S.R. – Soviet Socialist Republic
Sa. – Serra, Sierra
Sask. – Saskatchewan
Scot. – Scotland
Sd. – Sound
Sp. – Spain, Spanish
St. – Saint
Sta. – Santa
Ste. – Sainte
Sto. – Santo
Str. – Strait, Stretto
Switz. – Switzerland
Tanz. – Tanzania

Tas. – Tasmania
Tenn. – Tennessee
Terr. – Territory
Tex. – Texas
Trans. – Transvaal
U.K. – United Kingdom
U.S.A. – United States of America
U.S.S.R. – Union of Soviet Socialist Republics
Va. – Virginia
Vdkhr. – Vodokhranilishche
Ven. – Venezuela
Vic. – Victoria
Vt. – Vermont
W. – West
W. Va. – West Virginia
Wis. – Wisconsin
Wlkp. – Wielkopolski
Wyo. – Wyoming
Yorks. – Yorkshire
Yug. – Yugoslavia
Zam. – Zambia

A

A'Âlâ en Nîl □ ...45 8 50N 29 55 E
Aachen ...10 50 47N 6 4 E
Aalen ...10 48 49N 10 6 E
Aalsmeer ...9 52 17N 4 43 E
Aalst ...9 50 56N 4 2 E
Aare, R. ...10 47 37N 8 13 E
Aalten ...9 51 56N 6 35 E
Aargau □ ...10 47 26N 8 10 E
Aarhus Amt. □ ...25 56 15N 10 15 E
Aarschot ...9 50 59N 4 49 E
Aba ...44 5 10N 7 19 E
Aba Saud ...43 17 30N 44 10 E
Abadan ...41 30 22N 48 20 E
Abakan ...27 53 40N 91 10 E
Abashiri ...40 44 0N 144 15 E
Abaya, L. ...43 6 30N 37 50 E
Abaza ...26 52 39N 90 6 E
Abbeville ...6 50 6N 1 49 E
Abbottabad ...42 34 10N 73 15 E
Abéché ...45 13 50N 20 35 E
Abenrá ...25 55 3N 9 25 E
Abeokuta ...44 7 3N 3 19 E
Aberayron ...2 52 15N 4 16w
Aberdare ...2 51 43N 3 27w
Aberdeen, Australia .51 32 9s 150 56 E
Aberdeen, U.K. ...3 57 9N 2 6w
Aberdeen, S. Dak. ...59 45 30N 98 30w
Aberdeen, Wash. ...60 47 0N 123 58w
Aberdovey ...2 52 33N 4 3w
Aberfeldy ...3 56 37N 3 50w
Aberystwyth ...2 52 25N 4 6w
Abha ...43 18 0N 42 34 E
Abidjan ...44 5 26N 3 58w
Abilene, Kans. ...59 39 0N 97 16w
Abilene, Tex. ...59 32 22N 99 40w
Abingdon, U.K. ...2 51 40N 1 17w

Abingdon, U.S.A. ...58 36 46N 81 56w
Abkhaz A.S.S.R. □ ...31 43 0N 41 0 E
Abkit ...27 64 10N 147 10 E
Abohar ...32 30 10N 74 10 E
Abomey ...44 7 10N 2 5 E
Aboyne ...3 57 4N 2 48w
Abqaiq ...41 26 0N 49 45 E
Abri ...45 20 50N 30 27 E
Abruzzi □ ...18 42 15N 14 0 E
Absaroka Ra. ...60 44 40N 110 0w
Abū Arish ...43 16 53N 42 48 E
Abū Dhabī ...42 24 28N 54 36 E
Abū Dis ...45 19 12N 33 38 E
Abū Hamed ...45 19 32N 33 13 E
Abū Tig ...45 27 4N 31 15 E
Abū Zabad ...45 12 25N 29 10 E
Abū Zabi ...42 24 28N 54 36 E
Abukuma, R. ...40 38 2N 140 56 E
Acajutla ...61 13 36N 89 50w
Acámbaro ...61 20 0N 100 40w
Acapoueta ...61 22 30N 105 20w
Acapulco ...61 16 51N 99 56w
Acara ...64 2 11s 48 20w
Acarai, Serra ...63 1 50N 57 50w
Acatlán ...61 18 10N 98 3w
Acayucan ...61 17 59N 94 58w
Accra ...44 5 35N 0 6w
Accrington ...2 53 46N 2 22w
Achensee ...11 47 26N 11 45 E
Achill Hd. □ ...114 53 59N 10 15w
Achill I. ...4 53 58N 10 5w
Achinsk ...27 56 20N 90 20 E
Acireale ...20 37 37N 15 9 E
Aconcagua, Mt. ...65 27 0s 66 0w
Acquaviva delle Fonti ...20 40 53N 16 50 E
Acqui ...17 44 40N 8 28 E
Acre □ ...63 9 1s 71 0w
Acri ...20 39 29N 16 23 E
Ada, U.S.A. ...59 34 50N 96 45w

Ada, Yug. ...21 45 49N 20 9 E
Adamaoua Massif de l' ...46 7 20N 12 20 E
Adams ...58 43 50N 76 3w
Adam's Bridge ...33 9 15N 79 40 E
Adam's Pk. ...34 6 55N 80 45 E
Adana ...41 37 0N 35 16 E
Adant ...36 8 8s 131 7 E
Adda, R. ...17 45 8N 9 53 E
Addis Ababa = Addis Abeba ...43 9 2N 38 42 E
Addis Abeba ...43 9 2N 38 42 E
Adel ...58 31 10N 83 28w
Adelaide ...51 34 52s 138 30 E
Aden = Al' Adan ...43 12 50N 45 0 E
Aden, G. of ...43 13 0N 50 0 E
Adige, R. ...18 45 10N 12 20 E
Adirondack, Mts. ...58 44 0N 74 15w
Adler ...31 43 27N 39 55 E
Admiralty Is. ...51 2 0s 147 0 E
Adoni ...34 15 38N 77 17 E
Adour, R. ...7 43 32N 1 32w
Adra ...33 23 30N 86 42 E
Adrano ...20 37 40N 14 49 E
Adrar ...44 27 51N 0 11w
Adrar des Iforas ...44 19 40N 1 40 E
Adre ...45 13 40N 22 20 E
Adria ...18 45 4N 12 3 E
Adrian ...58 41 55N 84 0w
Adriatic Sea ...18 43 0N 16 0 E
Acwa ...43 27 15N 42 35 E
Adzhar A.S.S.R. ...31 42 0N 42 0 E
Aegean Sea ...23 37 0N 25 0 E
Aerht'ai Shan, Mts. ...38 48 0N 90 0 E
Aeós ...23 37 15N 21 50 E
Afghanistan ■ ...42 33 0N 65 0 E
Afgoi ...43 2 7N 44 59 E
Afognak, I. ...56 58 15N 152 30w
Afragola ...20 40 54N 14 15 E

Afyon ...41 38 20N 30 15 E
Agadez ...44 16 58N 7 59 E
Agadir ...44 30 28N 9 35w
Agano, R. ...40 37 57N 139 8 E
Agartala ...33 23 50N 91 23 E
Agats ...36 5 34s 138 5 E
Agboville ...44 5 55N 4 15w
Agdash ...31 40 38N 47 28 E
Agde ...7 43 19N 3 28 E
Agen ...7 44 12N 0 38 E
Aginskoye ...27 51 6N 114 32 E
Agira ...20 37 40N 14 30 E
Agra ...32 27 17N 77 58 E
Ağri Daği Mts. ...41 39 50N 44 15 E
Agrigento ...19 37 19N 13 33 E
Agrinion ...23 38 37N 21 27 E
Agua Clara ...64 20 25s 52 45w
Agua Prieta ...61 31 20N 109 32w
Aguadas ...63 5 40N 75 38w
Aguadilla ...62 18 27N 67 10w
Aguascalientes ...61 22 0N 102 12w
Aguascalientes □ ...61 22 0N 102 20w
Aguilar ...15 37 31N 4 40w
Aguilas ...16 37 23N 1 36w
Agulhas, K. ...47 34 52s 20 0 E
Agusan, R. ...36 9 0N 125 30 E
Ahaggar, Mts. ...44 23 0N 6 30 E
Ahaura ...54 42 20s 171 32 E
Ahlen ...10 51 45N 7 52 E
Ahmadabad ...32 23 0N 72 40 E
Ahmadnagar ...34 19 7N 74 46 E
Ahmadpur ...32 29 12N 71 10 E
Ahuachapán ...61 13 54N 89 52w
Aichi □ ...40 35 0N 137 15 E
Aihun ...27 50 13N 127 33 E
Aiken ...58 33 34N 81 50w
Ailsa Craig, I. ...3 55 15N 5 7w
Ain □ ...6 46 5N 5 20 E

Aïn Beida ...44 35 50N 7 35 E
Ain Ben Tili ...44 25 59N 9 27w
Aïn Sefra ...44 32 47N 0 37w
Ainsworth ...59 42 33N 99 52w
Aïr = Azbine □ ...44 18 30N 8 0 E
Airdrie ...3 55 53N 3 57w
Aire, R. ...6 49 19N 4 49 E
Aisne, R. ...6 49 26N 2 50 E
Aisne □ ...6 49 42N 3 40 E
Aitana, Sierra de ...16 38 35N 0 24w
Aitape ...51 3 11s 142 22 E
Aitolikón ...23 38 26N 21 21 E
Aitush ...38 39 54N 75 40 E
Aiud ...13 46 19N 23 44 E
Aix-en-Provence ...8 43 32N 5 27 E
Aix-les-Bains ...8 45 41N 5 53 E
Aíyina, I. ...23 37 45N 23 26 E
Aiyínion ...23 40 8N 22 38 E
Aiyion ...23 38 15N 22 5 E
Aizpute ...28 56 43N 21 40 E
Ajaccio ...8 41 55N 8 40 E
Ajman ...42 25 25N 55 30 E
Ajmer ...32 26 28N 74 37 E
Akaroa ...54 43 49s 172 59 E
Akashi ...40 34 45N 135 0 E
Akashi, Mts. ...40 35 18N 138 6 E
Akershus Fylke □ ...25 60 10N 11 15 E
Aketi ...46 2 38N 23 47 E
Akhaïa □ ...23 38 5N 21 45 E
Akhaltsikhe ...31 41 40N 43 0 E
Akharnaí ...23 38 5N 23 44 E
Akhelóös, R. ...23 38 36N 21 14 E
Akhmîm ...45 26 31N 31 47 E
Akhtubinsk ...31 48 27N 46 7 E
Akita ...40 39 45N 140 0 E
Akita □ ...40 39 40N 140 30 E
Akjoujt ...44 19 45 E 14 15w
Akko ...41 32 35N 35 4 E
Akkol ...26 43 36N 70 45 E
Akola ...32 20 42N 77 2 E

147

150

Delano 60 35 48N 119 13W
Delaware □ 58 39 0N 75 40W
Delft 9 52 1N 4 22E
Delfzijl 9 53 20N 6 55E
Delgado, C. 46 10 45S 40 40E
Delhi 32 28 38N 77 17E
Delicias 61 28 10N 105 30W
Delitzsch 10 51 32N 12 22E
Delmenhorst 10 53 3N 8 37E
Delnice 18 45 23N 14 50E
Delphi 23 38 30N 22 29E
Delray Beach 58 26 27N 80 4W
Delta 60 38 44N 108 5W
Delvina 23 39 59N 20 4E
Demba 46 5 28S 22 15E
Deming 60 32 10N 107 50W
Demopolis 58 32 30N 87 48W
Den Helder 9 52 57N 4 45E
Denain 6 50 20N 3 22E
Denau 26 38 16N 67 54E
Denbigh 2 53 12N 3 26W
Dendang 35 3 7S 107 56E
Dendermonde 9 51 2N 4 5E
Deniliquin 51 35 30S 144 58E
Denison 59 42 0N 95 18W
Denizli 41 37 42N 29 2E
Denmark 49 34 59S 117 18E
Denmark ■ 25 55 30N 9 0E
Denpaser 35 8 45S 115 5E
Denton 59 33 12N 97 10W
D'Entrecasteaux Is. 51 9 0S 151 0E
Denver 59 39 45N 105 0W
Deoband 32 29 42N 77 43E
Deoghar 33 21 32N 84 45E
Deolali 34 19 50N 73 50E
Deoria 33 26 31N 83 48E
Dera Ghazi Khan 32 30 5N 70 43E
Dera Ismail Khan 32 31 50N 70 50E
Derbent 31 42 5N 48 15E
Derby, Australia 49 17 18S 123 40E
Derby, U.K. 2 52 55N 1 28W
Derbyshire □ 2 52 55N 1 28W
Derg, L. 4 53 0N 8 20W
Derna 45 32 40N 22 35E
Derryveagh Mts. 4 55 0N 8 40W
Derudub 45 17 31N 36 7E
Derwent, R., Cumbria 2 54 38N 3 34W
Derwent, R., Yorks. 2 53 45N 0 57W
Derwentwater 2 53 34N 3 9W
Dervéni 23 38 8N 22 25E
Des Moines 59 41 35N 93 37W
Desenzano del Garda 17 45 28N 10 32E
Desert Center 60 33 45N 115 27W
Desna, R. 28 52 0N 33 15E
Dessau 10 51 49N 12 15E
Detmold 10 51 55N 8 50E
Detroit 58 42 20N 83 5W
Deurne, Belg. 9 51 12N 4 24E
Deurne, Neth. 9 51 27N 5 49E
Deutsche Bucht, B. 10 54 10N 7 51E
Deutschlandsberg 11 46 49N 15 14E
Deux Sevres □ 5 46 5N 22 0W
Deva 13 45 53N 22 55E
Devakottai 34 9 55N 78 45E
Dévaványa 12 47 2N 20 59E
Deventer 9 52 15N 6 10E
Devils Lake 59 48 5N 98 50W
Devizes 2 51 21N 2 0W
Devnya 22 43 13N 27 33E
Devon □ 2 55 50N 3 40W
Devonport, Australia 51 41 12S 146 28E
Devonport, N.Z. 54 36 49S 174 49E
Devonport, U.K. 2 50 23N 4 11W
Dewas 32 22 59N 76 3E
Dewsbury 2 53 42N 1 38W
Dezful 41 32 30N 48 30E
Dezhneva, Mys 27 66 10N 169 3E
Dharan 43 26 9N 50 10E
Dhamar 43 14 46N 44 23E
Dhamtari 33 20 42N 81 35E
Dhanbad 33 23 50N 86 30E
Dhar 32 22 35N 75 26E
Dharangaon 32 21 1N 75 16E
Dharapuram 34 10 45N 77 34E
Dharmapuri 34 12 10N 78 10E
Dharwar 34 15 29N 75 5E
Dhaulagiri, Mt. 33 28 45N 83 45E
Dheskati 23 39 55N 21 49E
Dhestina 23 38 25N 22 31E
Dhodhekánisos, Is. 23 36 35N 27 0E
Dholiana 23 39 54N 20 32E
Dholka 32 22 44N 72 29E
Dholpur 32 26 45N 77 59E
Dhomokos 23 39 10N 22 18E
Dhoraji 32 21 45N 70 37E
Dhrangadhra 32 22 59N 71 31E
Dhubri 33 26 2N 90 2E
Dhulia 32 20 58N 74 50E
Diablo Heights 61 8 58N 79 34W
Diamantina 64 18 5S 43 40W
Diamantina, R. 51 26 45S 139 10E
Diamantino 64 14 30S 56 30W
Diano Marini 17 43 55N 8 3E
Dibaya 46 6 20S 22 0E
Dibi 43 4 10N 41 52E
Dickinson 59 46 50N 102 40W
Dickson 58 36 5N 87 22W
Die 8 44 47N 5 22E
Diégo-Suarez 48 12 25S 49 20E
Dien Bien Phu 37 21 20N 103 0E
Dieppe 5 49 54N 1 4E
Diest 9 50 58N 5 4E
Differdange 9 49 31N 5 54E
Digby 57 44 41N 65 50W
Digne 8 44 5N 6 12E
Digoin 6 46 29N 3 58E
Digos 36 6 45N 125 20E
Digul, R. 36 7 7S 138 42E
Dijlah, Nahr, R. 41 31 0N 47 25E
Dijon 6 47 20N 5 0E
Dikson 26 73 40N 80 5E
Dikwa 45 12 4N 13 30E
Dili 36 8 39S 125 34E
Dillenburg 10 50 44N 8 17E
Dillon, Mont. 60 45 9N 112 36W
Dillon, S.C. 58 34 26N 79 20W
Dilolo 46 10 28S 22 18E
Dimashq 41 33 30N 36 18E
Dimbokor 44 6 45N 4 30W
Dimboola 51 36 28S 142 0E
Dimbovita, Reg. 13 45 0N 25 30E
Dimitrovgrad, Bulg. 22 42 5N 25 35E
Dimitrovgrad, Yug. 21 43 0N 22 48E
Dimitrovo = Pernik 21 42 36N 23 2E
Dimovo 21 43 43N 22 50E
Dinagat, I. 36 10 10N 125 40E
Dinajpur 33 25 33N 88 43E
Dinan 5 48 28N 2 2W
Dinant 9 50 16N 4 55E
Dinapore 33 25 38N 85 5E
Dinar 41 38 5N 30 15E
Dinara Planina 18 44 0N 17 30E
Dinard 5 48 38N 2 6W
Dindigul 34 10 25N 78 0E
Dingle 4 52 8N 10 15W
Dingle, B. 4 52 5N 10 15W
Dingwall 3 57 36N 4 26W
Dinosaur Nat. Monument 60 40 30N 108 45W
Dinuba 60 36 37N 119 22W
Diósgyor 12 48 7N 20 43E
Diourbel 44 14 39N 16 12W
Dipolog 36 8 36N 123 20E
Dire Dawa 43 9 35N 41 45E
Diriamba 62 11 51N 86 19W
Disappointment, C. 60 46 20N 124 0W
Disappointment, L. 49 23 20S 122 40E
Distrito Federal □ Brazil 64 15 45S 47 45W
Distrito Federal □ Mexico 61 19 15N 99 10W
Divinópolis 64 20 9S 44 54W
Divnoye 31 45 55N 43 27E
Dixon, Ill. 59 41 50N 89 30W
Dixon, N. Mex. 60 36 15N 105 57S
Dixon Entrance 56 54 30N 132 0W
Diyarbakir 41 37 55N 40 18E
Djajapura 36 2 28N 140 38E
Djajawidjaja, Pegunungan 36 7 0S 139 0E
Djakarta 36 6 9S 106 49E
Djambi □ 35 1 30S 103 0E
Djapara 36 6 30S 110 40E
Djatiberang 36 6 28S 108 18E
Djatinegara 36 6 13S 106 52E
Djelfa 44 34 40N 3 15E
Djema 46 6 9N 25 15E
Djember 36 8 11S 113 41E
Djibouti 43 11 30N 43 5E
Djidjelli 44 36 52N 5 50E
Djirlagne 37 11 44N 108 15E
Djombang 36 7 32S 112 12E
Djursholm 25 59 25N 18 6E
Dmitriev Lgovskiy 28 52 10N 35 0E
Dmitrov 29 56 25N 37 32E
Dnepr, R. 30 46 30N 32 18E
Dneprodzerzhinsk 30 48 32N 34 30E
Dneprodzerzhin-skoye Vdkhr. 30 49 0N 34 0E
Dnepropetrovsk 30 48 30N 35 0E
Dnestr, R. 30 46 18N 30 17E
Dnieper, R. = Dnepr, R. 30 46 30N 32 18E
Dno 28 57 50N 29 58E
Doba 45 8 40N 16 50E
Döbeln 10 51 7N 13 10E
Doberai, Djazirah 36 1 25S 133 0E
Dobo 36 5 45S 134 15E
Doboj 21 44 46N 18 6E
Dobra 13 53 34N 15 20E
Dobrich Bazargic = Tolbukhin 22 43 37N 27 49E
Dobrush 28 52 28N 30 35E
Dodge City 59 37 42N 100 0W
Dodoma 46 6 8S 35 45E
Doetinchem 9 51 59N 6 18E
Dona 42 25 17N 51 32E
Dohad 32 22 50N 74 15E
Dojo 36 35 51N 139 32E
Dol 5 48 34N 1 47W
Dolbeau 57 48 25N 72 18W
Dôle 6 47 7N 5 31E
Dolgellau 2 52 44N 3 53W
Dolinskaya 30 48 16N 32 36E
Dolisie 46 4 0S 13 10E
Dolj, Reg. 13 44 10N 23 30E
Dolni Dŭbnik 22 43 24N 26 26E
Dolo 18 45 25N 12 4E
Dolomiti, Mts. 18 46 30N 11 40E
Dolores 65 36 20S 57 40W
Dolphin & Union, Str. 56 69 30N 117 0W
Domažlice 11 49 28N 13 0E
Dombarovskiy 26 51 0N 59 10E
Dombasle 6 49 8N 6 24E
Dombóvár 12 46 21N 18 9E
Dominica, I. 62 15 20N 61 20W
Dominican Rep. ■ 62 19 0N 70 30W
Domodóssola 17 46 6N 8 19E
Don, R. Eng. 2 53 39N 0 59W
Don, R. Scot. 3 57 10N 2 4W
Don, R., U.S.S.R. 31 47 4N 39 18E
Don Benito 15 38 53N 5 51W
Donaldsonville 58 30 2N 91 50W
Donard, Slieve 4 54 10N 5 57W
Donawitz 11 47 22N 15 4E
Doncaster 2 53 31N 1 9W
Dondo 46 19 33S 34 36E
Dondra Head 34 5 55N 80 40E
Donegal 4 54 39N 8 8W
Donegal □ 4 54 53N 8 0W
Donegal, B. 4 54 30N 8 35W
Donetsk 30 48 0N 37 45E
Dong Hene 37 16 44N 105 14E
Dong Hoi 37 17 18N 106 36E
Dongara 49 29 14S 114 57E
Donggala 36 0 30S 119 40E
Dongou 46 2 0N 18 5E
Donji Vakuf 21 44 8N 17 24E
Donnelly's Crossing 54 35 42S 173 38E
Doon, R. 3 55 26N 4 38W
Dora Báltea, R. 17 45 11N 8 5E
Dora Riparia, R. 17 45 5N 7 44E
Dorada, Costa 16 40 45N 1 15E
Dorchester 2 50 42N 2 28W
Dordogne, R. 7 45 2N 0 35W
Dordogne □ 7 45 5N 0 40E
Dordrecht 9 51 48N 4 39E
Dornbirn 11 47 25N 9 45E
Dornoch 3 57 52N 4 0W
Dornoch Firth 3 57 52N 4 0W
Dorogobuzh 28 54 50N 33 10E
Dorohoi 13 47 56N 26 30E
Döröö Nuur 38 48 0N 93 0E
Dorrigo 51 30 19S 152 38E
Dorset □ 2 50 48N 2 25W
Dortmund 10 51 32N 7 28E
Doruma 46 4 42N 27 33E
Dos Hermanas 15 37 16N 5 55W
Dosso 44 13 0N 3 13E
Dothan 58 31 10N 85 25W
Douai 6 50 12N 121 25W
Douala 46 4 0N 9 45E
Douarnenez 5 48 6N 4 21W
Doubs, R. 6 46 54N 5 2E
Doubs □ 6 47 10N 6 20E
Doucet 57 48 15N 76 35W
Douglas, U.K. 2 54 9N 4 29W
Douglas, U.S.A. 60 31 21N 109 30W
Douglasville 58 33 46N 84 43W
Doullens 6 50 10N 2 20E
Dounreay 3 58 40N 3 28W
Dourada, Serra 64 13 10S 48 45W
Dourados 64 22 9S 54 50W
Douro, R. 15 41 8N 8 40W
Dove, R. 2 52 50N 1 35W
Dover, U.K. 2 51 7N 1 19E
Dover, U.S.A. 58 43 5N 70 51W
Dovey, R. 2 52 32N 4 0W
Dovrefjell 25 62 15N 9 33E
Down □ 4 54 20N 6 0W
Downham Market 2 52 36N 0 22E
Downpatrick 4 54 20N 5 43W
Drăgăsani 13 44 39N 24 17E
Dragocvet 21 44 0N 21 15E
Draguignan 8 43 30N 6 27E
Drake Passage 55 58 0S 68 0W
Drakensberg, Mts. 48 31 0S 25 0E
Dráma 23 41 9N 24 10E
Drammen 25 59 42N 10 12E
Drangajökull, Mt. 24 66 9N 22 15W
Drava, R. 21 45 30N 18 55E
Draveil 6 48 41N 2 25E
Dren 21 43 8N 20 44E
Drenthe □ 9 52 45N 6 30E
Dresden 10 51 2N 13 45E
Dresden □ 10 51 12N 14 0E
Dreux 5 48 44N 1 23E
Driffield 2 54 0N 0 25W
Drina, R. 21 44 53N 19 21E
Drogheda 4 53 45N 6 20W
Droichead Nua 4 53 11N 6 50W
Drôme, R. 8 44 46N 4 46E
Drôme □ 8 44 38N 5 15E
Dronfield 51 21 12S 140 3E
Dronne, R. 7 45 2N 0 9W
Dronning Maud Land 55 70 05 10 0E
Drumheller 56 51 25N 112 40W
Druya 28 55 45N 27 15E
Dryanovo 22 42 59N 25 28E
Duaringa 51 23 42S 149 42E
Dubayy 42 24 10N 55 20E
Dubbo 51 32 11S 148 35E
Dublin, Ireland 4 53 20N 6 18W
Dublin, U.S.A. 58 32 30N 83 0W
Dublin □ 4 53 24N 6 20W
Dubna 29 54 8N 36 52E
Dubno 28 50 25N 24 45E
Dubois 60 44 7N 112 9W
Dubossary Vdkhr. 30 47 30N 29 0E
Dubovka 31 49 5N 44 50E
Dubovskoye 31 47 28N 42 40E
Dubrajpur 33 23 48N 87 25E
Dubrovitsa 28 51 31N 26 35E
Dubrovnik 21 42 39N 18 6E
Dubrovskoye 27 58 55N 111 0E
Dubuque 59 42 30N 90 41W
Duchess 51 21 20S 139 50E
Ducie I. 53 24 47S 124 40W
Dudinka 27 69 30N 86 0E
Dudley 2 52 30N 2 5W
Dueñas 15 41 52N 4 33W
Duero, R. 15 41 8N 8 40W
Dugi Otok, I. 18 44 0N 15 0E
Duisburg 10 51 27N 6 42E
Dukelský průsmyk, pass 12 49 25N 21 43E
Dukhan 42 25 25N 50 50E
Dukhovshchina 28 55 15N 32 27E
Dulgopol 22 43 3N 27 22E
Dululu 51 23 48S 150 15E
Duluth 59 46 48N 92 10W
Dum-Dum 33 22 39N 88 26E
Dumai 35 1 35N 101 20E
Dumaring 36 1 46N 118 10E
Dumas, Ark. 59 33 52N 91 30W
Dumas, Tex. 59 35 50N 101 58W
Dûmat al Jandal 41 29 55N 39 40E
Dumbarton 3 55 58N 4 35W
Dumbrăveni 13 46 14N 24 34E
Dumfries and Galloway □ 3 55 5N 4 0W
Dumka 33 24 0N 87 22E
Dumyât 45 31 24N 31 48E
Dun Laoghaire 4 53 17N 6 9W
Dunarea, R., = Danube, R. 22 45 20N 29 40E
Dunaújváros 12 47 0N 18 57E
Dunav, R. = Danube, R. 22 45 20N 29 40E
Dunback 54 45 23S 170 36E
Dunbar 3 56 0N 2 32W
Dunblane 3 56 10N 3 58W
Duncan, Ariz. 60 32 46N 109 6W
Duncan, Okla. 59 34 25N 98 0W
Dundalk 4 53 55N 6 45W
Dundee, S. Afr. 48 28 12S 30 16E
Dundee, U.K. 3 56 29N 3 0W
Dundrum B. 4 54 12N 5 40W
Dunedin 54 45 50S 170 33E
Dunfermline 3 56 5N 3 28W
Dungannon 4 54 30N 6 47W
Dungannon □ 4 54 31N 6 47W
Dungarvan 4 52 6N 7 40W
Dungeness 2 50 54N 0 59E
Dunkeld 3 56 34N 3 36W
Dunkerque 6 51 2N 2 20E
Dunkirk 58 42 30N 79 18W
Dunkwa 44 6 0N 1 47W
Dunnellon 58 29 4N 82 28W
Dunoon 3 55 57N 4 56W
Dunstable 2 51 33N 0 31W
Durack Ra. 49 16 50S 127 40E
Durance, R. 8 43 55N 4 44E
Duranculak = Blatnitsa 22 43 41N 28 32E
Durango, Mexico 61 24 3N 104 39W
Durango, Spain 16 43 13N 2 40W
Durango, U.S.A. 60 37 10N 107 50W
Durango □ 61 25 0N 105 0W
Durant 59 34 0N 96 25W
Durazno 65 33 25S 56 38W
Durban 48 29 49S 31 1E
Durdevac 21 46 2N 17 3E
Duren 10 50 48N 6 30E
Durg 33 21 15N 81 22E
Durham, UK 2 54 47N 1 34W
Durham, U.S.A. 58 36 0N 78 55W
Durham □ 2 54 42N 1 45W
Durmitor, Mt. 21 43 18N 19 0E
Durresi 23 41 19N 19 28E
D'Urville, I. 54 40 50S 173 55E
Dushak 26 37 20N 60 10E
Dushanbe 26 38 40N 68 50E
Dusseldorf 10 51 15N 6 46E
Duzdab = Záhedán 42 29 30N 60 50E
Dvur Králové 11 50 27N 15 50E
Dyatkovo 28 53 48N 34 27E
Dyersburg 59 36 2N 89 20W
Dyfed □ 2 52 0N 4 30W
Dzerzhinsk 29 56 15N 43 15E
Dzhalal Abad 26 41 0N 73 0E
Dzhambul 26 43 10N 71 0E
Dzhankoi 30 45 40N 34 30E
Dzhetygara 26 52 10N 61 0E
Dzhezkazgan 26 47 10N 67 40E
Dzhizak 26 40 20N 68 0E
Dzhugdzur, Khrebet 27 57 30N 138 0E
Dzhungarskiye Vorota 26 45 0N 82 0E
Dzialdowo 14 53 15N 20 15E
Dzierzoniow 14 50 45N 16 39E
Dzungaria, Reg. 38 44 10N 88 0E
Dzuunbulag 39 46 58N 115 30E

E

Eagle Butte 59 45 1N 101 12W
Eagle Nest 60 36 33N 105 13W
Eagle Pass 59 28 45N 100 35W
Eaglehawk 51 36 43S 144 16E
Ealing 2 51 30N 0 19W
East China Sea 39 30 5N 126 0E
East Germany ■ 10 52 0N 12 0E
East Indies 62 0 0N 120 0E
East Liverpool 58 40 39N 80 35W
East London 48 33 0S 27 55E
East Point 58 33 40N 84 28W
East Retford 2 53 19N 0 55W
East Sussex □ 2 50 55N 0 16E
East Siberian Sea 27 73 0N 160 0E
Eastbourne, N.Z. 54 41 19S 174 55E
Eastbourne, U.K. 2 50 46N 0 18E
Easter I. 53 27 8S 109 23W
Eastern Ghats 34 15 0N 80 0E
Eastern Malaysia □ 35 4 0N 115 0E
Eastleigh 2 50 58N 1 21W
Eau Claire 59 44 46N 91 30W
Ebbw Vale 2 51 47N 3 12W
Ebensee 11 47 48N 13 46E
Eberbach 10 49 27N 8 59E
Eberswalde 10 52 49N 13 50E
Eboli 20 40 39N 15 2E
Ebro, R. 16 40 43N 0 54E
Echigo, Mts. 40 37 50N 139 50E
Ecija 15 37 30N 5 10W
Eckernförde 10 54 26N 9 50E
Ecuador ■ 63 2 0S 78 0W
Edam 9 52 31N 5 3E
Edapally 34 11 19N 78 3E
Eddystone 2 50 11N 4 16W
Ede 9 52 4N 5 40E
Eden 51 37 3S 149 55E
Eden, R. 2 54 57N 3 1W
Edenburg 47 29 43S 25 58E
Edenderry 4 53 21N 7 3W
Edenton 58 36 5N 76 36W
Edge Hill 2 52 7N 1 28W
Edhessa 23 40 48N 22 5E
Edievale 54 45 49S 169 22E
Edinburgh 3 55 57N 3 12W
Edmonton, Australia 51 16 55S 145 45E
Edmonton, Canada 56 53 50N 113 30W
Edmundston 57 47 23N 68 20W
Edson 56 53 40N 116 28W
Edward, L. = Idi Amin Dada, L. 46 0 25S 29 40E
Edwards Plat. 59 30 30N 101 5W
Eekloo 9 51 11N 3 33E
Eforie Sud 13 44 1N 28 37E
Égadi, Is. 19 37 55N 12 10E
Eger 12 47 53N 20 27E
Eger = Cheb 11 50 9N 12 20E
Egerton, Mt. 49 24 42S 117 44E
Egmont, Mt. 54 39 17S 174 5E
Egvekinot 27 66 19N 179 10W
Egypt ■ 45 28 0N 31 0E
Ehime □ 40 33 30N 132 40E
Eibar 16 43 11N 2 28W
Eichstatt 10 48 53N 11 12E
Eifel, Mts. 10 50 10N 6 45E
Eigersund 24 58 26N 6 1E
Eigg, I. 3 56 54N 6 10W
Eighty Mile Beach 49 19 30S 120 40E
Eli 43 8 0N 49 50E
Eilenburg 10 51 28N 12 38E
Einasleigh 51 18 32S 144 5E
Eindhoven 9 51 26N 5 30E
Eisenach 10 50 58N 10 18E
Eisenerz 11 47 32N 15 54E
Eisenhüttenstadt 10 52 9N 14 41E
Eisleben 10 51 31N 11 31E
Ekenäs 24 59 58N 23 26E
Eketahuna 54 40 38S 175 43E
Ekibastuz 26 51 40N 75 22E
Ekimchan 27 53 0N 133 0W
Eksjö 25 57 40N 14 58W
El Alamein 45 30 48N 28 58E
El' Arîsh 45 31 8N 33 50E
El Asnam 44 36 10N 1 20E
El Bawiti 45 28 25N 28 45E
El Bonillo 16 38 57N 2 35W
El Cajon 60 32 49N 117 0W
El Centro 60 32 50N 115 40W
El Cerro 63 17 30S 61 40W
El Djouf 44 20 0N 11 30E
El Dorado, Ark. 59 33 10N 92 40W
El Dorado, Kans. 59 37 55N 96 56W
El Faiyûm 45 29 19N 30 50E
El Fâsher 45 13 33N 25 26E
El Ferról 15 43 29N 3 14W
El Geneina 45 13 27N 22 45E
El Gîza 45 30 0N 31 10E
El Goléa 44 30 30N 2 50E
El Iskandarîya 45 31 0N 30 0E
El Istwâ 'ya □ 45 5 0N 31 0E
El Jadida 44 33 16N 9 31W
El Kab 45 19 27N 32 46E
El Kal 44 36 50N 8 30E
El Kef 44 36 12N 8 47E
El Khârga 45 25 30N 30 33E
El Khartûm 45 15 31N 32 55E
El Khartûm Bahrî 45 15 40N 32 31E
El Mahalla el Kubra 45 31 0N 31 0E
El Mansura 45 31 0N 31 19E
El Minyâ 45 28 7N 30 33E
El Obeid 45 13 8N 30 18E
El Oro 61 25 50N 105 20W
El Oued 44 33 20N 6 58E
El Paso 60 31 50N 106 30W
El Progreso 61 15 26N 87 51W
El Qâhira 45 30 1N 31 14E
El Qantara 45 30 51N 32 20E
El Qubba 45 11 10N 27 5E
El Reno 59 35 30N 98 0W
El Shallal 45 24 0N 32 53E
El Suweis 45 29 58N 32 31E
El Tigre 63 8 55N 64 15W
El Uqsur 45 25 41N 32 38E
El Wak 46 2 49N 40 56E
Elassón 23 39 55N 22 12E
Elaziğ 41 38 37N 39 22E
Elba, I. 17 42 48N 10 15E
Elbasani 23 41 9N 20 9E
Elbe, R. 10 53 50N 9 0E
Elbert, Mt. 60 39 12N 106 36W
Elbeuf 5 49 17N 1 2E
Elblag 14 54 10N 19 25E
Elbrus, Mt. 31 43 30N 42 30E
Elche 16 38 15N 0 42W
Elda 16 38 29N 0 47W
Eldoret 46 0 30N 35 25E
Elektrostal 29 55 41N 38 32E
Elephant Butte Res. 60 33 45N 107 30W
Eleuthera I. 62 25 0N 76 20W
Elevsís 23 38 4N 23 26E
Elgin, U.K. 3 57 39N 3 20W
Elgin, U.S.A. 58 42 2N 88 17W
Elgon, Mt. 46 1 10N 34 30E
Eliase 36 8 10S 130 55E
Elisabethville = Lubumbashi 46 11 32S 27 28E
Elista 31 46 25N 44 17E
Elizabeth, Australia 51 34 45S 138 39E
Elizabeth, U.S.A. 58 40 37N 74 12E
Elizabeth City 58 36 18N 76 16W
Elizabethton 58 36 20N 82 13W
Elk 14 53 50N 22 22E
Elk City 59 35 25N 99 25W

Fukui 40 36 0N 136 10 E
Fukui □ 40 36 0N 136 12 E
Fukuoka 40 33 30N 130 30 E
Fukushima 40 37 45N 140 28 E
Fukushima □ 40 37 30N 140 15 E
Fukuyama 40 34 35N 133 20 E
Fulda 10 50 32N 9 41 E
Fulda, R. 10 51 25N 9 39 E
Fullerton 60 33 52N 117 58W
Fulton 58 43 19N 76 25W
Fumel 7 44 30N 0 58 E
Funabashi 40 35 45N 14 0 E
Fundacion 63 10 31N 74 11W
Fundy, B. of 57 45 0N 66 0W
Funtua 44 11 30N 7 18 E
Furat. Nahr al, R. 41 33 30N 43 0 E
Furmanov 29 57 25N 41 3 E
Furmanovo 31 49 42N 49 25 E
Furneaux Group 51 40 10S 147 50 E
Furness 2 54 14N 3 8W
Fürstenfeld 11 47 3N 16 3 E
Fürstenfeldbruck 10 48 10N 11 15 E
Fürstenwalde 10 52 20N 14 3 E
Fürth 10 49 29N 11 0 E
Fushun 39 42 0N 123 59 E
Fusin 39 42 12N 121 33 E
Füssen 10 47 12N 121 33 E
Fuyuan 39 48 9N 134 3 E
Fylde 2 53 47N 2 56W
Fyn, I. 25 55 20N 10 30 E
Fyne, L. 3 56 0N 5 20W
Fyns Amt. □ 25 55 15N 10 30 E

G

Gabela 46 11 0S 14 37 E
Gabès 44 33 53N 10 2 E
Gabès, G. de 45 34 0N 10 30 E
Gabon ■ 46 0 10S 10 0 E
Gaborone 47 24 37S 25 57 E
Gabrovo 22 42 52N 25 27 E
Gach Saran 42 30 15N 50 45 E
Gacko 21 43 10N 18 33 E
Gadag 34 15 30N 75 45 E
Gádor, Sierra de 16 36 57N 2 45 E
Gadsden 58 34 1N 86 0W
Gadwal 34 16 10N 77 50 E
Găesti 13 44 48N 25 19 E
Gaeta 19 41 12N 13 35 E
Gaeta, G. di 19 41 0N 13 25 E
Gafsa 44 34 24N 8 51 E
Gagarin 28 55 30N 35 0 E
Gagra 31 43 20N 40 10 E
Gaillac 7 44 54N 1 54 E
Gainesville 58 34 17N 83 47W
Gainesville 59 33 40N 97 10W
Gainsborough 2 53 23N 0 46W
Gairdner, L. 49 31 30S 136 0 E
Gairloch, L. 3 57 43N 5 45W
Gal Oya Res. 34 8 5N 80 55 E
Galápagos, Arch. 53 0 0 89 0W
Galas, R. 37 4 55N 101 57 E
Galashiels 3 55 37N 2 50W
Galaţi 13 45 27N 28 2 E
Galatina 20 40 10N 18 10 E
Galátone 20 40 8N 18 3 E
Galdhøpiggen 25 61 38N 8 18 E
Galesburg 59 40 57N 90 23W
Galich 29 58 23N 42 18 E
Galicia □ 15 42 43N 8 0W
Gallarate 17 45 40N 8 48 E
Galle 34 6 5N 80 10 E
Galliate 17 45 27N 8 44 E
Gallinas, Pta 63 12 28N 71 40W
Gallipoli 20 40 8N 18 0 E
Gällivare 24 67 7N 20 32 E
Galloway Reg. 3 55 0N 4 25W
Galloway, Mull of 3 54 38N 4 50W
Gallup 60 35 30N 108 54W
Galty Mts. 4 52 22N 8 10W
Galtymore, Mts. 4 52 22N 8 12W
Galveston 59 29 15N 94 48W
Gálvez 65 32 0S 61 20W
Galway 4 53 16N 9 4W
Galway □ 4 53 16N 9 3W
Galway B. 4 53 10N 9 20W
Gamagori 40 34 50N 137 14 E
Gambia ■ 44 13 25N 16 0W
Gambia, R. 44 13 28N 16 34W
Gamboa 61 9 8N 79 42W
Ganàveh 42 29 35N 50 35 E
Gander 57 49 1N 54 33W
Gandia 16 33 58N 0 9W
Ganga, R. 33 23 22N 90 32 E
Ganganagar 32 29 56N 73 56 E
Gangavati 34 15 30N 76 36 E
Ganges, R. = Ganga, R. 33 23 22N 90 32 E
Gangtok 33 27 20N 88 40 E
Gannat 6 46 7N 3 11 E
Gannett Pk. 60 43 15N 109 47W
Gao 44 18 0N 1 0 E
Gaoual 44 11 45N 13 25W
Gap 8 44 33N 6 5 E
Garachiné 62 8 0N 78 12 E
Garanhuns 64 8 50S 36 30W
Garberville 60 40 11N 123 50W
Gard □ 8 44 2N 4 10 E
Garda, L. di 17 45 40N 10 40 E
Garden City 59 38 0N 100 45W
Gardez 42 33 31N 68 59 E
Gardiner 60 45 3N 110 53W
Gardo 43 9 18N 49 20 E
Gargano, Mte. 20 41 50N 16 0 E
Garland 60 41 47N 112 10 E
Garmisch Partenkirchen 10 47 30N 11 5 E
Garonne, R. 7 45 2N 0 36W
Garoe 43 8 35N 48 40 E
Garoua 46 9 19N 13 21 E
Garrison Res. 59 47 30N 102 0W
Gartempe, R. 5 46 48N 0 50 E
Gartok 38 5 35N 31 20 E
Garub 47 26 37S 16 0 E
Garut 36 7 14S 107 53 E
Garvie, Mts. 54 45 27S 169 59 E
Gary 58 41 35N 87 20W
Gasan Kul 26 37 40N 54 20 E
Gascogne, Reg. 7 43 45N 0 20 E
Gascogne, G. de 7 44 0N 2 0W
Gashiun Nor, L. 38 42 30N 100 30 E
Gaspé 57 48 52N 64 30W
Gaspé, C. 57 48 48N 64 7W
Gastonia 58 35 17N 81 10W
Gastoúni 23 37 51N 21 15 E
Gastoúri 23 39 34N 19 54 E
Gata, Sa. de 15 40 20N 6 20W
Gatchina 28 59 34N 30 8 E
Gateshead 2 54 57N 1 37W
Gaths 48 26 2S 30 32 E
Gatinais, Reg. 6 48 5N 2 40 E
Gâtine, Hauteurs de 5 46 35N 0 45W
Gatun 61 9 16N 79 55W
Gatun L. 61 9 7N 79 56W
Gatun Locks 61 9 16N 79 55W
Gatooma 48 18 21S 29 55 E
Gauhati 33 26 10N 91 45 E
Gávdhos, I. 23 34 50N 24 5 E
Gävle 25 60 41N 17 13 E
Gävleborgs Län □ 25 61 20N 16 15 E
Gavorrano 17 42 55N 10 55 E
Gawler 51 34 30S 138 42 E
Gaya, India 33 24 47N 85 4 E
Gaya, Nigér 44 11 58N 3 28 E
Gayndah 51 25 35S 151 39 E
Gaysin 30 48 57N 28 25 E
Gayvoron 30 48 22N 29 45 E
Gaza 41 31 30N 34 28 E
Gaziantep 41 37 6N 37 23 E
Gdańsk 14 54 22N 18 40 E
Gdańska, Zatoka 14 54 30N 19 20 E
Gdynia 14 54 35N 18 33 E
Gedaref 45 14 2N 35 28 E
Gedser 25 54 35N 11 55 E
Geelong 51 38 10S 144 22 E
Geesthacht 10 53 25N 10 20 E
Geili 45 16 1N 32 37 E
Geisingén 10 47 55N 8 37 E
Geita 46 2 48S 32 12 E
Gela 20 37 3N 14 15 E
Gela, G. di 20 37 0N 14 8 E
Gelderland □ 9 52 5N 6 10 E
Geldermalsen 9 51 53N 5 17 E
Geldrop 9 51 25N 5 32 E
Geleen 9 50 57N 5 49 E
Gelendzhik 30 44 33N 38 6 E
Gelsenkirchen 10 51 30N 7 5 E
Gembloux 9 50 34N 4 43 E
Gemona del Friuli 18 46 16N 13 7 E
Gendringen 9 51 52N 6 21 E
General Toshevo 22 43 42N 28 6 E
Geneva = Genève, Switz. 10 46 12N 6 9 E
Geneva, U.S.A. 58 42 53N 77 0W
Genève 10 46 12N 6 9 E
Genève, L. = Léman, L. 10 46 26N 6 30 E
Genichesk 30 46 11N 34 48 E
Genil, R. 15 37 42N 5 19W
Genjem 36 2 46S 140 12 E
Genk 9 50 58N 5 32 E
Gennargentu, Mti. del 19 40 0N 9 10 E
Genoa = Génova 17 44 24N 8 57 E
Génova 17 44 24N 8 57 E
Génova, G. di 17 44 0N 9 0 E
Gent 9 51 2N 3 37 E
Geokchay 31 40 39N 47 44 E
George 47 33 58S 22 29 E
George Town 37 5 25N 100 19 E
Georgetown, Guyana 63 6 50N 58 12W
Georgetown, U.S.A. 58 33 22N 79 15W
Georgia □ 58 32 0N 82 0W
Georgia S.S.R. □ 31 41 0N 45 0 E
Georgiu-Dezh 29 51 3N 39 20 E
Gera 10 50 53N 12 5 E
Gera □ 10 50 45N 11 30 E
Geraldton 49 28 48S 114 32 E
Gerlachovka, Mt. 12 49 11N 20 7 E
Germiston 48 26 15S 28 5 E
Gerolstein 10 50 12N 6 24 E
Gerona □ 16 42 11N 2 30 E
Gerona 16 41 58N 2 46 E
Gers, R. 7 44 9N 0 39 E
Gesso, R. 17 44 24N 7 33 E
Getafe 15 40 18N 3 44W
Gevgelija 21 41 9N 22 30 E
Geyser 60 47 17N 110 30W
Ghana ■ 44 6 0N 1 0W
Ghanzi, Reg. 47 21 50S 21 45 E
Ghardaia 44 32 31N 3 37 E
Ghazaouet 44 35 8N 1 50W
Ghaziabad 32 28 42N 77 35 E
Ghazipur 33 25 38N 83 35 E
Ghazni □ 42 33 0N 68 0 E
Ghedi 17 45 24N 10 16 E
Ghelinsor 43 6 35N 46 55 E
Gheorghe Gheorghe – Dej 13 46 17N 26 47 E
Gheorgheni 13 46 43N 25 36 E
Gherla 13 47 2N 23 55 E
Ghor □ 42 34 0N 65 0 E
Gia Nghia 37 12 0N 107 42 E
Giant's Causeway 4 55 15N 6 30W
Giarre 20 37 44N 15 10 E
Giaveno 17 45 3N 7 20 E
Gibraltar 15 36 7N 5 22W
Gibraltar, Str. of 15 35 55N 5 40W
Gibson Desert 49 24 0S 126 0 E
Giddings 59 30 11N 96 58W
Gien 6 47 40N 2 36 E
Giessen 10 50 34N 8 40 E
Gifu □ 40 36 0N 137 0 E
Gifu 40 35 30N 136 45 E
Gigant 31 46 30N 41 20 E
Giganta, Sa. de la 61 25 30N 111 30W
Giglio, I. 17 42 20N 10 52 E
Gijón 15 43 32N 5 42W
Gila, R. 60 32 43N 114 33W
Gila Bend 60 33 0N 112 46W
Gilan □ 41 37 0N 49 0 E
Gilbert Is. 52 0 30S 174 0 E
Gilgandra 51 31 43S 148 39 E
Gilgit 32 33 50N 74 15 E
Gillette 59 44 20N 105 38W
Gilliat 51 20 40S 141 28 E
Gillingham 2 51 23N 0 34 E
Ginosa 20 40 35N 16 45 E
Gióia del Colle 20 40 49N 16 55 E
Gióia Táuro 20 38 26N 15 53 E
Giovinazzo 20 41 10N 16 40 E
Gir Hills 32 21 0N 71 0 E
Girardot 63 4 18N 74 48W
Girga 45 26 17N 31 55 E
Giridih 33 24 10N 86 21 E
Gironde □ 7 44 45N 0 30W
Gironde, R. 7 45 20N 0 45W
Girvan 3 55 15N 4 50W
Gisborne 54 38 39S 178 5 E
Gisenyi 46 1 41S 29 30 E
Gislaved 25 57 19N 13 32 E
Gisors 6 49 15N 1 40 E
Giugliano in Campania 20 40 55N 14 12 E
Giulianova 18 42 45N 13 58 E
Giurgiu 13 43 52N 25 57 E
Givet 6 50 8N 4 49 E
Givors 8 45 35N 4 47 E
Gizhiga 27 62 0N 150 27 E
Gizhiginskaya Guba 27 61 0N 158 0 E
Giżycko 14 54 2N 21 48 E
Gjirokastra 23 40 7N 20 16 E
Gjøvik 25 60 47N 10 43 E
Glace, B. 57 46 11N 59 58W
Glacier Nat. Park 60 48 40N 114 0W
Gladstone, Queens. 51 23 52S 151 16 E
Gladstone, S. Austral. 51 33 15S 138 22 E
Glåma, R. 25 59 12N 10 57 E
Glarus 10 47 3N 9 4 E
Glasgow 3 55 52N 4 14 E
Glastonbury 2 51 9N 2 42W
Glauchau 10 50 50N 12 33 E
Glazov 29 58 0N 52 30 E
Glen Affric 3 57 15N 5 0W
Glen Canyon Dam 60 37 0N 111 25W
Glen Canyon Nat. Rec. Area 60 37 30N 111 0W
Glen Garry 3 57 3N 5 0W
Glen Innes 51 29 40S 151 39 E
Glen More 3 57 18N 4 25W
Glencoe 48 28 11S 30 11 E
Glendale, Ariz. 60 33 40N 112 8W
Glendale, Calif. 60 34 7N 118 18W
Glendale, Oreg. 60 42 44N 123 29W
Glendive 59 47 7N 104 40W
Glenelg 51 34 58S 138 31 E
Glengariff 4 51 45N 9 33W
Glenmorgan 51 27 14S 149 42 E
Glenns Ferry 60 43 0N 115 15W
Glenorchy 51 42 49S 147 18 E
Glen Falls 58 43 20N 73 40 E
Glittertind, Mt. 25 61 40N 8 32 E
Gliwice 12 50 22N 18 41 E
Globe 60 33 25N 110 53W
Gloggnitz 11 47 41N 15 56 E
Glossop 2 53 27N 1 56W
Gloucester, Australia 51 32 0S 151 59 E
Gloucester, U.K. 2 42 38N 2 15W
Gloucestershire □ 2 51 44N 2 10W
Gloversville 58 43 5N 74 18W
Glückstadt 10 53 46N 9 28 E
Glukhov 28 51 41N 33 53 E
Gmünd 11 48 45N 15 0 E
Gmunden 11 47 55N 13 48 E
Gniezno 14 52 30N 17 35 E
Gnowangerup 49 30 58S 117 59 E
Gô Công 37 10 22N 106 40 E
Goa □ 34 15 33N 73 59 E
Goat Fell, Mt. 3 55 37N 5 11W
Gobabis 47 22 16S 19 0 E
Gobi, Des. 39 43 0N 106 0 E
Gobichettipalayam 34 11 31N 77 21 E
Goch 10 51 40N 6 9 E
Godavari, R. 34 16 37N 82 18 E
Godhra 32 22 49N 73 40 E
Gödöllö 12 47 38N 19 25 E
Goeree, I. 9 51 50N 4 0 E
Goes 9 51 30N 3 55 E
Gogango 51 23 40S 150 2 E
Goiânia 64 16 35S 49 20W
Goias □ 64 12 10S 48 0W
Goisern 11 47 38N 13 38 E
Gojra 32 31 10N 72 40 E
Gökçeada, I. 23 40 10N 26 0 E
Gold Coast 51 28 0S 153 25 E
Golden Gate 60 37 54N 122 30W
Golden Vale 4 52 33N 8 17W
Goldsboro 58 35 24N 77 59W
Goleniów 14 53 35N 14 50 E
Golfito 62 8 41N 83 5W
Golija, Mt. 21 43 5N 18 45 E
Golmo 38 36 30N 95 10 E
Golspie 3 57 58N 3 58W
Goma 46 1 37S 29 10 E
Gomel 28 52 28N 31 0 E
Gómez Palacio 61 25 40N 104 40W
Gonaïves 62 19 20N 72 50W
Gonda 33 27 9N 81 58 E
Gondal 32 21 58N 70 52 E
Gonder 43 12 23N 37 30 E
Gondia 33 21 30N 80 10 E
Gondomar 15 41 10N 8 35W
Goniri 45 11 30N 12 15 E
Gonno-Altaysk 26 51 50N 86 5 E
Gónnos 23 39 52N 22 29 E
Good Hope, C. of 47 34 24S 18 30 E
Goole 2 53 42N 0 52W
Goondiwindi 51 28 30S 150 21 E
Goose Bay 57 53 15N 60 20W
Göppingen 10 48 42N 9 40 E
Gorakhpur 33 26 47N 83 32 E
Goražde 21 43 40N 18 56 E
Gordonia, Reg. 47 28 13S 21 10 E
Gordonvale 51 17 5S 145 50 E
Goré 45 8 12N 35 32 E
Gore 54 46 5S 168 58 E
Gorgàn 42 36 55N 54 30 E
Gorgona, I. 63 3 0N 78 10W
Gori 31 41 58N 44 7 E
Gorinchem 9 51 50N 4 59 E
Gorízia 18 45 56N 13 37 E
Gorki Byelorussian S.S.R. 28 54 18N 30 59 E
Gorki = Gorkiy R.S.F.S.R. 29 56 20N 44 0 E
Gorkiy 29 56 20N 44 0 E
Gorkovskoye Vdkhr. 29 57 2N 43 4 E
Görlitz 10 51 10N 14 59 E
Gorlovka 30 48 18N 38 3 E
Gorna Dzhumayo = Blagoevgrad 21 42 1N 23 6 E
Gorna Oryakhovitsa 22 43 7N 25 40 E
Gornji Milanovac 21 44 0N 20 29 E
Gornji Vakuf 21 43 57N 17 34 E
Gorno Filinskoye 26 60 5N 70 0 E
Gorodishche 30 53 13N 45 40 E
Gorodnya 28 51 55N 31 33 E
Gorodok 30 55 30N 30 3 E
Gorontalo 36 0 35N 123 13 E
Gorzów Wielkopolski 14 52 43N 15 15 E
Gosford 51 33 23S 151 18 E
Goshen 58 41 36N 85 46W
Goshen, Reg. 47 25 50S 25 0 E
Goslar 10 51 55N 10 23 E
Gospic 18 44 35N 15 23 E
Gosport 2 50 48N 1 8W
Gostiva 21 41 48N 20 57 E
Gostyn 14 51 50N 17 3 E
Gostynin 14 52 26N 19 29 E
Göta alv, R. 25 57 42N 11 52 E
Göta kanal 25 58 35N 14 15 E
Göteborg 25 57 43N 11 59 E
Göteborgs och Bohus Län □ 25 58 30N 11 30 E
Götene 25 58 33N 13 30 E
Gotha 10 50 56N 10 42 E
Gotland, I. 24 57 30N 18 30 E
Gotse Delchev 22 41 43N 23 46 E
Gotska Sandön, I. 24 58 24N 19 15 E
Göttingen 10 51 31N 9 55 E
Gottwaldov 12 49 14N 17 40 E
Gouda 9 52 1N 4 42 E
Gourdon 7 44 44N 1 23 E
Goulburn 51 34 44S 149 44 E
Governador Valadares 64 18 15S 41 57W
Gower 2 51 35N 4 10W
Goya 65 29 10S 59 10W
Goz Beïda 45 12 20N 21 30 E
Graaff-Reinet 47 32 13S 24 32 E
Grafton, Australia 51 29 38S 152 58 E
Grafton, U.S.A. 59 48 30N 97 25W
Gragnano 20 40 42N 14 30 E
Graham 58 36 5N 79 22W
Graham Land 55 65 0S 64 0W
Grahamstown 47 33 19S 26 31 E
Grajewo 14 53 39N 22 30 E
Grammichele 20 37 12N 14 37 E
Grampian □ 3 57 0N 3 0W
Grampian Highlands 3 56 50N 4 0W
Gran Chaco, Reg. 65 25 0S 61 0W
Gran Paradiso, Mt. 17 49 33N 7 17 E
Gran Sasso d'Italia, Mt. 18 42 25N 13 30 E
Granada, Spain 15 37 10N 3 35W
Granada, Nicaragua 62 11 58N 86 0W
Granada □ 15 37 5N 4 30W
Granby 57 45 25N 72 45W
Grand Bahama I. 62 26 40N 78 30W
Grand Bourg 62 15 53N 61 19W
Grand Canyon Nat. Park 60 36 15N 112 20W
Grand Cayman, I. 62 19 20N 81 20W
Grand Coulee Dam 60 48 0N 118 50W
Grand Forks 59 48 0N 97 3W
Grand Falls 57 47 2N 67 46W
Grand Island 59 40 59N 98 25W
Grand Junction 60 39 0N 108 30W
Grand Rapids, Canada 56 53 12N 99 19W
Grand Rapids, Mich. 58 42 57N 85 40W
Grand Rapids, Minn. 59 47 19N 93 29W
Grand St. Bernard, Col du 17 45 53N 7 11 E
Grand Teton, Mt. 60 43 45N 110 57W
Grande, B. 65 50 30S 68 20W
Grande, R. 64 53 48S 67 40W
Grande Prairie 56 55 15N 118 50W
Grangemouth 3 56 1N 3 43W
Grängesberg 25 60 6N 15 1 E
Granite City 59 38 45N 90 3W
Granite Pk. 60 45 8N 109 52W
Granity 54 41 39S 171 51 E
Granja 64 3 17S 40 50W
Granollers 16 41 39N 2 18 E
Grantham 2 52 55N 0 39W
Grantown-on-Spey 3 57 19N 3 36W
Grants Pass 60 42 30N 123 22W
Granville 5 48 50N 1 35W
Graskop 48 24 56S 30 49 E
Gräsö, I. 25 60 28N 18 35 E
Grass Valley 60 39 18N 121 0W
Grasse 8 43 38N 6 56 E
Graubünden □ 10 46 45N 9 30 E
Gravelines 6 51 0N 2 10 E
Gravesend 2 51 25N 0 22 E
Gravina di Púglia 20 40 48N 16 25 E
Graz 11 47 4N 15 27 E
Great Abaco I. 62 26 15S 77 10W
Great Australian Basin 51 26 0S 140 0 E
Great Australian Bight 49 33 30S 130 0 E
Great Barrier, I. 54 36 11S 175 25 E
Great Barrier Reef 51 19 0S 149 0 E
Great Basin 60 40 0N 116 30W
Great Bear, L. 56 65 0N 120 0W
Great Bend 59 38 25N 98 55W
Gt. Blasket I. 4 52 5N 10 30W
Great Divide, The 51 23 0S 146 0 E
Great Exuma I. 62 23 30N 75 50W
Great Falls 60 47 27N 111 12W
Great Fish R. 47 33 30S 27 8 E
Great Indian Des. 32 28 0N 72 0 E
Great Kei R. 48 32 41S 28 22 E
Great Ouse, R. 2 52 47N 0 22 E
Great Salt L. 60 41 0N 112 30W
Great Sandy Des. 49 21 0S 124 0 E
Great Slave, L. 56 61 30N 114 20W
Great Victoria Des. 49 29 30S 126 30 E
Great Whernside 2 54 9N 1 59W
Great Yarmouth 2 52 40N 1 45 E
Greater Manchester □ 2 53 30N 2 15W
Greater Sunda Is. 35 5 0S 110 0 E
Gredos, Sierra de 15 40 20N 5 0W
Greece ■ 23 40 0N 23 0 E
Greeley 59 40 30N 104 40W
Green Bay 59 44 30N 88 0W
Green Island 54 45 55S 170 26 E
Green River 60 41 32N 109 28W
Greenfield 58 42 38N 72 38W
Greenland ■ 57 66 0N 45 0W
Greenock 3 55 57N 4 45W
Greenore 4 54 2N 6 8W
Greenore Pt. 4 52 15N 6 20W
Greensboro 58 36 7N 79 46W
Greenville, Mich. 58 43 12N 85 14W
Greenville, Miss 59 33 25N 91 0W
Greenville, N.C. 58 35 37N 77 26W
Greenville, S.C. 58 34 54N 82 24W
Greenville, Tenn. 58 36 13N 82 51W
Greenville, Tex. 59 33 5N 96 5W
Greenwich 2 51 28N 0 0
Greenwood, Miss. 59 33 30N 90 4W
Greenwood, S.C. 58 34 13N 82 13W
Gregory, L. 49 20 5S 127 0 E
Gregory Ra. 51 19 0S 143 5 E
Greifswald 10 54 6N 13 23 E
Greiner Wald, Mts. 11 48 30N 15 0 E
Greiz 10 50 39N 12 12 E
Gremikha 26 67 50N 39 40 E
Grenå 25 56 26N 10 53 E
Grenada, I. 62 12 10N 61 40W
Grenoble 8 45 12N 5 42 E
Gretna Green 3 55 0N 3 3W
Grevená 23 40 4N 21 25 E
Grey Ra. 51 27 0S 143 30 E
Grey, R. 54 42 17N 171 35 E
Greybull 60 44 30N 108 3W
Greymouth 54 42 29S 171 13 E
Greytown 54 41 5S 175 29 E
Greytown 48 29 1S 30 36 E
Griffin 58 33 17N 84 14W
Griffith 51 34 14S 145 46 E
Grimsby 2 53 35N 0 5W
Grindelwald 10 46 38N 8 2 E
Grindsted 25 55 46N 8 55 E
Griqualand West, Reg. 47 28 40S 23 30 E
Grodersdal 48 25 15S 29 25 E
Grodno 28 53 42N 23 52 E
Grodzisk Mázowiecki 14 52 7N 20 37 E
Grodzisk Wlkp. 14 52 15N 16 22 E
Gronau 10 52 13N 7 2 E
Groningen □ 9 53 16N 6 40 E
Groningen 9 53 15N 6 35 E
Groot Karoo, Mts. 47 32 35S 23 0 E
Groot Namakwaland, Reg. 47 26 0S 18 0 E
Groot Winterhoek, Mt. 47 33 36S 24 58 E
Groote Eylandt, I. 50 14 0S 136 50 E
Grootfontein 47 19 31S 18 6 E
Gross Glockner, Mt. 11 47 5N 12 40 E
Grosseto 17 42 45N 11 7 E
Grottáglie 20 40 32N 17 25 E
Groznyy 31 43 20N 45 45 E
Grudziądz 14 53 30N 18 47 E
Grumo Ápulla 20 41 2N 16 43 E
Grums 25 59 22N 13 5 E
Gruyères 10 46 35N 7 4 E
Gryazi 29 52 30N 39 58 E
Gstaad 10 46 28N 7 18 E
Guacanayabo, G. de 62 20 40N 77 20 E
Guadalajara □ 16 40 47N 3 0W
Guadalajara 61 20 40N 103 20W

M

Morella 51 23 0s 143 47 E
Morelos □ 61 18 40N 99 10w
Morena, Sierra 15 38 20N 4 0w
Morenci 60 33 7N 109 20w
Moreton I. 51 27 10s 153 25 E
Morez 6 46 31N 6 2 E
Morgan City 59 29 40N 91 15w
Morgantown 58 39 39N 75 58w
Morioka 40 39 45N 141 8 E
Morlaix 5 48 36N 3 52w
Mornington 51 38 15s 145 5 E
Morocco ■ 44 32 0N 5 50w
Moroleón 61 20 8N 101 32w
Morombé 48 21 45s 43 22 E
Morón 62 22 0N 78 30w
Morón de la Frontera 15 37 6N 5 28w
Morondava 48 20 17s 44 17 E
Morozvsk 31 48 25N 41 50 E
Morpeth 2 55 11N 1 41w
Morrinhos 64 17 45s 49 10w
Morrinsville 54 37 40s 175 32 E
Morristown 58 36 18N 83 20w
Morro Bay 60 35 27N 120 54w
Morrosquillo, G. de 63 9 35N 75 40w
Mors, I. 25 56 50N 8 45 E
Morshansk 29 53 28N 41 50 E
Mortara 17 45 15N 8 43 E
Morteau 6 47 3N 6 35 E
Mortes, R. 64 11 45s 50 44w
Mortlake 51 38 5s 142 48 E
Morvan, Mts. du 6 47 5N 4 0 E
Morvern, Reg. 3 56 38N 5 44w
Morvi 32 22 25N 72 5 E
Morwell 51 38 10s 146 22 E
Moscos Is. 37 14 0N 97 45 E
Moscow 60 46 45N 116 59w
Moscow = Moskva 29 55 45N 37 35 E
Moselle □ 6 48 59N 6 33 E
Moselle, R. 6 50 22N 7 36 E
Mosgiel 54 45 53s 170 21 E
Moshi 46 3 22s 37 18 E
Mosjøen 24 65 51N 13 12 E
Moskva 29 55 45N 37 35 E
Mosonmagyaróvár 12 47 52N 17 18 E
Mosquera 63 2 35N 78 30w
Mosquitos, G. de los 62 9 15N 81 0w
Moss 25 59 27N 10 40 E
Moss Vale 51 34 32s 150 25 E
Mossaka 46 1 15s 16 45 E
Mossburn 54 45 41s 168 15 E
Mosselbaai 47 34 11s 22 8 E
Mossendjo 46 2 55s 12 42 E
Mossoró 64 5 10s 37 15w
Most 11 50 31N 13 38 E
Mostaganem 44 35 54N 0 5 E
Mostar 21 43 22N 17 50 E
Mosty 28 53 27N 24 38 E
Mosul = Al Mawsil 41 36 20N 43 5 E
Motala 25 58 32N 15 1 E
Motherwell 3 55 48N 4 0w
Motihari 33 26 37N 85 1 E
Motril 15 36 44N 3 37w
Móttola 20 40 38N 17 0 E
Motueka 54 41 7s 173 1 E
Motul 61 21 0N 89 20w
Moulins 6 46 35N 3 19 E
Moultrie 58 31 11N 83 47w
Moultrie, L. 58 33 25N 80 10w
Moundou 45 8 40N 16 10 E
Mt. Airy 58 36 31N 80 37w
Mount Barker 51 34 38s 117 40 E
Mount Clemens 58 42 35N 82 50w
Mount Douglas 51 21 35s 146 50 E
Mt. Eden 54 36 53s 174 46 E
Mount Enid 49 21 42s 116 26 E
Mount Gambier 51 37 50s 140 46 E
Mount Goldsworthy 49 20 20s 119 30w
Mount Isa 51 20 42s 139 26 E
Mount Lofty Ranges 51 34 35s 139 5 E
Mount Magnet 49 28 2s 117 47 E
Mount Morgan 51 23 40s 150 25 E
Mt. Pleasant, Iowa 59 41 0N 91 35w
Mt. Pleasant, Mich. 58 43 38N 84 46w
Mt. Pleasant, S.C. 58 32 45N 79 48w
Mount Surprise 51 18 10s 144 17 E
Mount Tom Price 49 22 50s 117 40 E
Mount Vernon, Ohio 58 40 20N 82 30w
Mount Vernon, Wash. 60 48 27N 122 18w
Mount Whaleback 49 23 18s 119 44 E
Mountain View 60 37 26N 122 5w
Mountmellick 4 53 7N 7 20w
Mourne Mts. 4 54 10N 6 0w
Mouscron 9 50 45N 3 12 E
Mowming 39 21 50N 110 32 E
Moyale 43 3 34N 39 4 E
Moyamba 44 8 15N 12 30w
Moyle □ 4 55 10N 6 15w
Mozambique ■ 48 19 0s 35 0 E
Mozambique Chan 48 20 0s 39 0 E
Mozdok 31 43 45N 44 48 E
Mozyr 28 52 0N 29 15 E
Mpanda 46 6 23s 31 40 E
Mrągowo 14 53 57N 21 18 E
Msaken 45 35 49N 10 33 E
Mtsensk 29 53 25N 36 30 E
Mtskheta 31 41 52N 44 45 E
Mtwara 46 10 20s 40 20 E
Muana 64 1 25s 49 15w
Muar, R. 37 2 3N 102 35 E
Muaraenim 35 3 40s 103 50 E
Muaratewe 35 0 50s 115 0 E
Muchkapskiy 29 51 52N 42 28 E
Muck, I. 3 56 50N 6 15w
Mucuri 64 18 0s 40 0w
Mudgee 51 32 32s 149 31 E
Mufulira 46 12 32s 28 15 E
Muhammad Qol 45 20 53N 37 9 E
Mühldorf 10 48 14N 12 23 E
Mühlhausen 10 51 12N 10 29 E
Mukallā 43 14 33N 49 2 E
Mukden = Shenyang 39 41 48N 123 27 E
Mukeiras 43 13 59N 45 52 E
Muktsar 32 30 30N 74 30 E
Mula 16 38 3N 1 33w
Mulatas, Arch. de las 62 6 51N 78 31w
Mulchén 65 37 45s 72 20w
Mulde, R. 10 51 10N 12 48 E
Mulgrave 57 45 38N 61 31w
Mülheim 10 51 26N 6 53w
Mulhouse 6 47 40N 7 20 E
Mull, I. 3 56 27N 6 0w
Muller Ra. 51 5 30s 143 0 E
Mullet Pen. 4 54 10N 10 2w
Mullewa 49 28 29s 115 30 E
Mullingar 4 53 31s 7 20w
Mullumbimby 51 28 30s 153 30 E
Multan 32 30 15N 71 30 E
Multan □ 32 30 29N 72 29 E
Muna, I. 36 5 0s 122 30 E
München 10 48 8N 11 33 E
Muncie 58 40 10N 85 20w
Münden 10 51 25N 9 42 E
Mundo, R. 16 38 19N 1 40w
Munera 16 39 2N 2 29w
Mungana 51 17 8s 144 27 E
Mungbere 46 2 36N 28 28 E
Munkfors 25 59 50N 13 30 E
Munku Sarbyk, Mt. 27 51 45N 100 32 E
Munster, Reg. 4 52 20N 8 40w
Münster 10 51 58N 7 37 E
Muntok 35 2 5s 105 10 E
Munyak 26 43 35N 59 30 E
Muong Soni 37 19 32N 102 47 E
Muonio 24 67 57N 23 40 E
Muonio älv 24 67 48N 23 25 E
Mur, R. 11 46 18N 16 53 E
Murashi 29 59 30N 49 0 E
Murat 7 45 7N 2 53 E
Murchison 54 41 49s 172 21 E
Murchison Ra. 49 20 0s 134 10 E
Murcia 16 38 2N 1 10w
Murcia □ 16 37 50N 1 30w
Mureș, Reg. 13 46 45N 24 40 E
Muret 7 43 30N 1 20 E
Murfreesboro 58 35 50N 86 21w
Murgab 26 38 10N 73 59 E
Murgon 51 26 15s 151 54 E
Muris 36 2 23s 140 5 E
Müritzsee, L. 10 53 25N 12 40 E
Murmansk 26 68 57N 33 10 E
Murom 29 55 35N 42 3 E
Muroran 40 42 25N 141 0 E
Muroto 40 33 18N 134 9 E
Murphysboro 59 37 50N 89 20w
Murray 60 40 41N 111 58w
Murray, R. 51 35 50s 147 40 E
Murray Bridge 51 35 6s 139 14 E
Murrumbidgee, R. 51 34 43s 143 12 E
Murrumburrah 51 34 30s 148 15 E
Murrurundi 51 31 42s 150 51 E
Murska Sobota 18 46 39N 16 12 E
Murwara 33 23 46N 80 28 E
Murwillumbah 51 28 18s 153 27 E
Mürzzuschlag 11 47 36N 15 41 E
Musala, Mt. 22 42 13N 23 37 E
Muscat = Masqat 42 23 37N 58 36 E
Muscatine 59 41 25N 91 5w
Musgrave Ra. 49 26 0s 132 0 E
Musi, R. 35 2 20s 104 56 E
Muskegon 58 43 15N 86 17w
Muskogee 59 35 50N 95 25w
Musmar 45 18 6N 35 40 E
Musoma 46 1 30s 33 48 E
Musselburgh 3 55 57N 3 3w
Mussidan 7 45 2N 0 22 E
Mussomeli 19 37 35N 13 43 E
Muswellbrook 51 32 16s 150 56 E
Mutankiang 39 44 35N 129 30 E
Muya 27 56 27N 115 39 E
Muzaffarnagar 32 29 26N 77 40 E
Muzaffarpur 33 26 7N 85 32 E
Mvadhi-Ousye 46 1 13N 13 12 E
Mwanza 46 2 30s 32 58 E
Mweelrea, Mt. 4 53 37N 9 48w
Mweru, L. 46 9 0s 29 0 E
My Tho 37 10 29N 106 23 E
Myanaung 37 18 25N 95 10 E
Myaungmya 37 16 30N 95 0 E
Myingxan 37 21 30N 95 30 E
Myitkyina 38 25 30N 97 26 E
Myrtle Beach 58 33 43N 78 50w
Myslowice 12 50 15N 19 12 E
Mysore 34 12 17N 76 41 E
Mytishchi 29 57 50N 37 50 E

N

Naantali 24 60 29N 22 2 E
Naas 4 53 12N 6 40w
Nabadwip 33 23 34N 88 20 E
Nabeul 45 36 30N 10 51 E
Nabha 32 30 26N 76 14 E
Naboomspruit 48 24 32s 28 40 E
Nabulus 41 32 14N 35 15 E
Nacka 25 59 17N 18 12 E
Nacogdoches 59 31 33N 95 30w
Nacozari 61 30 30N 109 50w
Nadiad 32 22 41N 72 56 E
Nadym 26 63 35N 72 42 E
Naestved 25 55 13N 11 44 E
Naga 36 13 38N 123 15 E
Nagano 40 36 40N 138 10 E
Nagano □ 40 36 15N 138 0 E
Nagaoka 40 37 27N 138 50 E
Nagappattinam 34 10 46N 79 51 E
Nagasaki 40 32 47N 129 50 E
Nagasaki □ 40 32 50N 129 40 E
Nagercoil 34 8 12N 77 33 E
Nagina 32 29 30N 78 30 E
Nagornyy 27 55 58N 124 57 E
Nagoya 40 35 10N 136 50 E
Nagpur 32 21 8N 79 10 E
Nagykanizsa 12 46 28N 17 0 E
Nagykörös 12 46 55N 19 48 E
Naha 39 26 13N 127 42 E
Nairn 3 57 35N 3 54w
Nairobi 46 1 17s 36 48 E
Naivasho 46 0 40s 36 30 E
Najafābād 42 32 40N 51 15 E
Najibabad 32 29 40N 78 20 E
Najin 39 42 12N 130 15 E
Nakhodka 27 43 10N 132 45 E
Nakhon Phanom 37 17 23N 104 43 E
Nakhon Ratchasima 37 14 59N 102 12 E
Nakina 57 50 10N 86 40w
Nakskov 25 54 50N 11 8 E
Nakło n Noteoja 14 53 8N 17 35 E
Nakuru 46 0 15s 35 5 E
Nalchik 31 43 30N 43 33 E
Nalgonda 34 17 6N 79 15 E
Nam Dinh 37 20 25N 106 5 E
Nam Tok 37 14 14N 99 4 E
Nam Tso, L. 38 30 40N 90 30 E
Namaland, Reg. 47 25 0s 17 0 E
Namangan 26 41 0N 71 40 E
Namber 36 1 2s 134 57 E
Nambour 51 26 32s 152 58 E
Namib Des 47 22 30s 15 0w
Namibia = South-West Africa ■ 47 22 0s 18 9 E
Nambucca Heads 51 30 37s 153 0 E
Namcha Barwa, Mt. 38 29 40N 95 10 E
Namlea 36 3 10s 127 5 E
Nampa 60 43 40N 116 40w
Nampula 46 15 6s 39 7 E
Namsos 24 64 29N 11 30 E
Namur 9 50 27N 4 52 E
Namur □ 9 50 17N 5 0 E
Namystow 14 51 6N 17 42 E
Nan 37 18 48N 100 46 E
Nan, R. 37 15 42N 100 11 E
Nan Shan, Mts. 38 38 30N 99 0 E
Nanaimo 56 49 10N 124 0w
Nanango 51 26 40s 152 0 E
Nanao 40 37 0N 137 0 E
Nanchang 39 28 34N 115 48 E
Nancheng 38 33 10N 107 2 E
Nanchung 38 30 47N 105 59 E
Nancy 6 48 42N 6 12 E
Nanda Devi, Mt. 33 30 30N 80 30 E
Nander 34 19 10N 77 20 E
Nandurbar 32 21 20N 74 15 E
Nandyal 34 15 30N 78 30 E
Nanga Eboko 46 4 41N 12 22 E
Nangarhar □ 42 34 20N 70 0 E
Nanking 39 32 5N 118 45 E
Nannine 49 26 51s 118 18 E
Nanning 38 22 48N 108 20 E
Nanping 39 26 45N 118 5 E
Nansei, Is. 40 34 22N 136 41 E
Nansei-Shoto, Is. 39 29 0N 129 0 E
Nantes 5 47 12N 1 33w
Nantou 39 23 57N 120 35 E
Nantua 6 46 10N 5 35 E
Nantung 39 32 0N 120 50 E
Nanuque 64 17 50s 40 21w
Nanyang 39 33 0N 112 32 E
Nanyuki 46 0 2N 37 4 E
Náousa 23 40 42N 22 9 E
Napa 60 38 18N 122 17w
Napier 54 39 30s 176 56 E
Naples = Nápoli 20 40 50N 14 5 E
Nápoli 20 40 50N 14 5 E
Nápoli, G. di 20 40 40N 14 10 E
Nara 40 34 40N 135 49 E
Nara □ 40 34 30N 136 0 E
Naracoorte 51 36 58s 140 45 E
Narasapur 34 16 26N 81 50 E
Narathiwat 37 6 40N 101 55 E
Narayanganj 33 23 31N 90 33 E
Narayanpet 34 16 45N 77 30 E
Narbonne 7 43 11N 3 0 E
Nardò 20 40 10N 18 0 E
Narew, R. 14 52 26N 20 42 E
Narmada, R. 32 21 35N 72 35 E
Narnaul 32 28 5N 76 11 E
Narni 18 42 30N 12 30 E
Naro 19 37 18N 13 48 E
Narrabri 51 30 19s 149 46 E
Narrandera 51 34 42s 146 31 E
Narrogin 49 32 58s 117 14 E
Narromine 51 32 12s 148 12 E
Narva 28 59 10N 28 5 E
Narva, R. 28 59 27N 28 2 E
Narvik 24 68 28N 17 26 E
Naryan Mar 26 68 0N 53 0 E
Narym 26 59 0N 81 58 E
Narymskoye 26 49 10N 84 15 E
Naryn 26 41 26N 75 58 E
Nassau 26 25 0N 77 30w
Naser, Buheiret en 45 23 0N 32 30 E
Nashville 58 36 12N 86 46w
Našice 21 45 32N 18 4 E
Nasik 34 20 2N 73 50 E
Nasirabad Bangladesh 33 24 42N 90 30 E
Nasirabad, India 32 26 15N 74 45 E
Nasser, L. = Naser, en Buheiret 45 23 0N 32 30 E
Nässjö 25 57 38N 14 45 E
Natal 64 5 47s 35 13w
Natal □ 48 28 30s 30 30 E
Natchez 59 31 35N 91 25w
Natchitoches 59 31 47N 93 4w
National City 60 32 45N 117 7w
Natron, L. 46 2 20s 36 0 E
Naturaliste, C. 49 33 32s 115 0 E
Naujoji Vilnia 28 54 48N 25 27 E
Naumburg 10 51 10N 11 48 E
Nauru Is. 52 0 25N 166 0 E
Nautla 61 20 20N 96 50w
Nava del Rey 15 41 22N 5 6w
Navarra □ 16 42 40N 1 40w
Navarre, Reg. 7 43 15N 1 20 E
Navia, R. 15 43 33N 6 44w
Navlya 28 52 53N 34 15 E
Navoi 26 40 9N 65 22 E
Navojoa 61 27 0N 109 30w
Návplion 23 37 33N 22 50 E
Navsari 32 20 57N 72 59 E
Nawabganj, Bangladesh 33 24 35N 81 14 E
Nawabganj, U.P. 33 28 32N 79 40 E
Nawabganj, U.P. 33 26 56N 81 14 E
Nawabshah 32 26 15N 68 25 E
Nawalgarh 32 27 50N 75 15 E
Náxos, I. 23 37 5N 25 30 E
Näy Band 42 27 20N 52 40 E
Nayakhan 27 62 10N 159 0 E
Nayarit □ 61 22 0N 105 0w
Nazaré 64 13 0N 39 0w
N'Délé 46 8 25N 20 36 E
Ndendé 46 2 29s 10 46 E
Ndjamena 45 12 4N 15 8 E
Ndola 46 13 0s 28 34 E
Neagh, Lough 4 54 35N 6 25w
Neamt, Reg. 13 47 0N 26 20 E
Neápolis 23 40 20N 21 24 E
Neápolis 23 35 15N 25 36 E
Near, Is. 56 53 0N 172 0w
Neath 2 51 39N 3 49w
Nebraska □ 59 41 30N 100 0w
Nébrodi, Mti. 20 37 55N 14 35 E
Neckar, R. 10 49 31N 8 26 E
Necochea 65 38 30s 58 50w
Needles 60 34 50N 114 35w
Needles, The 2 34 51N 114 37w
Neenah 59 44 10N 88 30w
Neepawa 56 50 20N 99 30w
Negaunee 58 46 30N 87 36w
Negele 43 5 20N 39 30 E
Negeri Sembilan 37 2 50N 102 10 E
Negombo 34 7 12N 79 50 E
Negotin 21 44 16N 22 37 E
Negotino 21 41 29N 22 9 E
Negra, Pta. 63 6 6s 81 10w
Negro, R. Arg. 65 41 25s 62 47w
Negro, R., Brazil 63 3 0s 60 0w
Negros, I. 36 10 0N 123 0 E
Negru Vodă 13 43 47N 28 21 E
Neikiang 38 29 35N 105 10 E
Neisse, R. 10 52 4N 14 46 E
Neiva 63 2 56N 75 18w
Nellikuppam 34 11 46N 79 43 E
Nellore 34 14 27N 79 59 E
Nelson, Canada 56 49 30N 117 20w
Nelson, N.Z. 54 41 18s 173 16 E
Nelson, U.K. 2 53 50N 2 14w
Nelson □ 54 42 11s 172 15 E
Nelson, R. 56 57 4N 92 30w
Nelspruit 48 25 29s 30 59 E
Neman, R. 28 55 18N 21 23 E
Neméa 23 57 49N 22 40 E
Nemira, Mt. 13 46 17N 26 19 E
Nemuro 40 43 20N 145 35 E
Nemuro, Chan. 40 43 20N 145 30 E
Nenagh 4 52 52N 8 11w
Nene, R. 2 52 48N 0 13 E
Nepal ■ 33 28 0N 84 30 E
Nephin, Mt. 4 54 1N 9 21w
Nerchinsk 27 52 0N 116 39 E
Nerchinskiy Zavod 27 51 10N 119 30 E
Nerekhta 29 57 26N 40 38 E
Neretvanski, Kan. 21 43 7N 17 10 E
Nes 24 60 34N 9 58 E
Nesebŭr 22 42 41N 27 46 E
Ness, L. 3 57 15N 4 30w
Netherdale 51 21 10s 148 33 E
Netherlands ■ 9 52 0N 5 30 E
Nettuno 19 41 29N 12 40 E
Neu-Ulm 10 48 23N 10 2 E
Neubrandenburg 10 53 33N 13 17 E
Neubrandenburg □ 10 53 30N 13 20 E
Neuchâtel 10 47 0N 6 55 E
Neuchâtel □ 10 47 0N 6 55 E
Neuchâtel, L. de 10 46 53N 6 50 E
Neufchâteau 6 48 21N 5 40 E
Neumünster 10 54 4N 9 58 E
Neunkirchen, Austria 11 47 43N 16 4 E
Neunkirchen, Germany 10 49 23N 7 6 E
Neuquén 65 38 0s 68 0 E
Neuruppin 10 52 56N 12 48 E
Neusiedler See 12 47 50N 16 47 E
Neuss 10 51 12N 6 39 E
Neustrelitz 10 53 22N 13 4 E
Neuweid 10 50 26N 7 29 E
Nevada □ 60 39 20N 117 0w
Nevada, Sierra 15 37 3N 3 15w
Nevanka 27 56 45N 98 55 E
Nevel 28 56 0N 29 55 E
Nevers 6 47 0N 3 9 E
Nevinnomyssk 31 44 40N 42 0 E
Nevis, I. 62 17 0N 62 30w
Nevrokop = Gotse Delchev 22 41 43N 23 46 E
New Amsterdam 63 6 15N 57 30w
New Bedford 58 41 40N 70 52w
New Bern 58 35 8N 77 3w
New Braunfels 59 29 43N 98 9w
New Brighton 54 43 29s 172 43 E
New Britain, I. 51 5 50s 150 20 E
New Brunswick 57 40 30N 74 28w
New Caledonia 52 21 0s 165 0 E
New Delhi 32 28 37N 77 13 E
New Forest 2 50 53N 1 40w
New Glasgow 57 45 35N 62 36w
New Hampshire □ 58 43 40N 71 40w
New Hanover, I. 51 2 30s 150 10 E
New Haven 58 41 20N 72 54w
New Hebrides 52 15 0s 168 0 E
New Iberia 59 30 2N 91 54w
New Ireland, I. 51 3 20s 151 50 E
New Jersey □ 58 39 50N 74 10w
New London 58 41 23N 72 8w
New Mexico □ 60 34 30N 106 0w
New Orleans 59 30 0N 90 5w
New Plymouth 54 39 4s 174 5 E
New Providence I. 62 25 0N 77 30w
New Rockford 59 47 44N 99 7w
New Ross 4 52 24N 6 58w
New South Wales □ 51 33 0s 146 0 E
New Westminster 56 49 10N 122 52w
New York 58 40 45N 74 0w
New York □ 58 42 40N 76 0w
New Zealand ■ 54 40 0s 176 0w
Newark, U.K. 2 53 6N 0 48w
Newark, N.J. 58 40 41N 74 12w
Newark, Ohio 58 40 5N 82 30w
Newbury 2 51 24N 1 19w
Newcastle, Australia 51 32 52s 151 49 E
Newcastle, Canada 57 47 1N 65 38w
Newcastle, S. Africa 48 27 49s 29 55 E
Newcastle-under-Lyme 2 53 2N 2 37w
Newcastle upon Tyne 2 54 59N 1 37w
Newcastle Waters 49 17 30s 133 28 E
Newdegate 49 33 6s 119 0 E
Newfoundland, I. 57 48 30N 56 0w
Newfoundland □ 57 48 28N 56 0w
Newham 2 51 31N 0 2 E
Newhaven 2 50 47N 0 4 E
Newmarket 2 52 15N 0 23 E
Newport, Gwent 2 51 35N 3 0w
Newport, I. of W. 2 50 42N 1 18w
Newport, U.S.A. 59 35 38N 91 15w
Newport Beach 60 33 40N 117 58w
Newport News 58 37 2N 76 54w
Newquay 2 50 24N 5 6w
Newry 4 54 10N 6 20w
Newry and Mourne □ 4 54 10N 6 15w
Newton, Iowa 59 41 40N 93 3w
Newton, Kans. 59 38 2N 97 30w
Newton Abbot 2 50 32N 3 37w
Newton Stewart 3 54 57N 4 30w
Newtownards 4 54 37N 5 40w
Newtown 2 52 31N 3 19w
Newtownabbey □ 4 54 45N 6 0w
Neyshābūr 42 36 10N 58 20 E
Nezhin 28 51 5N 31 55 E
Ngandjuk 36 7 32s 111 55 E
Ngaoundére 46 7 15N 13 35 E
Ngapara 54 44 57s 170 46 E
Ngawi 36 7 24s 111 26 E
Ngoring Nor, L. 38 34 50N 98 0 E
Ngum, R. 37 18 9N 103 6 E
Nguru 44 12 56N 10 29 E
Nha Trang 37 12 16N 109 10 E
Niagara, Falls 57 43 7N 79 5w
Niagara Falls 58 43 5N 79 0w
Niamey 44 13 27N 2 6 E
Niangara 46 3 50N 27 50 E
Nias, I. 35 1 0N 97 40 E
Nicaragua ■ 62 11 40N 85 30w
Nicaragua, L. de 62 12 50N 85 30w
Nicastro 20 39 0N 16 18 E
Nice 8 43 42N 7 14 E
Nichinan 40 31 38N 131 23 E
Nicosia 20 37 45N 14 22 E
Nicosia = Levkôsia 41 35 10N 33 25 E
Nicoya, Golfo de 62 10 0N 85 0w
Nida, R. 12 50 18N 20 52 E
Nidd, R. 2 54 1N 1 12w
Nidzica 14 53 25N 20 28 E
Niedere Tauern, Mts. 11 47 18N 14 0 E
Niederösterreich □ 11 48 25N 15 40 E
Niedersachsen □ 10 52 45N 9 0 E
Nienburg 10 52 38N 9 15 E
Nieuw Amsterdam 64 6 15N 57 30w
Nieuw Nickerie 64 6 0N 57 10w
Nièvre □ 6 47 10N 5 40 E
Nigel 48 26 27s 28 25 E
Niger ■ 44 13 30N 10 0 E
Niger, R. 44 5 33N 6 33 E
Nigeria ■ 44 8 30N 8 0 E
Nightcaps 54 45 57s 168 14 E
Nigrita 23 40 56N 23 29 E
Niigata 40 37 58N 139 0 E
Niigata □ 40 37 15N 138 45 E
Niihama 40 33 55N 133 10 E
Nijkerk 9 52 13N 5 30 E
Nijmegen 9 51 50N 5 52 E
Nijverdal 9 52 22N 6 27 E
Nikiniki 36 9 40s 124 30 E
Nikolayev 30 46 58N 32 7 E
Nikolayevsk 29 50 10N 45 35 E
Nikolayevsk-na-Amur 27 53 8N 140 44 E
Nikopol, Bulgaria 22 43 43N 24 54 E
Nikopol, U.S.S.R. 30 47 35N 34 25 E
Nikšić 21 42 50N 18 57 E
Nîl el Azraq □ 45 12 30N 34 30 E
Nîl, Nahr en 45 27 30N 30 30 E
Nile, R. = Nîl, Nahren 45 27 30N 30 30 E
Nîmes 8 43 50N 4 23 E
Nimneryskiy 27 58 0N 125 10 E
Nineveh 41 36 25N 43 10 E
Ningpo 39 29 53N 121 33 E
Ningsia-Hui A.R. □ 38 37 45N 106 0 E
Ningteh 39 26 45N 120 0 E
Ningwu 39 29 2N 112 15 E
Ninh Binh 37 20 15N 105 55 E
Ninove 9 50 51N 4 2 E

Ostuni **20** 40 44N 17 34E
Osúm, R. **22** 40 48N 19 52E
Osmui, Chan **40** 30 55N 131 0E
Osumi, Is. **40** 30 30N 130 45E
Osuna **15** 37 14N 5 8W
Oswego **58** 43 29N 76 30W
Oswestry **2** 52 52N 3 3W
Oswiecim **12** 50 2N 19 11E
Otago □ **54** 45 20S 169 20E
Otago, Harb. **54** 45 47S 170 42E
Otake **40** 34 12N 132 13E
Otaki **54** 40 45S 175 10E
Otaru **40** 43 10N 141 0E
Otaru, B = Ishikari, B. **4** 43 25N 141 1E
Otavi **47** 19 40S 17 24E
Otira, Gorge **54** 42 53S 171 33E
Otjiwarongo **47** 20 30S 16 33E
Otorohanga **54** 38 12S 175 14E
Otranto **20** 40 9N 18 28E
Otranto, Str. of **20** 40 15N 18 40E
Otsu **40** 35 0N 135 52E
Ottapalam **34** 10 46N 76 23E
Ottawa, Canada **57** 45 27N 75 42W
Ottawa, U.S.A. **58** 41 20N 88 55W
Ottawa, R. **57** 45 20N 73 58W
Ottumwa **59** 41 0N 92 25W
Oturkpo **44** 7 14N 8 08E
Otwock **14** 52 5N 21 20E
Ötztaler Alpen **11** 46 58N 11 0E
Ou-Sammyaku, Mts. **40** 39 20N 140 35E
Ouachita Mts. **59** 34 50N 94 30W
Ouagadougou **44** 12 25N 1 30W
Ouargla **44** 31 59N 5 25E
Oubangi, R. **46** 1 0N 17 50E
Ouche, R. **6** 47 11N 5 10E
Oudenaarde **9** 50 50N 3 37E
Oudtshoorn **47** 33 35S 22 14E
Ouessant, Île d' **5** 48 28N 5 6W
Ouesso **46** 1 37N 16 5E
Ouidah **44** 6 25N 2 0E
Oujda **44** 33 18N 1 25W
Oujeft **44** 20 2N 13 0W
Oulu **24** 65 1N 25 29E
Oulu □ **24** 65 0N 25 30E
Oulujärvi, L. **24** 64 25N 27 0E
Oum Hadjer **45** 13 13N 19 37E
Our, R. **9** 49 53N 6 18E
Ouro Preto **64** 20 20S 43 30W
Ourthe, R. **9** 50 38N 5 35E
Ouse, R. **2** 53 42N 0 41W
Oust, R. **5** 47 39N 2 6W
Outer Hebrides Is. **3** 57 30N 7 40W
Outjo **47** 20 5S 16 7E
Outreau **6** 50 40N 1 46E
Ouyen **51** 35 1S 142 22E
Ovalle **65** 30 33S 71 18W
Ovamboland, Reg. **47** 17 20S 16 20E
Ovar **15** 40 51N 8 40W
Over Flakkee, I. **9** 51 45N 4 5E
Overijssel □ **9** 52 25N 6 35E
Overpelt **9** 51 12N 5 20E
Övertornea **24** 66 23N 23 40E
Oviedo **15** 43 25N 5 50W
Oviedo □ **15** 43 20N 6 0W
Oviksfjällen, Mts. **25** 63 0N 13 49E
Ovruch **28** 51 25N 28 45E
Owatonna **59** 44 3N 93 17W
Owen Sound **57** 44 35N 80 55W
Owen Stanley Ra. **51** 8 30S 147 0E
Owens L. **60** 36 30N 118 0W
Owensboro **58** 37 40N 87 5W
Owosso **58** 43 0N 84 10W
Ox Mts. **4** 54 6N 9 0W
Oxelösund **25** 58 43N 17 15E
Oxford **2** 51 45N 1 15W
Oxfordshire □ **2** 51 45N 1 15W
Oxnard **60** 34 10N 119 14W
Oyama **40** 36 18N 139 48E
Oyo **44** 7 46N 3 56E
Oyonnax **6** 46 16N 5 40E
Ozamiz **36** 8 15N 123 50E
Ozark **58** 31 29N 85 39W
Ozarks, L. of the **59** 38 10N 93 0W
Ozd **12** 48 14N 20 15E
Ozona **59** 30 43N 101 11W
Ozorków **14** 51 57N 19 16E
Ozun **13** 45 57N 25 20E

P

Pa Sak, R. **37** 14 11N 100 40E
Paan **38** 16 45N 97 40E
Paarl **47** 33 45S 18 56E
Pab Hills **42** 26 30N 66 45E
Pabianice **14** 51 40N 19 20E
Pabna **33** 24 1N 19 20E
Pacaraima, Sa. **63** 6 0N 60 0W
Pacasmayo **63** 7 20S 79 35W
Paceco **19** 37 59N 12 32E
Pachino **20** 36 43N 15 4E
Pachuca **61** 20 10N 98 40W
Pacific Ocean **53** 10 0N 140 0W
Padang **35** 1 0S 100 20E
Paderborn **10** 51 42N 8 44E
Padeşul, Mt. **13** 45 40N 22 22E
Pádova **18** 45 24N 11 52E
Padstow **2** 50 33N 4 57W
Padua = Pádova **18** 45 24N 11 52E
Paducah, Ky. **58** 37 0N 88 40W
Paducah, Tex. **59** 34 3N 100 16W
Paeroa **54** 37 23S 175 41E
Pag, I. **18** 44 50N 15 0E
Pagadian **36** 7 55N 123 30E
Page **60** 47 11N 97 37W
Pahang, R. **37** 3 32N 103 28E
Pahang □ **37** 3 40N 102 20E
Pahiatua **54** 40 27S 175 50E
Paicheng **39** 45 50N 122 52E
Paignton **2** 50 26N 3 33W
Päijanne, L. **24** 61 30N 25 30E
Paimboeuf **5** 47 17N 2 0W
Painted Des. **60** 36 40N 112 0W
Paisley **3** 55 51N 4 27W
Paita **63** 5 5S 81 0W
Paiyin **38** 36 45N 104 4E
Paiyunopo **38** 42 10N 109 28E
Pajakumbun **35** 0 20S 100 35E
Pak Lay **37** 18 15N 101 27E
Pak Sane **37** 18 22N 103 39E
Pakanbaru **35** 0 30N 101 15E
Pakaraima, Mts. **63** 6 0N 60 0W
Pakhoi **38** 21 30N 109 10E
Pakistan ■ **32** 30 0N 70 0E
Pakokku **37** 21 30N 95 0E
Pakpattan **32** 30 25N 73 16E
Pakrac **21** 45 27N 17 12E
Paks **12** 46 38N 18 55E
Pakse **37** 15 15N 105 52E
Paktya □ **42** 33 0N 69 15E
Pala **45** 9 25N 15 5E
Palakol **34** 16 31N 81 46E
Palamás **23** 39 26N 22 4E
Palamós **16** 41 50N 3 10E
Palangkaraja **35** 2 16S 113 56E
Palanpur **32** 24 10N 72 25E
Palapye **47** 22 30S 27 7E
Palatka **58** 29 40N 81 40W
Palau Is. **36** 7 30N 134 30E
Palavas **7** 43 32N 3 56E
Palawan, I. **36** 10 0N 119 0E
Palawan Is. **35** 10 0N 115 30E
Palayancottai **34** 8 45N 77 45E
Palazzolo Acreide **20** 37 4N 14 43E
Pale **21** 43 50N 18 38E
Paleleh **36** 1 10N 121 50E
Palembang **35** 3 0S 104 50E
Palencia **15** 42 1N 4 34W
Palencia □ **15** 42 31N 4 33W
Palermo **19** 38 8N 13 20E
Palestine **59** 31 42N 95 35W
Paletwa **37** 21 30N 92 50E
Palghat **34** 10 46N 76 42E
Pali **32** 25 50N 73 20E
Palimé **44** 6 57N 0 37E
Palitana **32** 21 32N 71 49E
Palk Bay **34** 9 30N 79 30E
Palk Strait **34** 10 0N 80 0E
Palkonde Ra. **34** 13 50N 79 20E
Palm Is. **51** 18 40S 146 35E
Palm Springs **60** 33 51N 116 35W
Palma **16** 39 33N 2 39E
Palma, Bahía de **16** 39 30N 2 39E
Palma di Montechiaro **19** 37 12N 13 46E
Palmares **64** 8 41S 35 36E
Palmeirinhas, Pta. das **46** 9 2S 12 57E
Palmer **56** 61 35N 149 10W
Palmer Land **55** 73 0S 60 0W
Palmerston **54** 45 29S 170 43E
Palmerston N. **54** 40 21S 175 39E
Palmetto **58** 27 33N 82 33W
Palmi **20** 38 21N 15 51E
Palmira **63** 3 32N 76 16W
Palmyra = Tadmor **41** 34 30N 37 55E
Palmyra Is. **53** 5 52N 162 6W
Palni **34** 10 30N 77 30E
Palo Alto **60** 37 25N 122 8W
Palo del Colle **20** 41 4N 16 43E
Palopo **36** 3 0S 120 16E
Pamekasan **36** 7 10S 113 29E
Pamiers **7** 43 7N 1 39E
Pamirs, Mts. **26** 37 40N 73 0E
Pampa **59** 35 35N 100 58W
Pampanua **36** 4 22S 120 14E
Pampas, Reg. **65** 34 0S 64 0W
Pamplona, Colombia **63** 7 23N 72 39W
Pamplona, Spain **16** 42 48N 1 38E
Panagyurishte **22** 42 49N 24 15E
Panaji **34** 15 25N 73 50E
Panamá ■ **62** 8 48N 79 55W
Panamá **62** 9 0N 79 25W
Panamá, Golfo de **62** 8 4N 79 20W
Panama City **58** 30 10N 85 41W
Panay, I. **36** 11 0N 122 30E
Pančevo **21** 44 52N 20 41E
Pandharpur **34** 17 41N 75 20E
Panevezys **28** 55 42N 24 25E
Pangaíon Oros, Mts. **23** 40 50N 24 0E
Pangkiang **39** 43 4N 112 30E
Panipat **32** 29 25N 77 2E
Panjim = Panaji **34** 15 25N 73 50E
Pankalpinang **35** 2 0S 106 0E
Panorama **64** 21 21S 51 51W
Pantelleria, I. **19** 36 52N 12 0E
Pánuco **61** 22 0N 98 25W
Paochang **39** 41 46N 115 30E
Paoki **38** 34 25N 107 15E
Páola **20** 39 21N 16 2E
Paonia **60** 38 56N 107 37E
Paoshan **38** 25 7N 99 9E
Paoteh **39** 39 0N 110 45E
Paoting **39** 38 50N 115 30E
Paotow **38** 40 35N 110 3E
Paoua **46** 7 25N 16 30E
Papá **12** 47 22N 17 30E
Papakura **54** 37 45S 174 59E
Papaloapan, R. **61** 18 42N 95 38W
Papantla **61** 20 45N 97 21W
Papua, G. of **51** 9 0S 145 0E
Papua New Guinea ■ **51** 8 0S 145 0E
Papuk, Mts. **21** 45 30N 17 30E
Pará □ **64** 3 20S 52 0W
Pará = Belem **64** 1 20S 48 30W
Paracatú **64** 17 10S 46 50W
Paradise **60** 47 27N 114 54W
Paragua, R. **63** 6 55N 62 55W
Paraguanna, Pen. de **63** 12 0N 70 0W
Paraguay ■ **65** 23 0S 57 0W
Paraguay, R. **65** 27 18S 58 38W
Paraiba = João Pessoa **64** 7 10S 34 52W
Paraiba □ **64** 7 0S 36 0W
Parakhino Paddubye **28** 58 46N 33 10E
Parakou **44** 9 25N 2 40E
Paramagudi **34** 9 31N 78 39E
Paramaribo **64** 5 50N 55 10W
Paraná **65** 32 0S 60 30W
Paraná R. **65** 12 30S 48 14W
Paraná □ **65** 24 30S 51 0W
Paranaguá **65** 25 30S 48 30W
Paranapiacaba, Sa. do **65** 24 31S 48 35W
Paray-le-Monial **6** 46 27N 4 7E
Parbati, R. **32** 25 51N 76 54E
Parbhani **34** 19 8N 76 52E
Parchim **10** 53 25N 11 50E
Parczew **14** 51 9N 22 52E
Pardo, R. **64** 15 39S 38 57W
Pardubice **11** 50 3N 15 45E
Pare **36** 7 43S 112 12E
Parecis, Serra dos **13** 14 0S 60 0W
Paredes de Nava **15** 42 9N 4 42W
Paren **27** 62 45N 163 0E
Parepare **36** 4 0S 119 40E
Parima, Sa. **63** 2 30N 64 0W
Paris, France **6** 48 50N 2 20E
Paris, Tenn. **58** 36 20N 88 20W
Paris, Tex. **59** 33 40N 95 30W
Pariti **36** 9 55S 123 30E
Parker Dam **60** 34 13N 114 5W
Parkes **51** 33 9S 148 11E
Parlakimedi **34** 18 45N 84 5E
Parma **17** 44 50N 10 20E
Parnaíba **64** 3 0S 41 40W
Parnaíba, R. **64** 3 0S 41 50W
Parnassós, Mt. **23** 38 17N 21 30E
Párnis, Mt. **23** 38 14N 23 45E
Párnon Óros, Mts. **23** 37 15N 22 45E
Parnu **28** 58 12N 24 33E
Paroo, R. **51** 31 28S 143 32E
Páros, I. **23** 37 5N 25 12E
Parraburdoo **49** 23 14S 117 32E
Parral **65** 36 10S 72 0W
Parramatta **51** 33 48S 151 1E
Parras **61** 25 30N 102 20W
Parrett, R. **2** 51 13N 3 1W
Parry Sd. **57** 45 20N 80 0W
Parsons **59** 37 20N 95 10W
Partanna **19** 37 43N 12 51E
Parthenay **5** 46 38N 0 16W
Partille **25** 57 48N 12 18E
Partinico **19** 38 3N 13 6E
Paru, R. **64** 1 33S 52 38W
Pǎrvomay **22** 42 6N 25 13E
Pas de Calais □ **6** 50 30N 2 30E
Pasadena, Calif. **60** 34 5N 118 0W
Pasadena, Tex. **59** 29 45N 95 14W
Paşcani **13** 47 14N 26 45E
Pasco **60** 46 10N 119 0W
Pasewalk **10** 53 30N 14 0E
Pasing **10** 48 8N 11 27E
Paso Robles **60** 35 40N 120 45W
Passau **10** 48 34N 13 27E
Passero, C. **20** 36 42N 15 8E
Passo Fundo **65** 28 10S 52 30W
Passos **64** 20 43S 46 37W
Pasto **63** 1 13N 77 17W
Pasuruan **36** 7 40S 112 53E
Patagonia, Reg. **65** 45 0S 69 0W
Patan, Gujarat **32** 23 54N 72 14E
Patan, Maharashtra **34** 17 22N 73 48E
Patea **54** 39 45S 174 30E
Paternò **20** 37 34N 14 53E
Paterson **58** 40 55N 74 10W
Pathankot **32** 32 18N 75 45E
Pathfinder Res. **60** 52 0N 107 0W
Patiala **32** 30 23N 76 26E
Patmos, I. **23** 37 21N 26 36E
Patna **33** 25 35N 85 18E
Patos, L. dos **65** 31 20S 51 0W
Patos de Minas **64** 18 35S 46 32W
Pátrai **23** 38 14N 21 47E
Patrocínio **64** 18 57S 47 0W
Patuakhali **33** 22 20N 90 25E
Patuca, R. **62** 15 50N 84 18W
Pátzcuaro **61** 19 30N 101 40W
Pau **7** 43 19N 0 25W
Pauillac **7** 45 11N 0 46W
Paulhan **7** 43 33N 3 28E
Paulistana **64** 8 9S 41 9W
Paulo Afonso **64** 9 21S 38 15W
Paulpietersburg **48** 27 23S 30 50E
Paul's Valley **59** 34 40N 97 17W
Paungde **37** 18 29N 95 30E
Pauni **33** 20 48N 79 40E
Pavia **17** 45 10N 9 10E
Pavlikeni **22** 43 14N 25 20E
Pavlodar **26** 52 33N 77 0E
Pavlograd **30** 48 30N 35 52E
Pavlovo **29** 55 58N 43 30E
Pavlovsk **29** 50 26N 40 5E
Pavlovskaya **31** 46 17N 39 47E
Pavlovskiy-Posad **29** 55 37N 38 42E
Pavullo nel Frignano **17** 44 20N 10 50E
Payerne **10** 46 49N 6 56E
Payette **60** 44 0N 117 0W
Paysandú **65** 32 19S 58 8W
Paz, R. **61** 13 44N 90 10W
Pazardzhik **22** 42 12N 24 20E
Pazin **18** 45 14N 13 56E
Peace, R. **56** 59 0N 111 25W
Peace River **56** 56 15N 117 18W
Peak Hill, N.S.W. **51** 32 39S 148 11E
Peak Hill, W.A. **49** 25 35S 118 43E
Peale, Mt. **60** 38 25N 109 12W
Pearsall **59** 28 55N 99 8W
Pec **21** 42 40N 20 19E
Pechora, R. **26** 68 13N 54 10E
Pechorskaya Guba **26** 68 40N 54 0E
Pecos **59** 31 25N 103 35W
Pecos, R. **59** 29 42N 101 22W
Pécs **12** 46 5N 18 13E
Peddapuram **34** 17 5N 82 8E
Pedra Azul **64** 16 1S 41 16W
Pedro Juan Caballero **64** 22 34S 55 37W
Pedro Miguel **61** 9 1N 79 36W
Peebles **3** 55 39N 3 12W
Peel **2** 54 13N 4 40W
Pegasus Bay **54** 43 20S 172 55E
Pegu **37** 17 20N 96 29E
Pegu Yoma **37** 19 0N 96 0E
Pehan **39** 48 17N 120 31E
Pehpei **38** 29 44N 106 29E
Pehuajó **65** 36 0S 62 0W
Peine **10** 52 19N 10 12E
Peiping **39** 39 45N 116 25E
Pekalongan **36** 6 53S 109 40E
Pekan **37** 3 30N 103 25E
Pekin **59** 40 35N 89 40W
Peking = Peiping **39** 39 45N 116 25E
Pelat, Mt. **8** 44 16N 6 42E
Pélla □ **23** 40 52N 22 0E
Pellworm, I. **10** 54 30N 8 40E
Peloponnisos □ **23** 37 10N 22 0E
Pelorus, Sd. **54** 40 59S 173 59E
Pelotas **65** 31 42S 52 23W
Pelvoux, Massif de **8** 44 52N 6 20E
Pemalang **36** 6 53S 109 23E
Pematangsiantar **35** 2 57N 99 5E
Pemba I. **46** 5 0S 39 45E
Pemberton **49** 34 30S 116 0E
Pembroke, Canada **57** 45 50N 77 15W
Pembroke, U.K. **2** 51 41N 4 57W
Pen-y-Ghent **2** 54 10N 2 15W
Peña, Sierra de la **16** 42 32N 0 45W
Penapolis **64** 21 30S 50 0W
Peñarroya-Pueblonuevo **15** 38 19N 5 16W
Penas, G. de **65** 47 0S 75 0W
Pendleton **60** 45 35N 118 50W
Penglai **39** 37 49N 120 47E
Pengpu **39** 33 0N 117 25E
Peniche **15** 39 19N 9 22W
Penki **39** 41 20N 132 50E
Penmarch **5** 47 49N 4 21W
Penne **18** 42 28N 13 56E
Penner, R. **34** 14 50N 78 20E
Pennine Ra. **2** 54 50N 2 20W
Pennsylvania □ **58** 40 50N 78 0W
Penola **51** 37 25S 140 47E
Penong **49** 31 59S 133 5E
Penrhyn Is. **53** 9 0S 150 30W
Penrith, Australia **53** 33 43S 150 38E
Penrith, U.K. **2** 54 40N 2 45W
Pensacola **58** 30 30N 87 10W
Penticton **56** 49 30N 119 30W
Pentland **51** 20 32S 145 25E
Pentland Firth **3** 58 43N 3 10W
Pentland Hills **3** 55 48N 3 25W
Penza **29** 53 15N 45 5E
Penzance **2** 50 7N 5 32W
Penzhinskaya Guba **27** 61 30N 163 0E
Peoria **59** 40 40N 89 40W
Perak □ **37** 5 0N 101 0E
Perast **21** 42 31N 18 47E
Perche **5** 48 31N 1 1E
Perche, Collines du **5** 48 30N 2 5E
Pereira **63** 4 49N 75 43W
Pereslavl Zalesskiy **29** 56 45N 38 58E
Pereyaslav Khmelnitskiy **28** 50 3N 31 28E
Pergamino **65** 33 52S 60 30W
Pérgine Valsugano **18** 46 4N 11 15E
Perico **65** 24 20S 65 5W
Périgueux **7** 45 10N 0 42E
Perijá, Sierra de **63** 9 30N 73 3W
Periyakulam **34** 10 5N 77 30E
Perlas, Arch. de las **62** 8 41N 79 7W
Perlez **21** 45 11N 20 22E
Perlis □ **37** 6 30N 100 15E
Perm **26** 58 0N 57 10E
Pernambuco = Recife **64** 8 0S 35 0W
Pernambuco □ **64** 8 0S 37 0W
Pernik **21** 42 36N 23 2E
Perpignan **7** 42 42N 2 53E
Perry, Fla. **58** 30 9N 83 10W
Perry, Ga. **58** 32 25N 83 41W
Persepolis **42** 29 55N 52 50E
Persia = Iran ■ **42** 35 0N 50 0E
Persian Gulf = The Gulf **42** 27 0N 50 0E
Perstorp **25** 56 10N 13 25E
Perth, Australia **49** 31 57S 115 52E
Perth, U.K. **3** 56 24N 3 27W
Perth, U.S.A. **58** 40 33N 74 36E
Pertuis **8** 43 42N 5 30E
Peru ■ **63** 8 0S 75 0W
Peru **58** 40 42N 86 0W
Perúgia **18** 43 6N 12 24E
Pervomaysk **29** 54 53N 43 49E
Pervouralsk **26** 56 55N 60 0E
Pésaro **18** 43 55N 12 53E
Pescara **18** 42 28N 14 13E
Pescara, R. **18** 42 28N 14 13E
Péscia **17** 43 54N 10 40E
Peshawar **42** 34 2N 71 37E
Peshawar □ **42** 35 0N 72 50E
Peski **29** 51 14N 42 12E
Pessac **7** 44 48N 0 37W
Pest □ **12** 47 29N 19 5E
Petah Tiqwa **41** 32 6N 34 53E
Petaling Jaya **37** 3 4N 101 42E
Petange **9** 49 33N 5 55E
Petén Itzá, L. **61** 16 58N 89 50W
Peterboro' **57** 42 55N 71 59W
Peterborough, Australia **51** 33 0S 138 45E
Peterborough, U.K. **2** 52 35N 0 14W
Peterhead **3** 57 30N 1 49W
Petersburg **58** 37 17N 77 26W
Petlad **32** 22 30N 72 45E
Petone **54** 41 13S 174 53E
Petoskey **58** 45 21N 84 55W
Petrich **22** 41 24N 23 13E
Petrila **13** 45 29N 23 29E
Petrolina **64** 9 24S 40 30W
Petropavlovsk **26** 55 0N 69 0E
Petropavlovsk-Kamchatskiy **27** 53 16N 159 0E
Petrópolis **64** 22 33S 43 9W
Petroşeni **13** 45 28N 23 20E
Petrovac **21** 42 13N 18 57E
Petrovaradin **21** 45 16N 19 55E
Petrovsk **29** 52 22N 45 19E
Petrovsk-Zabaykalskiy **27** 51 26N 108 30E
Petrozavodsk **26** 61 41N 34 20E
Peureulak **35** 4 48N 97 45E
Peyruis **8** 44 1N 5 56E
Pézenas **7** 43 28N 3 24E
Pforzheim **10** 48 53N 8 43E
Pfungstadt **10** 49 47N 8 36E
Phan Rang **37** 11 40N 109 9E
Phan Thiet **37** 11 1N 108 9E
Phenix City **58** 32 30N 85 0W
Philadelphia **58** 40 0N 75 10W
Philippines ■ **36** 12 0N 123 0E
Philippopolis = Plovdiv **22** 42 8N 24 44E
Phitsanulok **37** 16 50N 100 12E
Phnom Penh **37** 11 33N 104 55E
Phoenix **60** 33 30N 112 10W
Phoenix Is. **53** 3 30S 172 0W
Phu Ly **37** 20 35N 105 50E
Phuket **37** 8 0N 98 28E
Phuoc Le **37** 10 39N 107 19E
Piabla **51** 25 20S 152 45E
Piacenza **17** 45 2N 9 42E
Piaseczno **14** 52 5N 21 2E
Piatra **13** 43 51N 25 9E
Piatra Neamţ **13** 46 56N 26 21E
Piauí □ **64** 7 0S 43 0W
Piave, R. **18** 45 32N 12 44E
Piazza Armerina **20** 37 21N 14 20E
Picardie □ **6** 50 0N 2 15E
Picardie, Pl. de **6** 50 0N 2 0E
Picton **54** 34 12S 150 34E
Pictou **57** 45 41N 62 42W
Piedmont = Piemonte **17** 45 0N 7 30E
Piedras Blancas Pt. **60** 35 45N 121 18W
Piedras Negras **61** 28 35N 100 35W
Piemonte □ **17** 45 0N 7 30E
Piería □ **23** 40 13N 22 25E
Pierre **59** 44 23N 100 20W
Pierrelatte **8** 44 23N 4 43E
Pieštany **12** 48 35N 17 50E
Piet Retief **48** 27 1S 30 50E
Pietermantzburg **48** 29 35S 30 25E
Pietersburg **48** 23 54S 29 25E
Pietrasanta **17** 43 57N 10 12E
Pietrosu, Mt. **13** 47 12N 25 8E
Pietrosul, Mt. **13** 47 35N 24 43E
Pihani **33** 27 36N 80 15E
Pikalevo **28** 59 37N 34 0E
Pikes Pk. **59** 38 50N 105 10W
Piketberg **47** 32 55S 18 40E
Pila **14** 53 10N 16 48E
Pilbara **49** 21 15S 118 19E
Pilibhit **33** 28 40N 79 50E
Pilica, R. **14** 51 52N 21 17E
Pílos **23** 36 55N 21 42E
Pinang □ **37** 5 25N 100 15E
Pinar del Rio **62** 22 26N 83 40W
Pincota **13** 46 20N 21 45E
Pindiga **44** 9 58N 10 53E
Pindos Óros, Mts. **23** 40 0N 21 0E
Pindus Mts = Pindos Óros **23** 40 0N 21 0E
Pine Bluff **59** 34 10N 92 0W
Pine Creek **49** 13 50S 131 49E
Pine Hill **51** 23 42S 147 0E
Pinerolo **17** 44 47N 7 21E
Pinetown **48** 29 48S 30 54E
Ping, R. **37** 15 40N 100 9E
Pingliang **38** 35 20N 106 40E
Pingsiang **38** 22 2N 106 55E
Pingtung **39** 22 36N 120 30E
Pinjarra **49** 32 37S 115 52E
Pinos, I. de **62** 21 40N 82 40W
Pinrang **36** 3 46S 119 34E
Pinsk **28** 52 10N 26 8E
Pinyug **26** 60 5N 48 0E
Pioche **60** 38 0N 114 35W
Piombino **17** 42 54N 10 30E
Pionki **14** 51 29N 21 28E
Piotrków Trybunalski **14** 51 23N 19 43E
Piracicaba **64** 22 45S 47 30W
Piracunica **64** 3 50S 41 50W
Piraiévs **23** 37 57N 23 42E
Pirapora **64** 17 20S 44 56W
Pirdop **22** 42 40N 24 10E
Pírgos **23** 37 40N 21 27E
Pirimopon **36** 6 45S 138 10E
Pirineous, Mts. **16** 42 40N 1 0E
Pirmasens **10** 49 12N 7 30E
Pirna **10** 50 57N 13 57E
Pirot **21** 43 9N 22 39E
Pisa **17** 43 43N 10 23E
Pisagua **63** 19 40S 70 15W
Pisco **63** 13 50S 76 5W
Písek **11** 49 19N 14 10E
Pisticci **20** 40 24N 16 33E
Pistóia **17** 43 57N 10 53E
Pisuerga, R. **15** 41 33N 4 52W
Pisz **14** 53 38N 21 49E
Pitcairn I. **53** 25 5S 130 5W
Piteälv **24** 65 44N 20 50W
Piteå **24** 65 20N 21 25E
Piteşti **13** 44 52N 24 54E
Pithapuram **34** 17 10N 82 15W
Píthion **23** 41 24N 26 40W
Pithiviers **6** 48 10N 2 13E

S

Semenov 29 56 43N 44 30E
Semiluki 29 51 41N 39 10E
Seminoe Res. 60 42 0N 107 0W
Seminole 59 35 15N 96 45W
Semiozernoye 26 52 35N 64 0E
Semipalatinsk 26 50 30N 80 10E
Semiyarskoye 26 50 55N 78 30E
Semmering P. 11 47 41N 15 45E
Semnān 42 35 55N 53 25E
Semnān □ 42 36 0N 54 0E
Semois, R. 9 49 53N 4 45E
Senai 37 1 38N 103 38E
Sendai, Kagoshima 40 31 50N 130 20E
Sendai, Miyagi 40 38 15N 141 0E
Seneca 60 44 10N 119 2W
Senegal ■ 44 14 30N 14 30W
Senegal, R. 44 15 48N 16 32E
Sengiley 29 53 58N 48 54E
Senigállia 18 43 42N 13 12E
Senja, I. 24 69 15N 17 30E
Sennâr 45 13 30N 33 35E
Senneterre 57 48 25N 77 15W
Sens 6 48 11N 3 15E
Senta 21 45 55N 20 3E
Sentolo 36 7 55s 110 13E
Seoni 33 22 5N 79 30E
Seoul=Sŏul 39 37 26N 126 55E
Sepik, R. 51 3 51s 144 34E
Sepone 37 16 45N 106 13E
Sept Îles 57 50 13N 66 22W
Septemvri 22 42 13N 24 6E
Sequoia Nat. Park 60 36 20N 118 30W
Seraing 9 50 35N 5 32E
Seram □ 36 3 10s 129 0E
Serampore 33 22 44N 88 30E
Serang 36 6 8s 106 10E
Seravezza 17 43 59N 10 13E
Serdobsk 29 52 28N 44 10E
Seregno 17 45 40N 9 12E
Seremban 37 2 43N 101 53E
Serenje 46 13 11s 30 52E
Sergipe □ 64 10 30s 37 30W
Serian 35 1 10N 110 40E
Sérifos, I. 23 37 9N 24 30E
Sérmide 18 45 0N 11 17E
Serov 26 59 40N 60 20E
Serowe 47 22 25s 26 43E
Serpa Pinto 46 14 48s 17 52E
Serpis, R. 16 39 59N 0 9W
Serpukhov 29 54 55N 37 28E
Serra do Navio 64 0 59N 52 3W
Sérrai 23 41 5N 23 37E
Serres 8 44 26N 5 43E
Serrinha 64 11 39s 39 0W
Serui 36 1 45s 136 10E
Sérvia 23 40 9N 21 58E
Sesia, R. 17 45 5N 8 37E
Sessa Aurunca 19 41 14N 13 55E
Sestao 15 43 18N 3 0W
Sesto S. Giovanni 17 45 32N 9 14E
Sestri Levante 17 44 17N 9 22E
Sète 7 43 25N 3 42E
Sete Lagôas 64 19 27s 44 16W
Sétif 44 36 9N 5 26E
Seto 40 35 14N 137 6E
Setonaikai, Inland Sea 40 34 10N 133 10E
Settat 44 33 0N 7 40W
Setté Cama 46 2 32s 9 57E
Séttimo 17 45 9N 7 46E
Settle 2 54 5N 2 18W
Setubal 15 38 30N 8 58W
Setúbal □ 15 38 25N 8 35W
Seulimeum 35 5 27N 95 15E
Sevan, Ozero 31 40 20N 45 20E
Sevastopol 30 44 35N 33 30E
Severn, R. 2 51 35N 2 40W
Severnaya Dvina, R. 26 64 32N 40 30E
Severnaya Zemlya 27 79 0N 100 0E
Severo-Kurilsk 27 50 40N 156 8E
Severo-Yeniseyskiy 27 60 22N 93 1E
Severočeský □ 11 50 35N 14 15E
Severodinsk 26 64 27N 39 58E
Severodonetsk 31 48 50N 38 30E
Severomoravský □ 12 49 38N 17 40E
Sevilla 15 37 23N 6 0W
Sevilla □ 15 37 0N 6 0W
Sevlievo 22 43 1N 25 6E
Seward 56 60 0N 149 40W
Seward, Pen. 56 65 0N 164 0W
Sewer 36 5 46s 134 40E
Seydhisfjördhur 24 65 16N 14 0W
Seymour 51 36 58s 145 10E
Seyssel 8 45 57N 5 49E
Sezze 19 41 30N 13 3E
Sfânti Gheorghe 13 45 52N 25 48E
Sfax 45 34 49N 10 48E
's-Gravenhage 9 52 7N 4 17E
Shabani 48 20 17s 30 2E
Shabla 22 43 31N 28 32E
Shadrinsk 26 56 5N 63 38E
Shaftesbury 2 51 0N 2 12W
Shahabad 33 27 36N 79 56E
Shahi 42 36 30N 52 55E
Shajahanpur 33 27 54N 79 57E
Shahpur 32 22 12N 77 58E
Shahrud 42 36 30N 55 0E
Shajapur 32 23 20N 76 15E
Shakhty 31 47 40N 40 10E
Shala, L. 43 7 30N 38 30E
Shamo, L. 43 5 45N 37 30E
Shan □ 37 21 30N 98 30E
Shanghai 39 31 10N 121 25E
Shangjao 39 28 25N 117 57E
Shangklu 39 34 28N 115 42E
Shangshui 39 33 42N 115 4E
Shannon 54 40 33s 175 25E
Shannon, R. 4 52 36N 9 41W
Shansi □ 39 38 20N 112 0E
Shantow 39 23 25N 116 40E
Shantung □ 39 36 0N 118 0E
Shaohing 39 30 0N 120 32E
Shaoyang 39 27 10N 111 30E
Sharjah 42 25 23N 55 26E
Shark, B. 49 25 15s 133 20E
Sharon 58 41 18N 80 30W
Sharya 29 58 12N 45 40E
Shasi 39 30 16N 112 20E
Shasta, Mt. 60 41 45N 122 0W
Shasta Res. 60 40 50N 122 15W
Shatsk 29 54 0N 41 45E
Shatt al Arab, R. 41 30 0N 48 31E
Shaunavon 56 49 35N 108 40W
Shawano 59 44 45N 88 38W
Shawnee 59 35 15N 97 0W
Shchekino 29 54 1N 37 28E
Shchigry 29 51 55N 36 58E
Shchors 28 51 48N 31 56E
Shchuchiosk 26 52 56N 70 12E
Shebelle, Wabi, R. 43 0 1s 42 45E
Sheboygan 59 43 46N 87 45W
Sheelin, L. 4 53 48N 7 20W
Sheerness 2 51 26N 0 47E
Sheffield 2 53 23N 1 28W
Sheikh, J. ash, Mt. 41 33 26N 35 51E
Shekhupura 32 25 9N 85 53E
Sheki 31 41 10N 47 5E
Shekki 39 22 30N 113 15E
Sheklung 39 23 5N 113 55E
Shelburne 57 43 47N 65 20W
Shelby, Mont. 60 48 30N 111 59W
Shelby, N.C. 58 35 18N 81 34W
Shelikhova, Zaliv 27 59 30N 157 0E
Shellharbour 51 34 31s 150 51E
Shelton 60 47 15N 123 6W
Shenandoah, R. 58 39 19N 77 44W
Shendı 45 16 46N 33 33E
Shensi □ 38 35 0N 109 0E
Shenyang 39 41 35N 123 30E
Shepetovka 28 50 10N 27 0E
Shepparton 51 36 18s 145 25E
Sherborne 2 50 56N 2 31W
Sherbrooke 57 45 24N 71 57W
Sheridan 60 44 50N 107 0W
Sherman 59 33 40N 96 35W
Sherpur 33 25 1N 90 3E
Sherridon 56 55 10N 101 5W
's-Hertogenbosch 9 51 41N 5 19E
Sherwood Forest 2 53 5N 1 5W
Shetland Is. 3 60 30N 1 30W
Shetland □ 3 60 30N 1 30W
Shevchenko 26 44 25N 51 20E
Shiel, L. 3 56 48N 5 32W
Shiga □ 40 35 20N 136 0E
Shigatse 38 29 10N 89 0E
Shihkiachwang 39 38 0N 114 32E
Shihwei 39 51 28N 119 59E
Shikarpur 32 28 17N 78 7E
Shikoku, I. 40 33 30N 133 30E
Shikoku □ 40 33 30N 133 30E
Shilka 27 52 0N 115 55E
Shillelagh 4 52 46N 6 32W
Shilovo 29 54 25N 40 57E
Shimada 40 34 49N 138 19E
Shimane □ 40 35 0N 132 30E
Shimizu 40 35 0N 138 30E
Shimodate 40 36 20N 139 55E
Shimoga 34 13 57N 75 32E
Shimonoseki 40 33 58N 131 0E
Shimpek 26 44 50N 74 10E
Shin, L. 3 58 7N 4 30W
Shinano, R. 40 37 56N 139 3E
Shinyanga 46 3 45s 33 27E
Shirane-San, Mt. 40 36 38N 138 32E
Shiraz 42 29 42N 52 30E
Shiukwan 39 24 58N 113 3E
Shivpuri 32 25 18N 77 42E
Shizuoka 40 35 0N 138 30E
Shizuoka □ 40 35 15N 138 40E
Shklov 28 54 10N 30 15E
Shkodra 23 42 6N 19 20E
Shoeburyness 2 51 31N 0 49E
Sholapur 34 17 43N 75 56E
Shoshone 60 43 0N 114 27W
Shostka 28 51 57N 33 32E
Show Low 60 34 16N 110 0W
Shreveport 59 32 30N 93 50W
Shrewsbury 2 52 42N 2 45W
Shropshire=Salop □ 2 52 36N 2 45W
Shumerlya 29 55 30N 46 10E
Shumikha 26 55 15N 63 30E
Shungay 31 48 30N 46 45E
Shur, R. 42 29 59N 54 50E
Shuya 29 56 50N 41 28E
Shwebo 37 22 30N 95 45E
Si Kiang, R. 39 22 25N 113 23E
Sihan Ra. 42 27 30N 64 40E
Sialkot 32 32 32N 74 30E
Siam=Thailand ■ 37 16 0N 101 0E
Siam, Gulf of 37 11 30N 101 0E
Sian 38 34 2N 109 0E
Siang Kiang, R. 39 27 10N 112 45E
Siangfan 39 32 15N 112 2E
Siangtan 39 28 0N 112 55E
Siao Hingan Ling, Mts. 39 49 0N 127 0E
Siauliai 28 55 56N 23 15E
Siazan 31 41 3N 48 7E
Sibenic 18 43 48N 15 54E
Siberut, I. 35 1 30s 99 0E
Sibiu 13 45 45N 24 9E
Sibolga 35 1 50N 98 45E
Sibu 35 2 19N 111 51E
Sichang 38 28 0N 102 10E
Sicilia, I. 19 37 30N 14 30E
Sicilia □ 19 37 30N 14 30E
Sicilian Chan. 19 37 25N 12 30E
Sicuani 63 14 10s 71 10W
Sid 21 45 6N 19 16E
Siderno Marina 20 38 16N 16 17E
Sidhirókastron 23 37 20N 21 46E
Sidhpur 32 23 56N 71 25E
Sîdi Barrâni 45 31 32N 25 58E
Sidi bel Abbès 44 35 13N 0 10W
Sidlaw Hills 3 56 32N 3 10W
Sidmouth 2 50 40N 3 13W
Sidoardjo 36 7 30s 112 46W
Siedlce 14 52 10N 22 20E
Sieg, R. 10 50 45N 7 5E
Siegburg 10 50 48N 7 12E
Siegen 10 50 52N 8 2E
Siena 18 43 20N 11 20E
Sienyang 38 34 20N 108 48E
Sieradz 14 51 37N 18 41E
Sierpc 14 52 55N 19 43E
Sierra Blanca 60 31 11N 105 17W
Sierra Leone ■ 44 9 0N 12 0W
Sierra Nevada, Mts. 60 39 0N 120 30W
Sierre 10 46 17N 7 31E
Sífnos, I. 23 37 0N 24 45E
Sighet 13 47 57N 23 52E
Sighişoara 13 46 12N 24 50E
Sigli 35 5 25N 96 0E
Siglufjörður 24 66 12N 18 55W
Siguiri 44 11 31N 9 10W
Sikandarabad 32 28 30N 77 39E
Sikar 32 27 39N 75 10E
Sikasso 44 11 7N 5 35W
Sikeston 59 36 52N 89 35W
Sikhote Alin, Khrebet 27 46 0N 136 0E
Sikkim □ 33 27 50N 88 50E
Silba 18 44 24N 14 41E
Siliguri 33 26 45N 88 25E
Silinhot 39 43 16N 116 0E
Silistra 22 44 6N 27 19E
Siljan, L. 25 60 55N 14 45E
Silkeborg 25 56 10N 9 32E
Sillajhuay, Mt. 63 19 40s 68 40W
Silute 28 55 21N 21 33E
Silva Porto 46 12 22s 16 55E
Silver City, Panama Canal Zone 61 9 21N 79 53W
Silver City, Calif. 60 36 19N 119 44W
Silver City, N. Mex. 60 32 50N 108 18W
Simanggang 35 1 15N 111 25E
Simenga 27 62 50N 107 55E
Simeria 13 45 51N 23 1E
Simeulue, I. 35 2 45N 95 45E
Simferopol 30 44 55N 34 3E
Sími, I. 23 36 35N 27 50E
Simla 32 31 2N 77 15E
Simojärvi 24 66 5N 27 10E
Simojoki, R. 24 65 37N 25 3E
Simonstown 47 34 14s 18 26E
Simpang 37 1 3s 110 6E
Simplonpass 10 46 15N 8 0E
Simpson Des. 49 25 0s 137 0E
Simrishamn 25 55 33N 14 22E
Sinabang 35 2 30N 46 30E
Sinai, Pen=Gebel es Sînâ 45 29 0W 34 0E
Sinaloa □ 61 25 50N 108 20W
Sinalunga 18 43 12N 11 43E
Sincelejo 63 9 18N 75 24E
Sincorá, Sa. do 64 13 30s 41 0W
Sindangbarang 36 7 27s 107 9E
Singa 45 13 10N 33 57E
Singapore ■ 37 1 17N 103 51E
Singapore, Straits of 37 1 15N 104 0E
Singaradja 35 8 15s 115 10E
Singen 10 47 45N 8 50E
Singkawang 35 1 0N 109 5E
Singleton 51 32 33s 151 10E
Singtai 39 37 2N 114 30E
Singtze 29 29 30N 116 4E
Sinhailien 39 34 31N 119 0E
Sinhsien 39 38 25N 112 45E
Sinhwa 39 27 36N 111 6E
Sining 38 36 35N 101 50E
Sinkat 45 18 55N 36 49E
Sinkiang 39 35 35N 111 25E
Sinkiang-Uigur A.R. □ 38 42 0N 86 0E
Sinnamary 64 5 23N 52 57W
Sinoia 48 17 20s 30 8E
Sinsiang 39 35 15N 113 55E
Sinskoye 27 61 8N 126 48E
Sintai 38 30 59N 105 0E
Sintang 35 0 5N 111 35E
Sintra 15 38 47N 9 25W
Sinŭiju 39 40 5N 124 20E
Sinyang 39 32 6N 114 2E
Sion 10 46 14N 7 20E
Sioux City 59 42 32N 96 25W
Sioux Falls 59 43 35N 96 40W
Sioux Lookout 56 50 10N 91 50W
Siquia, R. 62 12 10N 84 20W
Siracusa 20 37 4N 15 17E
Sirajganj 33 24 25N 89 47E
Siret 13 47 55N 26 5E
Siret, R., 13 45 27N 28 1E
Sironj 32 24 5N 77 45E
Síros, I. 23 37 28N 24 57E
Sirsa 32 29 33N 75 4E
Sisak 18 45 30N 16 21E
Sisaket 37 15 8N 104 23E
Sisophon 37 13 31N 102 59E
Sistan Baluchistan □ 42 27 0N 62 0E
Sistema Central, Mts. 15 40 40N 5 55W
Sistema Ibérico, Mts. 16 41 0N 2 10W
Sisteron 8 44 12N 5 57E
Sitapur 33 27 38N 80 45E
Sitges 16 41 17N 1 47E
Sithoniá, Pen. 23 40 0N 23 45E
Sitía 23 35 13N 26 6E
Sittang, R. 37 17 10N 96 58E
Sittard 9 51 0N 5 52E
Sivakasi 34 9 24N 77 47E
Sivas 41 39 43N 36 58E
Siwalik Ra. 33 28 0N 83 0E
Siwan 33 26 13N 84 27E
Sizewell 2 52 13N 1 38E
Sjaelland, I. 25 55 30N 11 30E
Skadarsko, Jezero 21 42 8N 19 20E
Skagafjörður 24 65 55N 19 35W
Skagastølstindane, Mt. 25 61 25N 8 10E
Skagen 25 57 43N 10 35E
Skagerrak, Str. 25 57 30N 9 0E
Skagway 56 59 30N 135 20W
Skalat 30 94 23N 25 55E
Skanderborg 25 56 2N 9 55E
Skare 25 58 25N 13 30E
Skaraborg Län □ 25 58 20N 13 30E
Skarźysko Kamienna 14 51 7N 20 52E
Skegness 2 53 9N 0 20E
Skelllefte älv 24 65 30N 18 30E
Skellefteå 24 64 45N 20 59E
Skelleftehamn 24 64 41N 21 14E
Skíathos, I. 23 39 12N 23 30E
Skiddaw, Mt. 2 54 39N 3 9W
Skien 25 59 12N 9 35E
Skierniewice 14 51 58N 20 19E
Skikda 44 36 50N 6 58E
Skipton 2 53 57N 2 1W
Skíros 23 38 55N 24 34E
Skíros, I. 23 38 55N 24 34E
Skive 25 56 33N 9 2E
Skjálfandafljót 24 65 15N 17 25W
Skjalfandi, B. 24 66 5N 17 30W
Skjern 25 55 57N 8 30E
Skónsberg 25 62 25N 17 21E
Skópelos, I. 23 39 9N 23 47E
Skopin 29 53 55N 39 32E
Skopje 21 42 1N 21 32E
Skövde 25 58 24N 13 52E
Skovorodino 27 53 59N 123 55E
Skowhegan 58 44 49N 69 40W
Skutskär 25 60 37N 17 25E
Skwierzyna 14 52 46N 15 30E
Skye, I. 3 57 15N 6 10W
Slagelse 25 55 23N 11 19E
Slaney, R. 4 52 21N 6 30W
Slano 21 42 48N 17 53E
Slantsy 28 59 7N 28 5E
Slaný 11 50 13N 14 6E
Slatina 13 44 28N 24 22E
Slave, R. 56 61 18N 113 39W
Slavgorod 26 53 10N 78 50E
Slavonska Pozega 21 45 20N 17 40E
Slavonski Brod 21 45 11N 18 0E
Slavuta 28 50 15N 27 2E
Slavyansk 30 49 0N 37 30E
Slavyansk-na-Kubani 30 45 15N 38 11E
Sławno 14 54 22N 16 40E
Sleaford 2 53 0N 0 22W
Sleat, Sd. of 3 57 5N 5 47W
Sleman 36 7 40s 110 20E
Sliedrecht 9 51 50s 4 45E
Sligo 4 54 17N 8 28W
Sligo □ 4 54 10N 8 30W
Slite 24 57 42N 18 48E
Sliven 22 42 42N 26 19E
Slivnitsa 21 42 50N 23 0E
Slobodskoy 29 58 40N 50 6E
Slobozia 13 44 30N 25 14E
Slonim 28 53 4N 25 19E
Slough 2 51 30N 0 35W
Slovakian Ore Mts.=Slovenské Rudohorie, Mts. 12 50 25N 13 0E
Slovenija □ 18 45 58N 14 30E
Slovenská Socialisticka Rep. □ 12 48 40N 19 0E
Slovenské Rudohorie, Mts. 12 50 25N 13 0E
Slovensko, Reg. 12 48 50N 20 0E
Slunchev Bryag 22 42 40N 27 41E
Slyne Hd. 4 53 25N 10 10W
Smederevo 21 44 40N 20 57E
Smedjebacken 25 60 8N 15 25E
Smela 30 49 30N 32 0E
Smidevich 27 48 36N 133 49E
Smithton 51 31 0s 152 48E
Smithville 58 30 2N 97 12W
Smolensk 28 54 45N 32 0E
Smolyan 22 41 36N 24 38E
Snaefell, Mt. 24 54 18N 4 26W
Snaefellsjökull 24 64 50N 23 49W
Snake, R. 60 46 12N 119 2W
Sneek 9 53 2N 5 40E
Snezhnoye 31 48 0N 38 58E
Sniardwy, Jeżoro, L. 14 53 46N 21 44E
Snigirevka 30 47 2N 32 35E
Snizort, L. 3 57 33N 6 28W
Snøhetta, Mt. 25 62 19N 9 16E
Snowdon 2 53 4N 4 8W
Snowtown 51 33 46s 138 14E
Snowy Mts. 51 36 30s 148 20E
Snyder 59 32 45N 100 57W
Sobinka 29 56 0N 40 0E
Sobral 64 3 50s 40 30W
Sochaczew 14 52 15N 20 13E
Soche 38 38 24N 77 20E
Sochi 31 43 35N 39 40E
Society Is. 53 17 0s 151 0W
Socorro 60 34 3N 106 58W
Socotra, I. 43 12 30N 54 0E
Socúellamos 16 39 16N 2 47W
Soda Springs 60 42 4N 111 40W
Söderhamn 25 61 18N 17 10E
Söderkoping 25 58 31N 16 35E
Södermanlands Län □ 25 59 10N 16 30E
Södertälje 25 59 12N 17 50E
Soekmekaar 48 23 30s 29 55E
Soest, Netherlands 9 52 9N 5 19E
Soest, W. Germany 10 51 34N 8 7E
Sofala 48 19 30s 34 52E
Sofia=Sofiya 22 42 45N 23 20E
Sofiya 22 42 45N 23 20E
Sogn og Fjordane □ 24 61 40N 6 0E
Sognefjorden 25 61 10N 5 50E
Sohâg 45 26 27N 31 43E
Soignies 9 50 35N 4 5E
Soissons 6 49 25N 3 19E
Sok, R. 29 53 24N 50 8E
Sokal 28 50 31N 24 15E
Sokhós 23 40 48N 23 22E
Sokol 29 59 30N 40 5E
Sokołka 14 53 25N 23 30E
Sokolov 11 50 12N 12 40E
Sokoto 44 13 2N 5 16E
Sokołow Podlaski 14 52 25N 22 15E
Sol, Costa del 15 36 30N 4 30W
Sol Iletsk 26 51 10N 55 0E
Solano 36 16 25N 121 15E
Solec Kujawski 14 53 5N 18 14E
Soledad, Col. 63 10 55N 74 46W
Soledad, U.S.A. 60 36 27N 121 16W
Soledad, Ven. 63 8 10N 63 34W
Solent 2 50 45N 1 25W
Solesmes 6 50 10N 3 30E
Soligorsk 28 52 48N 27 32E
Solikamsk 26 59 38N 56 50E
Solimões, R. 63 0 5s 50 0W
Solingen 10 51 10N 7 4E
Sollefteå 25 63 12N 17 20E
Sollentuna 25 59 26N 17 56E
Solna 25 59 22N 18 1E
Solnechnogorsk 29 56 10N 36 57E
Sologne, Reg. 6 47 40N 2 0E
Solok 35 0 55s 100 40E
Sololá 61 14 49N 91 10E
Solomon Is. 52 6 0s 155 0E
Solomon Sea 51 7 0s 150 0E
Solothurn 10 47 13N 7 32E
Solothurn □ 10 47 18N 7 40E
Solta, I. 20 43 24N 16 15E
Soltau 10 52 59N 9 50E
Solunska Gl, Mt. 21 41 44N 21 31E
Sölvesborg 25 56 5N 14 35E
Solway Firth 2 54 45N 3 38W
Solwezi 46 12 20s 26 21E
Somatino 19 37 20N 14 0E
Somali Rep. ■ 43 7 0N 47 0E
Sombor 21 45 46N 19 17E
Somerset 62 32 20N 64 55W
Somerset, I. 56 73 30N 93 0W
Somerset □ 2 51 9N 3 0W
Somerset East 47 32 42s 25 35E
Somerset West 47 34 8s 18 50E
Somerton 60 32 41N 114 47W
Somma Lombardo 17 45 41N 8 42E
Somma Vesuviana 20 40 52N 14 23E
Somme, B. de la 5 5 22N 1 30E
Somme, R. 6 50 11N 1 39E
Somme □ 6 50 0N 2 20E
Sommesous 6 48 44N 4 12E
Somogy □ 12 46 19N 17 30E
Somport, Col du 7 42 48N 0 31W
Son 5 42 43N 8 58W
Son, R. 33 25 40N 84 51E
Sonamukhi 33 23 18N 87 27E
Soncino 17 45 24N 9 52E
Sønderborg 25 54 55N 9 49E
Sønderjylland Amt. □ 25 55 10N 9 10E
Sóndrio 17 46 10N 9 53E
Sonepat 32 29 0N 77 5E
Song Cau 37 13 20N 109 18E
Sonkovo 29 57 50N 37 5E
Sonneberg 10 50 22N 11 10E
Sonora □ 61 28 0N 111 0W
Sonsonate 61 13 43N 89 44W
Sonthofen 10 47 31N 10 19E
Soochow 39 31 18N 120 41E
Sopot 14 54 27N 18 31E
Sopotnica 21 41 23N 21 13E
Sopron 12 47 41N 16 37E
Sør-Trøndelag □ 24 63 0N 11 0E
Sora 19 41 45N 13 36E
Sorel 57 46 0N 73 10W
Soresina 17 45 17N 9 51E
Sorgues 8 44 1N 4 53E
Soria 16 41 43N 2 32W
Soria □ 16 41 46N 2 28W
Sorø 25 55 26N 11 32E
Sorocaba 65 23 31s 47 35W
Soroki 30 48 8N 28 12E
Soroti 46 1 43N 33 35E
Sørøya, I. 24 14 9s 73 17W
Sørøysunddet 24 70 25N 23 0E
Sorrento 20 40 38N 14 23E
Sosnowiec 12 50 20N 19 10E
Sotterille 5 49 24N 1 5E
Souanke 46 2 10N 14 10E
Sŏul 39 37 33N 126 58E
Soure 15 40 4N 8 38W
Sousse 45 35 50N 10 38E
South, I. 54 43 0s 170 0E
South Africa ■ 47 32 0s 25 0E
South Andaman, I. 37 11 50N 92 45E
South Australia □ 49 32 0s 139 0E
South Bend 58 41 38N 86 20W
South Carolina □ 58 33 45N 81 0W
South China Sea 35 20 0N 115 0E
South Dakota □ 59 45 0N 100 0W
South Downs 2 50 53N 0 10W
South Esk, R. 3 55 53N 3 4W
South Foreland 2 51 7N 1 23E
South Georgia, I. 55 54 30s 37 0W
South Glamorgan □ 2 51 30N 3 20W
South Grafton 51 29 41s 152 47E
South Haven 58 42 22N 86 20W
South Korea ■ 39 36 0N 128 0E
South Milwaukee 59 42 50N 87 52W
South Orkney Is. 55 63 0s 45 0W
South Portland 58 43 38N 70 15W
South Ronaldsay, I. 3 58 46N 2 58W
South Saskatchewan, R. 56 53 15N 105 5W
South Shetland Is. 55 62 0s 59 0W
South Shields 2 54 59N 1 26W
South Uist, I. 3 57 10N 7 10W
South Vietnam ■ 37 14 0N 108 40E
South-West Africa ■ 47 22 0s 18 9E
South Yemen ■ 43 15 0N 48 0E
South Yorkshire □ 2 53 30N 1 20W
Southampton 2 50 54N 1 23W
Southend 2 51 32N 0 43E
Southern Alps 54 43 41s 170 11E
Southern Cross 49 31 12s 119 15E
Southern Ocean 55 62 0s 160 0W
Southern Uplands 3 55 30N 4 0W
Southport, Australia 51 27 58s 153 25E
Southport, U.K. 2 53 38N 3 1W
Southwold 2 52 19N 1 41E
Soutpansberge, Mts. 48 23 0s 29 30E
Sovetsk, Lithuania 28 55 6N 21 50E
Sovetsk, R.S.F.S.R. 29 57 38N 48 53E

Villafranca di Verona 17 45 20N 10 51E
Villaguay 65 32 0S 58 45W
Villahermosa, Mexico 61 17 45N 92 50W
Villahermosa, Spain 16 38 46N 2 52W
Villalpando 15 41 51N 5 25W
Villanueva de Arzobispo 16 38 10N 3 0W
Villanueva de Córdoba 15 38 20N 4 38W
Villanueva y Geltrú 16 41 13N 1 40E
Villareal 16 39 55N 0 3W
Villarosa 20 37 36N 14 9E
Villarrica 65 39 15S 72 30W
Villarrubia de los Ojos 15 39 14N 3 36W
Villarrobledo 16 39 18N 2 36W
Villazón 63 22 0S 65 35W
Ville de Paris □ 6 48 50N 2 20E
Villefranche-de-Rouergue 7 44 21N 2 2E
Villena 16 38 39N 0 52W
Villeneuve 6 48 42N 2 25E
Villeneuve-lès-Avignon 8 43 57N 4 49E
Villeneuve-sur-Lot 7 44 24N 0 42E
Villerupt 6 49 28N 5 55E
Villeurbanne 8 45 46N 4 55E
Villupuram 34 11 59N 79 31E
Vilnius 28 54 38N 25 25E
Vils 11 47 33N 10 37E
Vilvoorde 9 50 56N 4 26E
Vilyuy, R. 27 63 58N 125 0E
Vilyuysk 27 63 40N 121 20E
Vimercate 17 45 38N 9 25E
Vimmerby 25 57 40N 15 55E
Viña del Mar 65 33 0S 71 30W
Vindeln 24 64 12N 19 43E
Vindhya Ra. 32 22 50N 77 0E
Vinh 37 18 45N 105 38E
Vinkovci 21 45 19N 18 48E
Vinnitsa 30 49 15N 28 30E
Viqueque 36 8 42S 126 30E
Viramgam 32 23 5N 72 0E
Virden 56 49 50N 101 0W
Virginia 59 47 30N 92 32W
Virginia □ 58 37 45N 78 0W
Virje 21 46 4N 16 59E
Virovitica 21 45 51N 17 21E
Virpaza 21 42 15N 19 5E
Virtsu 28 58 32N 23 33E
Virudunagar 34 9 30N 78 0E
Vis, I. 18 43 0N 16 10E
Vis Kanal 18 43 4N 16 5E
Visalia 60 36 25N 119 18E
Visayan Sea 36 11 30N 123 30E
Visby 24 57 37N 18 18E
Visegrad 21 43 47N 19 17E
Viseu 15 40 40N 7 55W
Viseu □ 15 40 40N 7 55W
Viseu de Sus 13 47 44N 24 22E
Vishakhapatnam 34 17 45N 83 20E
Vishnupur 33 23 8N 87 20E
Visnagar 32 23 42N 72 33E
Viso, Mte. 17 44 38N 7 5E
Vitebsk 28 55 12N 30 11E
Viterbo 18 42 25N 12 6E
Vitim 27 59 28N 112 34E
Vitim, R. 27 59 26N 112 34E
Vitória 64 20 20S 40 22W
Vitoria 16 42 51N 2 40W
Vitória da Conquista 64 14 51S 40 51W
Vitré 5 48 8N 1 12W
Vitry-le-François 6 48 43N 4 33W
Vittória 20 36 58N 14 30E
Vittório Véneto 18 45 59N 12 18E
Vivero 15 43 39N 7 38W
Vivonne 7 46 36N 0 15E
Vivsta 25 62 30N 17 18E
Vizcaya □ 16 43 15N 2 45W
Vizianagaram 34 18 6N 83 10E
Vizille 8 45 5N 5 46E
Viziru 13 45 0N 27 43E
Vizzini 20 37 9N 14 43E
Vlaardingen 9 51 55N 4 21E
Vlădeasa, Mt. 13 46 47N 22 50E
Vladimir 29 56 0N 40 30E
Vladimir Volynskiy 28 50 50N 24 18E
Vladivostok 27 43 10N 131 53E
Vlasenica 21 44 11N 18 59E
Vlašić, Mt. 21 44 19N 17 37E
Vlieland, I. 9 53 30N 4 55E
Vlissingen 9 51 26N 3 34E
Vlora 23 40 32N 19 28E
Vltava 11 50 21N 14 30E
Vöcklabruck 11 48 1N 13 39E
Vodnjan 18 44 59N 13 52E
Vogelsberg 10 50 30N 9 15E
Voghera 17 44 59N 9 1E
Voi 46 3 25S 38 32E
Voiotía □ 23 38 20N 23 0E
Voiron 8 45 22N 5 35E
Voitsberg 11 47 3N 15 9E
Voiviïs, L. 23 39 30N 22 45E
Volcano Is. 52 25 0N 141 0E
Volchansk 29 50 17N 36 58E
Volchya, R. 30 48 0N 36 8E
Volga, R. 31 45 55N 47 52E
Volgodonsk 31 47 33N 42 5E
Volgograd 31 48 40N 44 25E
Volgogradskoye Vdkhr. 29 50 0N 45 20E
Völklingen 10 49 15N 6 50E
Volkovysk 28 53 10N 24 28E
Volksrust 48 27 24S 29 53E
Volnovakha 30 47 36N 37 31E
Vologda 29 59 12N 39 55E
Vólos 23 39 21N 22 56E
Volsk 29 52 5N 47 28E
Volta, L. 44 7 30N 0 15E
Volta Redonda 64 22 31S 44 5W
Volturno, R. 19 41 1N 13 55E
Vólvi, L. 23 40 40N 23 34E
Volzhsk 29 55 57N 48 23E
Volzhskiy 31 48 56N 44 46E
Vónitsa 23 38 53N 20 58E
Voorburg 9 52 5N 4 24E
Vopnafjördur 24 65 45N 14 40W
Vorarlberg □ 11 47 20N 10 0E
Vóras Óros, Mts. 23 40 57N 21 45E
Vordingborg 25 55 0N 11 54E
Voríai Sporádhes, Is. 23 39 15N 23 30E
Vorkuta 26 67 48N 64 20E
Voronezh 29 51 40N 39 10E
Voroshilovgrad 31 48 38N 39 15E
Vöru 28 57 50N 27 1E
Vosges, Mts. 6 48 20N 7 10E
Vosges □ 6 48 12N 6 20E
Voskresensk 29 55 27N 38 31E
Voss 24 60 38N 6 26E
Vostochnyy Sayan, Mts. 27 54 0N 96 0E
Vostok I. 53 10 5S 152 23W
Votkinsk 26 57 0N 53 55E
Vouziers 6 49 22N 4 40E
Voznesenka 27 52 24N 70 12E
Voznesensk 30 47 34N 31 20E
Vrancea, Reg. 13 45 50N 26 45E
Vrancei, Munții, Mts. 13 46 0N 26 30E
Vrangelya, Ostrov 27 71 0N 180 0E
Vranica, Mt. 21 43 59N 18 0E
Vranje 21 42 34N 21 54E
Vratsa 22 43 13N 23 30E
Vrbas 21 45 0N 17 27E
Vrbas, R. 21 45 6N 17 31E
Vrbnik 18 45 4N 14 32E
Vrbovsko 18 45 24N 15 5E
Vrchlabí 11 49 38N 15 37E
Vrede 48 27 24S 29 6E
Vrindaban 32 27 37N 77 40E
Vrpolie 21 43 42N 16 1E
Vršac 21 45 8N 21 18E
Vrsacki Kanal 21 45 15N 21 0E
Vryburg 47 26 55S 24 45E
Vsetín 12 49 20N 18 0E
Vučitrn 21 42 49N 20 59E
Vught 9 51 38N 5 20E
Vukovar 21 45 21N 18 59E
Vulcan 13 45 23N 23 17E
Vulcano, I. 20 38 25N 14 58E
Vyatskiye Polyany 29 56 5N 51 0E
Vyazemskiy 27 47 32N 134 45E
Vyazma 28 55 10N 34 15E
Vyazniki 29 56 15N 42 10E
Vyborg 26 60 42N 28 45E
Vychodné Beskydy, Mts. 12 49 30N 22 0E
Vychodočeský □ 11 50 20N 15 45E
Východoslovenský □ 12 48 50N 21 0E
Vyksa 29 55 18N 42 11E
Vyrnwy, L. 2 52 47N 3 30W
Vysokovsk 29 56 22N 36 30E
Vyšší Brod 11 48 36N 14 20E
Vytegra 26 61 15N 36 40E

W

Waal, R. 9 51 55N 4 30E
Wąbrzeźno 14 53 16N 18 57E
Waco 59 31 33N 97 5W
Wad Banda 45 13 10N 27 50E
Wâd Medanî 45 14 28N 33 30E
Waddenzee 9 53 15N 5 15E
Wadi Halfa 45 21 53N 31 19E
Wageningen 9 51 58N 5 40E
Wagga Wagga 51 35 7S 147 24E
Wagin 49 33 17S 117 25E
Wagrowiec 14 52 48N 17 19E
Wahpeton 59 46 20N 96 35W
Waiau 54 42 39S 173 3E
Waibeem 36 0 30S 132 50E
Waidhofen 11 48 49N 15 17E
Waihi 54 37 23S 175 52E
Waihou, R. 54 37 10S 175 32E
Waikabubak 36 9 45S 119 25E
Waikari 54 42 58S 172 41E
Waikato, R. 54 37 23S 174 43E
Waikokopu 54 39 3S 177 52E
Waikouaiti 54 45 36S 170 41E
Waimakariri, R. 54 43 24S 172 42E
Waimarino 54 40 40S 175 20E
Waimate 54 44 53S 171 3E
Wainwright 56 52 50N 110 50W
Waiouru 54 39 28S 175 41E
Waipara 54 43 3S 172 46E
Waipawa 54 39 56S 176 38E
Waipu 54 35 59S 174 29E
Waipukurau 54 40 1S 176 33E
Wairakei 54 38 37S 176 6E
Wairau, R. 54 41 32S 174 7E
Wairoa 54 39 3S 177 25E
Waitara 54 38 59S 174 15E
Wakasa, B. 40 34 45N 135 30E
Wakatipu, L. 54 45 5S 168 33E
Wakayama 40 34 15N 135 15E
Wakayama □ 40 33 50N 135 30E
Wake I. 52 19 18N 166 36E
Wakefield, N.Z. 54 41 24S 173 5E
Wakefield, U.K. 2 53 41N 1 31W
Wakema 37 16 40N 95 18E
Wakkanai 40 45 28N 141 35E
Wakkerstroom 48 27 24S 30 10E
Wałbrzych 14 50 45N 16 18E
Walcheren, I. 9 51 30N 3 35E
Wałcz 14 53 17N 16 27E
Waldbröl 10 50 52N 7 36E
Wales ■ 2 52 30N 3 30W
Walgett 51 30 0S 148 5E
Walkerston 51 21 11S 149 8E
Walla Walla 60 46 3N 118 25W
Wallaroo 51 33 55S 137 33E
Wallasey 2 53 26N 3 2W
Wallis Arch. 52 13 18S 176 10W
Wallowa 60 45 40N 117 35W
Wallsend, Australia 51 32 55S 151 40E
Wallsend, U.K. 2 54 59N 1 30W
Walney, I. 2 54 5N 3 15W
Walsall 2 52 36N 1 59W
Walvisbaai 47 23 0S 14 28E
Wanaka, L. 54 44 33S 169 7E
Wanapiri 36 4 30S 135 50E
Wanganui 54 39 35S 175 3E
Wangaratta 51 36 20S 146 7E
Wanhsien 38 30 50N 108 30E
Wankie 47 18 18S 26 30E
Wanyang Shan, Mts. 39 26 30N 114 0E
Warandab 43 7 20N 44 2E
Warangal 34 17 58N 79 45E
Ward 54 41 49S 174 11E
Wardak □ 42 34 15N 68 0E
Warden 48 27 50S 29 0E
Wardha 32 20 45N 78 39E
Waren 10 53 30N 12 41E
Warialda 51 29 29S 150 33E
Warkopi 36 1 12S 134 9E
Warkworth 54 55 22N 1 38W
Warley 2 52 30N 2 0W
Warmbad 48 19 14S 13 51E
Warnemünde 10 54 9N 12 5E
Warner Ra. 60 41 30N 120 20W
Warragul 51 38 1S 145 57E
Warrego, R. 51 30 24S 145 21E
Warren, Australia 51 31 42S 147 51E
Warren, U.S.A. 59 33 35N 92 3W
Warrenton 47 28 9S 24 47E
Warrina 49 28 12S 135 50E
Warrington, U.K. 2 53 25N 2 38W
Warrington, U.S.A. 58 30 22N 87 16W
Warrnambool 51 38 12S 142 31E
Warsak Dam 42 34 10N 71 25E
Warszawa 14 52 13N 21 0E
Warta, R. 14 52 35N 14 39E
Warwick, Australia 51 28 10S 152 1E
Warwick, U.K. 2 52 17N 1 36W
Warwickshire □ 2 52 20N 1 30W
Wasatch Ra. 60 40 30N 111 15W
Wasco 60 35 37N 119 16W
Washington D.C. 58 38 52N 77 0W
Washington, Ohio 58 39 34N 83 26W
Washington I. 53 4 43N 160 25W
Washington □ 60 47 45N 120 30W
Wasian 36 1 47S 133 19E
Wassenaar 9 52 8N 4 24E
Watampone 36 4 29S 120 25E
Waterberg, Mts. 48 24 14S 28 0E
Waterbury 58 41 32N 73 0W
Waterford 4 52 16N 7 10W
Waterford □ 4 51 10N 7 40W
Waterloo, Belgium 9 50 43N 4 25E
Waterloo, S. Leone 44 8 26N 13 8W
Waterloo, U.S.A. 59 42 27N 92 20W
Watertown, N.Y. 58 43 58N 75 57W
Watertown, S.D. 59 44 57N 97 5W
Watertown, Wis. 59 43 15N 88 45W
Waterville 58 44 35N 69 40W
Wates 36 7 53S 110 6E
Watford 2 51 38N 0 23W
Watrous 56 51 40N 105 25W
Watson Lake 56 60 12N 129 0W
Watsonville 60 37 58N 121 49W
Wattwil 10 47 18N 9 6E
Waukegan 58 42 22N 87 54W
Wausau 59 44 57N 89 40W
Wauwatosa 59 43 6N 87 59W
Waveney, R. 2 52 28N 1 45E
Waverley 54 39 46S 174 37E
Wavre 9 50 43N 4 38E
Wâw 45 7 45N 28 1E
Waxahachie 59 32 22N 96 53W
Waycross 58 31 12N 82 25W
Waynesville 58 35 31N 83 0W
Wazirabad 32 32 30N 74 8E
Wear, R. 2 54 55N 1 22W
Webster Green 59 38 38N 90 20W
Weddell Sea 55 72 30S 40 0W
Weed 60 41 29N 122 22W
Weert 9 51 15N 5 43E
Weglinièc 14 51 17N 15 13E
Weiden 10 49 40N 12 10E
Weifang 39 36 47N 119 10E
Weihai 39 37 30N 122 10E
Weilheim 10 47 50N 11 9E
Weimar 10 51 0N 11 20E
Weinheim 10 49 33N 8 40E
Weipa 51 12 24S 142 0E
Weiz 11 47 13N 15 39E
Wejherow 14 54 35N 18 12E
Welkom 47 28 0S 26 50E
Welland, R. 2 52 53N 0 2E
Wellesley Is. 51 17 20S 139 30E
Wellingborough 2 52 18N 0 41W
Wellington, Australia 51 32 30S 149 0E
Wellington, N.Z. 54 41 19S 174 46E
Wellington, S. Africa 47 33 38S 18 57E
Wellington, U.K. 2 52 42N 2 31W
Wellington, I. 65 49 30S 75 0W
Wellington □ 54 40 8S 175 36E
Wells, Norfolk 2 52 57N 0 51E
Wells, Somerset 2 51 12N 23 39W
Wells 60 41 8N 115 0W
Wels 11 48 9N 14 1E
Welshpool 2 52 40N 3 9W
Wem 2 52 52N 2 45W
Wenatchee 60 47 30N 120 17W
Wenchow 39 28 0N 120 35E
Wepener 47 29 42S 27 3E
Werdau 10 50 45N 12 20E
Weri 36 3 10S 132 30E
Wernigerode 10 51 49N 0 45E
Werribee 51 37 54S 144 40E
Wersar 36 1 30S 131 55E
Weser, R. 10 52 32N 8 34E
Wesiri 36 7 30S 126 30E
West Bengal □ 33 25 0N 90 0E
West Bromwich 2 52 32N 2 1W
West Germany ■ 10 52 0N 9 0E
West Glamorgan □ 2 51 48N 3 55W
West Midlands □ 2 52 14N 1 58W
West Palm Beach 58 26 44N 80 3W
West Point 59 33 36N 88 38W
West Sussex □ 2 50 50N 0 35W
West Virginia □ 58 39 0N 18 0W
West Wyalong 51 33 56S 147 10E
West Yorkshire □ 2 53 55N 1 40W
Western Australia □ 49 25 0S 118 0E
Western Ghats 34 15 30N 74 30E
Western Isles □ 3 58 0N 7 0W
Western Malaysia □ 37 5 0N 100 0E
Western Sahara ■ 44 25 0N 13 0W
Western Samoa ■ 52 14 0S 172 0W
Westerschelde 9 51 25N 3 45E
Westerwald, Mts. 10 50 39N 8 0E
Westfalen □ 10 51 50N 7 30E
Westland □ 54 43 33S 169 59E
Westmeath □ 4 53 30N 7 30W
Weston 35 5 10N 115 35E
Weston-super-Mare 2 51 20N 2 59W
Westport, Ireland 4 53 44N 9 31W
Westport, N.Z. 54 41 46S 171 37E
Westray, I. 3 59 18N 3 0W
Wetar, I. 36 7 30S 126 30E
Wetaskiwin 56 52 55N 113 24W
Wetteren 9 51 0N 3 53E
Wetzlar 10 50 33N 8 30E
Wewak 51 3 29S 143 28E
Wexford 4 52 20N 6 28W
Wexford □ 4 52 30N 6 30W
Weyburn 56 49 40N 103 50W
Weymont 57 47 50N 73 50W
Weymouth 2 50 36N 2 28W
Whakatane 54 37 57S 177 1E
Whangamomona 54 39 8S 174 44E
Whangarei 54 35 43S 174 21E
Wharfe, R. 2 53 51N 1 7W
Wheeler Pk. 60 38 57N 114 15W
Wheeling 58 40 2N 80 41W
Whernside 2 54 14N 2 24W
Whitby 2 54 29N 0 37W
White Butte, Mt. 59 46 23N 103 25W
White Horse, Vale of 2 51 39N 1 35W
White Russia □ = Byelorussian S.S.R. 28 53 30N 27 0E
Whitecliffs 54 43 26S 171 55E
Whitehaven 2 54 33N 3 35W
Whitehorse 56 60 45N 135 10W
Whiteville 58 34 20N 78 40W
Whitianga 54 36 47S 175 41E
Whitney, Mt. 60 36 35N 118 14W
Whitstable 2 51 21N 1 2E
Whittier 56 60 46N 148 48W
Whyalla 51 33 2S 137 30E
Wichita 59 37 40N 97 29W
Wichita Falls 59 33 57N 98 30W
Wick 3 58 26N 3 5W
Wickenburg 60 33 58N 112 45W
Wicklow 4 53 0N 6 2W
Wicklow Hd. 4 52 59N 6 3W
Wicklow Mts. 4 53 5N 6 25W
Wicklow □ 4 52 59N 6 25W
Widnes 2 53 22N 2 44W
Wielbork 14 53 24N 20 55E
Wieluń 14 51 15N 18 40E
Wien 12 48 12N 16 22E
Wiener Neustadt 12 47 49N 16 16E
Wierden 9 52 22N 6 35E
Wiesbaden 10 50 7N 8 17E
Wigan 2 53 33N 2 38W
Wight, I. of 2 50 40N 1 20W
Wigtown 3 54 52N 4 27W
Wigtown B. 3 54 46N 4 15W
Wil 10 47 28N 9 3E
Wildspitze, Mt. 11 46 53N 10 53E
Wilhelm, Mt. 51 5 50S 145 1E
Wilhelmsburg 10 53 28N 10 1E
Wilhelmshaven 10 53 30N 8 9E
Wilkes Barre 58 41 15N 75 52E
Wilkes Land 55 69 0S 120 0E
Wilkie 56 52 27N 108 42W
Willcox 60 32 13N 109 53W
Willemstad 62 12 5N 69 0W
Williams 60 35 16N 112 11W
Williams Lake 56 52 20N 122 10W
Williamsburg 58 37 17N 76 44W
Williamsport 58 41 18N 77 1W
Williamstown 51 37 51S 144 52E
Williston, S. Africa 47 31 20S 20 53E
Williston, Fla. 58 29 25N 82 28W
Williston, N.D. 59 48 10N 103 35W
Willmar 59 45 5N 95 0W
Wilmington, Del. 58 39 45N 75 32W
Wilmington, N.C. 58 34 14N 77 54W
Wilson 58 35 44N 77 54W
Wilson, Mt. 60 37 55N 105 3W
Wilsons Promontory 51 38 55S 146 25E
Wilton 2 51 5N 1 51W
Wiltshire □ 2 51 20N 2 0W
Wiluna 49 26 36S 120 14E
Winburg 47 28 30S 27 2E
Winchester, U.K. 2 51 4N 1 19W
Winchester, U.S.A. 58 39 14N 78 8W
Wind River Ra. 60 43 0N 109 40W
Windermere 2 54 24N 2 56W
Windhoek 47 22 35S 17 4E
Windrush, R. 2 51 42N 1 25W
Windsor, Australia 51 33 37S 150 50E
Windsor, N.S. 57 44 59N 64 5W
Windsor, Ont. 57 42 25N 83 0W
Windsor, U.K. 2 51 28N 0 36W
Windward Is, Pacific Oc. 53 19 0S 153 0W
Windward Is, W. Indies 62 13 0N 63 0W
Winfield 59 37 15N 97 0W
Winnebago, L. 59 44 0N 88 20W
Winnemucca 60 41 0N 117 45W
Winnibigoshish L. 59 47 25N 94 12W
Winnipeg 56 49 50N 97 15W
Winnipeg, L. 56 52 30N 98 0W
Winona 59 44 2N 91 45W
Winooski 58 44 31N 73 11W
Winschoten 9 53 9N 7 3E
Winslow 60 35 2N 110 41W
Winston-Salem 58 36 7N 80 15W
Winter Haven 58 28 0N 81 42W
Winterswijk 9 51 58N 6 43E
Winterthur 10 47 30N 8 44E
Winton, Australia 51 22 24S 143 3E
Winton, N.Z. 54 46 8S 168 20E
Wirral 2 53 25N 3 0W
Wisbech 2 52 39N 0 10E
Wisconsin □ 59 44 30N 90 0W
Wisconsin Rapids 59 44 25N 89 50W
Wishaw 3 55 46N 3 55W
Wisła, R. 14 54 22N 18 55E
Wismar 10 53 53N 11 23E
Wissembourg 6 48 57N 7 57E
Witbank 48 25 51S 29 14E
Witham, R. 2 52 56N 0 4E
Withernsea 2 53 43N 0 2W
Witney 2 51 47N 1 29W
Witten 10 51 26N 7 19E
Wittenberg 10 51 51N 12 39E
Wittenberge 10 53 0N 11 44E
Wittenoom 49 22 15S 118 20E
Wittlich 10 50 0N 6 54E
Wittow, I. 10 54 37N 13 21E
Wittstock 10 53 10N 12 30E
Wkra, R. 14 52 27N 20 44E
Wladyssawowo 14 52 6N 18 28E
Wlingi 36 8 5S 112 25E
Wloclawek 14 52 40N 19 3E
Wokam, I. 36 5 45S 134 28E
Wolfenbüttel 10 52 10N 10 33E
Wolfsberg 11 46 50N 14 52E
Wolfsburg 10 52 27N 10 49E
Wolin 14 53 40N 14 37E
Wollongong 51 34 25S 150 54E
Wolomin 14 52 19N 21 15E
Wolverhampton 2 52 35N 2 6W
Wondai 51 26 20S 151 49E
Wŏnju 39 37 20N 127 59E
Wŏnsan 39 39 11N 127 27E
Woodend 51 37 20S 144 33E
Woodland 60 38 40N 121 50W
Woodlark, I. 51 9 10S 152 50E
Woodroffe, Mt. 49 26 20S 131 45E
Woods, L. 49 17 50S 133 30E
Woods, L. of the 59 49 30N 94 30W
Woodstock, Canada 57 46 11N 67 37W
Woodstock, U.K. 2 51 51N 1 20W
Woodville 54 40 20S 175 53E
Woodward 59 36 24N 99 28W
Woolgoolga 51 30 6S 153 11E
Woombye 51 26 40S 152 55E
Woomera 51 31 11S 136 47E
Worcester, S. Africa 47 33 40S 19 28E
Worcester, U.K. 2 52 12N 2 12W
Worcester, U.S.A. 58 42 14N 71 49W
Wörgl 11 47 29N 12 3E
Workington 2 54 39N 3 34W
Worksop 2 53 19N 1 9W
Worms 10 49 37N 8 21E
Wörther See 11 46 37N 14 19E
Worthing 2 50 49N 0 21W
Wrangell 56 56 30N 132 25E
Wrangell, Mts. 56 61 30N 144 0W
Wrath, C. 3 58 38N 5 0W
Wrexham 2 53 5N 3 0W
Wrocław 14 51 5N 17 5E
Września 14 52 21N 17 36E
Wu Kiang, R. 38 29 40N 107 25E
Wuchang, Heilungkiang 39 44 55N 127 10E
Wuchang, Hupeh 39 30 30N 114 15E
Wuchih Shan, Mt. 39 18 45N 109 45E
Wuchow 39 23 26N 111 19E
Wuchung 38 38 0N 106 12E
Wudham 42 23 49N 57 34E
Wuhan 39 30 35N 114 15E
Wuhu 39 31 18N 118 20E
Wulumuchi 38 43 48N 87 35E
Wuppertal 10 51 15N 7 8E
Würzburg 10 49 46N 9 55E
Wurzen 10 51 21N 12 45E
Wusih 39 31 30N 120 30E
Wutunghliao 38 29 24N 104 0E
Wuwei 38 37 55N 102 48E
Wuyi Shan, Mts. 39 26 40N 116 30E
Wuying 39 48 10N 129 20E
Wyandotte 58 42 14N 83 13W
Wyandra 51 27 12S 145 56E
Wye, R. 2 51 36N 2 39W
Wynberg 47 34 2S 18 28E
Wyndham 49 15 33S 128 3E
Wynnum 51 27 27S 153 9E

Alternative spellings

NOTE: The following list gives the principal places where new names or spellings (given first) have been adopted. Earlier forms still in use are cross referenced to the new form. Place names of which the national spelling varies considerably from the English form, e.g. Livorno—Leghorn, are also included.

Chilumba: Deep Bay
Chipata: Fort Jameson
Chitipa: Fort Hill
Choibalsan: Bayan Tumen
Colomb-Béchar, *see* Béchar
Cologne: Köln
Congo (Kinshasa), *see* Zaïre
Constantinople, *see* Istanbul
Copenhagen: København
Corfu, *see* Kerkira
Costermansville, *see* Bukavu
Courtrai, *see* Kortrijk
Coquilhatville, *see* Mbandaka
Craigavon: Lurgan and Portadown
Crete, *see* Kriti
Cuidad Trujillo, *see* Santo Domingo
Cyclades, *see* Kikladhes

Dahomey, *see* Benin
Dakhla: Villa Cisneros
Dairen, *see* Lu-ta
Damascus, *see* Esh Sham
Damietta, *see* Dumyat
Danzig, *see* Gdansk
Daugavpils: Dvinsk
Deep Bay, *see* Chilumba
Dimitrovgrad: Caribrod
Dimitrovo, *see* Pernik
Djajapuru: Hollandia, Kota Baru and Sukarnapura
Djakarta: Batavia
Djambi, *see* Telanaipura
Djibouti: Jibuti
Donetsk: Stalino
Droichead Nua: Newbridge
Dublin, *see* Baile Átha Cliath
Dumyat: Damietta
Dunaujvaros: Sztalinvaros
Dunkerque: Dunquerque, Dunkirk
Dushanbe: Stalinabad
Dvinsk, *see* Daugavpils
Dzaudzhikau, *see* Ordzhonikidze
Dzhargalantu, *see* Hovd
Dzhibkhalantu, *see* Ulyasutay

East Pakistan, *see* Bangladesh
Edirne: Adrianople
Edward, L., *see* Idi Amin Dada, L.
Eisenhuttenstadt: Stalinstadt
El Asnam: Orléansville
El Iskandariya: Alexandria
El Qahira: Cairo
El Suweis: Suez
Elizabethville, *see* Lubumbashi
Ellice Is., *see* Tuvalu
Esh Sham: Damascus
Essaouira: Mogador
Evvoia: Euboea

F'Dérik: Fort Gouraud
Fernando Póo, *see* Macias Nguema Biyoga
Firenze, *see* Florence
Fiume, *see* Rijeka
Flanders: Vlaanderen
Florence: Firenze
Flushing, *see* Vlissingen
Foochow: Minhow
Formosa, *see* Taiwan
Fort de Polignac, *see* Illizi
Fort Gouraud, *see* F'Dérik
Fort Hall, *see* Muranga
Fort Jameson, *see* Chipata
Fort Rosebery, *see* Mansa
Fort Hill, *see* Chitipa
Fort Manning, *see* Mchinji
Fort Trinquet, *see* Bir Mogreïn
Fortaleza: Ceará
Frunze: Pishpek

Gallipoli, *see* Gelibolu
Gand, *see* Gent
Gdansk: Danzig

Gelibolu: Gallipoli
Geneva, Lake, *see* Leman, Lac
Genoa: Genova
Gent: Gand, Ghent
Gliwice: Gleiwitz
Gökçeada: Imroz
Gorki: Nijni Novogorod
Göteborg: Gothenburg
Gottwaldov: Zlin
Guardafui, C., *see* Ras Asir
Guinea-Bissau: Portuguese Guinea
Guyana: British Guiana

Halab: Aleppo
Hämeenlinna: Tavastehus
Hebron, *see* Al Khalih
Helsinki: Helsingfors
Hollandia, *see* Djajapura
Hovd: Jargalant, Dzhargalantu, Kobdo
Huambo: Nova Lisboa

Idi Amin Dada, L.: Edward, L.
Ieper: Ypres
Ilebo: Port Francqui
Illizi: Fort de Polignac
Imroz, *see* Gökçeada
India: Bharat
Iraklion: Candia
Iran: Persia
Isiro: Paulis
Iskenderon: Alexandretta
Istanbul: Constantinople
Ivano-Frankovsk: Stanislav
Izmir: Smyrna

Jadotville, *see* Likasi
Javhlant, *see* Ulyasutay
Jelenia Góra: Hirschberg
Jesselton, *see* Kota Kinabalu
Jibuti, *see* Djibouti

Kabwe: Broken Hill
Kalemie: Albertville
Kaliningrad: Königsberg
Kananga: Luluabourg
Karl Marx Stadt: Chemnitz
Karlovy Vary: Carlsbad
Katowice: Stalinogrod
Kells, *see* Ceanannus Mór
Kenitra: Port Lyautey
Kerkira: Corfu
Khemis Miliana: Affreville
Khmer Rep., *see* Cambodia
Khodzhent, *see* Leninabad
Kikladhes: Cyclades
Kinshasa: Leopoldville
Kirovgrad: Kirovo, Zinovyevsk
Kisangani: Stanleyville
Klaipeda: Memel
Kobdo, *see* Hovd
København: Copenhagen
Kolarovgrad, *see* Šumen
Kolberg: Kolobrzeg
Kolchugino, *see* Leninsk Kuznetski
Köln, *see* Cologne
Kolobrzeg: Kolberg
Kommunarsk: Voroshilovsk, Stavropol
Königsberg, *see* Kaliningrad
Kortrijk: Courtrai
Kota Baru, *see* Djajapura
Kota Kinabalu: Jesselton
Kozhikode, *see* Calicut
Kriti: Krete, Crete
Ksar el Kebir: Alcazarquivir
Kunming: Yunnan
Kutaradja, *see* Banda Atjeh
Kwangchow, *see* Canton

Laibach, *see* Ljubljana
Latakia, *see* Al Ladhiqiyah

Leghorn: Livorno
Legnica: Liegnitz
Leman, Lac: Geneva, Lake
Leninbad: Khodzhent
Leninsk Kuznetski: Kolchugino
Leopoldville, *see* Kinshasa
Lesotho: Basutoland
Leuven: Louvain
Liegnitz, *see* Legnica
Likasi: Jadotville
Livorno, *see* Leghorn
Ljubljana: Laibach
Lod: Lydda
Lourenço Marques, *see* Maputo
Louvain, *see* Leuven
Lubumbashi: Elizabethville
Lugansk, *see* Voroshilovgrad
Luluabourg, *see* Kananga
Lurgan, *see* Craigavon
Lu-ta: Port Arthur and Dairen
Lydda, *see* Lod

Maas, *see* Meuse
Macias Nguema Biyoga: Fernando Póo
Makasar, *see* Ujung Pandang
Majorca, *see* Mallorca
Malawi: Nysasland
Malawi, L.: Nyasa, L.
Malines, *see* Mechelen
Mallorca: Majorca
Maputo: Lourenço Marques
Mansa: Fort Rosebery
Mantova: Mantua
Marsa Susa: Apollonia
Masulipatnam: Bandar
Mbala: Abercorn
Mbandaka: Coquilhatville
Mbuji-Mayi: Bakwanga
Mchinji: Fort Manning
Mechelen: Malines
Memel, *see* Klaipeda
Menorca: Minorca
Meuse: Maas
Minhow, *see* Foochow
Minorca, *see* Menorca
Mobutu Sese Seko, L.: Albert, L.
Mogador, *see* Essaouira
Molotov, *see* Perm
Molotovsk, *see* Severodvinsk
Monastir, *see* Bitolj
Montgomery, *see* Sahiwal
Mosul, *see* Al Mawsil
Muar: Bandar Maharani
Mukden: Shenyang, Fengtien
Munich: München
Muranga: Fort Hall
Muscat & Oman, *see* Oman
Mymensingh, *see* Nasirabad

Nasirabad: Mymensingh
Neisse, *see* Nysa
Neustettin, *see* Szczecinek
Nevalat: Beit Nabala
Newbridge (Ire.), *see* Droichead Nua
Newtownbarry, *see* Bunclody
Nijni Novgorod, *see* Gorki
Northern Rhodesia, *see* Zambia
Nouadhibou: Port Etienne
Nova Lisboa: Huambo
Novokuznetsk: Stalinsk
Novomoskovsk: Stalinogorsk
Nyasa, L., *see* Malawi, L.
Nyasaland, *see* Malawi
Nysa: Neisse
Nystad, *see* Uusikapunki

Odenburg, *see* Sorpon
Ordzhonikidze: Dzaudzihikau
Orléansville, *see* El Asnam
Osipendo, *see* Berdyansk
Oświęcim: Auschwitz
Oulu: Uleåborg

Pagalu: Annobón
Para, *see* Belém
Paulis, *see* Isiro
Perm: Molotov
Pernambuco, *see* Recife
Pernik: Dimitrovo
Persia, *see* Iran
Persian Gulf: Arabian G., The Gulf
Philippeville, *see* Skikda
Philippopolis, *see* Plovdiv
Pilsen, *see* Plzen
Pishpek, *see* Frunze
Plovdiv: Philippopolis
Plzen,: Pilsen
Podgorica, *see* Titograd
Ponthierville, *see* Ubundi
Port Arthur, *see* Lu-ta
Port Etienne, *see* Nouadhibou
Port Francqui, *see* Ilebo
Port Lyautey, *see* Kenitra
Portadown, *see* Craigavon
Portuguese Guinea, *see* Guinea-Bissau
Porvoo: Borgå
Praha: Prague
Pressburg, *see* Bratislava

Qeisari: Caesarea
Quelpart, *see* Cheju-do

Raahe: Brahestad
Raheng, *see* Tak
Ras Asir: Cape Guardafui
Rashid: Rosetta
Ratisbon, *see* Regensburg
Recife: Pernambuco
Regensburg: Ratisbon
Revel, *see* Tallinn
Rezâiyeh, L.: Urmia, L.
Rhodesia: Southern Rhodesia
Rijeka: Fiume
Rosetta, *see* Rashid
Rybinsk: Shcherbakov

Sahiwal: Montgomery
Salonika, *see* Thessaloniki
Santo Domingo: Cuidad Trujillo
Saragossa, *see* Zaragoza
Scutari (Albania), *see* Shkodër
Scutari (Turkey), Uskūdar
Severodvinsk: Molotovsk
's Gravenhage: The Hague
Shcherbakov, *see* Rybinsk
Shenyang, *see* Mukden
Shkodër: Scutari, Shkodra
Siam, *see* Thailand
Simbirsk, *see* Ulyanovsk
Skikda: Philipeville
Skopje: Skoptje, Usküb
Smyrna, *see* Izmir
Soche: Yarkand
Sofala: Beira
Soochow: Wuhsien
Sorpon: Odenburg
Southern Rhodesia, *see* Rhodesia
Sovetsk: Tilsit
Spanish Sahara, *see* Western Sahara
Sri Lanka: Ceylon
Stalin, *see* Varna
Stalinabad, *see* Dushanbe
Stalingrad, *see* Volgograd
Staliniri, *see* Tskhinvali
Stalino, *see* Donetsk
Stalinogorsk, *see* Novomoskovsk
Stalinogrod, *see* Katowice
Stalinsk, *see* Novokuznetsk
Stalinstad, *see* Eisenhuttenstadt
Stanislav, *see* Ivano-Frankovsk
Stanleyville, *see* Kisangani
Stavropol, *see* Kommunarsk
Stettin, *see* Szczecin
Suez, *see* El Suweis
Sukarnapura, *see* Djajapura
Sulawesi: Celebes

Šumen: Kolarovgrad
Sur: Tyre
Szczecin: Stettin
Szczecinek: Neustettin
Sztalinvaros, *see* Dunaujvaros

Taiwan: Formosa
Tak: Raheng
Tallinn: Revel
Tampere: Tammefors
Tanzania: Tanganyika and Zanzibar
Tarabulus, *see* Tripoli
Tavastehus, *see* Hämeenlinna
Tbilisi: Tiflis
Tchad, *see* Chad
Telanaipura: Djambi
Thailand: Siam
The Gulf, *see* Persian Gulf
The Hague, *see* 's Gravenhage
Thessaloniki: Salonika
Tiflis, *see* Tbilisi
Tihwa, *see* Urumchi
Tilsit, *see* Sovetsk
Titograd: Podgorica
Tombouctou: Timbuktu
Trèves: Trier
Tripoli: Tarabulus
Trucial States, *see* United Arab Emirates
Tselinograd: Akmolinsk
Tskhinvali: Staliniri
Turin: Torino
Turku: Åbo
Tuvalu: Ellice Is.
Tver, *see* Kalinin
Tyre, *see* Sur

Ubundi: Ponthierville
Ujung Pandang: Makasar
Ulan Ude: Verkhneudinsk
Uleåborg, *see* Oulu
Ulyanovsk: Simbirsk
Ulyasutay: Javhlant, Dzhibkhalantu
United Arab Emirates: Trucial States
Urmia, L., *see* Rezâiyeh, L.
Urumchi: Tihwa
Usküb, *see* Skopje
Usküdar: Scutari
Ussurysk: Voroshilov
Usumbura, *see* Bujumbura
Uusikaarlepy: Nykarleby
Uusikaupunki: Nystad

Varanasi: Banaras, Benares
Varna: Stalin
Verkhneudinsk, *see* Ulan Ude
Vjalar, *see* Tissemsilt
Viborg: Vipuri, Vyborg
Vienna: Wien
Villa Cisneros, *see* Dakhla
Vlaanderen, *see* Flanders
Vlissingen: Flushing
Volgograd: Stalingrad
Voroshilov, *see* Ussurysk
Voroshilovgrad: Lugansk
Voroshilovsk, *see* Kommunarsk

Western Sahara: Spanish Sahara
Wien, *see* Vienna
Wroclaw: Breslau
Wuhsien, *see* Soochow

Yarkland, *see* Soche
Ypres, *see* Ieper
Yunnan, *see* Kunming

Zaïre: Congo (Kinshasa)
Zambia: Northern Rhodesia
Zaragoza: Saragossa
Zinovyevsk, *see* Kirovgrad
Zlin, *see* Gottwaldov

Picture credits

Photo research by Annette Brown.
The publishers would like to thank the following photographers, organizations, tourist offices and embassies for supplying photographs for use in this book. Our special thanks go to SAS who supplied a superb selection.

Photographs have been credited by page number. Where more than one photo appears on the page, references are made from left to right and then top to bottom.

Some references have, for reasons of space, been abbreviated as follows:
Australian Information Service: AIS
British Tourist Authority: BTA
Scandinavian Airline Systems: SAS
South African Tourist Corporation: SATOUR
Tourist Office: T.O.
United States Travel Service: USTS

Front cover: R. Adshead/SAS/SAS/SAS. **Back cover:** USTS/Swiss National T.O./SAS/SAS. **Endpapers:** D. Arnold. **Page 1:** D. Arnold. **2:** USTS. **4:** Swiss National T.O. **6:** A. Huxley. **8:** H. Angel. **10:** SAS. **15:** SAS/D. Gibson. **17:** European Communities Commission. **18:** BTA/R. Adshead. **20:** BTA/BTA/BTA. **22:** Irish Tourist Board – B. Lynch/BTA. **24:** French Government T.O. **26:** French Government T.O./French Government T.O. **27:** French Government T.O./French Government T.O. **29:** Frency Government T.O. **30:** Belgian T.O. **31:** Luxembourg T.O./Netherlands National T.O. **33:** SAS. **34:** R. Adshead/Goethe Institute/Swiss National T.O. **37:** Austrian National T.O. **38:** SAS/SAS. **39:** Rumanian National T.O. **40:** SAS/SAS. **43:** H. Angel/Portuguese T.O. **44:** H. Angel. **47:** Italian T.O. **48:** R. Adshead/Italian T.O. **49:** Italian T.O./Italian T.O. **50:** Italian T.O. **51:** H. Angel. **53:** SAS. **54:** SAS/SAS. **55:** A. Huxley/A. Huxley. **56:** A. Huxley/A. Huxley. **59:** SAS/Finnish T.O. **60:** SAS. **61:** SAS/SAS. **62:** SAS/Danish T.O. **65:** Novosti/SAS. **67:** Novosti. **69:** Novosti. **70:** Novosti. **71:** Novosti. **72:** H. Angel. **73:** Ruposhi Bangla. **74:** A. Huxley/Air India/R. Adshead. **76:** Indonesian Embassy. **79:** SAS/Thai Embassy/Thai Embassy. **80:** R. Adshead/J. Mason/J. Mason. **81:** SAS. **82:** SAS. **84:** R. Adshead/R. Adshead. **86:** Japanese National T.O./Japanese National T.O. **89:** Turkish T.O. **90:** Cyprus T.O./Israeli Government T.O. **91:** Ministry of Tourism, Jordan. **92:** Shell Photo. **94:** SATOUR. **95:** R. Adshead/Moroccan T.O. **96:** Algerian T.O./SAS. **97:** SAS. **98:** H. Angel. **100:** P. H. Ward. **101:** P. H. Ward/Zambia National T.O. **102:** H. Angel/H. Angel. **104:** SATOUR/SATOUR/SATOUR. **106:** SATOUR. **107:** H. Angel. **109:** AIS. **110:** AIS. **111:** AIS/AIS/AIS. **112:** AIS. **115:** B. Hill. **116:** New Zealand High Commission. **117:** B. Hill/H. Angel. **118:** B. Hill/H. Angel. **119:** G. Maxwell. **120:** USTS. **123:** Canadian Film Library. **124:** Canadian Film Library. **125:** USTS/USTS. **126:** USTS/USTS. **129:** USTS/USTS/USTS. **130:** USTS/SAS. **132:** Mexican National Tourist Council/P. Morris/Mexican National Tourist Council. **134:** Bahamas T.O./Tate & Lyle Limited. **135:** C. A. Walker. **137:** H. Angel/SAS. **138:** P. Morris. **140:** SAS/SAS. **141:** SAS. **142:** SAS/D. Fisher. **143:** SAS.

PRINTED BY proost Turnhout (Belgium)

PRINTED IN BELGIUM